English Folk Songs
from the
Southern Appalachians

English Folk Songs from the Southern Appalachians

Collected by
Cecil J. Sharp

Comprising two hundred and seventy-four Songs and Ballads with nine hundred and sixty-eight Tunes

Including thirty-nine Tunes contributed by
Olive Dame Campbell

Edited by
Maud Karpeles

Volume I

Geoffrey Cumberlege
OXFORD UNIVERSITY PRESS
London New York Toronto

Original publication by
Oxford University Press, Amen House, London E.C. 4
GLASGOW NEW YORK TORONTO MELBOURNE WELLINGTON
BOMBAY CALCUTTA MADRAS CAPE TOWN
Geoffrey Cumberlege, Publisher to the University

Reprinted for
CAMSCO Music
145 Hickory Corner Road, East Windsor, NJ 08520

Loomis House Press, 2012
www.loomishousepress.com

ISBN 978-1-935243-17-5 (paper)
ISBN 978-1-935243-18-2 (cloth)

FIRST PUBLISHED 1932
SECOND IMPRESSION 1952

Cover photo: Cecil Sharp, Maud Karpeles, and
Lucindy (Mrs Doc) Pratt, Kentucky, USA, 1916-1918.
Licensed from Heritage Images

PRINTED IN THE UNITED STATES OF AMERICA

INTRODUCTION

"The Book." When my older relatives were singing and made reference to 'the book,' had there been people listening, they would not have realized this was the only book they considered worth giving a second glance to when discussing the old 'lovesongs.' In all honesty, they really didn't have the need to reference any book when it came to the singing of songs they had learned as children from grandparents, parents, aunts, uncles, siblings and other family members of the small mountain community many of them had lived in their entire lives. Every word to literally hundreds of songs, was tucked away in their minds. None had learned a single word from a sheet of music or the page of a book, They learned the same way I was being taught—by listening to the song over and over until I 'caught' it. The oral tradition Granny called "Old-timey knee-to-knee" was still going strong in Sodom in 1958.

But even as a child, I knew the importance of the book though I was not allowed to even lift the cover. I had rubbed my hand over the brown paper that covered Granny's copy many a time, longing to hold it, to turn the pages, look at the words and see them set to music. And, when I was old enough, I held it often.

Vergie, Cas' wife, was the one who took pity on a curious little girl of five-years-old and allowed me my first glimpse of the title and what was between the covers, *English Folk Songs from the Southern Appalachians* and had given me the names of Cecil Sharp and Maud Karpeles.

"Who was them people?"

"Them was the two folks what wrote it—they come all the way from the homeland, honey, to set and listen to our family sing the old songs. Cas' uncle Mitch said that woman wrote the words down in little squiggles and dots and dashes. Beat all, he said. And while she was a squiggling, that feller—why, he could write a tune fast as greased lightening using them round notes. He always had on a white suit and a big, fine hat and she was always wearing a dress and stockings and hit hotter than blue blazes."

Vergie leaned over the book in her lap and carefully turned several pages. With forehead puckered in concentration, often pausing to run a finger along a line of words as she read to herself lips moving silently with each word. Then her face lifted and I was struck by the sparkle in her bright green eyes. I was more amazed as she slid the book into my lap and pointed at a whole page of music and words.

"Now this here lovesong were give to him by Mary Sands. I knowed she'd sung a version fer him of the Silk Merchant's Daughter on account of Cas' uncle setting on this same porch and telling us all about it. And here it is, almost word fer word the one Cas sings. Lord you ought to have heard his brother Jeter sing. He were the best singer of these old lovesongs in this part of the world. Him and Chappell moved off up to…" and the story would spin on with me looking longingly at the page, barely able to make out

"No. 64
The Silk Merchant's Daughter
A
Sung by Mrs. Mary Sands at Allenstand, N.C., July 31, 1916"

At Mars Hill College twelve years later I would sit at a table in the Rare Books room and satisfy all my childhood questions concerning The Book. And, forty years later an MFA student, Judy Rhodes, would be asking me questions about Sharp's book and would determine that he collected songs from 56 members of my family and 30 songs from Mary Bullman Sands, half sister to Jess and Doug Wallin who were my great-grandfathers.

If you haven't read Sharp's introduction to the first edition, you really should. He could've been a prophet on some of the predictions he made—he totally missed on others. But, on the whole, he nailed 85% of what would eventually become of the tradition I hold with such reverence. Here's one of his most impressive observations, however ominous it now seems:

> "Again, the value of such songs as these as material for the general education of the young cannot be overestimated. For, if education is to be cultural and not merely utilitarian, if its aim is to produce men and women capable, not only of earning a living, but of holding a dignified and worthy position upon an equality with the most cultivated of their generation, it will be necessary to pay at least as much attention to the training and development of the emotional, spiritual, and imaginative faculties as to those of the intellect. And this, of course, can be achieved only by the early cultivation of some form of artistic expression, such as singing, which, for reasons already given, seems of all the arts to be the most natural and the most suitable one for the young. Moreover, remembering that the primary purpose of education is to place the children of the present generation in possession of the cultural achievements of the past, so that they may as quickly as possible enter into their racial inheritance, what better form of music or of literature can we give them than the folk-songs and folk-ballads of the race to which they belong, or of the nation whose language they speak? To deny them these is to cut them off from the past and rob them of that which is theirs by right of birth. To put it another way, the aim of the educationist should be not to forge the first link of a new chain but to add a fresh link to an old one.
>
> That culture is primarily a matter of inheritance and not of education is, perhaps, a mere truism, but it is one, nevertheless, which educationists often forget…
>
> Of the supreme cultural value of an inherited tradition, even when unenforced by any formal school education, our mountain community in the Southern Highlands is an outstanding example…
>
> When he sings his aim is to forget himself and everything that reminds him of his everyday life; and so it is that he has come to create an imaginary world of his own and to people it with characters quite as wonderful, in their way, as the elfish creations of Spenser."

As Sharp so accurately determined, the educational system showed little or no interest in maintaining or nourishing a tradition which, in their opinion, did nothing to move an American child forward into a quickly changing world based on scientific advancement.

My mother said it best, "Right before the start of World War II, I had just graduated from Asheville Normal Teachers College. I had already begun to feel inferior in many ways to the other young women—most of this inferiority having to do with where I was born, the dialect I spoke and words I used. Oh I worked hard to forget as much of my childhood as possible. And the old songs, well they were so closely tied to the bone crushing poverty I wanted nothing to do with them. Thinking about what I've just said, I guess my generation threw away its heritage with both hands. What a sad thought that is. All those beautiful old lovesongs I can still hear in my memories but can't recall but a line or two here and there. My mother sang so many of them. What a loss."

"Talk out one of the lines you remember, Mommy," I said.

Her eyes grew distant and softly she said, "There was a rich merchant in London did right…"

She stopped and sighed, "That's all I remember, honey. I'm sorry."

And I picked it up and sang the entire version I'd learned from Cas Wallin when I was twelve.

Sharp predicted the tradition of passing down the traditional ballads would die out in the southern Appalachians by 1950. Maud Karpeles, in her note to the preface, remarks on a return visit to the mountains of Virginia, North Carolina and Tennessee. And despite her acknowledgement of finding the change she'd expected in mountain life, she admits, "Nevertheless traditions dies hard. Memory may weaken, but the love of the songs remains and with a little encouragement it springs up anew."

I learned many songs from my older relatives and as I grow older, amazingly I am remembering those I wasn't drawn to at the time I learned them. And, if I can only recall a verse or two I go to my bookcase and without even looking, because it has always had its special place where I could put my hands on it immediately, I take down The Book, the only book I consider worth glancing through for a verse to a song I learned over fifty years ago sitting knee-to-knee with an older relative.

Whether Sharp was an idealistic dreamer or a self-promoting academic doesn't matter one whit to me. I am just grateful—perhaps he had hopes that someone would see the importance and beauty in songs of an ancient tradition having been passed from loving voice to loving voice enough to keep it alive until it reached down through all those generations and found a little girl who would be entranced with a story that came to life when it was sung. And with a loving voice pass it down to other young people who would carry it into the 21st Century. I wonder at his reaction if he could hear my four-year-old grandson, Ezra, singing the songs in much the same way my ancestor, Mary Sands, sang for him in 1916. I wonder if he would feel the satisfaction I do? My guess is he would be astounded. Perhaps not—he was, after all a dreamer and sometimes dreams do indeed come true.

SHEILA KAY ADAMS
Madison County, North Carolina, USA

CONTENTS

VOLUME I

PREFACE	xii
INTRODUCTION TO THE FIRST EDITION, 1917	xxi

BALLADS:

1.	The Elfin Knight .	1
2.	The False Knight upon the Road	3
3.	Lady Isabel and the Elf Knight .	5
4.	Earl Brand	14
5.	The Two Sisters	26
6.	The Cruel Brother	36
7.	Lord Randal	38
8.	Edward	46
9.	Sir Lionel .	54
10.	The Cruel Mother	56
11.	The Three Ravens	63
12.	The Two Brothers	65
13.	Young Beichan	77
14.	Lizzie Wan	89
15.	The Cherry-Tree Carol	90
16.	Fair Annie .	95
17.	Lady Maisry	97
18.	Young Hunting	101
19.	Lord Thomas and Fair Ellinor	115
20.	Fair Margaret and Sweet William	132
21.	Lord Lovel	146
22.	The Wife of Usher's Well	150
23.	Little Musgrave and Lady Barnard	161
24.	Barbara Allen	183
25.	Giles Collins	196
26.	The Lowlands of Holland	200
27.	Lamkin	201
28.	The Maid Freed from the Gallows	208
29.	Johnie Scot	215
30.	The Bailiff's Daughter of Islington	219
31.	Sir Hugh	222
32.	The Death of Queen Jane	230
33.	The Gypsy Laddie .	233
34.	Geordie	240
35.	The Daemon Lover	244
36.	The Grey Cock	259

Contents

37. THE SUFFOLK MIRACLE	261
38. OUR GOODMAN	267
39. THE WIFE WRAPT IN WETHER'S SKIN	271
40. THE FARMER'S CURST WIFE	275
41. THE GOLDEN VANITY	282
42. THE MERMAID	291
43. JOHN OF HAZELGREEN	294
44. THE BROWN GIRL	295
45. THE TROOPER AND THE MAID	305
46. THE BLIND BEGGAR'S DAUGHTER	308
47. THE BABES IN THE WOOD	309
48. IN SEAPORT TOWN	310
49. THE CRUEL SHIP'S CARPENTER	317
50. SHOOTING OF HIS DEAR	328
51. THE LADY AND THE DRAGOON	333
52. THE BOATSMAN AND THE CHEST	338
53. THE HOLLY TWIG	341
54. POLLY OLIVER	344
55. THE RICH OLD LADY	348
56. EDWIN IN THE LOWLANDS LOW	350
57. AWAKE! AWAKE!	358
58. THE GREEN BED	365
59. THE SIMPLE PLOUGHBOY	369
60. THE THREE BUTCHERS	370
61. WILLIAM TAYLOR	373
62. THE GOLDEN GLOVE	377
63. PRETTY NANCY OF YARMOUTH	379
64. THE SILK MERCHANT'S DAUGHTER	381
65. JACK WENT A-SAILING	385
66. THE BOLD LIEUTENANT	396
67. THE BANKS OF SWEET DUNDEE	399
68. THE COUNCILLOR'S DAUGHTER	402
69. CAROLINE OF EDINBORO' TOWN	404
70. THE CLOTHIER	405
71. THE MILLER'S APPRENTICE, OR THE OXFORD TRAGEDY	407
72. STILL GROWING	410
NOTES ON BALLADS Nos. 1–72	411
BIBLIOGRAPHY	427
INDEX OF TITLES	431

Contents

VOLUME II

SONGS:

73.	Married and Single Life	3
74.	Betsy	4
75.	If You Want to go A-Courting	6
76.	Pretty Saro	10
77.	My Dearest Dear	13
78.	I'm Going to Georgia	14
79.	Macafee's Confession, or Harry Grey	15
80.	Locks and Bolts	17
81.	William and Nancy	20
82.	George Reilly	22
83.	Johnny Doyle	27
84.	Lazarus	29
85.	Black is the Colour	31
86.	The Single Girl	32
87.	John Hardy	35
88.	Betty Anne	37
89.	My Boy Billy	38
90.	Soldier, won't You Marry Me?	40
91.	Swannanoa Town	42
92.	The Keys of Heaven	45
93.	Putman's Hill	50
94.	The False Young Man	51
95.	Pretty Peggy O	59
96.	My Parents Treated Me Tenderly	62
97.	The Sheffield Apprentice	66
98.	The Broken Token	70
99.	Wild Bill Jones	74
100.	The Shoemaker	75
101.	The Brisk Young Lover	76
102.	Seven Long Years	79
103.	Come All You Young and Handsome Girls	80
104.	Loving Reilly	81
105.	The Awful Wedding	83
106.	Sweet William	84
107.	Good Morning, My Pretty Little Miss	90
108.	My Mother Bid Me	93
109.	The Rejected Lover	96
110.	The Lover's Lament	103
111.	The Dear Companion	109
112.	The Rocky Mountain Top	110
113.	The Warfare is Raging	111
114.	The True Lover's Farewell	113
115.	Katie Morey	119

Contents

116.	Rain and Snow	122
117.	The Wagoner's Lad	123
118.	Come All You Fair and Tender Ladies	128
119.	Ibby Damsel	137
120.	Handsome Sally	138
121.	William and Polly	139
122.	Hicks's Farewell	142
123.	Poor Omie	144
124.	The Virginian Lover	149
125.	Early, Early in the Spring	151
126.	Green Bushes	155
127.	I'm Seventeen Come Sunday	156
128.	I Must and I Will Get Married	159
129.	The Lost Babe	160
130.	The Noble Man	162
131.	St. James's Hospital	164
132.	Springfield Mountain	166
133.	Tarry Trousers	168
134.	Whistle Daughter	169
135.	Brennan on the Moor	170
136.	The Battle of Shiloh	172
137.	The Foggy Dew	174
138.	The Bold Privateer	175
139.	Waterloo	176
140.	The Cuckoo	177
141.	The Derby Ram	184
142.	The Green Brier Shore	188
143.	I'm Going to Get Married Next Sunday	189
144.	The Riddle Song	190
145.	The Nightingale	192
146.	One Cold Winter's Morning	195
147.	The Lonesome Grove	197
148.	The Lily of the West	199
149.	Devilish Mary	200
150.	Ha, Ha, Ha	201
151.	Tom Bolynn	202
152.	The Gambling Man	204
153.	When Boys go A-Courting	205
154.	Will the Weaver	207
155.	Sally and Her Lover, or Lady Leroy	210
156.	Green Grows the Laurel	211
157.	The Rebel Soldier, or The Poor Stranger	212
158.	No-e in the Ark	216
159.	Sally Buck	217
160.	The Horse's Complaint	220
161.	The Miller's Will	221

Contents

162.	THE SONS OF LIBERTY	224
163.	LOVING NANCY	226
164.	THE BOY ON THE LAND	228
165.	THE SILVER DAGGER	229
166.	NIAGARA FALLS	231
167.	IN OLD VIRGINNY	232
168.	THE SAUCY SAILOR	235
169.	THE LONESOME PRAIRIE	236
170.	OLD ARKANSAS	238
171.	WILLIAM HALL	239
172.	FAREWELL DEAR ROSANNA	243
173.	BONEY'S DEFEAT	245
174.	THE FATEFUL BLOW	246
175.	THE SLIGHTED SOLDIER	247
176.	BILLY GRIMES	248
177.	THE COURTING CASE	249
178.	THE DEAF WOMAN'S COURTSHIP	252
179.	COME ALL YE SOUTHERN SOLDIERS	253
180.	THE IRISH GIRL	254
181.	JOHNNY GERMAN	256
182.	HARM LINK	258
183.	OLD JOE CLARKE	259
184.	THE POOR COUPLE	260
185.	SUSANNAH CLARGY	261
186.	THE SUNNY SOUTH	262
187.	TRUE LOVE FROM THE EASTERN SHORE	264
188.	THE DRUMMER AND HIS WIFE	265
189.	EVERY NIGHT WHEN THE SUN GOES IN	268
190.	I LOVE MY LOVE	269
191.	IN NOTTAMUN TOWN	270
192.	SAMUEL YOUNG	271
193.	WHEN ADAM WAS CREATED	272
194.	DANIEL IN THE LION'S DEN	273
195.	JESSE COLE	273
196.	BARBARA BUCK	274
197.	CLAY MORGAN	274
198.	WAY DOWN THE OHIO	275
199.	THE CROW-FISH MAN	275
200.	BARBER'S CRY	276
201.	LULIE	276
202.	A MONDAY WAS MY COURTING DAY	277
203.	BLACK GIRL	278
204.	HARDING'S DEFEAT	278
205.	COME MY LITTLE ROVING SAILOR	279
206.	THE TREE IN THE WOOD	281
207.	THE TEN COMMANDMENTS	283

Contents

HYMNS:

208. The Sinner-Man	289
209. Hold On	292
210. Christ was Born in Bethlehem	293
211. 'Tis a Wonder	294
212. Jacob's Ladder	295

NURSERY SONGS:

213. Cocky Robin	299
214. The Three Huntsmen	303
215. The Bird Song	304
216. Sourwood Mountain	305
217. The Foolish Boy	307
218. The Farmyard	310
219. I Whipped my Horse	311
220. A Frog He went A-Courting	312
221. The Frog in the Well	320
222. The Carrion Crow	324
223. The Old Grey Mare	326
224. The Bridle and Saddle	329
225. The Squirrel	330
226. The Old Black Duck	332
227. What are Little Boys made of?	334
228. What'll we do With the Baby?	336
229. Poor Old Maid	337
230. The Good Old Man	338
231. The Ground Hog	340
232. Bye, Bye, Baby	341
233. Mammy Loves	341
234. The Mocking Bird	342
235. The Old Woman and the Little Pigee	343
236. The Old Grey Goose	345
237. Phoebe in Her Petticoat	346
238. Snake Baked a Hoe-cake	346
239. The Tottenham Toad	347

JIGS:

240. Sally Anne	351
241. Cripple Creek	352
242. The Opossum	353
243. Liza Anne	355
244. Eliza Jane	356
245. Sugar Babe.	357
246. Give the Fiddler a Dram	358
247. Gone to Cripple Creek	358
248. Run, Nigger, Run	359

Contents

249.	Porto Rico	359
250.	The Hog-eyed Man	360
251.	The Jackfish	361
252.	Marina Girls	362
253.	O this Door Locked	363
254.	The Shad	364

PLAY-PARTY GAMES:

255.	Yonder Stands Young Couple	367
256.	Old Doc Jones	368
257.	Up she Rises	368
258.	Maria's Gone	369
259.	Old Roger	370
260.	Will You wear Red?	371
261.	Going to Boston	371
262.	Chase the Buffalo	372
263.	Sad Condition	372
264.	Early Sunday Morning	373
265.	Old Bald Eagle	374
266.	Philadelphia	374
267.	Charlie's Sweet	375
268.	The Higher up the Cherry Tree	377
269.	The Chickens They are Crowing	378
270.	Swing a Lady	379
271.	Reap, Boys, Reap	380
272.	Soldier Boy for Me	381
273.	I Wish I was a Child Again	383
274.	Some Love Coffee	383

NOTES ON SONGS Nos. 73–274	385
BIBLIOGRAPHY	400
INDEX OF TITLES	404

PREFACE

THIS publication represents the second and enlarged edition of folk-songs and ballads collected by Cecil Sharp and Olive Dame Campbell from the Southern Appalachian Mountains.

The original edition[1] comprising 122 songs (323 variants) included a selection of the material collected by Cecil Sharp during his first visit to the mountains in 1916, together with 32 songs (42 variants) from the collection of Olive Dame Campbell[2]—mainly songs and ballads from Kentucky (Clay, Knott, and Lee Counties) and Georgia (Habersham and Rabun Counties) noted by her during the years 1907 to 1910.

In the present publication the contents of the earlier edition are reproduced,[3] in addition to songs and ballads subsequently collected by Cecil Sharp.

Except for a few minor omissions, Cecil Sharp's Introduction to the 1917 edition is reprinted in full. Written after a brief sojourn of only nine weeks in the mountains, it is necessarily an incomplete survey of the work which requires some amplification in view of later experiences, but, nevertheless, it gives a true and vivid picture of the more remote mountain people as they were during the period of the first World War, and it sums up the main characteristics of their songs.

Cecil Sharp spent a total period of 46 weeks in the mountains—9 weeks in 1916, 19 weeks in 1917, and 18 weeks in 1918. I accompanied him throughout his travels, collaborating with him by taking down the words of the songs whilst he recorded the tunes. In this way, we noted songs from 281 different singers, obtaining a total of 1,612 tunes, representing about 500 different songs. For practical reasons it was not possible to publish the whole collection[4] in these volumes, and so those songs and variants which are of minor interest, or which show but slight variation from the published versions, have been excluded.

[1] *English Folk Songs from the Southern Appalachians, Comprising 122 Songs and Ballads and 323 Tunes*, collected by Olive Dame Campbell and Cecil J. Sharp: G. P. Putnam's Sons, 1917. Out of print.

[2] The songs collected by Olive Dame Campbell are Nos. 3 B, 3 C, 4 D, 7 E, 10 B, 13 B, 18 E, 18 F, 19 B, 19 J, 19 K, 20 B, 23 D, 23 G, 24 A, 24 B, 24 C, 24 F, 25 C, 35 C, 39 B, 44 F (no tune), 49 C, 56 C, 65 B, 65 C, 76 B, 80 E, 94 D, 95 A, 101 A, 102, 103, 104 A, 105, 117 B, 118 B, 123 A, 207 B (no tune), 207 C (no tune), 216 A, and 217 A.

[3] Three songs which appeared in the first edition, viz. versions of 'Lady Isabel and the Elf Knight', and 'The Bird Song', and 'Sing Said the Mother', have been excluded from this collection: the first two for the reason that they were collected outside the Southern Appalachian area, and the third because Cecil Sharp discovered after its publication that it was not a genuine folk-song.

[4] Cecil Sharp's original manuscript collection is in the Clare College Library at Cambridge, and there are also complete copies in the Harvard College Library, Cambridge, Massachusetts, and in the New York Public Library.

Preface

The following table shows the distribution of the tunes between the various States and the time spent in each:

State	Number of weeks	Tunes collected
North Carolina	14½	559
Kentucky	15	524
Virginia	12½	407
Tennessee	3½	116
West Virginia	½	6

And a closer geographical analysis is shown by the following tabularized itinerary:

Date		State	County	Place	Number of Tunes
1916	July 25	N. Carolina	(Buncombe)	(Asheville)	
	27	,,	Madison	White Rock	9
		,,	,,	*Alleghany*	
	30	,,	,,	Allenstand	44
	Aug. 5	,,	,,	(White Rock)	
	7	,,	,,	Alleghany	37
		,,	,,	*Carmen*	
	12	,,	,,	White Rock	1
	14	,,	,,	Big Laurel	38
		,,	,,	*Rice Cove*	
	18	,,	,,	(White Rock)	
	19		(Buncombe)	(Asheville)	
	23	,,	Madison	Hot Springs	29
	25	,,	(Buncombe)	(Asheville)	
	26	,,	(Madison)	(White Rock)	
	28	,,	,,	Alleghany	20
	,,	,,	,,	*Carmen*	
	30	Tennessee	Unicoi	Rocky Fork	58
		,,	,,	*Flag Pond*	
	Sept. 5	N. Carolina	Madison	Alleghany	9
		,,	,,	*Carmen*	
		,,	,,	*Spillcorn*	
	7	,,	Buncombe	Asheville	6
		,,	,,	*Swannanoa*	
	11	,,	Madison	Hot Springs	66
	16	,,	(Buncombe)	(Asheville)	
	18	,,	,,	Black Mountain	26
	20	Virginia	Albemarle	Charlottesville	42
	to 28	,,	,,	*Woodridge*	
		,,	,,	*Brown's Cove*	
1917	April 11	Tennessee	Knox	Knoxville	2
	14		Sevier	Sevierville	4
	16	,,	,,	Mount Smoky	24
	20			Sevierville	6
	21		(Knox)	(Knoxville)	

Settlements visited while staying at another centre are printed in italics.

xiii

Preface

Date	State	County	Place	Number of Tunes
1917 April 24	Tennessee	Claiborne	Harrogate	22
30	Kentucky	Bell	Pineville *Wasioto*	20
May 4	,,	Harlan	Harlan	0
5	,,	(Bell)	(Pineville)	
6		Knox	Barbourville	65
19	,,	Madison	Berea	81
31 to June 6	,,	Bell	Pineville	30
July 26	N. Carolina	Buncombe	Asheville	1
27	,,	Madison	Hot Springs	7
28	,,	Jackson	Balsam	7
31	,,	,,	Sylva	0
		,,	*Dillsboro'*	1
Aug. 1	,,	,,	Balsam	0
		Haywood	*Clyde*	5
3	,	(Buncombe)	(Asheville)	
6	Kentucky	Knox	Barbourville	7
9	,,	Clay	Manchester	29
16	,,	,,	Oneida *Teges*	38
22	,,	,,	Manchester	16
	,,	Knox	*Barbourville*	7
25	,,	Bell	Pineville	7
28	,,	Harlan	Pine Mountain	36
Sept. 1	,,	(Bell)	(Pineville)	
3	,,	Fayette	Lexington	2
4	,,	Lee	Beattyville *St. Helen's*	42
9	,,	Breathitt	Jackson	4
	,,	Lee	*St. Helen's*	14
13	,,	Perry	Hazard *Krypton*	5
17	,,	Knott	Hindman	62
24	,,	(Perry)	(Hazard)	
28	,,	Leslie	Hyden	48
Oct. 10	,,	Breathitt	Jackson	0
to 14	,,	Lee	*St. Helen's*	11
1918 April 16	Virginia	Shenandoah	Woodstock	0
18	,,	Rockingham	Harrisonburg	1
22	,,	Nelson	Afton	20
	,,	Albemarle	*Greenwood Crozet*	10
29	,,	Rockbridge	Buena Vista	21
May 3	,,	,,	Natural Bridge	0
6	,,	Nelson	Massie's Mills	0
7 to 10	,,	,,	Nash *White Rock*	37
17	,,	Albemarle	Charlottesville	1

xiv

Preface

Date	State	County	Place	Number of Tunes
1918 May 19	Virginia	(Nelson)	(Afton)	
20	,,	Nelson	Nellysford	27
24	,,	,,	Beechgrove	18
25	,,	,,	(Afton)	
27	W. Virginia	Greenbrier	Ronceverte	0
	,,	,,	Lewisberg	3
29	,,	Summers	Pence Springs	3
31	Virginia	(Alleghany)	(Clifton Forge)	
June 1	,,	Botetourt	Blue Ridge Springs	16
to 19	,,	Bedford	*Villamont*	
	,,	,,	*Montvale*	87
	,,	,,	*Dewey*	
July 24	,,	,,	Peaks of Otter	20
31	,,	,,	Reba	2
Aug. 2	,,	,,	Montvale	5
5	,,	(Roanoke)	(Roanoke)	
8	,,	Montgomery	Crockett Springs	1
9	,,	Franklin	(Rocky Mount)	
12	,,	,,	St. Peter's	67
21	,,	,,	Endicott	27
23	,,	,,	Shooting Creek	0
24	,,	Patrick	Woolwine	3
26	,,	,,	Stuart	2
27	,,	,,	Meadows of Dan	16
30	N. Carolina	Forsyth	Winston Salem	5
Sept. 2	,,	McDowell	Marion	
	,,	,,	*Clinchfield*	49
	,,	,,	*Garden City*	
11	,,	Yancey	Burnsville	
to Oct. 10	,,	,,	*Micaville*	199

On the whole, the most fertile ground was on either side of the big mountain range (known as the 'Great Divide') which separates the States of North Carolina and Tennessee, and this was, perhaps, to be expected, for it was in this region that the most primitive conditions prevailed. It was, however, in Kentucky that we obtained the best ballad-texts despite the intrusion of industrialism consequent on the finding of coal and oil; and the finest tunes came, perhaps, from Virginia, although the general progress of civilization had made further advances there than in the other mountain areas which we visited. West Virginia, where we spent only a few days, did not appear to be a promising field of research. Songs and ballads were undoubtedly to be found (see John Harrington Cox's *Folk-Songs of the South*), but owing to the disturbance of rural life by the big coal industry, they did not lie so ready to hand as in the other States.

Cecil Sharp, after his first visit to the mountains, predicted that the conditions prevailing at that time, which were so favourable to the preservation of traditional

Preface

culture, would not long be maintained, and this supposition was further strengthened by his subsequent experiences in other parts of the mountains.

It is surprising and sad to find how quickly the instinctive culture of the people will seem to disappear when once they have been brought into touch with modern civilization, and how soon they will imitate the manners and become imbued with the tastes of 'polite Society.' As one of our singers contemptuously remarked of the people living in a near-by settlement where a coal-mine had recently been opened, 'They have got rich before they have any money.' And the singing of traditional songs is relegated almost immediately to that past life, which has not only been outgrown, but which has no apparent bearing on the present existence. The explanation of the Kentucky women, who, when asked for songs, said that where she was 'raised' they were sung only by the common, rough people, a class to which she did not belong, was typical of the general attitude in certain districts, as was also the remark, 'We make it a rule never to swear, and never to sing love songs before the children.'[1]

This attitude is no doubt encouraged by the normal educational system, but mention should here be made of the few enlightened schools, of which the Pine Mountain Settlement School was perhaps the most shining example, where a real endeavour was made to maintain a sense of continuity in the lives of the people by strengthening, instead of destroying, their traditional culture, and grafting on to it those intellectual acquirements which are demanded by our present-day mode of life.

The innate courtesy and good breeding which Cecil Sharp extolled in the people of the Laurel Country was not peculiar to them. Throughout our travels we were never once asked what was our business, nor did any one ever show the slightest sign of curiosity or surprise at our visits, even when the appearance of strangers was a rare, if not a unique, event.

During our travels in 1917 and 1918, we sometimes benefited by the hospitality of a school or missionary settlement, as during our first visit to the mountains, but more often we were out of reach of any such institution and had to find lodgings amongst the mountain people. At the county seat there was usually a house rather larger than the rest, which was glorified by the name of 'hotel', and there it was the practice to accommodate travellers, or 'take care' of them, as the expression went. In other settlements we had to depend upon the kindness of those who were willing to extend to us the

---

For other accounts of the mountain people see *The Southern Highlander and his Homeland*, by John C. Campbell: Russell Sage Foundation, New York, 1921; *Our Southern Highlanders*, by Horace Kephart: Outing Publishing Company, New York, 1916 (first printed 1913); *The Land of Saddle-bags*, by James Watt Raine: Council of Women for Home Missions and Missionary Education Movement of the United States and Canada, New York, 1924; *Folk-Songs du Midi des États-Unis* by Josiah H. Combs: Les Presses Universitaires de France, Paris, 1925. See also p. xx.

Preface

hospitality of their homes, and, except on one occasion when rumour had it that we were German spies, the mountain people were always willing and glad to receive us and give us of their best.

The following entry in Cecil Sharp's diary written at the end of a week's stay in a very humble home indicates what was our normal experience on these occasions:—'We said good-bye with genuine reluctance. They are thoroughly nice people with nice feelings. They never did anything snobbish, or affected, or unpleasant, and were not in the least shy or overawed. They took us as we were and were obviously interested in our lives, which were so different from their own.' That is one side of the picture: the other was given me by our hostess, who remarked, 'I could go on listening for hours to Mr. Sharp talking. He is so educating.'

Cecil Sharp refers in his Introduction to the use of certain words in an archaic sense, and bearing this in mind I would quote a remark that was made by an old lady from whom we were taking our leave. She said: 'My husband and I are sorry you are going. We like you—you are so nice and common.' That was a compliment which Cecil Sharp treasured above all others. That he never 'talked down' to the people, but met them always on an equal footing, was perhaps one cause of the happy relationship which existed between him and the singers, ensuring a complete readiness on their part to reveal to him their store of treasured songs.

How great was the mountain people's love and appreciation of their songs can, perhaps, be shown by relating two incidents.

The first occurred whilst we were noting songs from Mrs. Wheeler at Buena Vista, when her family of thirteen children—seven of her own and six step-children—were present as eagerly interested spectators of the strange proceedings. They listened quietly for some time until their mother started 'The Green Bed' (see No. 58 D). Then almost as though impelled by some unseen power they softly joined in the singing of this beautiful air, and the haunting loveliness of their young voices, subdued to an undertone so as not to disturb their mother's singing, was an unforgettable experience.

On another occasion when we had been listening to the ballad of 'The Death of Queen Jane' (see No. 32), Mr. Sharp told the singer some of the historical facts which are referred to in the ballad. 'There now', she said triumphantly, 'I always said the song must be true, because it is so beautiful.'

The singers often expressed their appreciation of our endeavours to perpetuate their songs. 'Singing is a great power in the world', said one of them 'and you are doing a noble work.' The pleasure and bewilderment with which they regarded the process of notation is described by Cecil Sharp, but one particular instance must be recorded, when an old man was shown the musical notation of the song which he had just sung. 'There is your song', said Mr. Sharp, handing his note-book, and the old man, who could neither read nor write, peered thoughtfully at the page of manuscript, carefully scrutinizing the blobs, dashes and dots, and then, shaking his head, said, 'Well, I can hardly recognize it.'

Cecil Sharp refers to the decadence of dancing, but at that time he only knew by hearsay of the 'set-running', for it was not until August, 1917, that he saw an actual performance. This, although the only form of dance that is known to the mountain people, has an infinite variety of figure and is a finely constructed dance expressive of great beauty and forceful emotion. A full description is given elsewhere,[1] and it is therefore unnecessary to give further details here, except to add that the dance appears to be allied to the Square-Dance which is widely distributed throughout the North American Continent.

The instrumental tunes which were played as accompaniments to the dance were of little value. A few dance-tunes were noted by Cecil Sharp, but these apart from the method and style of their playing have but little interest, and so I have not reproduced them.

Of greater interest were the Jigs (see Nos. 240-54), which were sung often as ditties on their own account, but their primary purpose was apparently to serve as an accompaniment to step-dances, or 'hoe-downs', as they were called, and for this reason, perhaps, they were frowned upon by certain sections of the community. The words appeared to be chosen from a large stock of phrases and fitted at random to the tune.

It may be that some of the songs classified under Play-party Games (see Nos. 255-74) are actually Jigs. Only in a few cases did we see a performance of the Games, but from the words and the descriptions which were given us it is apparent that they have but little dramatic action and are in the nature of dance-games, though the actual dance-movements are elementary and insignificant. In the majority of games the main interest centres around the 'choosing' of partners.[2]

The dulcimer, which is described in the Introduction on p. xxvii, we saw and heard only in some of the Kentucky mountains-schools and never in the homes of the people, where it is evidently but rarely to be found. The history of its introduction into the mountains is obscure, but it may be noted that a similar instrument, catalogued as a German zither of the eighteenth century, is exhibited in the New York Metropolitan Museum of Art,[3] and if this classification is

---

[1] *The Country Dance Book*, Part V, by Cecil J. Sharp and Maud Karpeles: Novello and Co., London, 1918.

[2] For a further description of the Play-party Game see *The Play-Party in Indiana*, by Leah Jackson: Indiana Historical Commission, Indianapolis, 1916; and two articles in *The Journal of American Folk Lore*, viz. 'The Missouri Play Party', by Mrs. L. D. Ames, vol. xxvii, p. 289; and 'Some Play-Party Games of the Middle West', by Edwin F. Piper, vol. xxviii, p. 262.

[3] Crosby Brown Collection of Musical Instruments, No. 988.

Preface

correct it is possible that the instrument was introduced by the early German settlers, who drifted into the mountains from Pennsylvania.

The endeavour has been to present the tunes in these volumes as far as possible in accordance with the system of modal classification which Cecil Sharp adopted in the earlier edition (see pp. xxx–xxxiv of this volume). That involved two decisions: (1) the position of the 'weak' notes in hexatonic and heptatonic tunes; and (2) the position of the tonic.

(1) It will be seen from the chart given on p. xxxii that the hexatonic and heptatonic scales are given as derivates of the pentatonic and that they are formed by filling in the 'gaps' which occur in the latter scales. This in the earlier edition was done in two ways: by making the mediate note of the upper gap either B♭ or B♮, the mediate note of the lower gap remaining constant as E♮ in both cases. But in order to allow for the classification of tunes collected at a later date, Cecil Sharp afterwards found it necessary to add to these two possible combinations a third, in which the lower gap of the pentatonic is filled by E♭ and the upper by B♭. With this expansion of the system it will be seen that heptatonic tunes will be classified thus according to the position of the 'weak' notes :—

Heptatonic.	'Weak' Notes.	Pentatonic Mode.
Ionian	3rd and 7th	1
	4th and 7th	3
Dorian	3rd and 7th	1
	2nd and 6th	2
	3rd and 6th	4
Phrygian	2nd and 6th	2
	2nd and 5th	5
Lydian	4th and 7th	3
Mixolydian	3rd and 7th	1
	4th and 7th	3
	3rd and 6th	4
Aeolian	2nd and 6th	2
	3rd and 6th	4
	2nd and 5th	5

But since in a given tune it is often difficult to determine which are the 'weak' notes, I have refrained from making a decision, and accordingly this part of Cecil Sharp's scheme has not been applied to the hexatonic and heptatonic tunes which do not appear in the first edition.

(2) The position of the tonic is more vital, because on that depends a good deal of the musical feeling of the tune. In most cases the position is obvious, but in a few others it has to be a matter of individual judgement. I have given mine for what it may be worth, indicating it by the key-signature, and

Preface

also by a superscription when—as often occurs—the final note is not the tonic.

The list of those to whom we are indebted has greatly increased since Cecil Sharp wrote the concluding paragraph of his Introduction, and space forbids the inclusion of the names of all who helped us in our work, but of the many friends who gave us hospitality I would acknowledge the kindness of Mr. and Mrs. Guy Corbett of Afton, Va.; of Mr. and Mrs. Storey of Mount Smokey, Tenn.; and of the Principals and Staff of the following schools and colleges :— Lincoln Memorial University, Harrogate, Tenn.; Berea College, the Hindman, Oneida, and Pine Mountain Schools in Kentucky; and St. Peter's School, Virginia. Nor can I refrain from mentioning my gratitude to Dr. Packard and the late Mr. John Campbell, who made a two days' journey over the mountains to come to my assistance on one of the several occasions on which Cecil Sharp was suddenly stricken with fever and lay seriously ill.

I would also acknowledge my indebtedness to Mr. Fox Strangways, Miss A. G. Gilchrist, and Dr. Vaughan Williams for their help and advice in the preparation of these volumes, and finally, to Mr. Percy Grainger, to whose generosity the publication of this work is largely due.

1931
MAUD KARPELES

NOTE TO PREFACE

In the summer of 1951, with the assistance of the Library of Congress, I spent three-and-a-half weeks in the mountains of Virginia, North Carolina, and Tennessee, accompanied by Mrs. Sidney Robertson Cowell. With a tape-recording machine lent by the Library we recorded ninety-one songs and instrumental tunes, of which sixty-nine were from singers who had previously sung to Cecil Sharp or from near relations of these singers.

I found, as I had been led to expect, that mountain life has been completely revolutionized during the last twenty to twenty-five years. Roads and electricity have brought 'civilization' to the mountains. The roads have made markets accessible and the people are now so busy making money in order to buy electric appliances and to improve the general material standard of life that they no longer have the leisure that they formerly possessed. The radio, which now operates in nearly every mountain home, has let loose a flood of 'hilly-billy' and other popular music, and this is gradually submerging the traditional songs. Primary education is another force that is weakening the hold of tradition.

Nevertheless tradition dies hard. Memory may weaken, but the love of the songs remains and with a little encouragement it springs up anew. To many a singer it was a great delight to be able to re-learn from these volumes a song that he had sung to Cecil Sharp over thirty years ago and had since forgotten. Thus, a song, originating in England and carried to America, lives there by oral tradition for some hundreds of years; it is written down and taken back to England by Cecil Sharp; then some thirty years later the song is carried back in printed form to the country of its adoption and takes on a new lease of life. Such are the devious ways of tradition.

1951
M. K.

INTRODUCTION TO THE FIRST EDITION, 1917

THE effort that has been made to collect and preserve in permanent form the folk-songs of England during the last twenty or thirty years has resulted in the salvage of many thousands of beautiful songs. It was pardonable, therefore, if those who, like myself, had assisted in the task had come to believe that the major part of the work had been completed. So far as the collection in England itself was concerned, this belief was no doubt well founded. Nevertheless, in arriving at this very consolatory conclusion, one important, albeit not very obvious consideration had been overlooked, namely, the possibility that one or other of those English communities that lie scattered in various parts of the world might provide as good a field for the collector as England itself, and yield as bountiful and rich a harvest. The investigation which my colleague Mrs. Campbell began, and in which later on I came to bear a hand, has proved that at least one such community does in fact exist in the Southern Appalachian Mountains of North America. The region is an extensive one, covering some 110,000 square miles, and is considerably larger than England, Wales, and Scotland combined. It includes about one-third of the total area of the States of North and South Carolina, Tennessee, Virginia, West Virginia, Kentucky, Alabama, and Georgia. The total population exceeds five millions, or, excluding city dwellers, about three millions.

THE COUNTRY AND ITS INHABITANTS. The reader will, I think, be in a better position to appreciate and assess the value of the songs and ballads which form the major part of this volume if, by way of preface, I give some account of the way in which they were collected and record the impression which the inhabitants of this unique country made upon me. But I must bid him remember that I claim to speak with authority only with respect to that part of the mountain district into which I penetrated, and that the statements and opinions which are now to follow must be accepted subject to this qualification.

I spent nine weeks only in the mountains, accompanied throughout by Miss Maud Karpeles, who took down, usually in shorthand, the words of the songs we heard, while I noted the tunes. Mr. John C. Campbell, Director of the Southern Highland Division of the Russell Sage Foundation, went with us on our first expedition and afterwards directed our journeyings and, in general, gave us the benefit of his very full knowledge of the country and its people. Our usual procedure was to stay at one or other of the Presbyterian Missionary Settlements and to make it our centre for a week or ten days while we visited the singers who lived within a walking radius. In this way we successively visited White Rock, Allanstand, Alleghany and Carmen, Big Laurel and Hot Springs, in North Carolina, and thus succeeded in exploring

Introduction to the First Edition, 1917

the major portion of what is known as the Laurel Country. Afterwards we spent ten days at Rocky Fork, Tenn., and a similar period at Charlottesville, Va. I should add that had it not been for the generous hospitality extended to us by the heads of the Missionary Settlements at which we sojourned, it would have been quite impossible to prosecute our work.

The present inhabitants of the Laurel Country are the direct descendants of the original settlers who were emigrants from England and, I suspect, the lowlands of Scotland. I was able to ascertain with some degree of certainty that the settlement of this particular section began about three or four generations ago, i.e. in the latter part of the eighteenth century or early years of the nineteenth. How many years prior to this the original emigration from England had taken place, I am unable to say; but it is fairly safe, I think, to conclude that the present-day residents of this section of the mountains are the descendants of those who left the shores of Britain some time in the eighteenth century.

The region is from its inaccessibility a very secluded one. There are but few roads—most of them little better than mountain tracks—and practically no railroads. Indeed, so remote and shut off from outside influence were, until quite recently, these sequestered mountain valleys that the inhabitants have for a hundred years or more been completely isolated and cut off from all traffic with the rest of the world. Their speech is English, not American, and, from the number of expressions they use which have long been obsolete elsewhere, and the old-fashioned way in which they pronounce many of their words, it is clear that they are talking the language of a past day, though exactly of what period I am not competent to decide. One peculiarity is perhaps worth the noting, namely the pronunciation of the impersonal pronoun with an aspirate—'hit'—a practice that seems to be universal.

Economically they are independent. As there are practically no available markets, little or no surplus produce is grown, each family extracting from its holding just what is needed to support life, and no more. They have very little money, barter in kind being the customary form of exchange.

Many set the standard of bodily and material comfort perilously low, in order, presumably, that they may have the more leisure and so extract the maximum enjoyment out of life. The majority live in log-cabins, more or less water-tight, usually, but not always, lighted with windows; but some have built larger and more comfortable homesteads.

They are a leisurely, cheery people in their quiet way, in whom the social instinct is very highly developed. They dispense hospitality with an open-handed generosity and are extremely interested in and friendly toward strangers, communicative and unsuspicious. 'But surely you will tarry with us for the night?' was said to us on more than one occasion when, after paying an afternoon's visit, we rose to say good-bye.

Introduction to the First Edition, 1917

They know their Bible intimately and subscribe to an austere creed, charged with Calvinism and the unrelenting doctrines of determinism or fatalism. The majority we met were Baptists, but we met Methodists also, a few Presbyterians, and some who are attached to what is known as the 'Holiness' sect, with whom, however, we had but little truck, as their creed forbids the singing of secular songs.

They have an easy unaffected bearing and the unselfconscious manners of the well-bred. I have received salutations upon introduction or on bidding farewell, dignified and restrained, such as a courtier might make to his Sovereign. Our work naturally led to the making of many acquaintances, and, in not a few cases, to the formation of friendships of a more intimate nature, but on no single occasion did we receive anything but courteous and friendly treatment. Strangers that we met in the course of our long walks would usually bow, doff the hat, and extend the hand, saying, 'My name is ——; what is yours?' an introduction which often led to a pleasant talk and sometimes to singing and the noting of interesting ballads. In their general characteristics they reminded me of the English peasant, with whom my work in England for the past fifteen years or more has brought me into close contact. There are differences, however. The mountaineer is freer in his manner, more alert, and less inarticulate than his British prototype, and bears no trace of the obsequiousness of manner which, since the Enclosure Acts robbed him of his economic independence and made of him a hired labourer, has unhappily characterized the English villager. The difference is seen in the way the mountaineer, as I have already said, upon meeting a stranger, removes his hat, offers his hand and enters into conversation, where the English labourer would touch his cap, or pull his forelock, and pass on.

A few of those we met were able to read and write, but the majority were illiterate. They are, however, good talkers, using an abundant vocabulary racily and often picturesquely. Although uneducated, in the sense in which that term is usually understood, they possess that elemental wisdom, abundant knowledge, and intuitive understanding which those only who live in constant touch with Nature and face to face with reality seem to be able to acquire. It is to be hoped that the schools which are beginning to be established in some districts, chiefly in the vicinity of the Missionary Settlements, will succeed in giving them what they lack without infecting their ideals, or depriving them of the charm of manner and the many engaging qualities which so happily distinguish them.

Physically, they are strong and of good stature, though usually spare in figure. Their features are clean-cut and often handsome; while their complexions testify to wholesome, out-of-door habits. They carry themselves superbly, and it was a never-failing delight to note their swinging, easy gait and the sureness with which they would negotiate the foot-logs over the creeks,

Introduction to the First Edition, 1917

the crossing of which caused us many anxious moments. The children usually go about barefooted, and on occasion their elders too, at any rate in the summer time. Like all primitive peoples, or those who live under primitive conditions, they attain to physical maturity at a very early age, especially the women, with whom marriage at thirteen, or even younger, is not unknown.

I have been told that in past days there were blood-feuds—a species of vendetta—which were pursued for generations between members of certain families or clans; but, whenever circumstances connected with these were related to me, I was always given to understand that this barbarous custom had long since been discontinued. I have heard, too, that there is a good deal of illicit distilling of corn spirit by 'moonshiners', as they are called, in defiance of the State excise laws; but of this, again, I personally saw nothing and heard but little. Nor did I see any consumption of alcohol in the houses I visited. On the other hand, the chewing or snuffing of tobacco is a common habit amongst young and old; but, curiously enough, no one smokes.[1] Indeed, many looked askance at my pipe, and I rarely succeeded in extracting more than a half-hearted assent to my request for permission to light it.

That the illiterate may nevertheless reach a high level of culture will surprise those only who imagine that education and cultivation are convertible terms. The reason, I take it, why these mountain people, albeit unlettered, have acquired so many of the essentials of culture is partly to be attributed to the large amount of leisure they enjoy, without which, of course, no cultural development is possible, but chiefly to the fact that they have one and all entered at birth into the full enjoyment of their racial heritage. Their language, wisdom, manners, and the many graces of life that are theirs, are merely racial attributes which have been gradually acquired and accumulated in past centuries and handed down generation by generation, each generation adding its quotum to that which it received. It must be remembered, also, that in their everyday lives they are immune from that continuous grinding, mental pressure, due to the attempt to 'make a living', from which nearly all of us in the modern world suffer. Here no one is 'on the make'; commercial competition and social rivalries are unknown. In this respect, at any rate, they have the advantage over those who habitually spend the greater part of every day in preparing to live, in acquiring the technique of life, rather than in its enjoyment.

I have dwelt at considerable length upon this aspect of the mountain life because it was the first which struck me and further, because, without a realization of this background, it will be difficult for the reader to follow intelligently what I have to say. But before I leave this part of my subject I must, in self-justification, add that I am aware that the outsider does not

[1] The custom with regard to smoking varies in the different districts. In parts of Kentucky women habitually smoke clay-pipes.—M. K.

Introduction to the First Edition, 1917

always see the whole of the game, and that I am fully conscious that there is another and less lovely side of the picture which in my appreciation I have ignored. I have deliberately done so because that side has, I believe, already been emphasized, perhaps with unnecessary insistence, by other observers.

THE SINGERS AND THEIR SONGS. My sole purpose in visiting this country was to collect the traditional songs and ballads which I had heard from Mrs. Campbell, and knew from other sources, were still being sung there. I naturally expected to find conditions very similar to those which I had encountered in England when engaged on the same quest. But of this I was soon to be agreeably disillusioned. Instead, for instance, of having to confine my attention to the aged, as in England, where no one under the age of seventy ordinarily possesses the folk-song tradition, I discovered that I could get what I wanted from pretty nearly every one I met, young and old. In fact, I found myself for the first time in my life in a community in which singing was as common and almost as universal a practice as speaking. With us, of course, singing is an entertainment, something done by others for our delectation, the cult and close preserve of a professional caste of specialists. The fact has been forgotten that singing is the one form of artistic expression that can be practised without any preliminary study or special training; that every normal human being can sing just as every one can talk; and that it is, consequently, just as ridiculous to restrict the practice of singing to a chosen few as it would be to limit the art of speaking to orators, professors of elocution, and other specialists. In an ideal society every child in his earliest years would as a matter of course develop this inborn capacity and learn to sing the songs of his forefathers in the same natural and unselfconscious way in which he now learns his mother tongue and the elementary literature of the nation to which he belongs.

And it was precisely this ideal state of things that I found existing in the mountain communities. So closely, indeed, is the practice of this particular art interwoven with the ordinary avocations of everyday life that singers, unable to recall a song I had asked for, would often make some such remark as, 'Oh, if only I were driving the cows home I could sing it at once!' On one occasion, too, I remember that a small boy tried to edge himself into my cabin in which a man was singing to me and, when I asked him what he wanted, he said, 'I always like to go where there is sweet music.' Of course, I let him in and, later on, when my singer failed to remember a song I had asked for, my little visitor came to the rescue and straightway sang the ballad from beginning to end in the true traditional manner, and in a way which would have shamed many a professional vocalist (see No. 18 B). I have no doubt but that this delightful habit of making beautiful music at all times and in all places largely compensates for any deficiencies in the matter of reading and writing.

Introduction to the First Edition, 1917

But, of course, the cultural value of singing must depend upon the kind of songs that are sung. Happily, in this matter the hillsman is not called upon to exercise any choice, for the only music, or, at any rate, the only secular music, that he hears and has, therefore, any opportunity of learning is that which his British forefathers brought with them from their native country and has since survived by oral tradition.

When, by chance, the text of a modern street-song succeeds in penetrating into the mountains it is at once mated to a traditional tune (e.g. No. 99) and sometimes still further purified by being moulded into the form of a traditional ballad (see No. 87). But this happens but rarely, for, strange as it may seem, these mountain valleys are in fact far less affected by modern musical influences than the most remote and secluded English village, where there is always a parsonage or manor-house, or both, to link it to the outside world.

We found little or no difficulty in persuading those we visited to sing to us. To prove our interest in the subject and to arouse their memories, we would ourselves sometimes sing folk-songs that I had collected in England, choosing, for preference, those with which they were unacquainted. Very often they misunderstood our requirements and would give us hymns instead of the secular songs and ballads which we wanted; but that was before we had learned to ask for 'love-songs', which is their name for these ditties. It was evident, too, that it was often assumed that strangers like ourselves could have but one object and that to 'improve', and their relief was obvious when they found that we came not to give but to receive.

It is no exaggeration to say that some of the hours I passed sitting on the porch (i.e. verandah) of a log-cabin, talking and listening to songs were amongst the pleasantest I have ever spent. Very often we would call upon some of our friends early in the morning and remain till dusk, sharing the mid-day meal with the family, and I would go away in the evening with the feeling that I had never before been in a more musical atmosphere, nor benefited more greatly by the exchange of musical confidences.

The singers displayed much interest in watching me take down their music in my note-book, and when at the conclusion of a song I hummed over the tune to test the accuracy of my transcription they were as delighted as though I had successfully performed a conjuring trick.

The mountain singers sing in very much the same way as English folk-singers, in the same straightforward, direct manner, without any conscious effort at expression, and with the even tone and clarity of enunciation with which all folk-song collectors are familiar. Perhaps, however, they are less unselfconscious and sing rather more freely and with somewhat less restraint than the English peasant; I certainly never saw any one of them close the eyes when he sang nor assume that rigid, passive expression to which collectors in England have so often called attention.

Introduction to the First Edition, 1917

They have one vocal peculiarity, however, which I have never noticed amongst English folk-singers, namely, the habit of dwelling arbitrarily upon certain notes of the melody, generally the weaker accents. This practice, which is almost universal, by disguising the rhythm and breaking up the monotonous regularity of the phrases, produces an effect of improvisation and freedom from rule which is very pleasing. The effect is most characteristic in $\frac{6}{8}$ tunes, as, for example, No. 19 G, in which in the course of the tune pauses are made on each of the three notes of the subsidiary triplets.

The wonderful charm, fascinating and well-nigh magical, which the folk-singer produces upon those who are fortunate enough to hear him is to be attributed very largely to his method of singing, and this, it should be understood, is quite as traditional as the song itself. The genuine folk-singer is never conscious of his audience—indeed, as often as not, he has none—and he never, therefore, strives after effect, nor endeavours in this or in any other way to attract the attention, much less the admiration of his hearers. So far as I have been able to comprehend his mental attitude, I gather that, when singing a ballad, for instance, he is merely relating a story in a peculiarly effective way which he has learned from his elders, his conscious attention being wholly concentrated upon what he is singing and not upon the effect which he himself is producing. This is more true, perhaps, of the English than of the American singers, some of whom I found were able mentally to separate the tune from the text—which English singers can rarely do—and even in some cases to discuss the musical points of the former with considerable intelligence.

I came across but one singer who sang to an instrumental accompaniment, the guitar, and that was in Charlottesville, Va. (No. 12 B). Mrs. Campbell, however, tells me that in Kentucky, where I have not yet collected, singers occasionally play an instrument called the dulcimer,[1] a shallow, wooden box, with four sound-holes, in shape somewhat like a flat, elongated violin, over which are strung three (sometimes four) metal strings, the two (or three) lower of which are tonic-drones, the melody being played upon the remaining and uppermost string, which is fretted. As the strings are plucked with the fingers and not struck with a hammer, the instrument would, I suppose, be more correctly called a psaltery.

The only instrumental music I heard were jig tunes played on the fiddle. I took down several of these from the two fiddlers, Mr. Reuben Hensley and Mr. Michael Wallin, who were good enough to play to me. Wherever possible they used the open strings as drones, tuning the strings—which, by the way, were of metal—in a particular way for each air they were about to perform. I have not included any of these in this collection, but I hope, later on, to publish some of them when I have had further opportunities of examining this peculiar and unusual method of performance.[2]

See Preface, p. xviii.—M. K.   See Preface, p. xviii.—M. K.

Introduction to the First Edition, 1917

Many of the singers whose songs are recorded in the following pages had very large repertories. Mrs. Reuben Hensley, with the assistance of her husband and her daughter Emma, sang me thirty-five songs; while Mrs. Sands of Allanstand gave me twenty-five; Mr. Jeff Stockton of Flag Pond, Tenn., seventeen; Mr. N. B. Chisholm of Woodridge, Va., twenty-four; Mrs. Tom Rice of Big Laurel, twenty-six; and Mrs. Jane Gentry of Hot Springs, no less than sixty-four. Attention has often been called to the wonderful and retentive memories of folk-singers in England, and I can vouch for it that these American singers are, in this respect, in no way inferior to their English contemporaries.

None of the singers whom I visited possessed any printed song-sheets, but some of them produced written copies, usually made by children, which they called 'ballets', a term which the English singer reserves for the printed broadside.

It will be seen that in many cases we give several variants or different versions of the same song and that we have made no attempt to discriminate between these. The fact that no two singers ever sing the same song in identically the same way is familiar to all collectors, and may be interpreted in either of two ways. The upholder of the individualistic theory of origin contends that these variants are merely incorrect renderings of some original, individual composition which, never having been written down, has orally survived in various corrupt forms. On the other hand, there are those—and I count myself amongst them—who maintain that in these minute differences lie the germs of development; that the changes made by individual singers are akin to the 'sports' in the flower or animal worlds, which, if perpetuated, lead to further ideal development and, perhaps, ultimately to the birth of new varieties and species. There is no doubt that if this problem is ever to be solved it will be through the examination and analysis of genuine, authentic variants, such as we have done our best faithfully to record; and we make no apology, therefore, for printing so many of them.

For very much the same reason, in addition to the variants derived from different singers, we have in many cases recorded the changes made by the individual singer in the successive repetitions of the tune in the course of his song. These are often of great interest and significance and sometimes show an inventiveness on the part of the singer that is nothing less than amazing as, for example, in Mr. Jeff Stockton's version of 'Fair Margaret' (No. 20 A).

THE BALLADS. The distinction between the ballad and the song is more or less arbitrary and is not easy to define with precision. Broadly speaking, however, the ballad is a narrative song, romantic in character and, above all, impersonal, that is to say, the singer is merely the narrator of events with which he personally has no connexion and for which he has no responsibility. The song, on the other hand, is a far more emotional and passionate utterance,

Introduction to the First Edition, 1917

and is usually the record of a personal experience—very frequently of an amatory nature. The ballads have, probably, the longer history behind them; at any rate, they attracted the attention of collectors earlier than the songs— the reason, perhaps, why the ballads have suffered, far more than the songs, from the unscrupulous editing of literary meddlers.

The ballad air is necessarily of a straightforward type, as it is sung indifferently to verses often varying very widely in emotional character. Nevertheless, many of the ballad tunes are very lovely, as the musician who studies the contents of this volume will readily perceive. Such airs, for instance, as Nos. 4, 18, 22, 23, 33, 35, 41, 45, and 49 [1] make really beautiful music and are fully capable of standing alone, divorced from their texts, and of being played or sung as absolute music. The most perfect type of ballad, however, is that in which the tune, whilst serving its purpose as an ideal vehicle for the words, is of comparatively little value when divorced from its text. 'The False Knight upon the Road' (No. 2) is a good instance of this and, in my opinion, a splendid example of the genuine ballad at its highest pitch.

It is greatly to be deplored that the literature of the ballad has, in the past, attracted so much more attention than the music. Properly speaking, the two elements should never be dissociated; the music and the text are one and indivisible, and to sever one from the other is to remove the gem from its setting. Early poetry, to which category the traditional ballad belongs, was always sung or chanted; it was addressed to the ear, not the eye. While language appeals primarily to the intelligence, its sound acts upon and arouses the emotions, the more especially when the words have been artfully chosen, thrown into metrical rhythm and wedded to beautiful music. Of all human creations, language is perhaps the most distinctive and characteristic; its development has proceeded step by step with the progress of mankind from the savage to the cultivated being of the present day; and in the course of this evolution the ballad has played by no means an insignificant part.

THE SONGS. The song-melodies differ in many respects from those of the ballads. Structurally, many of them are built upon larger and more elaborate lines, while emotionally, for reasons already given, they are far more intense and more heavily charged with sentiment. Several of the mountain song-tunes are, in my opinion, very characteristic and beautiful; Nos. 88, 106, 109, 110, 111, 115, 118, and 122,[2] for instance, will challenge the very finest of the folk-tunes that have been found in England. Some of them too, while conforming in type to the regular English folk-tune, are yet in a measure so different that they may fairly be considered a fresh contribution to the subject.

From the later collection Nos. 10 J, 18 H, 34 D, and 64 D might be added to this list.—M. K.
See also Nos. 126, 140 C, and 145 E collected at a later date.—M. K.

Introduction to the First Edition, 1917

The literature of the traditional song does not, as a whole, compare favourably with that of the ballad. Many of the lines printed in this volume are corrupt and unintelligible, while some of them are the merest doggerel. Nevertheless, a few of the verses are very beautiful, not merely by contrast but intrinsically. Stanzas, for example, such as

> When I see your babe a-laughing,
> It makes me think of your sweet face;
> But when I see your babe a-crying,
> It makes me think of my disgrace,

and

> When your heart was mine, true love,
> And your head lay on my breast,
> You could make me believe by the falling of your arm
> That the sun rose up in the West.
>
> There's many a girl can go all round about
> And hear the small birds sing,
> And many a girl that stays at home alone
> And rocks the cradle and spins.
>
> There's many a star that shall jingle in the West,
> There's many a leaf below,
> There's many a damn that will light upon a man
> For treating a poor girl so.

contain all the essentials of genuine poetry and, in their feeling, in their artlessness, in the directness and simplicity of their verbal expression and the absence of circumlocution, reach a high level of imaginative and poetic expression.

One curious hiatus in the repertories of the mountain-singers struck me very forcibly, viz. the total absence of songs of a ritual nature, e.g. Harvest-Home songs, Carols (with one notable exception, No. 15), May-day songs and others of religious origin, such as those associated with the Morris and Sword-dance ceremonies. The reason for this, I take it, is because ritual observances belong to, and are bound up so closely with, the soil of a country that they do not readily survive transplantation; and partly, too, because the mountain people for the most part live in isolated dwellings and at considerable distances from one another and do not congregate in villages as in older and more settled countries like England, a condition that would inevitably lead to the discontinuance of seasonal and other communal festivals. This latter reason may also account for the decadence of dancing[1] amongst the mountaineers, although I have no doubt that religious scruples have also been a contributory cause—I noticed that in reply to my inquiries on this subject the euphemism 'playing games' was always substituted for 'dancing' by my informants.

SCALES AND MODES.[2] Very nearly all these Appalachian tunes are cast in

See Preface, p. xviii.—M. K.   See also Preface, pp. xix-xx.—M. K.

Introduction to the First Edition, 1917

'gapped scales, that is to say, scales containing only five, or sometimes six, notes to the octave, instead of the seven with which we are familiar, a 'hiatus' or 'gap' occurring where a note is omitted.

To trace the history of this particular scale is to venture upon controversial ground. Personally, I believe that is was the first form of scale evolved by the folk which was in any way comparable with our modern major or minor scale. Originally, as may be gathered from the music of primitive tribes, the singer was content to chant his song in monotone, varied by occasional excursions to the sounds immediately above or below his single tone, or by a leap to the fourth below. Eventually, however, he succeeded in converting the whole octave, but, even so, he was satisfied with fewer intermediate sounds than the seven which comprise the modern diatonic scale. Indeed, there are many nations at the present day which have not yet advanced beyond the two-gapped or pentatonic scale, such as, for instance, the Gaels of Highland Scotland; and, when we realize the almost infinite melodic possibilities of the 5-note scale, as exemplified in Celtic folk-music and, for that matter, in the tunes printed in this volume, we can readily understand that singers felt no urgent necessity to increase the number of notes in the octave. A further development in this direction was, however, eventually achieved by the folk-singer, though, for a long while, as was but natural, the two medial notes, required to complete the scale, were introduced speculatively and with hesitation. There are many instances in Irish folk-music, for example, in which the pitch or intonation of these added sounds is varied in the course of one and the same tune. This experimental and transitional period, however, eventually came to a close and the final stage was reached, so far as the folk-singer was concerned, when the diatonic scale, i.e. the 7-note scale represented by the white notes of the pianoforte, became definitely settled. And this is the scale which is commonly used by the English folk-singer of the present day. But even then, and for a long period after, the mediate sounds remained 'weak' and were employed only as auxiliary notes or connecting links, rather than structural or cadential notes, so that the gaps, though covered up, were not concealed. And it was left to the art-musician to take the final step and evolve the 7-note scale of which every note could be used with equal freedom and certainty.

Of the tunes in this volume, some are pentatonic; others belong to the transitional period and are hesitatingly hexatonic, or even heptatonic; while a few are frankly in the major mode, i.e. diatonic 7-note tunes in which no indication of a pentatonic origin can be traced. For the benefit of those interested in this technical question, particulars concerning scale and mode are given at the head of every tune in the text. The names and characteristics of the 7-note diatonic modes need no explanation; but with regard to the pentatonic modes, which are but rarely employed by art-musicians, it may be

Introduction to the First Edition, 1917

Pentatonic Modes

* With the combination of E♭ and B♭ (see Preface, p. xix) the heptatonic scales will be:—(1) Dorian, (2) Phrygian, (3) Mixolydian, and (4) Aeolian.—M. K.

Introduction to the First Edition, 1917

as well, perhaps, to explain the method of classification and nomenclature adopted in this volume. This is set out in the chart on p. xxxii.

The five pentatonic modes there given have been derived in the following way:

If from the white-note scale of the pianoforte the two notes E and B be eliminated we have the pentatonic scale with its two gaps in every octave, between D and F and between A and C. As in each one of the five notes of the system may in turn be chosen as tonic, five modes emerge, based, respectively, upon the notes C, D, F, G, and A. The gaps, of course, occur at different intervals in each scale, and it is this distinguishing feature which gives to each mode its individuality and peculiar characteristic.

The one-gapped or hexatonic scale, and the 7-note or heptatonic scale are, as we have already seen, derivates of the original pentatonic obtained by the filling in, respectively, of one or both of the gaps. Miss Gilchrist (see *Journal of the Folk-Song Society*, iv, pp. 150–3), whose very clear exposition of this matter I am in the main following, allows the lower gap, i.e. between D and F, to be completed by the insertion of either E-flat or E-natural, and the upper gap, i.e. between A and C, by the addition of B-flat; and by this method she has succeeded in classifying very satisfactorily her material, which consists entirely of Gaelic tunes. When, however, I came to apply this method to the mountain-tunes I found it necessary to make the following modification, viz. to take E-natural as the constant and invariable mediate note of the lower gap, and either B-flat or B-natural of the upper.[1] The chart shown on p. xxxii has, therefore, been constructed on this plan, i.e. Miss Gilchrist's, modified in the way just explained.

This description will, it is hoped, enable the reader to understand the modal and scale index attached to each of the tunes printed in this volume. His attention must, however, still be called to two points.

In some tunes it has been difficult to decide with certainty upon the tonic, for in pentatonic airs, or, at any rate, in these mountain melodies, the tonic is frequently and patently *not* the final note of the tune. Airs of this kind are called 'circular', because the final phrase is fashioned so that it may lead into the initial phrase without pause or break of continuity and thus complete the melodic circle. Strictly speaking, the singer on the final repetition of a circular tune should vary the last phrase so as to conclude upon the tonic; but this singers very rarely do—No 29 A is the only tune in this Collection in which this is done.

Again, it will be seen that a heptatonic tune may, so far as its notes are concerned, be assigned indifferently to one or other of two modes. An ionian air, for instance, may belong to Mode 1, or Mode 3; a dorian to Modes 2 or 4, and so forth. The true classification in such cases is determined by

[1] See Preface, p. xix.—M. K.

Introduction to the First Edition, 1917

detecting the 'weak' notes, which, by disclosing the places in the scale where the gaps originally occurred, will thereby show the mode, of which the tune in question is a derivative. An ionian tune, for example, will be assigned to Mode 1 if its third be a weak note (as well as its seventh), and to Mode 3 if, instead of the third, the fourth be the weak one. Similarly a dorian air will be classified second or fourth Mode according as the second or third scale-degree be the weak note.

ETHNOLOGICAL ORIGIN OF THE SINGERS. If the prevalence of the gapped scale in the mountain tunes is any indication of the ethnological origin of the singers, it seems to point to the North of England, or to the Lowlands, rather than the Highlands, of Scotland, as the country from which they originally migrated. For the Appalachian tunes, notwithstanding their 'gapped' characteristics, have far more affinity with the normal English folk-tune than with that of the Gaelic-speaking Highlander (cf. *Journal of the Folk-Song Society*, v, pp. 157–269), and may, therefore, very well have been derived from those who, dwelling on the borders of the Highland Kingdom, had become infected to some extent with the musical proclivities of their neighbours. It will be observed, moreover, that the Notes contain a large number of references to Dean Christie's *Traditional Ballad Airs*, and to the late Gavin Greig's *Folk-Songs of the North-East*, and both of these are collections of traditional songs from Lowland, not Highland, Scotland.[1]

There is, however, another possible explanation. For all that we know—and there is really no trustworthy evidence on this point—the English folk-singer of the eighteenth century may still have been using the gapped scale and may not have advanced to the understanding and use of the 7-note scale until the following century. And if this supposition be made—and it is at least a possible one—we may argue that the ancestors of our mountain singers hailed originally from England and that they sang in the gapped scale because that was the habit which then prevailed amongst their contemporaries. An analysis of the names of the singers recorded in this volume does not help us very much, but it seems to support rather than to contradict this latter supposition.

However, it is not a matter of any great importance which of these two hypotheses we accept, because, in either event, the tunes in question would quite correctly be called English. For, as folk-lorists will, I think, agree, England and the English-speaking parts of Scotland must, so far as folk-tales, folk-songs, and other folk-products are concerned, be regarded as one homogeneous area.

THE CULTURAL SIGNIFICANCE OF TRADITION. The words and the tunes in this Collection are typical and authentic examples of the beginnings and foundations of English literature and music. The history of man is the history of his efforts to express himself, and the degree to which he has at any given moment succeeded in doing this is the measure of the civilization to

[1] See also Gavin Greig's *Last Leaves*, in which several of the tunes bear a resemblance to those in this collection. M. K.

Introduction to the First Edition, 1917

which he has attained. The method by which he has sought to achieve this end has been through the exercise and development of certain inborn and basic human faculties; and his achievements are concretely to be seen in the literature, music, painting, dancing, sculpture, and other art-works which each nation has created and accumulated and in which it finds reflected its own peculiar and distinctive characteristics. The process is a cumulative one, the children of each generation receiving from their fathers that which, with certain modifications and additions of their own, they bequeath to their children. The historian, however, will point out that this process is not uniformly progressive; that nations in the course of their development pass through different phases, and that, in consonance with these, their artistic output varies in character and quality from period to period. These variations, however, fluctuate within certain clearly defined limits, and are superficial rather than radical; so that, while each may reflect with greater or less fidelity the specific outlook of a particular epoch, the form of expression remains fundamentally true to one type, and that the national type. And this national type is always to be found in its purest, as well as in its most stable and permanent form, in the folk-arts of a nation.

Although this theory of nationalism in art is now very generally accepted, the fact that it is based upon the intimate relationship which the art of the folk must always bear to that of the self-conscious, cultivated, and trained individual artist is too often overlooked. But, bearing this in mind, the significance and value of the contents of such a book as this become immediately apparent. We talk glibly of the creative musician, but, however clever and inspired he may be, he cannot, magician-like, produce music out of nothing; and if he were to make the attempt he would only put himself back into the position of the primitive savage. All that he can do and, as a matter of fact, does, is to make use of the material bequeathed to him by his predecessors, fashion it anew and in such manner that he can through it, and by means of it, express himself. It is my sober belief that if a young composer were to master the contents of this book, study and assimilate each tune with its variants, he would acquire just the kind of education that he needs, and one far better suited to his requirements than he would obtain from the ordinary conservatoire or college of music.

Again, the value of such songs as these as material for the general education of the young cannot be overestimated. For, if education is to be cultural and not merely utilitarian, if its aim is to produce men and women capable, not only of earning a living, but of holding a dignified and worthy position upon an equality with the most cultivated of their generation, it will be necessary to pay at least as much attention to the training and development of the emotional, spiritual, and imaginative faculties as to those of the intellect. And this, of course, can be achieved only by the early cultivation of some

Introduction to the First Edition, 1917

form of artistic expression, such as singing, which, for reasons already given, seems of all the arts to be the most natural and the most suitable one for the young. Moreover, remembering that the primary purpose of education is to place the children of the present generation in possession of the cultural achievements of the past, so that they may as quickly as possible enter into their racial inheritance, what better form of music or of literature can we give them than the folk-songs and folk-ballads of the race to which they belong, or of the nation whose language they speak? To deny them these is to cut them off from the past and to rob them of that which is theirs by right of birth. To put it another way, the aim of the educationist should be not to forge the first link of a new chain, but to add a fresh link to an old one.

That culture is primarily a matter of inheritance and not of education is, perhaps, a mere truism, but it is one, nevertheless, which educationists often forget. My knowledge of American life may be too slender for an opinion of mine to carry much weight, but I cannot withhold the criticism—advanced with the greatest diffidence—that the educational authorities of some of the larger cities in the United States are too ready to ignore the educational and cultural value of that national heritage which every immigrant brings with him to his new home, and to rest too confidently upon their educational system, which is often almost wholly utilitarian and vocational, to create the ideal American citizen. I admit that the problem which faces the educationist in America is a peculiarly difficult one, but it will, I am convinced, never be satisfactorily solved until the education given to every foreign colonist is directly based upon, and closely related to, his or her national inheritance of culture.

Of the supreme cultural value of an inherited tradition, even when unenforced by any formal school education, our mountain community in the Southern Highlands is an outstanding example. Another, though negative, instance of the truth of the same principle may be seen in the contents of a book which Professor Lomax has recently compiled, concerning the songs of the cowboys of Texas.[1] Let me ask the reader to compare these with the songs of the Southern Highlanders. The comparison is a fair one, for the cowboys live a communal life almost as isolated and shut off from the world as that of the mountaineers, and feel, accordingly, the same compelling desire to express themselves in song. They are not, or at any rate they would not, I imagine, consider themselves, in any way inferior to their neighbours; they are, I take it, less illiterate, while the life they lead is more vivid and exciting and far richer in incident. Why, then, is it that their songs compare so unfavourably with those of the mountain singers? It can only be because the cowboy has been despoiled of his inheritance of traditional song; he has nothing behind him. When, therefore, he feels the need of self-expression, having no inherited fund of poetic literature upon which to draw, no

[1] *Cowboy Songs and other Frontier Ballads.* Sturgis and Walton, 1916.

Introduction to the First Edition, 1917

imaginative world into which to escape, he has only himself and his daily occupations to sing about, and that in a self-centred, self-conscious way, e.g. 'The cowboy's life is a dreadful life'; 'I'm a poor lonesome cowboy'; 'I'm a lonely bull-whacker'—and so forth.

Now this, of course, is precisely what the folk-singer never does. When he sings his aim is to forget himself and everything that reminds him of his everyday life; and so it is that he has come to create an imaginary world of his own and to people it with characters quite as wonderful, in their way, as the elfish creations of Spenser.

We have in the following pages printed the songs exactly as we took them down from the lips of the singers, without any editing or 'adornments' whatsoever, and we have done so because we are convinced that this is the only way in which work of this kind should be presented, at any rate in the first instance. Later on, we may harmonize and publish a certain number of the songs and so make a wider and more popular appeal.

But this can be done at leisure. The pressing need of the moment is to complete our collection while there is yet the opportunity—and who can say how long the present ideal conditions will remain unaltered? Already the forests are attracting the attention of the commercial world; lumber companies are being formed to cut down and carry off the timber, and it is not difficult to foresee the inevitable effect which this will have upon the simple, Arcadian life of the mountains. And then, too, there are the schools, which, whatever may be said in their favour, will always be the sworn enemies of the folk-song collector.

I cannot allow myself to conclude these remarks without expressing my gratitude to the many friends who have assisted me in my investigations. There are those in particular, who were kind enough to entertain me in their mountain homes:—Dr. and Mrs. Packard of White Rock; Miss Edith Fish of Allanstand; Mrs. Hamilton and Miss Bacon of Alleghany; Miss Ollie Henricks of Big Laurel; and Miss Jennie Moor of Rocky Fork. Nor can I omit the names of some, at least, of those by whose help and advice I have so greatly profited:—Mrs. J. J. Storrow, who gave me assistance of a most practical kind; Professor Alphonso Smith, and Mr. John M. Glenn of the Russell Sage Foundation.

CECIL J. SHARP

27 Church Row,
   Hampstead,
      London, N.W.

MAP SHOWING THE COUNTIES IN WHICH THE SONGS WERE COLLECTED

BALLADS

The Elfin Knight

A

Pentatonic. Mode 3 (Tonic G).
Sung by Mrs. Cis Jones
at Manchester, Clay Co., Ky., Aug. 24, 1917

1. Go tell him to clear me one acre of ground,

Se-ther wood, sale, rose-ma-ry and thyme, Be twixt the sea and the

sea land side, And then he'll be a true lo-ver of mine.

2 Tell him to plough it all up with an old leather plough,
    Sether wood, etc.
  And hoe it all over with a pea-fowl's feather,
    And then he'll be, etc.

3 Go tell him to plant it all over with one grain of corn,
    Sether wood, etc.
  And reap it all down with an old ram's horn,
    And then he'll be, etc.

4 Go tell him to shock it in yonder sea,
    Sether wood, etc.
  And return it back to me all dry,
    And then he'll be, etc.

5 Go tell her to make me a cambric shirt,
    Sether wood, etc.
  Without any needle or needle's work,
    And then she'll be a true lover of mine.

6 Go tell her to wash it in yonders well,
    Sether wood, etc.
  Where rain nor water never fell,
    And then she'll be, etc.

7 Go tell her to hang it on yonders thorn,
    Sether wood, etc.
  Where man nor thorn was never seen born,
    And then she'll be a true lover of mine.

The Elfin Knight
B

Sung by Mrs. POLLY MITCHELL
at Burnsville, N.C., Sept. 22, 1918

Pentatonic. Mode 3.

1. I saw a young lady a walking all out, A-walking all out in the yonders green field. So sav'ry was said come marry in time, And she shall be a true lover of mine.

2. So tell that young lady to buy me a new cambric shirt,
   And make it without needles or yet needles' work.
       So sav'ry, etc.

3. So tell that young lady to wash it all out,
   And wash it all out in yonders well,
   Where never was water nor rain never fell.

4. So tell that young lady to deemens her work,
   And bring on my new cambric shirt.

5. I saw a young man a-walking all out,
   A-walking all out in the yonders green field,
       So sav'ry was said come marry in time,
   And he shall be a true lover of mine.

6. So tell that young man to buy me an acre of land,
   Betwixt the sea and the sun.
       So sav'ry, etc.
       And he shall be, etc.

7. So tell that young man to sow it all down,
   And sow it all down in pepper and corn.

8. So tell that young man to plough it all in,
   And plough it all in with that little ram's horn.

9. So tell that young man to haul it all in,
   And haul it all in on a chee-chicken feather.

10. So tell that young man to crib it all in,
    And crib it all in a little mouse's hole.

11. So tell that young man to thresh it all out,
    And thrash it all out in the corner of the house,
    On the peril of his life to not lose a grain.

12. Go tell that young man to deemens his work
    For to bring on the pepper and corn.

No. 2

The False Knight Upon the Road
A

Hexatonic. Mode 4, b.

Sung by Mrs. T. G. Coates
at Flag Pond, Tenn., Sept. 1, 1916

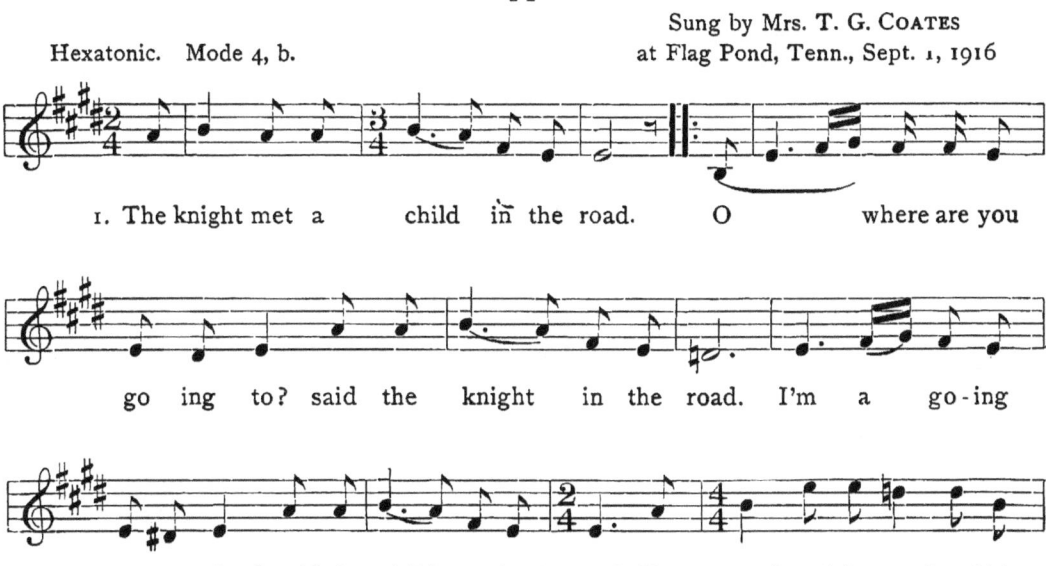

1. The knight met a child in the road. O where are you going to? said the knight in the road. I'm a going to my school, said the child as he stood. He stood and he stood and it's well because he stood. I'm a going to my school, said the child as he stood.

2 O what are you going there for?
  For to learn the Word of God.

3 O what have you got there?
  I have got my bread and cheese.

4 O won't you give me some?
  No, ne'er a bite nor crumb.

5 I wish you was on the sands.
  Yes, and a good staff in my hands.

6 I wish you was in the sea.
  Yes, and a good boat under me.

7 I think I hear a bell.
  Yes, and it's ringing you to hell.

The False Knight Upon the Road
B

Mode 3, b (no 6th).

Sung by Mrs. Jane Gentry
at Hot Springs, N. C., Sept. 12, 1916

1. Where are you go ing? Says the knight in the road. I'm a

go-ing to my school, said the child as he stood. He stood and he stood, He

well thought on he stood. I'm a - go-ing to my school, said the child as he stood.

2 What are you eating?
  I'm a-eating bread and cheese.

3 I wish'd you was in the sea.
  A good boat under me.

4 I wish'd you was in the well.
  And you that deep in hell.

No. 3
Lady Isabel and the Elf Knight
A

Pentatonic. Mode 3 (Tonic G).

Sung by Mrs. Mary Sands
at Allanstand, N. C., Aug. 2, 1916

1. Get down, get down, get down, says he, Pull off that fine silk

gown; For it is too fine and cost ly To rot in the salt-wa-ter

sea, sea, sea, To rot in the salt wa-ter sea.

2 Turn yourself all round and about
   With your face turned toward the sea.
   And she picked him up so manfully
   And over'd him into the sea.

3 Pray help me out, pray help me out,
   Pray help me out, says he,
   And I'll take you to the old Scotland
   And there I will marry thee.

4 Lie there, you false-hearted knight,
   Lie there instead of me,
   For you stripped me as naked as ever I was born,
   But I'll take nothing from thee.

5 She jumped upon the milk-white steed
   And she led the dapple grey,
   And she rode back to her father's dwelling
   Three long hours before day.

Lady Isabel and the Elf Knight

B

Pentatonic. Mode 3 (Tonic G).

Sung by Mrs. BISHOP, Clay Co., Ky., on July 16, 1909

1. Pull off that silk, my pretty Polly, Pull off that silk, said he, For it is too fine and too costly To rot in the briny, briny sea, To rot in the briny sea.

    2 Turn your back, sweet Willie, said she,
      O turn your back unto me,
      For you are too bad a rebel
      For a naked woman to see.

    3 She picked him up in her arms so strong
      And she threw him into the sea,
      Saying: If you have drowned six kings' daughters here,
      You may lay here in the room of me.

    4 Stretch out your hand, O pretty Polly,
      Stretch out your hand for me,

      And help me out of the sea.

    5 She picked up a rock and threw on him, saying:
      Lay there, lay there, you dirty, dirty dog,
      Lay there in the room of me.
      You're none too good nor too costly
      To rot in the briny, briny sea.

    6 Hush up, hush up, my pretty parrot,
      Hush up, hush up, said she.
      You shall have a golden cage with an ivory lid
      Hung in the willow tree.

Lady Isabel and the Elf Knight

C

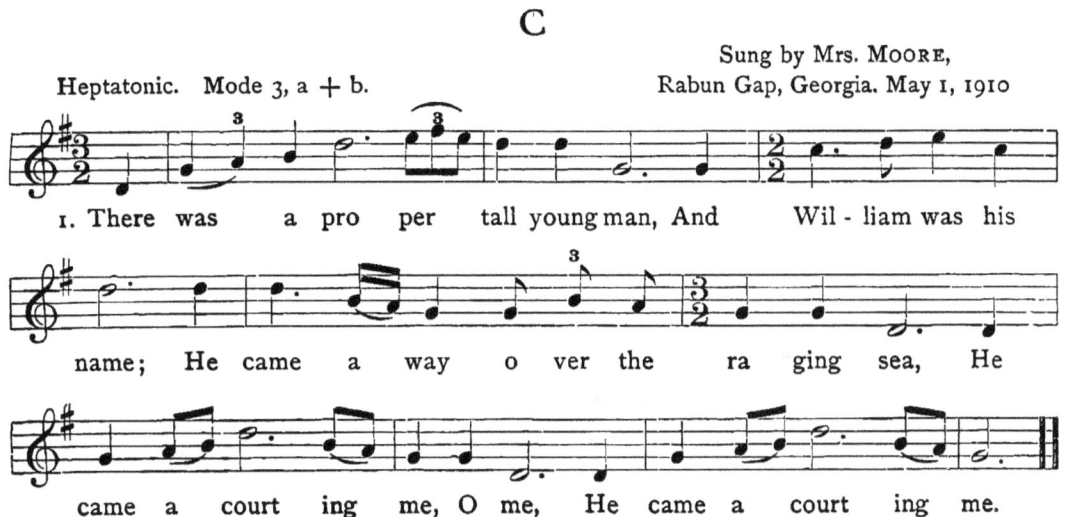

Heptatonic. Mode 3, a + b.

Sung by Mrs. Moore,
Rabun Gap, Georgia. May 1, 1910

1. There was a proper tall young man, And William was his name; He came away over the raging sea, He came a courting me, O me, He came a courting me.

2 He followed me up, he followed me down,
   He followed me in my room.
   I had no wings for to fly away,
   No tongue to say him nay.

3 He took part of my father's gold,
   Half of my mother's fee;
   He took two of my father's stable steeds,
   For there stood thirty and three.

4 The lady rode the milk-white steed,
   The gentleman rode the grey.
   They rode all down by the north green land
   All on one summer's day.

5 Light off, light off, my pretty fair miss,
   I tell you now my mind.
   Six pretty fair maids I've drownded here,
   The seventh one you shall be.

6 Hush up, hush up, you old vilyun,
   That hain't what you promised me.
   You promised to carry me over the raging sea,
   And then for to marry me.

7 Turn your back and trim those nettles
   That grow so near the brim;
   They'll tangle in my golden hair
   And tear my lily-white skin.

Lady Isabel and the Elf Knight

8 He turned his back to trim those nettles
   That growed so near the brim;
   This young lady with her skilfulness
   She tripped her false love in.

9 Lie there, lie there, you old vilyun,
   Lie there in the place for me.
   You have nothing so fine nor costly
   But to rot in the salt water sea.

10 First she rode the milk-white steed
   And then she rode the grey.
   She returned back to her father's house
   Three long hours before it was day.

D

Sung by Mrs. NANCY E. SHELTON
at Carmen, N. C., Aug. 8, 1916

Pentatonic. Mode 3 (Tonic G).

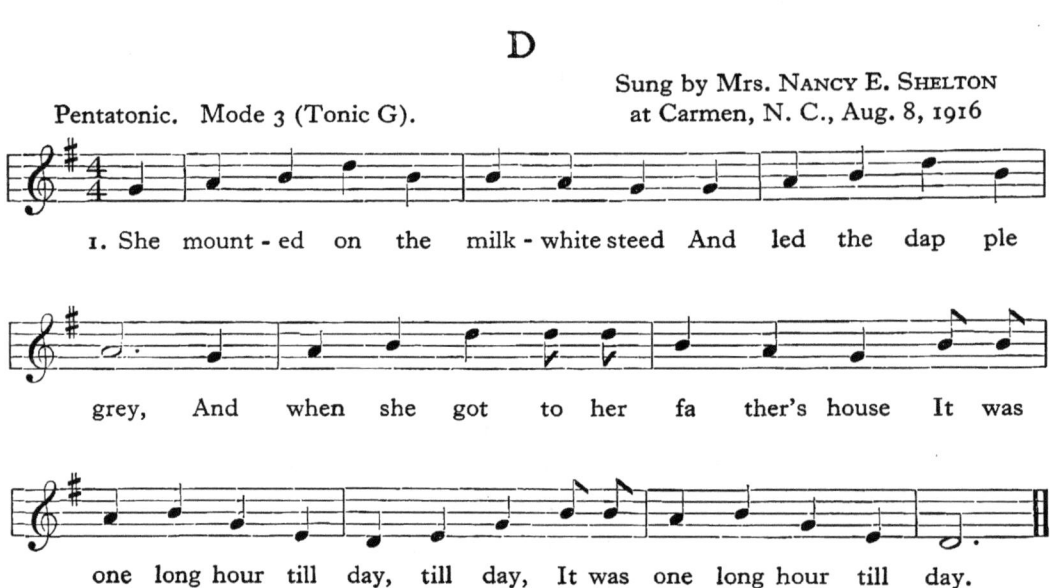

1. She mounted on the milk-white steed And led the dapple grey, And when she got to her father's house It was one long hour till day, till day, It was one long hour till day.

Lady Isabel and the Elf Knight

E

Sung by Mrs. Laura Virginia Donald
at Dewey, Va., June 6, 1918

Pentatonic. Mode 3 (Tonic A).

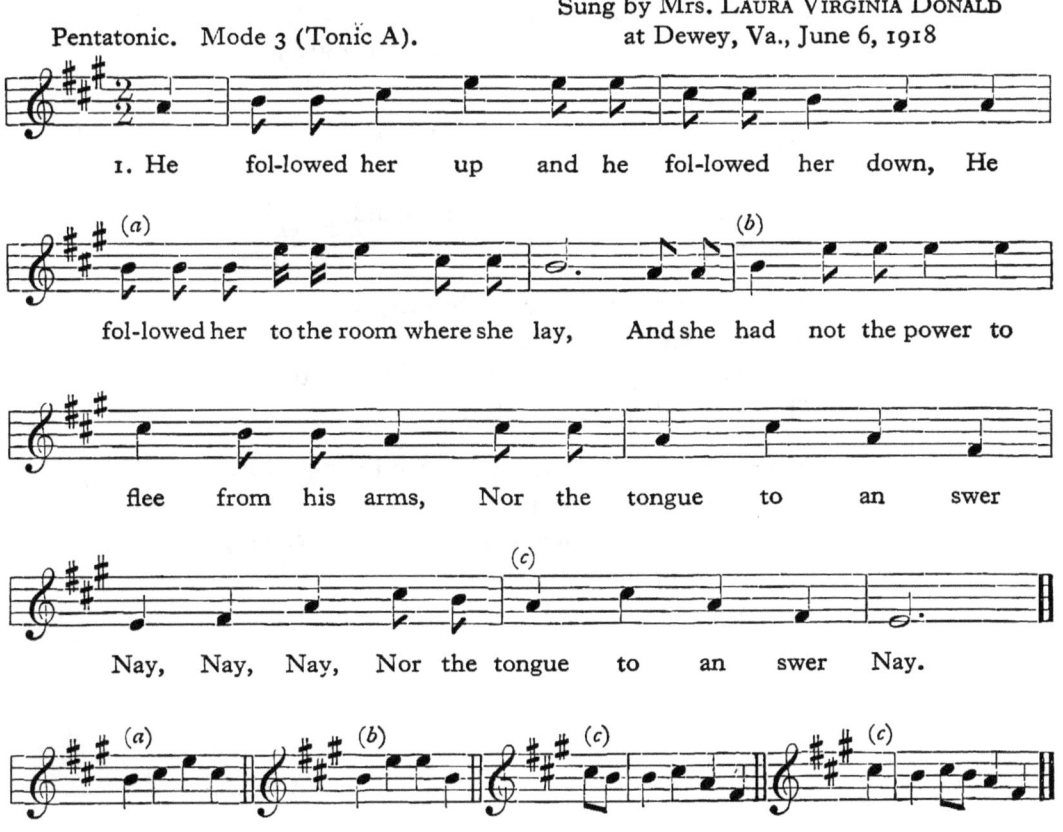

1. He followed her up and he followed her down, He followed her to the room where she lay, And she had not the power to flee from his arms, Nor the tongue to answer Nay, Nay, Nay, Nor the tongue to answer Nay.

2 She got on her pony, pony brown,
  He got on the iron-grey.
  They rode till they came to the blue water sea
  In the length of a long summer day.

3 Get down, get down, my pretty little Miss,
  Get down, these words I say.
  Here I've drownded nine kings' daughters,
  And you the tenth shall be.

4 Pull off, pull off that fine silken gown,
  And lie it on yonders stone,
  For it cost your father too much money
  For to rot in the salt sea foam.

5 Turn your face around and about,
  Turn to the green leaves on the tree,
  For I don't think as nice a gentleman as you
  A naked lady should see.

Lady Isabel and the Elf Knight

6 She picked him up and she plunged him in,
  She plunged him in the depths of the sea,
  Lie there, lie there, you false-hearted soul,
  In the place of poor me.

7 Hand me down your soft silk hand,
  O hand it down to me,
  O hand me down your soft silk hand,
  And married we shall be.

8 She got on her pony, pony brown,
  And she led her iron grey.
  She rode till she came to her father's gate,
  'Twas just three hours till day.

9 My pretty little parrot, my pretty little parrot,
  Don't tell no tales on me,
  Your cage shall be made out of yellow beaten gold
  And hung in the willow tree.

F

Heptatonic. Dorian.

Sung by Mrs. JOE VANHOOK
at Berea College, Madison Co., Ky., May 20, 1917

1. Come rise you up, my pret-ty Pol-ly, And go a long with

me. I'll take you to the North Scot-land, And mar-ried we will be.

2 Go bring me a bag of your father's gold,
  Likewise your mother's fee,
  And two of the best horses that stand in the stall,
  For there stand thirty and three.

Lady Isabel and the Elf Knight

3 She brought him a bag of her father's gold,
　Likewise her mother's fee,
　And two of the best horses that stand in the stall,
　For there stand thirty and three.

4 She lit upon her nimble going brown,
　She mounted the dapple grey,
　And when they reached the North Scotland
　Just three hours before the day.

5 Light you down, light you down, my pretty Polly,
　Light you down at my command.
　Six kings' daughters here have I drowned,
　And the seventh you shall be.

6 Pull off, pull off those fine gay clothes,
　And hang on yonder tree,
　For they are too fine and they cost too much
　For to rest in the salt lake sea.

7 Go get those sickles for to cut those nettles
　That grow so close to the brine,
　For they may tangle in my long, yellow hair,
　And stain my snowy white skin.

8 He got those sickles for to cut those nettles
　That grow so close to the brine;
　And poor, kind Polly with a pitifully wish
　And shoved false William in.

9 Lie there, lie there, you low William,
　Lie there in the room of me.
　Six kings' daughters you here have drowned,
　And you the seventh shall be.

10 Hush up, hush up, you pretty parrot bird,
　Tell none of your tales on me.
　Your cage shall be made of the yellow beating gold,
　And your doors of ivory.

11 Up speaks, up speaks that good old man
　In his room wherever he be:
　What's the matter, what's the matter with my pretty parrot bird,
　She's talking so long before it is day?

12 Here sits three cats at my cage door,
　My life expecting to betray;
　I was just calling up my pretty, golden bee
　For to drive those cats away.

Lady Isabel and the Elf Knight

G

Pentatonic. Mode 3 (Tonic G).

Sung by Mrs. SARAH V. CANNADY
at Endicott, Va., Aug. 23, 1981

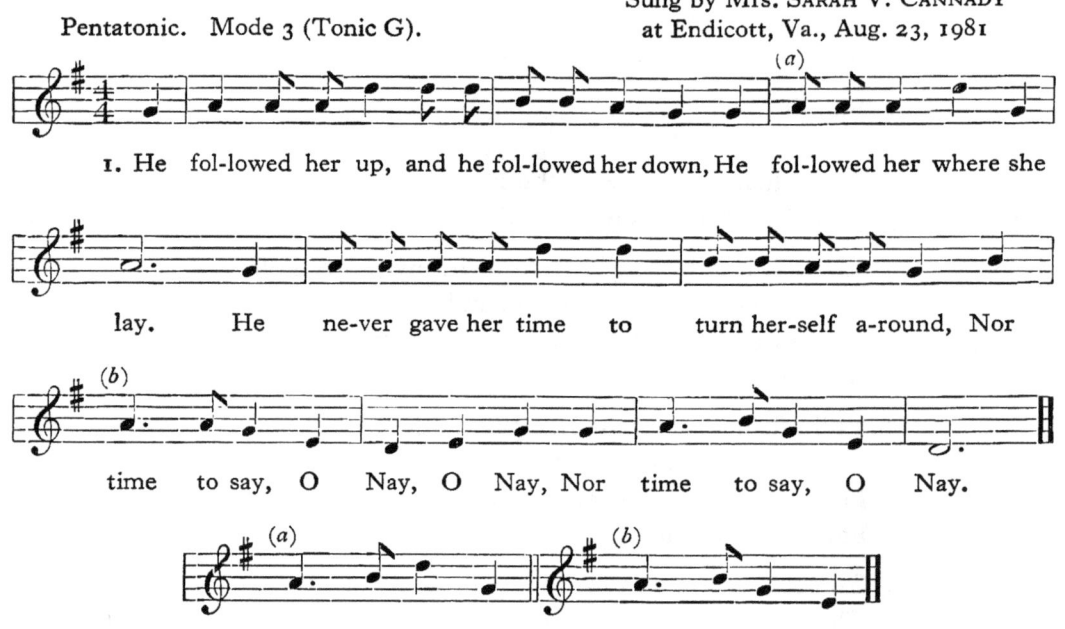

1. He fol-lowed her up, and he fol-lowed her down, He fol-lowed her where she lay. He ne-ver gave her time to turn her-self a-round, Nor time to say, O Nay, O Nay, Nor time to say, O Nay.

Pull off, pull off that new silken gown,
And hang it on a thorn.
Some other gay lady will wear this dress
When you are dead and gone.

H

Heptatonic. Dorian.

Sung by Mrs. LAUREL WHEELER
at Buena Vista, Va., May 2, 1918

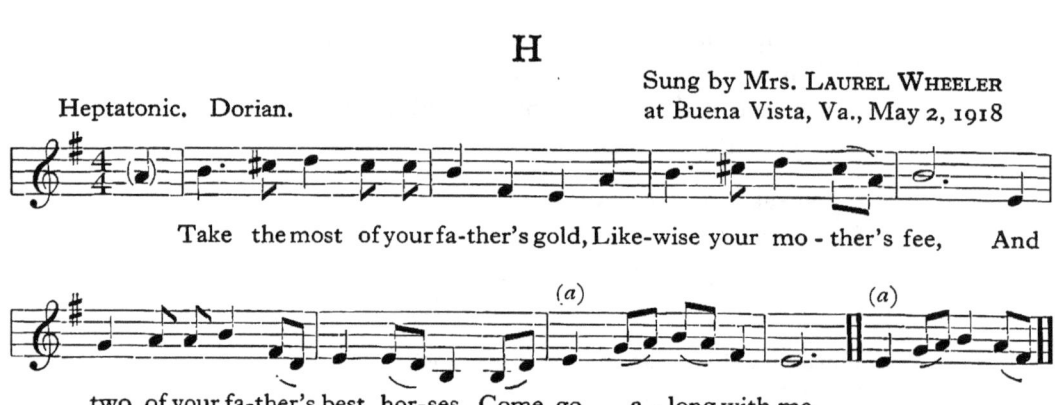

Take the most of your fa-ther's gold, Like-wise your mo-ther's fee, And two of your fa-ther's best hor-ses, Come go a-long with me.

Lady Isabel and the Elf Knight

I

Sung by Miss MAY RAY
at the Lincoln Memorial University, Harrogate,
Claiborne Co., Ky., April 29, 1917

Heptatonic. Mixolydian.

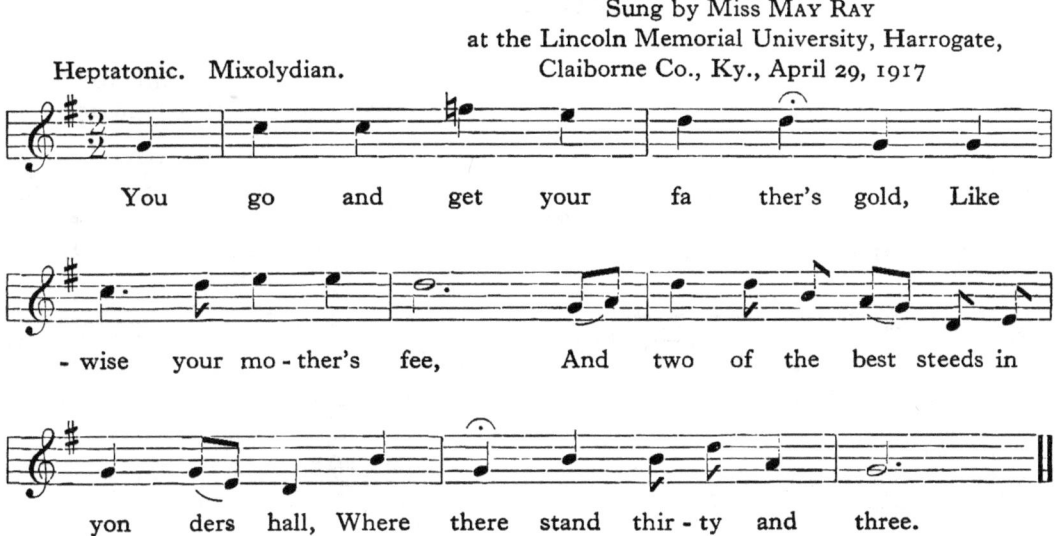

You go and get your father's gold, Likewise your mother's fee, And two of the best steeds in yonders hall, Where there stand thirty and three.

J

Sung by Mrs. ALICE SLOAN
at Barbourville, Knox Co., Ky., May 7, 1917

Heptatonic. Ionian (Tonic D).

You promised to take me to the sea-shore, And there to marry me. You promised to take me to the sea-shore, And there to marry me, And there to marry me.

No. 4

Earl Brand

A

Hexatonic. Mode 3, a.

Sung by Mrs. Polly Shelton
at White Rock, N. C., July 28, 1916

O rise you up, ye sev'n breth-e-rens, And bring your sis-ter down; It

nev-er shall be said that a stew-ard's son Had ta-ken her out of town.

2 I thank you kindly, sir, he says,
   I am no steward's son.
   My father is of a regis king, *
   My mother's a quaker's queen.

3 He mound (mounted) her on a milk-white steed,
   He rode a dapple grey.
   He swung a bugle horn all round about his neck
   And so went blowing away.

4 He had not gone three mile out of town
   Till he looked back again,
   And saw her father and seven bretherens
   Come tripping over the plain.

5 Sit you down, fair Ellender, he said,
   And hold this steed by the rein,
   Till I play awhile with your father
   And your seven bretherens.

6 Fair Ellender she sat still.
   It wasn't long till she saw
   Her own dear seven bretherens
   All wallowing in their blood.

* The richest of kings? (see version D).

Earl Brand

7 Fair Ellender she sat still,
  She never changed a note
  Till she saw her own father's head
  Come tumbling by her foot.

8 Saying: Love runs free in every vein,
  But father you have no more,
  If you're not satisfied with this,
  I wish you were in some mother's chamber
  And me in some house or room.

9 If I was in my mother's chamber
  You'd be welcome there.
  I'll wind you east, I'll wind you west,
  I'll wind along with you.

10 He mound her on a milk-white steed,
   He rode the dapple grey,
   He swung a bugle horn all round about his neck
   And so went bleeding away.

11 As he rode up to his father's gate
   He tingled at the ring,
   Saying: O dear father, asleep or awake,
   Arise and let me in.

12 O sister, sister, make my bed,
   My wounds are very sore.
   Saying: O dear mother, O bind up my head.
   For me you'll bind no more.

13 It was about three hours till day,
   The cock began to crow.
   From every wound that he received
   His heart blood began to flow.

14 Sweet William he died like it might be to-day,
   Fair Ellender tomorrow.
   Sweet William he died for the wounds he received,
   Fair Ellen died for sorrow.

15 Fair Ellender was buried by the church door,
   Sweet William was buried by her;
   And out of her breast sprung a blood red rose
   And out of his a briar.

16 They growed, they growed to the top of the church
   Till they could grow no higher,
   And there they tied a true love's knot
   And the rose ran round the briar.

Earl Brand
B

Pentatonic. Mode 3.

Sung by Mrs. MARY SANDS
at Allanstand, N. C., Aug. 1, 1916

1. He rode up to her fa-ther's gate, So bold-ly he did say: You may

keep your old-est daugh-ter at home, For the young-est I'll take a-way.

The pause-notes were sung as minims.

2. He jumped upon the milk-white steed
   And she rode the dapple grey,
   And he hung a bugle horn all about his neck
   And so went sounding away.

3. He had not got but a mile or two
   Till he looked back over the main,
   And he saw her father and her seven brothers all
   Come trippling over the lane.

4. Get down, get down, get down, says he,
   And hold this steed by the mane,
   Till I play awhile with your father, he says,
   Yes, and your seven brethren.

5. She got down and never spoke,
   Nor never cheeped
   Till she saw her own father's head
   Come trinkling by her feet.

6. Hold your hand, sweet William, she says,
   Pray hold your hand for sure,
   For love runs free in every vein,
   But father I'll have no more.

Earl Brand

7 If you hain't pleased at this, he says,
   If you hain't pleased, says he,
   I'll wished you was at home in your mother's chambery
   And me in some house or room.

8 Go wind you east, go wind you west,
   I will go along with you.
   And he hung a bugle all round about his neck,
   And so went bleeding away.

9 But when he got to his mother's hall,
   He jingled at the ring;
   O dear mother, sleep or awake,
   Rise and let me in.

10 Sister, sister make my bed,
   My wounds are very sore.
   O dear mother, bind my head,
   You'll never bind it more.

11 It was about three hours before day,
   The chickens began to crow,
   And every breath that he did draw
   His heart's blood begin to flow.

12 Sweet William died of the wounds he got
   And Barbary died for sorrow,
   And the old woman died for the love of them both
   And was buried on Easter Monday.

C

Hexatonic. Mode 3, a.

Sung by Mrs. Hester House at Hot Springs, N. C., Sept. 14, 1916

1. He rode up to the old man's gate, So boldly he did say, Saying: Keep your youngest daughter at home, For the oldest I'll take away.

Earl Brand

Verses 5 and 6

2 He holp her on his milk-white steed,
  And he rode the apple grey.
  He swung a bugle horn all round about her neck
  And so went winding away.

3 He hadn't got more than a mile out of town,
  Till he looked back again.
  He saw her own dear seven brothersen
  Come trippling over the plain.

4 Set you down, fair Ellinor, he said,
  And hold the steed by the rein,
  Till I play awhile with your own dear father
  And your seven brothersen.

5 Fair Ellinor she sat still
  And never changed a word,
  Till she saw her own dear seven brothersen
  All wallowing in their blood.

6 Fair Ellinor she sat still
  And never changed a note,
  Till she saw her own dear father's head
  Come tumbling by her feet.

7 He holp her on her milk-white steed
  And he rode the apple grey,
  Till he swung a bugle horn all around her neck
  And so went winding away.

8 He rode up to his mother's gate
  And tingled on the ring,
  Saying: O dear mother, asleep or awake,
  Arise and let me in.

9 Sister, sister, fix my bed,
  My wounds are very sore.
  Saying: O dear mother, bind up my head,
  For me you'll bind no more.

Earl Brand

10 Sweet William he died from the wounds received,
   Fair Ellinor died with sorrow;
   Sweet William died with the wounds received
   And Ellinor died with sorrow.

11 Sweet William was buried at the upper church yard
   And Ellinor was buried close by.
   Out of William's grave spring a blood red rose
   And out of hers a briar.

12 They grew, they grew to the top of the church
   Where could not grow any higher.
   They wound, they tied in a true love knot,
   The rose wrapped round the briar.

D

Pentatonic. Mode 3.

Sung by Mrs. MOORE,
Rabun Co., Georgia, in May, 1909

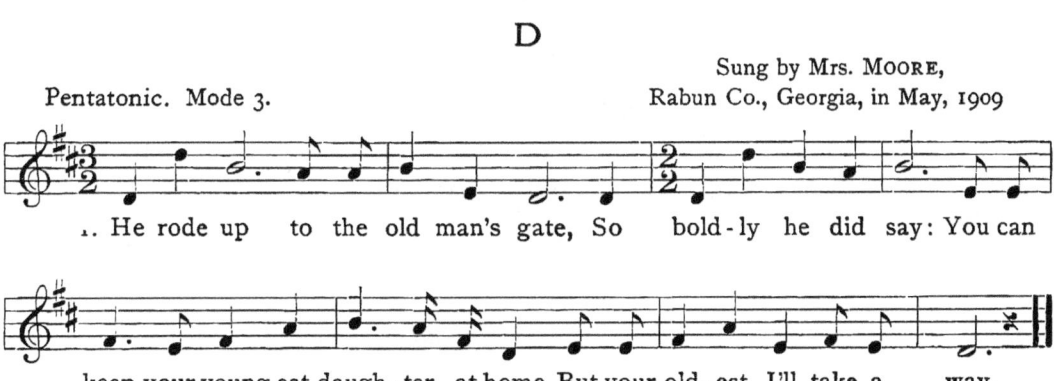

1. He rode up to the old man's gate, So bold-ly he did say: You can keep your young-est daugh-ter at home, But your old-est I'll take a way.

2 O rise you up, you seven brothers all,
  And bring your sister down,
  It never can be said that a steward's son
  Shall take her out of town.

3 I thank you, kind sir, said he,
  I am no steward's son;
  My father's of the richest of kings
  And my mother's a Quaker's queen.

4 She lit on the milk-white steed,
  And he rode on the brown.

5 Then they rode about three miles from town,
  And then he cast his eyes all around,
  And saw her father and seven brothers all
  Come trickling down the plain.

Earl Brand

6 O, light you off, fair Ellen, said he,
   And hold my steed by the rein,
   Till I play awhile with your father
   And seven brothers all.

7 Fair Ellen she still stood there
   And never changed a word
   Till she saw her own dear seven brothers all
   A-wallowing in their own blood.

8 Fair Ellen she still stood there
   And never changed a note,
   Till she saw her own dear father's head
   Come tumbling by her foot.

9 O hold your hand, sweet William, said she,
   Love runs free in every vein,
   But father I have no more.
   If you are not satisfied with this
   I wish you were in your mother's chamberee
   And I'se in some house or room.

10 If I was in my mother's chamberee,
   You'd be welcome there.
   I'll wind you East, I'll wind you West,
   I'll trip along with thee.

11 He rode up to his mother's gate
   And jangled at the ring:
   O mother, dear mother, asleep or awake,
   Arise and let me in.

12 O sister, O sister, make my bed,
   For my wound is very sore.
   O mother, O mother, bind up my head,
   For me you'll bind no more.

13 It was about three hours till day,
   And the chickens crowing for day,
   When every wound sweet William received,
   The blood began to pour.

14 Sweet Willlam he died like it was to-day,
   Fair Ellender tomorrow;
   Sweet William died from the wounds he received,
   Fair Ellender died of sorrow.

Earl Brand
E

Heptatonic. Mixolydian.

Sung by Mrs LIZZIE GIBSON
at Crozet, Va., April 26, 1918

1. Wake you up, wake you up, you seven sleep-ers, And do take warn-ing of me; O do take care of your old-est daugh-ter dear, For the young-est are go-ing with me.

2 He mounted her up on his bonny, bonny brown,
   Himself on the dark apple grey;
   He drew his buckles down by his side,
   And away he went singing away.

3 Get you up, get you up, my seven sons bold,
   Get on your arms so bright,
   For it never shall be said that a daughter of mine
   Shall lie with a lord all night.

4 He rode, he rode that livelong day,
   Along with this lady so dear,
   Until she saw her seventh brother come
   And her father were walking so near.

5 Get you down, get you down, Lady Margaret, he cried,
   And hold my horse for a while,
   Until I can fight your seventh brother bold,
   And your father is walking so nigh.

6 She held, she held, she bitter, bitter (or, better) held,
   And never shedded one tear
   Until she saw her seventh brother fall
   And her father she loved so dear.

Earl Brand

7 Do you choose for to go, Lady Margaret, he cried,
  Do you choose for to go or to stay?
  O I'll go, I'll go, Lord Thomas, she cried,
  For you've left me without any guide.

8 He mounted her up on his bonny, bonny brown,
  Himself on the dark apple grey;
  He drew his buckles down by his side,
  And away he went bleeding away.

9 He rode, he rode that livelong night
  Till he came to his mother's stand.
  Get you down, get you down, Lady Margaret, he cried.
  So that we can rest for a while.

10 It's mother, mother, make my bed,
   And fix it smooth and wide,
   And lie my lady down by my side
   So that we can rest for a while.

11 Lord Thomas he died by midnight,
   Lady Margaret before it were day,
   And the old woman for the loss of her son,
   And there was several lives lost.

F

Sung by Mr. PHILANDER H. FITZGERALD
at Nash, Va., May 7, 1918

Heptatonic. Dorian.

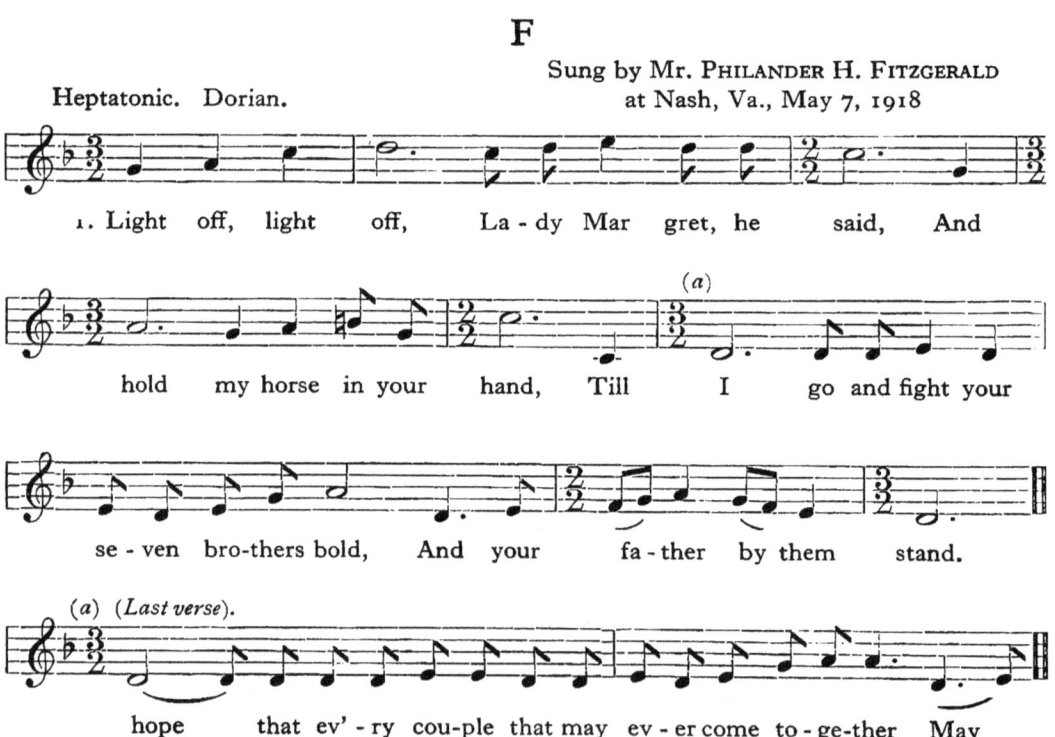

1. Light off, light off, Lady Margret, he said, And hold my horse in your hand, Till I go and fight your seven brothers bold, And your father by them stand.

(a) (Last verse).

hope that ev'ry couple that may ev-er come to-gether May

Earl Brand

2 She held, she held, she better, better held,
  And she never shed one tear
  Until that she saw her last brother fall
  And her father she loved more dear.

3 O hold, O hold, Lord William, she cried,
  Your strokes are now full sore,
  For many a true love I might have had,
  But a father I can have no more.

4 She pullèd out her silk handkerchief,
  Which was both soft and fine,
  And she wipèd off her father's bloody wounds
  Till they ran more clearer than wine.

5 Lord William he mounted his milk-white steed,
  Lady Margaret mounted her bay,
  And he drew his buckler down by his side,
  And so they went riding away.

6 They rode, they rode, yes, they bitter, bitter (*or* better) rode,
  They rode by the light of the moon,
  Until they came to their own mother's door,
  Crying: Dear mother, are you at home?

7 O mother, mother, dig my grave,
  Dig it both wide and deep,
  And lay my true love down by my side,
  That the better I may sleep.

8 Lord William died about midnight,
  Lady Margaret a while before day.
  And I hope that every couple that may ever come together
  They (May?) see more pleasure than they.

G

Sung by Mr. CLINTON FITZGERALD
at Royal Orchard, Afton, Va., April 28, 1918

Heptatonic. Dorian.

La-dy Mar-gret she mounted her milk-white steed, Lord William his dappled grey. He drew his buckler down by his side, And so he went riding away.

23

No. 5

The Two Sisters
A

Pentatonic. Mode 3.

Sung by Mrs. Jane Gentry
at Hot Springs, N. C., Sept, 11, 1916

1. O sister, O sister, come go with me, Go with me down to the sea.

Ju - ry flow-er gent the rose-ber - ry, The ju - ry hangs o - ver the rose-ber - ry.

We'll take them and we'll make harp screws.
We'll take it and we'll make harp strings.

2 She picked her up all in her strong arms
   And threwed her sister into the sea.

3 O sister, O sister, give me your glove,
   And you may have my own true love.

4 O sister, O sister, I'll not give you my glove,
   And I will have your own true love.

5 O sister, O sister, give me your hand,
   And you may have my house and land.

6 O sister, O sister, I'll not give you my hand,
   And I will have your house and land.

7 O the farmer's wife was sitting on a rock,
   Tying and a-sewing of a black silk knot.

8 O farmer, O farmer, run here and see
   What's this a-floating here by me.

9 It's no fish and it's no swan,
   For the water's drowned a gay lady.

10 The farmer run with his great hook
   And hooked this fair lady out of the sea.

11 O what will we do with her fingers so small?
   We'll take them and we'll make harp screws.

The Two Sisters

12 O what will we do with her hair so long?
   We'll take it and we'll make harp strings.

13 O the farmer was hung by the gallows so high,
   And the sister was burned by the stake close by.

B

Sung by Mr. WESLEY BATTEN at Mount Fair,
Albermarle County, Va., Sept. 22, 1916

Heptatonic. Mode 4, a + b (dorian).

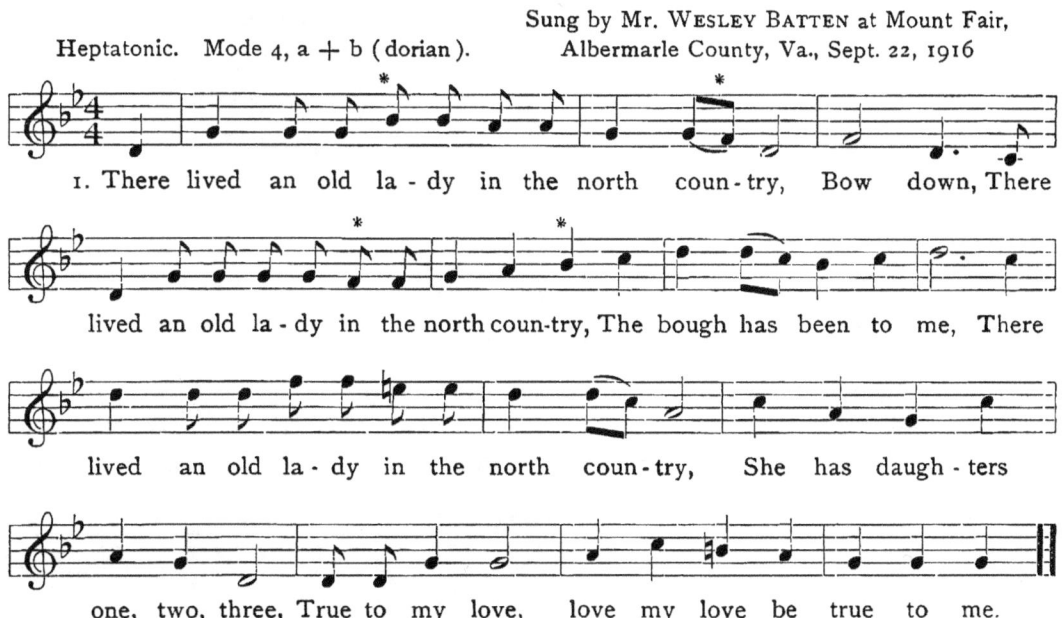

1. There lived an old la-dy in the north coun-try, Bow down, There lived an old la-dy in the north coun-try, The bough has been to me, There lived an old la-dy in the north coun-try, She has daugh-ters one, two, three, True to my love, love my love be true to me.

* These B's and F's were ordinarily sung as written; but the singer occasionally sharpened them, making the B's natural and the F's sharp.

    2 There came a young man a-courting there,
       And he made the choice of the youngest there.

    3 He made her a present of a beaver's hat,
       The oldest thought a heap of that.

    4 O sister, O sister, just walk out
       To see those vessels a-sailing about.

    5 The oldest pushed the youngest in.
       She did struggle and she did swim.

    6 O sister, O sister, give me your hand,
       And I will give you my house and land.

    7 I will not give you my hand,
       But I will marry that young man.

    8 The miller picked up his drab hook,
       And then he fished her out of the brook.

The Two Sisters

9 The miller got her golden ring,
  The miller pushed her back again.

10 The miller was hung at his mill gate
  For drownding my poor sister Kate.

C

Sung by Miss LOUISA CHISHOLM
at Woodridge, Va., Sept. 23, 1916

Heptatonic. Major Mode.

1. There lived an old lord by the north-ern sea, Bow down, There
lived an old lord by the north-ern sea, The boughs they bent to me. There
lived an old lord by the north-ern sea, And he had daughters one, two, three.
That will be true, true to my love, Love and my love will be true to me.

2 A young man came a-courting there,
  He took choice of the youngest there.

3 He gave this girl a beaver hat,
  The oldest she thought much of that.

4 O sister, O sister, let's we walk out
  To see the ships a-sailing about.

5 As they walked down the salty brim,
  The oldest pushed the youngest in.

6 O sister, O sister, lend me your hand,
  And I will give you my house and land.

7 I'll neither lend you my hand or glove,
  But I will have your own true love.

8 Down she sank and away she swam,
  And into the miller's fish pond she ran.

9 The miller came out with his fish hook
  And fished the fair maid out of the brook.

The Two Sisters

10 And it's off her finger took five gold rings,
And into the brook he pushed her again.

11 The miller was hung at his mill gate
For drowning of my sister Kate.

D

Heptatonic. Mode 1, a + b (mixolydian influence).

Sung by Mr. NUEL WALTON at Mt. Fair, Va., Sept. 26, 1916

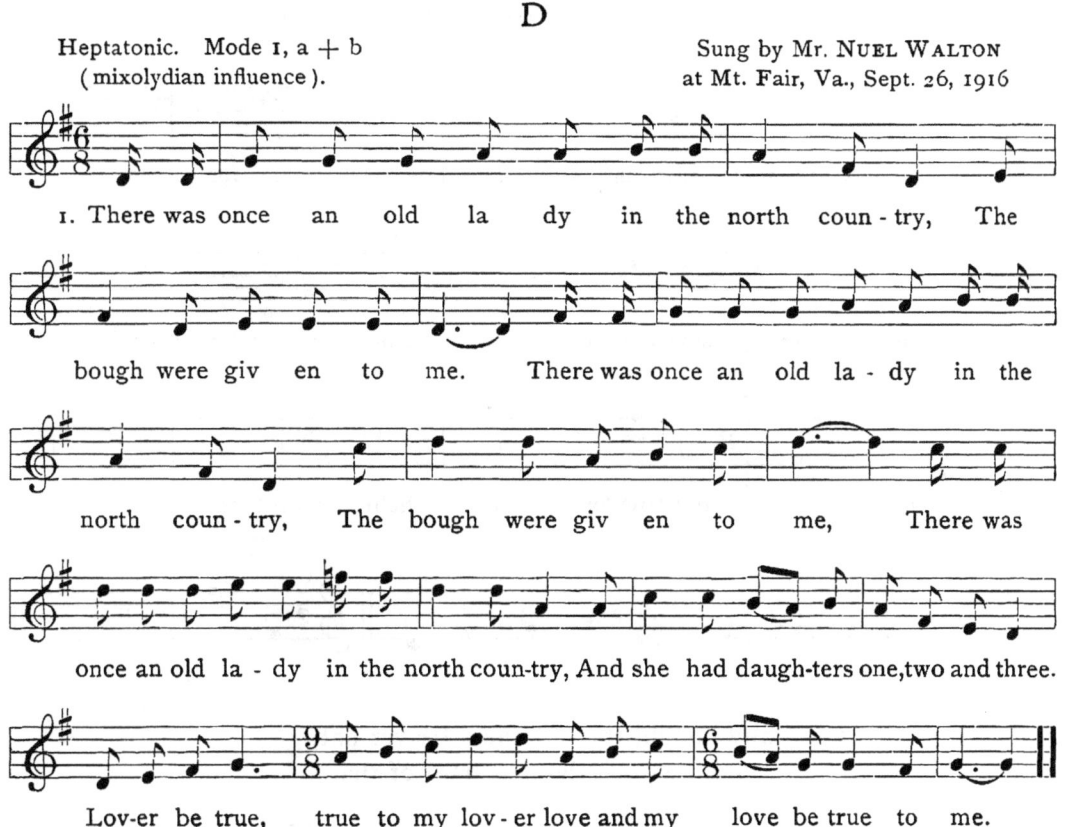

1. There was once an old lady in the north country, The bough were given to me. There was once an old lady in the north country, The bough were given to me, There was once an old lady in the north country, And she had daughters one, two and three. Lov-er be true, true to my lov-er love and my love be true to me.

2 That young man bought a beaver hat,
The oldest one thought hard of that.

The Two Sisters

E

Pentatonic. Mode 3.

Sung by Mrs. Clercy Deeton
at Mine Fork, Burnsville, N. C., Sept. 19, 1918

1. Two little sisters side and side, Sing I dum, sing I day.
Two little sisters side and side, The boys are bound for me.
Two little sisters side and side, The oldest one for Johnny cried.
I'll be kind to my true love If he'll be kind to me.

2 Johnny bought the old one a beaver hat,
The youngest one thought hard of that.

3 Johnny bought the young one a gay gold ring,
He never bought the old one a single thing.

4 Two little sisters a-going down stream;
The oldest one put the young one in.

5 She floated on down to the miller's dam;
The miller brought her safe to land.

6 The miller was hung on the gallows so high;
The oldest one was hung close by.

The Two Sisters
H

Sung by Mrs. Effie Mitchell
at Burnsville, N. C., Sept. 27, 1918

Hexatonic (no 7th).

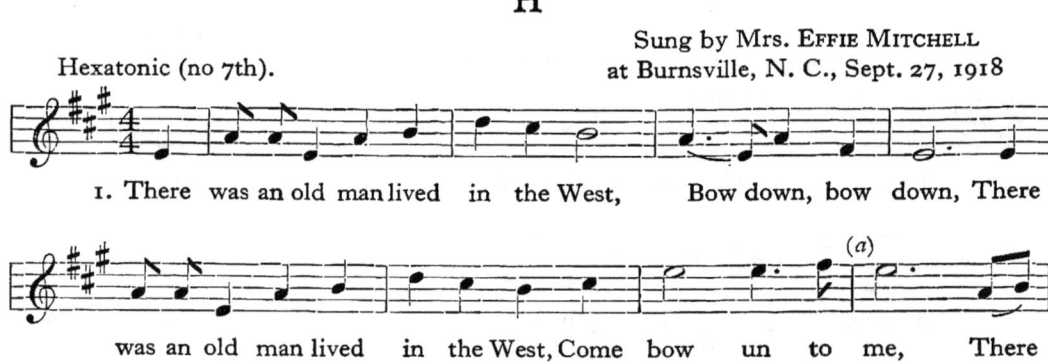

1. There was an old man lived in the West,
   Bow down, bow down,
   There was an old man lived in the West,
   Come bow un to me,
   There was an old man lived in the West,
   He liked the youngest sister best.
   True, true, true to my love,
   My love is true to me.

2 He gave the youngest a gilbern hat;
  The oldest sister didn't much like that.

3 He gave the youngest a gay gold ring;
  The oldest sister didn't much like that.

4 It's come, dear sister, and let's take a walk
  All down yon green river-side.

5 The oldest sister pushed the youngest in.
  She first did float and then did sink.

6 Pull me out, pull me out, I'll give you my cloak.
  I won't pull you out unless you give me your love.

7 She swum on down to the miller's gate

8 The miller cast about his hook,
  And caught her in her petticoat.

9 He robbed her of her gay gold ring,
  And then he pushed her in again.

10 This old miller was hung at the gate,
   And the oldest sister was burned at the stake.

The Two Sisters

I

Sung by Miss ELSIE COMBS
at Hindman School, Knott Co., Ky.,
Sept. 20, 1917

Pentatonic. Mode 3.

There lived a lord in the old country, Bow down, There lived a lord in the old country, Bow down to me, There lived a lord in the old country, He had daughters one, two, three. I'll be true to my love If my love be true to me.

J

Sung by Mrs. FLORENCE FITZGERALD
at Royal Orchard, Afton, Va., April 25, 1928

Heptatonic. Ionian.

There was an old man in the North Countree, And he had daughters one, two, three, Says I'll be true to my love, My love 'll be true to me.

The Two Sisters

K

Hexatonic (no 6th).

Sung by Mr. Joe Blackett
at Meadows of Dan, Va., Aug. 28, 1918

There was an old wo-man who lived by the sea, Bow down, There was an old wo-man who lived by the sea, The vows she made to me, There was an old wo-man lived by the sea, And daugh-ters she had one, two, three. I'll be true to my love If my love 'll be true to me.

L

Hexatonic (no 7th).

Sung by Mrs. Franklin
at Barbourville, Knox Co., Ky., May 7, 1917

There was an old wo-man lived on the sea-shore, Bow down, bow down, There was an old wo-man lived on the sea-shore, And thou hast bent to me, There was an old wo-man lived on the sea-shore, She had some daugh-ters, some three or four. And I'll be true to my love, My love will be true to me.

The Two Sisters

M

Hexatonic (no 7th).

Sung by Mrs. Delie Hughes
at Cane River, Burnsville, N. C., Oct. 9, 1918

O come, dear sister, and let's take a walk,
Bow un to me, O come, dear sister, and
let's take a walk, All on the green river-side. True, true,
true to my love, And my love is true to me.

N

Heptatonic. Mixolydian.

Sung by Mrs. Jenny L. Combs
at Berea, Madison Co., Ky., May 30, 1917

He gave to her a beaver hat, Bow down, He
gave to her a beaver hat, These vows were sent to
me, He gave to her a beaver hat, The old-est she thought
much of that. I'll be true, true to my love, If my
love will be true to me.

No. 6

The Cruel Brother
A

Hexatonic. Mode 3, b.

Sung by Mrs. Hester House
at Hot Springs, N. C., Sept. 15, 1916

1. There's three fair maids went out to play at ball, I o the li ly gay, There's

three land-lords come court them all, And the rose smells so sweet I know.

2 The first landlord was dressed in blue.
He asked his maid if she would be his true.

3 The next landlord was dressed in green.
He asked his maid if she'd be his queen.

4 The next landlord was dressed in white.
He asked his maid if she'd be his wife.

5 It's you may ask my old father dear,
And you may ask my mother too.

6 It's I have asked your old father dear,
And I have asked your mother too.

7 Your sister Anne I've asked her not,
Your brother John and I had forgot.

8 Her old father dear was to lead her to the yard,
Her mother too was to lead her to the step.

9 Her brother John was to help her up.
As he holp her up he stabbed her deep.

10 Go ride me out on that green hill,
And lay me down and let me bleed.

11 Go haul me up on that green hill,
And lay me down till I make my will.

12 It's what will you will to your old father dear?
This house and land that I have here.

13 It's what will you will to your mother, too?
This bloody clothing that I have wear.

The Cruel Brother

14 Go tell her to take them to yonders stream,
   For my heart's blood is in every seam.

15 It's what will you will to your sister Anne?
   My new gold ring and my silver fan.

16 It's what will you will to your brother John's wife?
   In grief and sorrow the balance of her life.

17 It's what will you will to your brother John's son?
   It's God for to bless and to make him a man.

18 It's what will you will to your brother John?
   A rope and a gallows for to hang him on.

B

Sung by Mrs. Julie Williams
at Hot Springs, Madison Co., N. C., July 27, 1917

Hexatonic (no 7th).

No. 7

Lord Randal

A

Pentatonic. Mode 3.

Sung by Mrs. Dora Shelton
at Allanstand, N. C., Aug. 2, 1916

1. What you will to your fa-ther, Jim-my Ran-dolph my son? What you

will to your fa-ther, my old-est, dear-est one? My hors-es, my bug-gies, Moth-er,

make my bed soon, For I am sick-heart-ed And I want to lie down.

    2 What you will to your brothers.
       My mules and waggons.

    3 What you will to your sisters.
       My gold and my silver.

B

Pentatonic. Mode 3.

Sung by Mrs. Mary Sands
at Allanstand, N. C., Aug. 3, 1916

1. What did you eat for your sup-per, Jim-my Ran-dal my son? What did you

eat for your sup-per, my own dear-est one? Cold poi-son, cold poul-try. Moth-er

make my bed soon, For I am sick-heart-ed and I want to lie down.

    2 What will you will to your mother.
       My gold and my silver.

    3 What will you will to your father
       My mules and my wagons.

Lord Randal

4 What will you will to your sister.
   My land and my houses.

5 What will you will to your brothers.
   My trunks and my clothing.

6 What will you will to your sweetheart.
   Two tushes bulrushes and them both parched brown,
   For she is the cause of my lying down.

C

Pentatonic. Mode 3.

Miss EMMA HENSLEY
at Carmen, N. C., Aug. 28, 1916

1. It's what did you eat for your breakfast, Jimmy Randal my son? It's what did you eat for your breakfast, My own dearest son? It's cold pie and cold coffee. Mother, make my bed soon, For I'm sick at the heart and I want to lie down.

(Mrs. HENSLEY's version)

2 It's what will you will to your father
   My mules and my wagons.

3 It's what will you will to your mother
   My trunk and my clothing.

4 It's what will you will to your brother
   My house and plantation.

5 It's what will you will to your sister
   My gold and my silver.

Lord Randal

6 It's what will you will to your sweetheart
 Bulrushes, bulrushes, and them half parched brown,
 For she's the whole cause of my lying down.

7 Where do you want to be buried
 By my little baby.

D

Sung by Mr. WILLIAM F. WELLS
at Swannanoah, N. C., Sept. 9, 1916

Pentatonic. Mode 3.

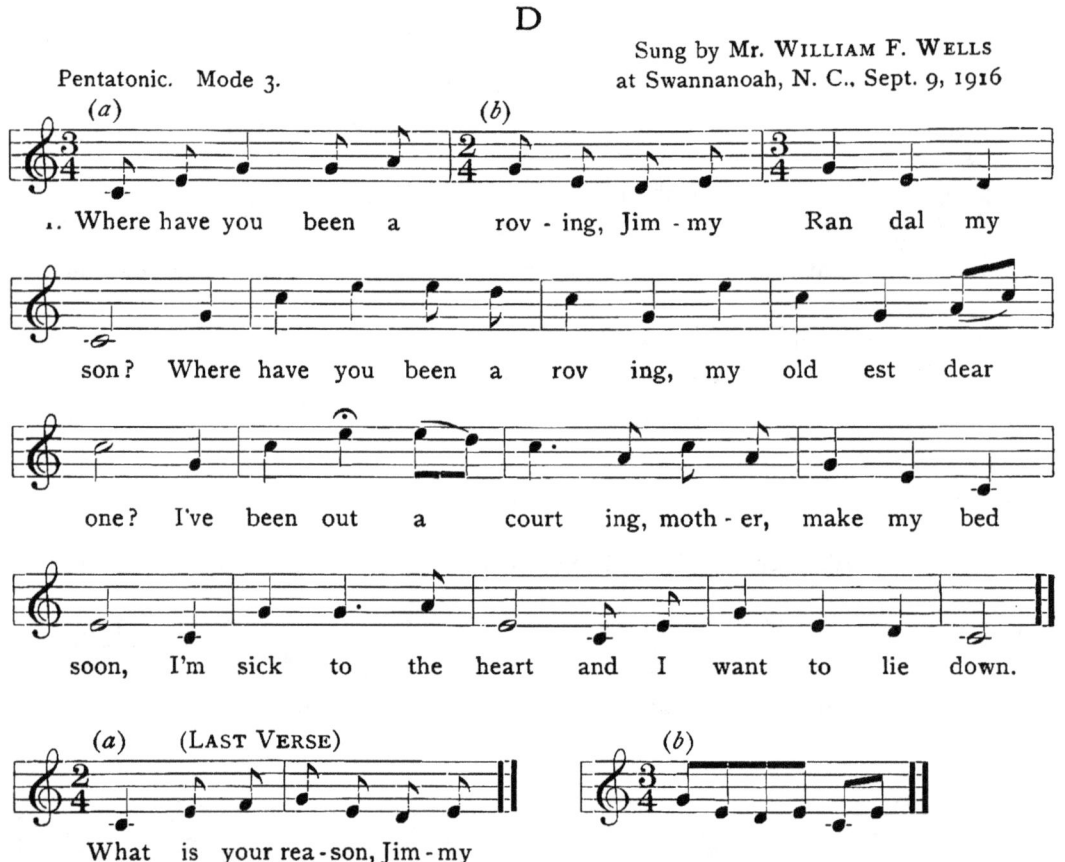

1. Where have you been a rov-ing, Jim-my Randal my son? Where have you been a rov-ing, my old-est dear one? I've been out a court-ing, moth-er, make my bed soon, I'm sick to the heart and I want to lie down.

(LAST VERSE) What is your rea-son, Jim-my

2 What did you will to your mother
 My houses and my lands.

3 What did you will to your father
 My waggon and my team.

4 What did you will to your brother
 My horn and my hounds.

5 What did you will to your sister
 My rings off my finger.

Lord Randal

6 What did you will to your sweetheart
A cup of strong poison.

7 What is your reason
Because she poisoned me.

E

Pentatonic. Mode 3.

Sung by Miss Florence McKinney
at Habersham Co., Georgia, June 2, 1910

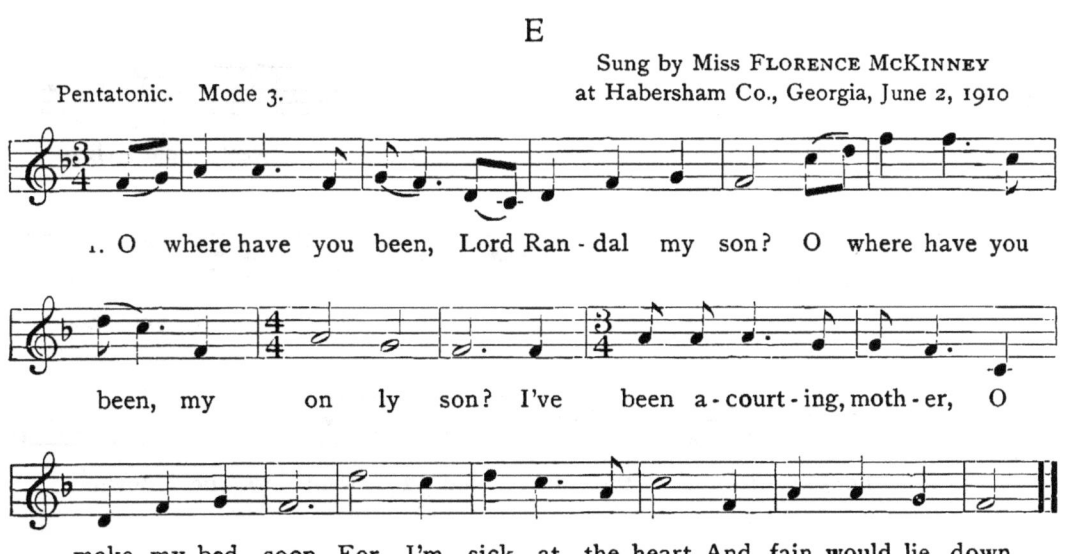

1. O where have you been, Lord Ran-dal my son? O where have you been, my on ly son? I've been a-court-ing, moth-er, O make my bed soon, For I'm sick at the heart And fain would lie down.

2 What did you have for your supper.
A cup of cold poison.

3 What would you leave your father.
My wagon and oxen.

4 What would you leave your mother
My coach and six horses.

5 What would you leave your sweetheart
Ten thousand weights of brimstone to burn her bones brown,
For she was the cause of my lying down.

Lord Randal

F

Hexatonic (no 3rd).

Sung by Mrs. Margaret Dunagan
at St. Helen's, Lee Co., Ky., Sept. 9, 1917

1. O where did you stay last night, O Randal, my son? O where did you stay last night, my sweet darling one? I stayed with my sweet-heart. Mother, make my bed soon, For I'm sick to the heart, and I want to lie down.

2 What did you eat for your supper, O Randal, my son?
   What did you eat for your supper, my sweet darling one?
   It was dill and dill broth. Mother, make my bed soon,
   For I'm sick to the heart and I want to lie down.

3 What colour was it, etc.
   It was brown and speckled, etc.

4 What'll you give to your sister, etc.
   My coach and my horses, etc.

5 What'll you give to your sweetheart, etc.
   Fire out of yon burning kiln for to burn her bones brown,
   For she is the occasion of my lying down;
   Fire out of yon burning kiln for to burn her bones brown,
   For she is the occasion of my lying down.

Lord Randal

G

Sung by Mrs. MAPLES at Bird's Creek, Sevierville, Sevier Co., Tenn., April 17, 1917

Pentatonic. Mode 3.

1. What you will to your mo-ther, my ram-bling young son? What you will to your mo-ther, my dear-est fair one? My hor-ses and cat-tle. Mo-ther, make my bed soon; I am sick to the heart and I fain would lie down.

H

Sung by Mrs. ADA MADDOX at Buena Vista, Va., April 30, 1918

Heptatonic. Mixolydian.

What for your sup-per, John Randolph, my son? What for your sup-per, my dar ling one? Eel soup and vin'-gar, has made my bed soon. Mo-ther, I'm sick at the heart and want to lie down.

* Bars of this rhythm, which occur constantly in this tune, were sung so that each of the first two notes were given rather more than their face value, i. e. the first note was nearly a crotchet, the second nearly a minim. The whole melody was sung quite slowly.

I

Sung by Mrs. LAUREL WHEELER at Buena Vista, Va., May 2, 1918

Heptatonic. Mixolydian.

What for your sup-per, John Ran-dolph, my son, What for your sup-per? Pray tell me, lit-tle one. Eel soup and vin-e-gar; go make my bed sound. I'm sick at the poor heart and want to lie down.

Lord Randal

2 Where were you last night, etc.
　I stayed at my love's house, etc.

3 What you will to your father, etc.
　My six hounds and musket, etc.

4 What you will to your sweetheart, etc.
　It's hot lead and brimstone for to parch her soul brown, etc.

J

Sung by Mrs. Sina Boone
at Shoal Creek, Burnsville, N. C., Sept. 28, 1918

(No 4th or 6th.)

What did you have for sup-per, Jim-my Ran-dolph, my son, What did you have for sup-per, my last man? Fried eels and fresh but-ter. Mother fix my bed soon, For I am faint heart-ed and I can no long-er stand.

K

Sung by Mrs. Ella Campbell
at Buena Vista, Va., May 1, 1918

Pentatonic. Mode 3.

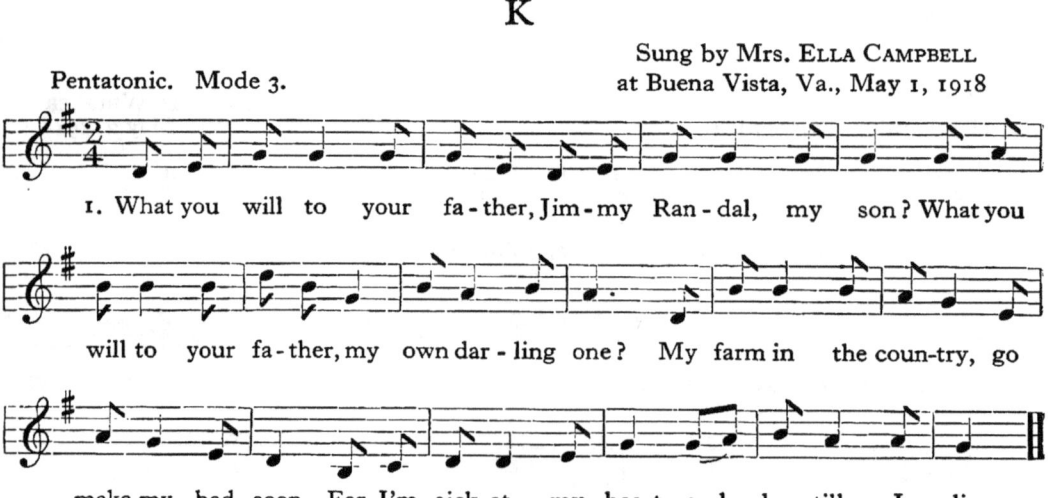

1. What you will to your fa-ther, Jim-my Ran-dal, my son? What you will to your fa-ther, my own dar-ling one? My farm in the coun-try, go make my bed soon, For I'm sick at my heart and be till I die.

44

Lord Randal

L

Heptatonic. Ionian.

Sung by Mrs. Emma Chisholm
at Nellysford, Va., May 21, 1918

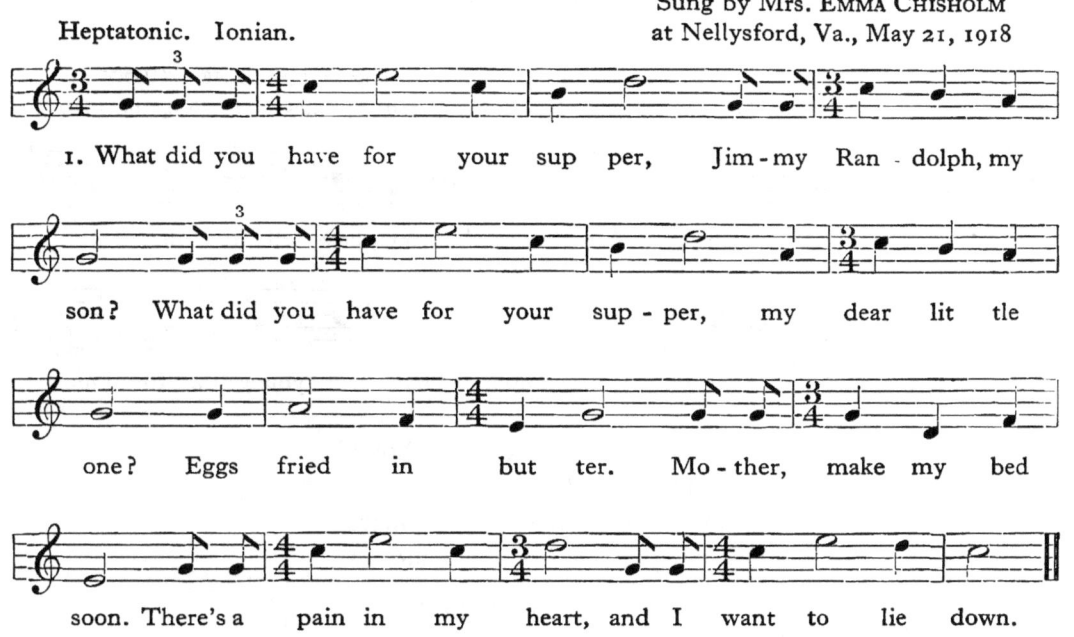

1. What did you have for your supper, Jimmy Randolph, my son? What did you have for your supper, my dear little one? Eggs fried in butter. Mother, make my bed soon. There's a pain in my heart, and I want to lie down.

M

Hexatonic (no 4th).

Sung by Mrs. Frances Richards
at St. Peter's School, Callaway, Va., Aug. 18, 1918

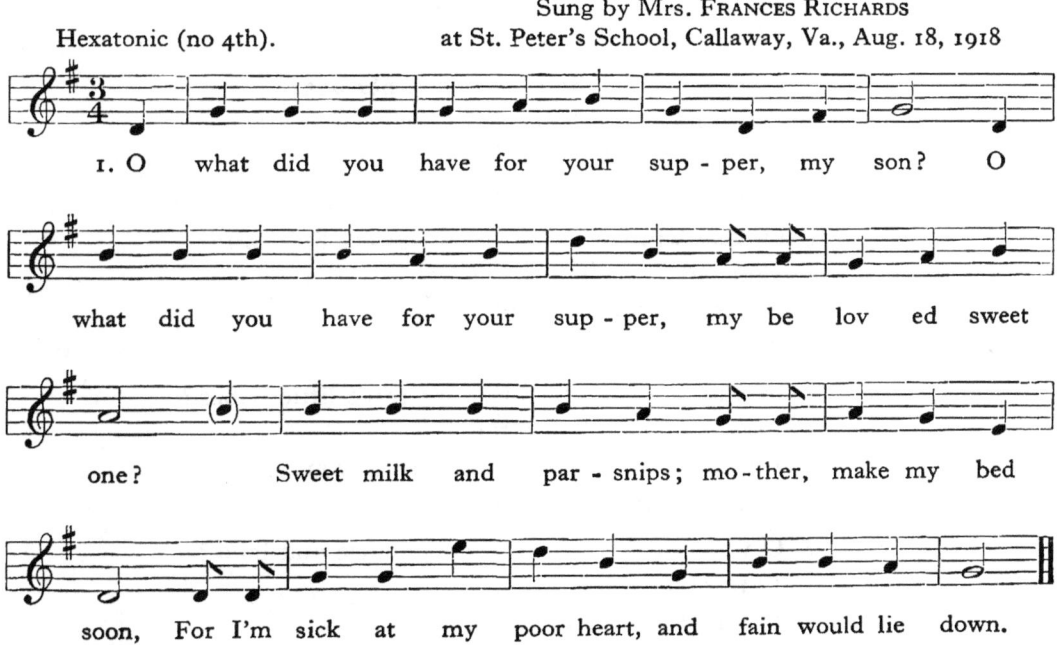

1. O what did you have for your supper, my son? O what did you have for your supper, my beloved sweet one? Sweet milk and parsnips; mother, make my bed soon, For I'm sick at my poor heart, and fain would lie down.

No. 8

Edward
A

Heptatonic. Mode 4, a + b (mixolydian).

Sung by Mrs. Jane Gentry
at Hot Springs. N. C., Aug. 24, 1916

1. How come that blood on your shirt sleeve? Pray, son, now tell to me. It

is the blood of the old grey-hound That run young fox for me.

2. It is too pale for that old greyhound.
   Pray, son, now tell to me.
   It is the blood of the old grey mare
   That ploughed that corn for me.

3. It is too pale for that old grey mare.
   Pray, son, now tell to me.
   It is the blood of my youngest brother
   That hoed that corn for me.

4. What did you fall out about?
   Pray, son, now tell to me.
   Because he cut yon holly bush
   Which might have made a tree.

5. O what will you tell to your father dear
   When he comes home from town?
   I'll set my foot in yonder ship
   And sail the ocean round.

6. O what will you do with your sweet little wife?
   Pray, son, now tell to me.
   I'll set her foot in yonder ship
   To keep me company.

7. O what will you do with your three little babes?
   Pray, son, now tell to me.
   I'll leave them here in the care of you
   For to keep you company.

8. O what will you do with your house and land?
   Pray, son, now tell to me.
   I'll leave it here in care of you
   For to set my children free.

Edward

Edward

2 It does look too pale for the old grey horse
That ploughed that field for you, you, you,
That ploughed that field for you.

3 What has come this blood on your shirt sleeve?
O dear love, tell me.
This is the blood of the old greyhound
That traced that fox for me, me, me,
That traced that fox for me.

4 It does look too pale for the old greyhound
That traced that fox for you, you, you,
That traced that fox for you.

5 What has come this blood on your shirt sleeve?
O dear love, tell me.
This is the blood of my brother-in-law
That went away with me, me, me,
That went away with me.

6 And it's what did you fall out about?
O dear love, tell me.
About a little bit of bush
That soon would have made a tree, etc.

7 And it's what will you do now, my love?
O dear love, tell me.
I'll set my foot in yanders ship,
And I'll sail across the sea, etc.

8 And it's when will you come back, my love?
O dear love, tell me.
When the sun sets into yanders sycamore tree,
And it's that will never be, be, be,
And it's that will never be.

Edward

E

Pentatonic. Mode 3 (Tonic G).

Sung by Mrs. MEG SHOOK
at Clyde, Haywood Co., N. C., Aug. 2, 1917

1. How came that blood on the point of your knife? My son, come tell to

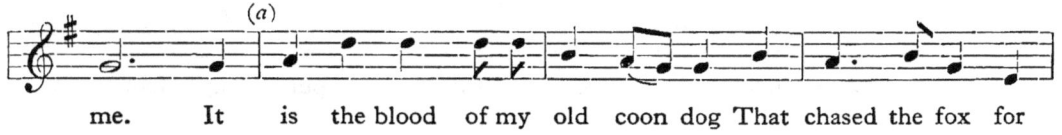

me. It is the blood of my old coon dog That chased the fox for

me, me, me, That chased the fox for me.

2 How come that blood, etc.
   It is the blood of that old horse
   That ploughed that field for me, etc.

3 How come that blood, etc.
   It is the blood of one of my brothers [1]
   Which fell out with me, etc.

4 What did you fall out about?
   My son, etc.
   We fell out about a holly-bush
   That would have made a tree, etc.

5 What will you do when your father comes home?
   I'll put my foot in a bunkum boat
   And sail across the sea.

6 What will you do with your dear little wife?
   I'll put her foot in a bunkum boat
   And sail across the sea.

7 What will you do with your dear little babe?
   I'll leave it here in this lone world
   To dandle on your knee.

8 And what will you do with your old gobbler?
   I'll leave it here with you when I'm gone
   To gobble after me.

[1] Mrs. Shook said that the name of the brother was Edward and that this line was sometimes sung, 'It is the blood of Edward'.

Edward

F

Hexatonic (no 3rd).

Sung by Mrs. J. L. Long
at Villamont, Va., June 4, 1918

1. O what are you going to do when your father comes home? O son, come tell to me. I'll put my foot in yonders boat, And sail across the sea.

G

Heptatonic. Mixolydian.

Sung by Mr. Ebe Richards
at St. Peter's School, Callaway, Va., Aug. 18, 1918

1. Where did you get your little blood red? My son, come tell to

me. I got it out of the little grey hawk That sits on yonders tree.

2 That little grey hawk's blood was never so red.
   My son, come tell to me.
   I got it out on that little red (*sometimes*, grey) colt
   That ploughed on yonders field.

3 That little grey (*or* red) colt's blood was never so red.
   My son, come tell to me.
   I got it out of my poor little brother
   That rode away with me.

4 What are you going to do when your papa comes home?
   My son, come tell to me.
   I'll set my foot in the bottomless ship,
   And sail across the sea.

5 When are you coming back, my son?
   My son, come tell to me.
   When the moon and sun sets in yonders hill,
   And that will never be.

Edward

H

Sung by Mrs. S. V. Cannady
at Endicott, Va., Aug. 23, 1918

Pentatonic. Mode 4.

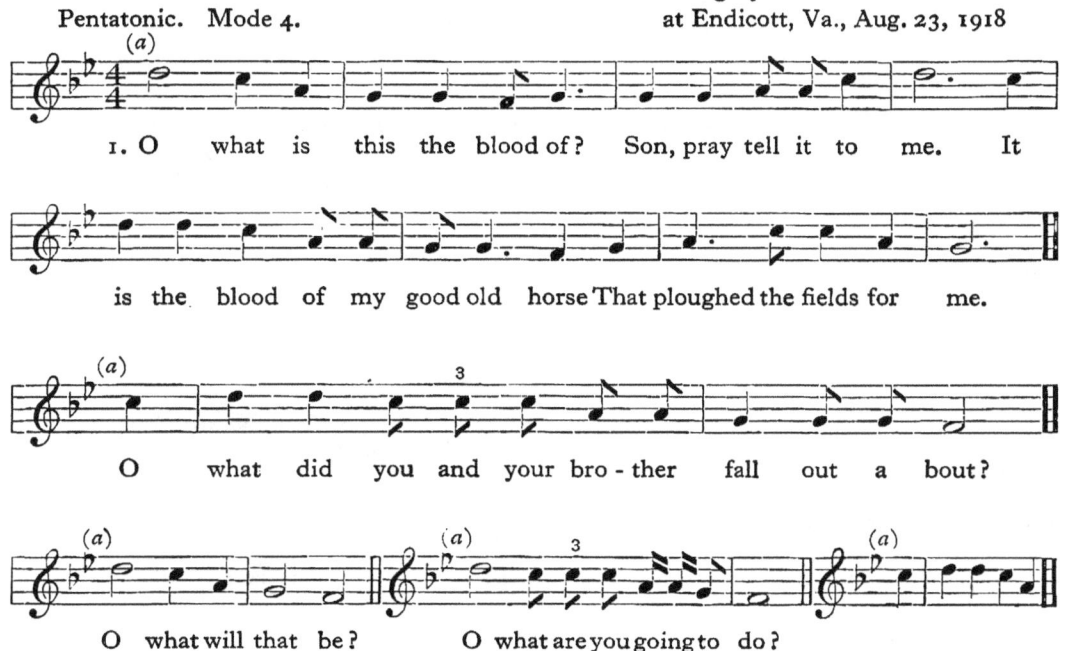

1. O what is this the blood of? Son, pray tell it to me. It is the blood of my good old horse That ploughed the fields for me.

O what did you and your bro-ther fall out a bout?

O what will that be? O what are you going to do?

2. It is too red for your good old horse.
   Son, pray tell it to me.
   It is the blood of my good old cow
   That gave the milk for me.

3. It is too red for your good old cow.
   Son, pray tell it to me.
   It is the blood of my good old dog
   That ran the deer for me.

4. It is too red for your good old dog.
   Son, pray tell it to me.
   It is the blood of my good old brother
   That walked the road with me.

5. O what did you and your brother fall out about?
   Son, pray tell it to me.
   We fell out about a hazel-nut bush
   Which might have made a hazel-nut tree.

6. O what are you going to do?
   Son, pray tell it to me.
   I'll set my foot on yonders shore,
   And I'll sail across the sea.

Edward

7 What are you going to do with your pretty little wife?
   Son, pray tell it to me.
   I'll set her foot on yonders shore,
   And she'll sail by the side of me.

8 What are you going to do with your sweet little babe?
   Son, pray tell it to me.
   I'll leave it here with my papa
   Till I come home again.

I

Pentatonic. Mode 3 (Tonic C).*

Sung by Mrs. NANNIE WEAVER
at Woolwine, Va., Aug. 25, 1918

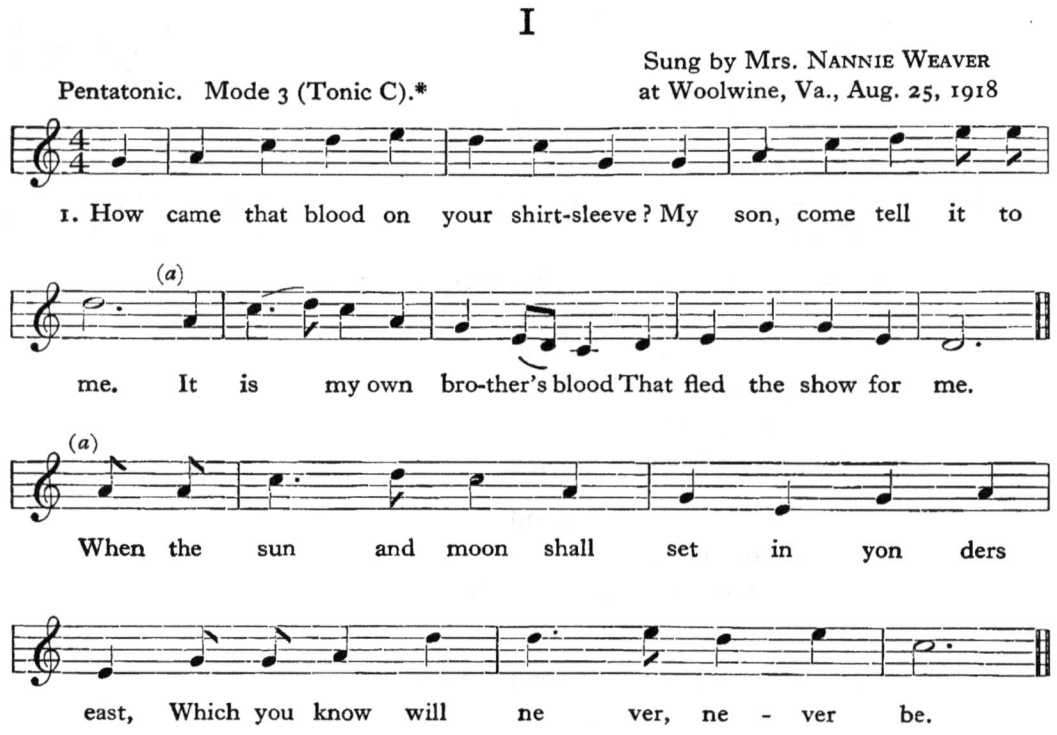

1. How came that blood on your shirt-sleeve? My son, come tell it to me. It is my own brother's blood That fled the show for me. When the sun and moon shall set in yonders east, Which you know will never, never be.

This variant is of the last verse, and, although corrupt and irregular, it may be that the tune ended on C in the last repetition. Mrs. Weaver only remembered two verses.

Last Stanza

When will you return again?
My son, come tell it to me.
When the sun and moon shall set in yonders east,
Which you know will never be.

* Mode 4 if D be tonic.

Edward

J

Pentatonic. Mode 3 (Tonic G).

Sung by Mrs. Mary Gibson
at Marion, N. C., Sept. 3, 1918

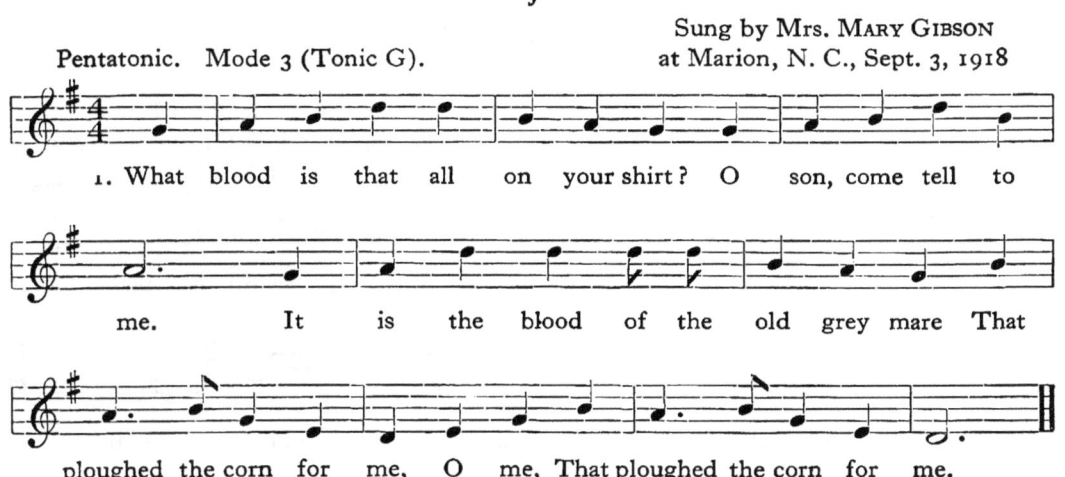

1. What blood is that all on your shirt? O son, come tell to me. It is the blood of the old grey mare That ploughed the corn for me, O me, That ploughed the corn for me.

2. It is too red for the old grey mare.
   O son, etc.
   It is the blood of the old grey hound
   That run the deer for me, etc.

3. It is too red for the old grey hound.
   It is the blood of the little guinea-pig
   That eat the corn for me.

4. It is too red for the little guinea-pig.
   It is the blood of my oldest brother
   That travelled along with me.

5. What did you fall out about?
   About a little holly bush
   That might have made a tree.

6. What will you do when your father comes home?
   I'll set my foot in a bunkum boat
   And sail all on the sea.

7. What will you do with your pretty little wife?
   I'll take her on a bunkum boat
   And sail along with me.

8. What will you do with your oldest son?
   I'll leave him here for you to raise
   And dance around your knees.

9. What will you do with your oldest daughter?
   I'll leave her here for you to raise
   For to remember me.

No. 9

Sir Lionel

A

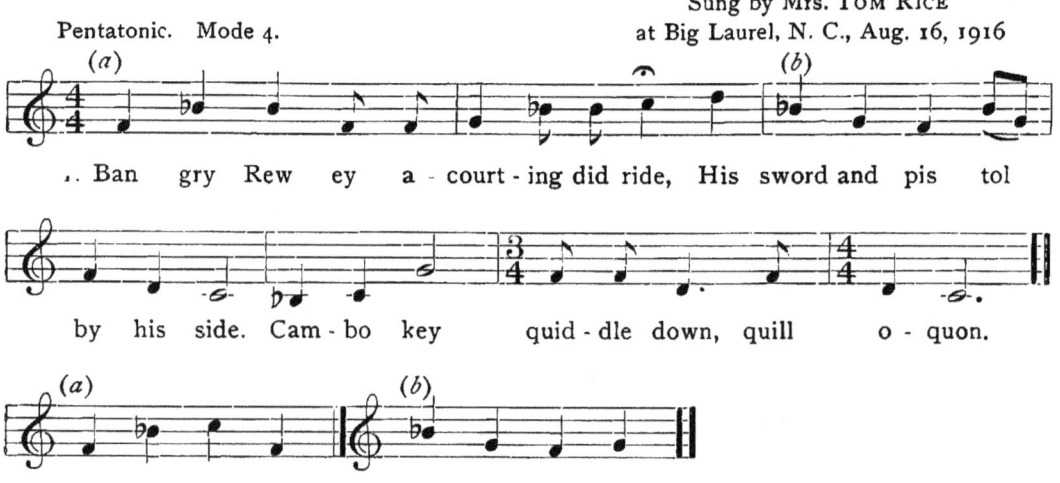

Sung by Mrs. Tom Rice
at Big Laurel, N. C., Aug. 16, 1916

Pentatonic. Mode 4.

1. Bangry Rewey a-courting did ride, His sword and pistol by his side. Cambo key quid-dle down, quill o-quon.

2 Bangry rode to the wild boar's den
  And there spied the bones of a thousand men.

3 Then Bangry drew his wooden knife
  To spear the wild boar of his life.

B

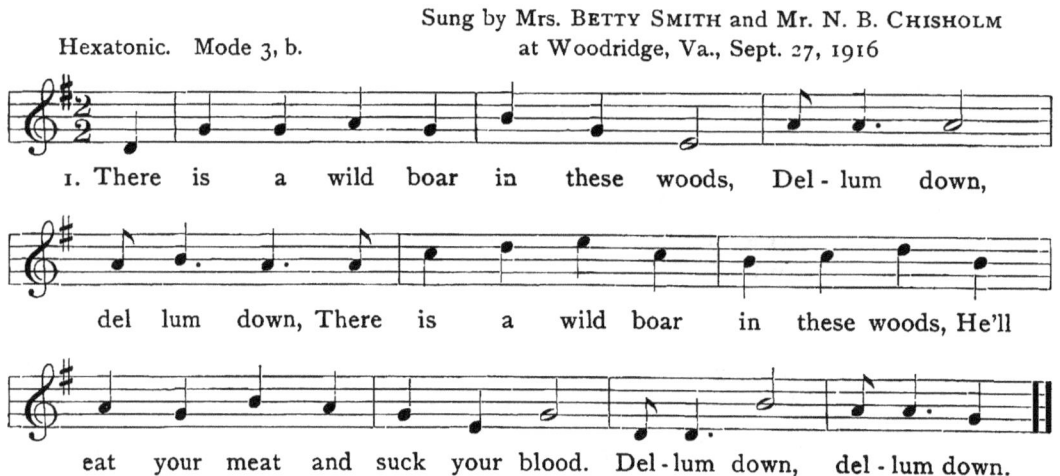

Sung by Mrs. Betty Smith and Mr. N. B. Chisholm
at Woodridge, Va., Sept. 27, 1916

Hexatonic. Mode 3, b.

1. There is a wild boar in these woods, Del-lum down, del lum down, There is a wild boar in these woods, He'll eat your meat and suck your blood. Del-lum down, del-lum down.

2 Bangrum drew his wooden knife
  And swore he'd take the wild boar's life.

3 The wild boar came in such a flash,
  He broke his way through oak and ash.

Sir Lionel

C

Hexatonic (no 6th).

Sung by Mrs. Mollie Broghton
at Barbourville, Knox Co., Ky., May 10, 1917

1. I went out a hunting one day, Del-lum down dil-lum,
I went out a-hunting one day, And I found there where a wild boar lay,
Come a call, cut him down, Quil-ly quo qua.

2 I hunted over hills and mountains,
And there I found him on his way.

3 The wild boar came in such a dash,
He cut his way through oak and ash.

4 I called up my army of men;
He killed one, two, three score of them.

D

Heptatonic. Ionian.

Sung by Miss Violet Henry
at Berea, Madison Co., Ky., May 21, 1917

O Bangum would a hunting ride, Cub-by kye,
cud-da' O Bangum would a hunting ride, Cud-dal down
O Bangum would a hunting ride, Sword and pistol
by his side, Cub-by kye, cud-dal down, kil-ly quo quam.

No. 10

The Cruel Mother

A

Heptatonic. Mode 1, a + b (mixolydian).

Sung by Mrs. ROSIE HENSLEY at Carmen, N. C., Aug. 10, 1916

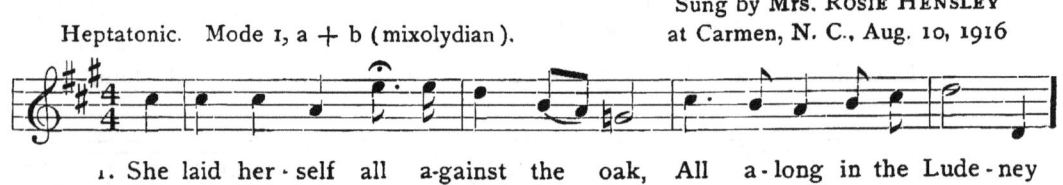

1. She laid her-self all a-gainst the oak, All a-long in the Lude-ney

And first it bent and then it broke, Down by the green-wood side.

2 She leaned herself all against the thorn,
And there she had two fine babes born.

3 She pulled out her snow-white breast,
And she bid them a-suck for that would be the last.

4 She pulled down her yellow hair,
And she bound it around their little feet and hands.

5 She pulled out her little penknife,
And she pierced all in their tender little hearts.

6 She was setting in her father's hall,
And she saw her babes a-playing with their ball.

7 O babes, O babes, if you were mine,
I would dress you in the silk so fine.

8 O mother, O mother, when we were thine,
You neither dressed us in the coarse silk nor fine.

B

Hexatonic. Minor mode (Aeolian influence, no 6th).

Sung by Mrs. MOORE at Rabun Co., Georgia, May 1, 1909

1. Christ-mas time is a roll-ing on, When the nights are long and cool, When three lit-tle babes come run-ning down And run in their moth-er's room.

The Cruel Mother

2 As she was going to her father's hall,
   All down by the greenwood side,
  She saw three little babes a-playing ball.
   All down by the greenwood side.

3 One was Peter and the other was Paul,
   All down, etc.
  And the other was as naked as the hour it was born.
   All down, etc.

4 O babes, O babes, if you were mine,
  I'd dress you in the silk so fine.

5 O mother, O mother, when we were young,
  You neither dressed us coarse nor fine.

6 You took your penknife out of your pocket,
  And you pierced it through our tender hearts.

7 You wiped your penknife on your shoe,
  And the more you wiped it the bloodier it grew.

8 You buried it under the marble stone,
  You buried it under the marble stone.

9 The hell gates are open and you must go through,
  The hell gates are open and you must go through.

C

Pentatonic. Mode 3.

Sung by Mr. T. Jeff Stockton
at Flag Pond, Tenn., Sept. 4, 1916

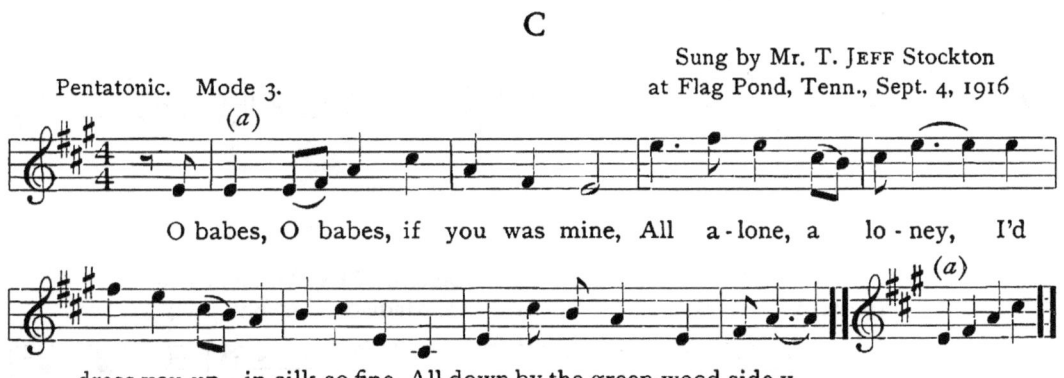

O babes, O babes, if you was mine, All a-lone, a lo-ney, I'd dress you up in silk so fine. All down by the green-wood side-y.

D

Heptatonic. Mode 1,
a + b (mixolydian).

Sung by Mr. N. B. Chisholm
at Woodridge, Va., Sept. 21, 1916

O ba by, O ba by, if you were mine,

The Cruel Mother

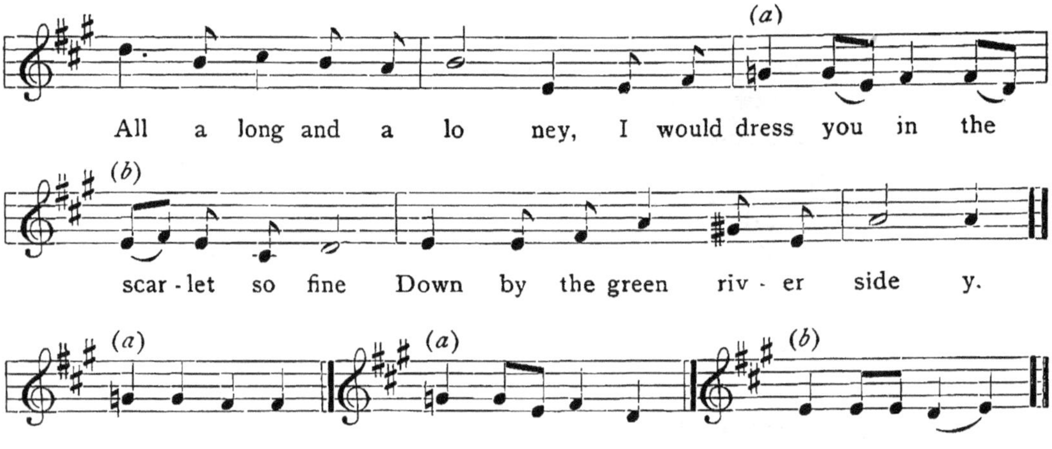
(a)
All a long and a lo ney, I would dress you in the
(b)
scar-let so fine Down by the green riv-er side y.
(a)
(a)
(b)

E

Sung by Mr. Riley Shelton
at Alleghany, N. C., Aug. 29, 1916

Pentatonic. Mode 2

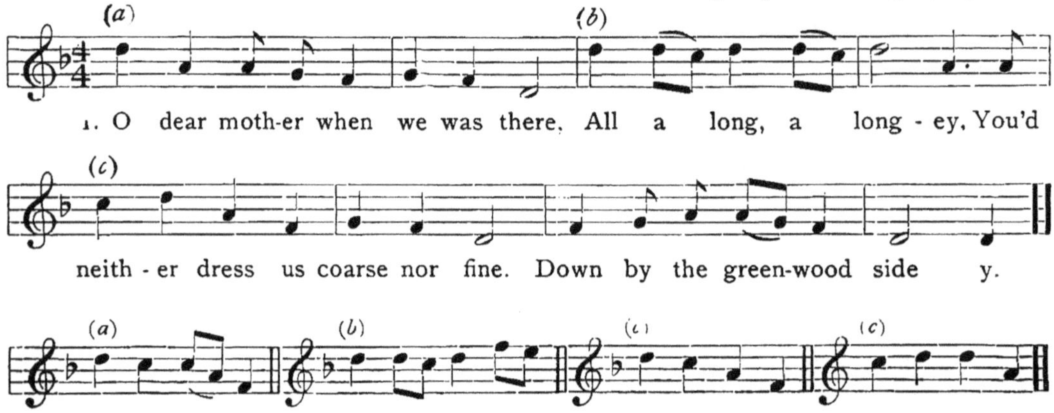
(a)
(b)
1. O dear moth-er when we was there, All a long, a long-ey, You'd
(c)
neith-er dress us coarse nor fine. Down by the green-wood side y.
(a)
(b)
(c)
(c)

F

Sung by Mrs. Maud Kilburn
at Berea, Madison Co., Ky., May 31, 1917

Hexatonic (no 7th).

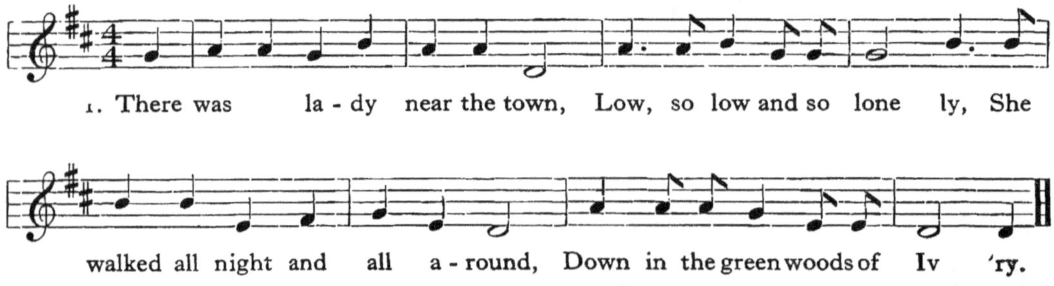
1. There was la-dy near the town, Low, so low and so lone ly, She
walked all night and all a-round, Down in the green woods of Iv 'ry.

The Cruel Mother

2 She had two pretty little babes,
　　Low, so low, etc.
　　She thought one day she'd take their lives,
　　　　Down in the green woods, etc.

3 She got a rope so long and neat,
　　And tied them down both hands and feet.

4 She got a knife so keen and sharp,
　　And pierced it through each tender heart.

5 Then she went out one moonlit night;
　　She saw two babes all dressed in white.

6 O babes, O babes, if you were mine,
　　I'd dress you up in silk so fine.

7 O mamma, O mamma, when we were yours,
　　You dressed us in our own heart's blood.

8 In seven years you'll hear a bell,
　　In seven years you'll land in hell.

G

Sung by Mrs. Doc. Pratt
at Hindman, Knott Co., Ky., Sept. 22, 1917

Hexatonic (no 6th).

1. There was a young lady so fair, Down in the loney, o ney, O, She was courted by the king's son so great, Down by the green wood sid eys, O.

2 He courted her for seven long years,
　　Until one evening she went walking.

3 It's first she leaned against an oak;
　　First it bent and then it broke.

4 The next she leaned against a pine;
　　Two sweet little babes to her was born.

5 She took her garter from her leg,
　　And there she tied her sweet little babes.

6 She took her penknife from her side,
　　Then she took their sweet little lives.

7 She was sitting one day in her father's hall;
　　She saw two sweet little babes playing.

The Cruel Mother

8 Saying: Babes, sweet babes, if you was mine,
  I'd dress you up in silk so fine.

9 O yes, false mother, we once was thine;
  You neither dressed us coarse nor fine.

10 O babes, sweet babes, can you tell me,
   What'll be my fate for killing you?

11 O yes, false mother, we can tell you.
   A false character you will bear.

12 Until your soul is scorched away,
   And then will hell scorch your bones.

H

Sung by Mrs. MARY GIBSON
at Marion, N. C., Sept. 3, 1918

Pentatonic. Mode 3.

1. There was a lady in New York, All a-long lit-tle O my, She fell in love with her father's clerk, All down by the green-wood sid ey.

2 She was a-going across the bridge,
  She found herself a-growing big.

3 She leant herself against an oak;
  First it bent and then it broke.

4 She leant herself against a thorn;
  And there she had two little babes born.

5 She carried a penknife both keen and sharp;
  She pierced those little babes to the heart.

6 She buried them under a bunch of rue;
  She prayed to the Lord they'd never come to.

7 When she was a-walking across the porch,
  She saw two little babes at play.

8 O babes, O babes, if you were mine,
  I'd dress you up in silk so fine.

9 Mother, O mother, when we were yours
  You neither gave us coarse nor fine.

10 Mother, O mother, for our sakes
   You'll always carry the keys of Hell's gates.

The Cruel Mother

The Cruel Mother

L

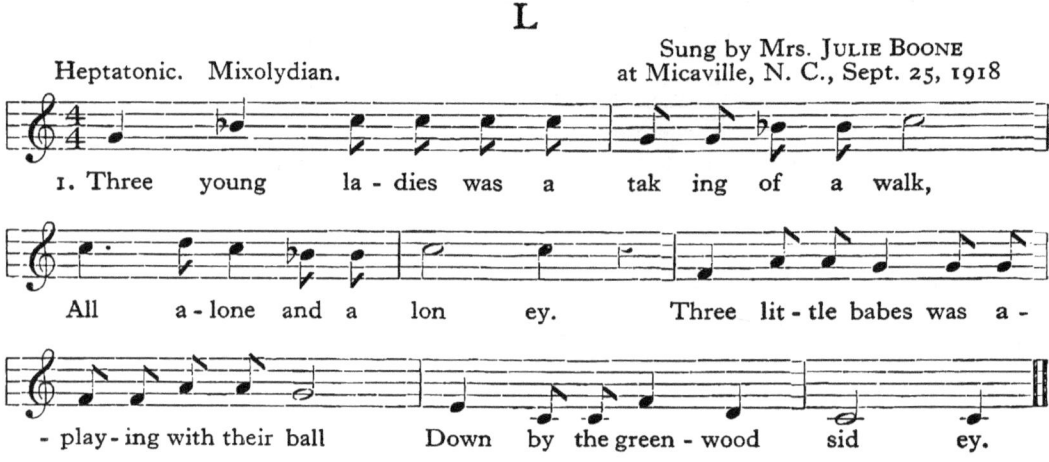

Heptatonic. Mixolydian.

Sung by Mrs. JULIE BOONE
at Micaville, N. C., Sept. 25, 1918

1. Three young ladies was a taking of a walk,
All alone and a loney.
Three little babes was a-playing with their ball
Down by the green-wood sidey.

2 One was Peter, the other was Paul,
The other was as naked as the hour it was born.

3 O babe, O babe, if you was mine,
Dress you up in silk so fine.

4 You took your knife out of your pocket,
Primmed[1] me of my little sweet life.

5 You buried me under the marble stone,
Then you turned as fair maid home.

6 Seven long years a-ringing of a bell,
Seven long years you'll prim[1] us in hell.

These words were very indistinctly pronounced. They might have been, and probably were, 'twinned' (deprived) in the fourth stanza (see Child, versions B and E), and 'twin' (part with) in the sixth stanza.

M

Hexatonic (no 7th).

Sung by Mrs. EMILY T. SNIPES
at Marion, N. C., Sept. 5, 1918

Mother, mother, do so no more, All lee little O-ney, For this you shall carry the keys of hell's door, All down by the green wad sid-ey.

No. 11

The Three Ravens

A

Heptatonic. Mode 1,
a + b (mixolydian).

Sung by Mr. Ben Burgess
at Charlottesville, Va., Sept. 28, 1916

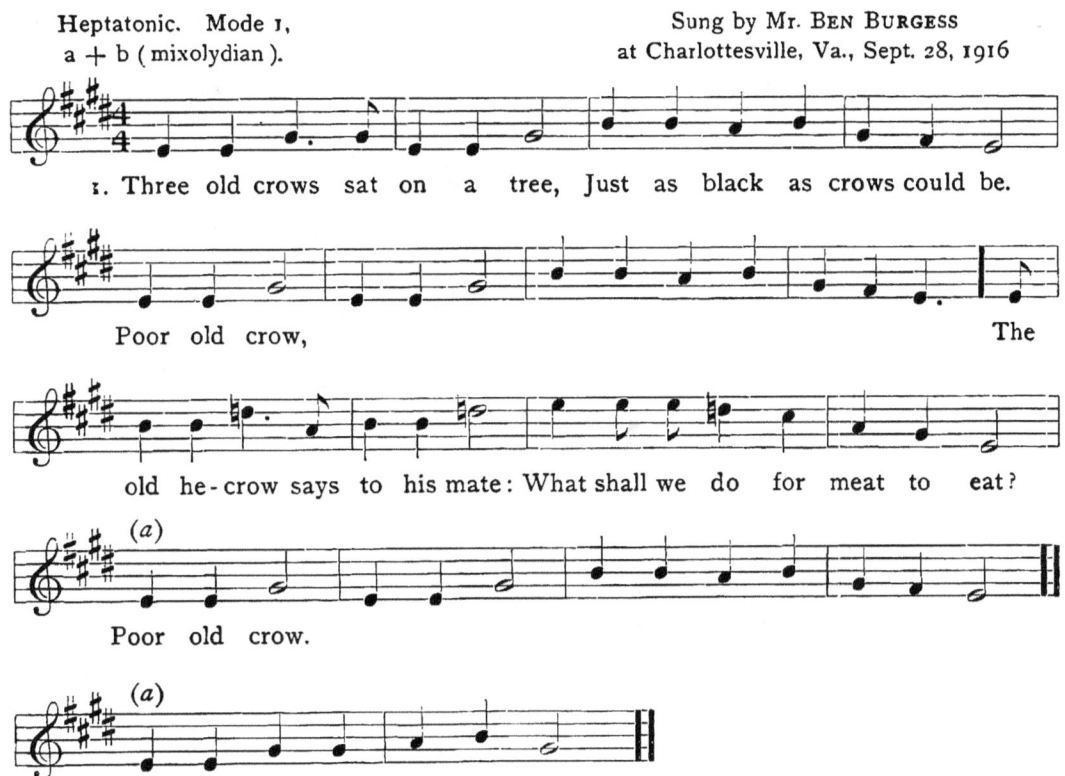

1. Three old crows sat on a tree, Just as black as crows could be.
Poor old crow, The old he-crow says to his mate: What shall we do for meat to eat?
Poor old crow.

The Three Ravens

B

Heptatonic. Ionian.

Sung by Mrs. ADA MADDOX
at Loch Laird, Buena Vista, Va., May 3, 1918

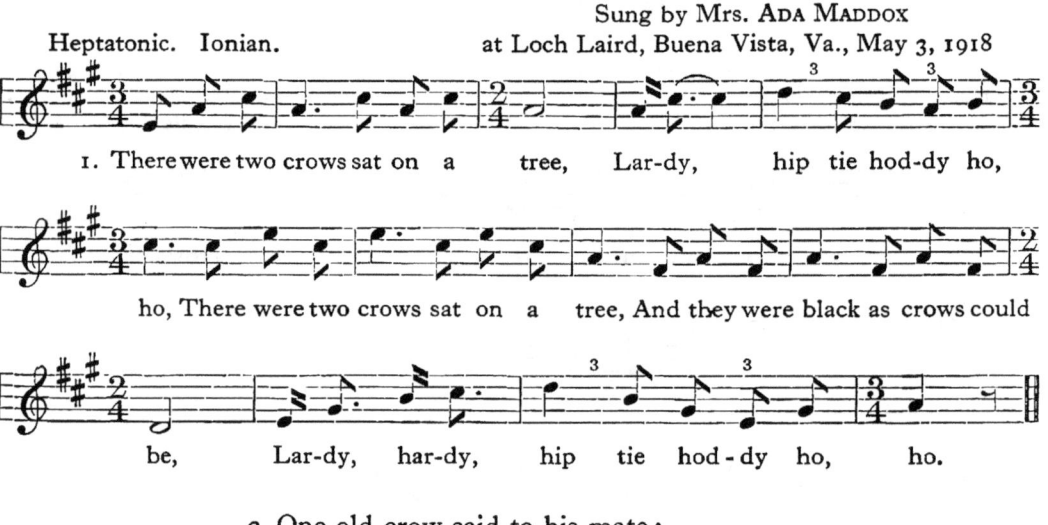

2 One old crow said to his mate:
   Lardy, etc.,
   One old crow said to his mate:
   What shall we have to-day to eat?

3 Yonder lies a horse in yonders lane,
   Whose body has not been very long slain.

4 We'll press our feet on his breast-bone,
   And pick his eyes out one by one.

C

(No 4th or 6th.)

Sung by Mrs. QUEENIE WOODS
at Buena Vista, Va., May 2, 1918

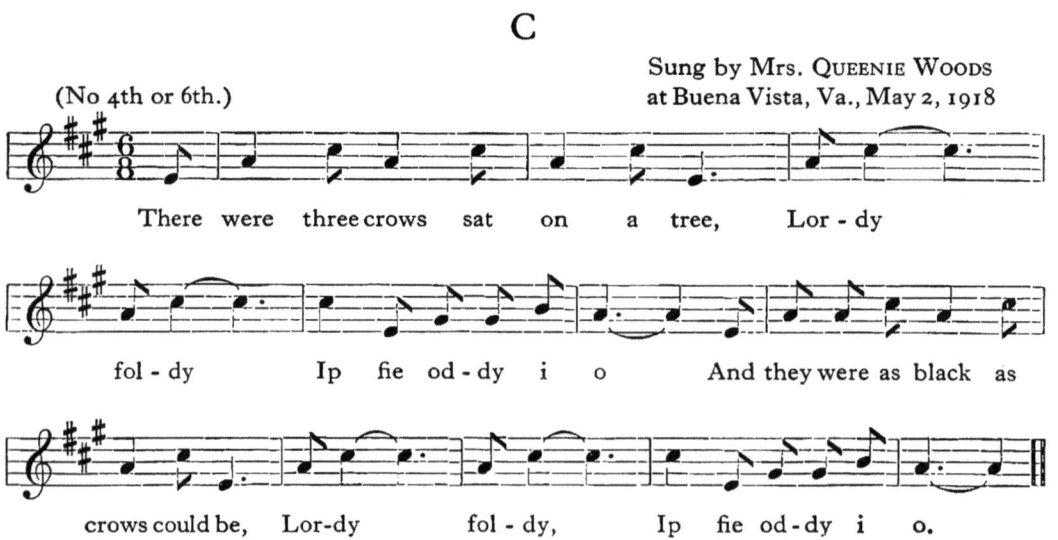

No. 12

The Two Brothers
A

Hexatonic. Mode 3, a.

Sung by Mrs. Lizzie Roberts and Mrs. Smith at Hot Springs, N. C., Sept. 15, 1916

1. Mon - day morn - ing go to school, Fri - day eve - ning home.

Broth - er, comb my sweet-heart's hair As we go walk - ing home.

2 Brother, won't you play a game of ball?
  Brother, won't you toss a stone?
  Brother, won't you play no other game
  As we go marching home?

3 I can't play no game of ball,
  I can't toss no stone,
  I can't play no other game.
  Brother, leave me alone.

4 Brother took out his little penknife,
  It was sharp and keen.
  He stuck it in his own brother's heart,
  It caused a deadly wound.

5 Brother, take off your little check shirt,
  Stitched from gore to gore;
  Bind it around the deadly wound.
  It won't bleed no more.

6 Brother took off his little check shirt,
  Stitched from gore to gore;
  Bound it around the deadly wound.
  It didn't bleed no more.

7 Brother, O brother, go dig my grave,
  Dig it wide and deep.
  Bury my bible at my head,
  My hymn book at my feet.

The Two Brothers

8 He buried his bible at his head,
His hymn book at his feet,
His bow and arrow by his side,
And now he's fast asleep.

B

Heptatonic. Mode 3, a + b (ionian).

Sung by Mrs. ROSIE SMITH
at Charlottesville, Va., Sept. 25, 1916

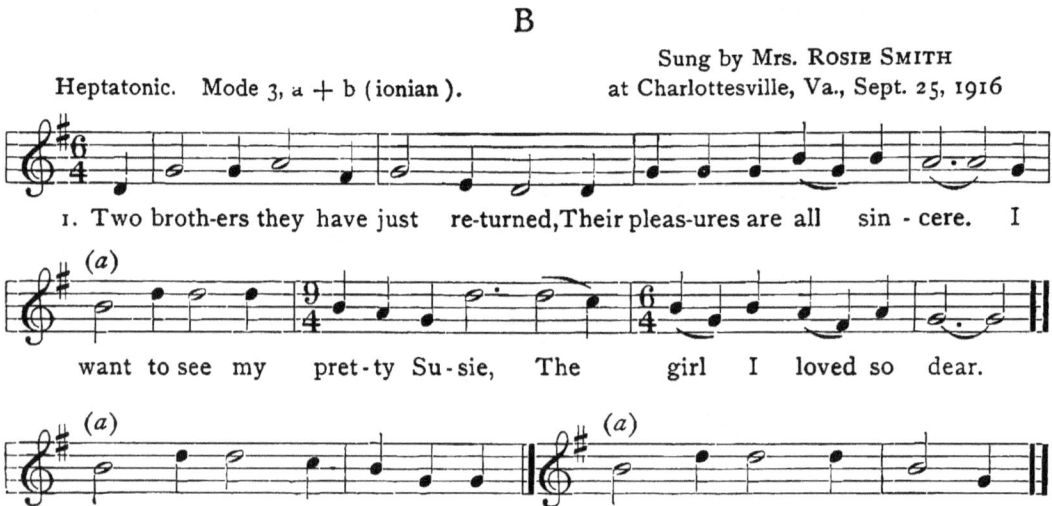

1. Two broth-ers they have just re-turned, Their pleas-ures are all sin-cere. I want to see my pret-ty Su-sie, The girl I loved so dear.

2 You're not the one that loves Susie,
And here I'll spill your blood.
He drew a knife both keen and sharp
And pierced it through his heart.

3 What will you tell my father dear
When he calls for his son John?
I'll tell him you're in the western woods
A-learning your hounds to run.

4 What will you tell my mother dear
When she calls for her son John?
I'll tell her you're in the Tennessee
A lesson there to learn.

5 What will you tell my pretty Susie
When she calls for true love John?
I'll tell her you're in your silent grave,
Where never no more to return.

6 She took her bible in her hand,
A-moaning she went on.
She moaned till she came to his silent grave.
In search of her true love John.

The Two Brothers

7 What do you want, my pretty Susie?
  What do you want with me?
  I want a kiss from your clay-cold lips,
  'Tis all I ask of thee.

8 If I were to kiss your rosy cheeks
  My breath it is too strong.
  If I were to kiss your ruby lips,
  You would not stay here long.

9 So now go home, my pretty Susie,
  And moan no more for me,
  For you may moan to Eternity,
  My face no more you'll see.

C

Heptatonic. Mode 1, a + b
(mixolydian influence).

Sung by Mr. NUEL WALTON
at Mount Fair, Va., Sept. 26th, 1916

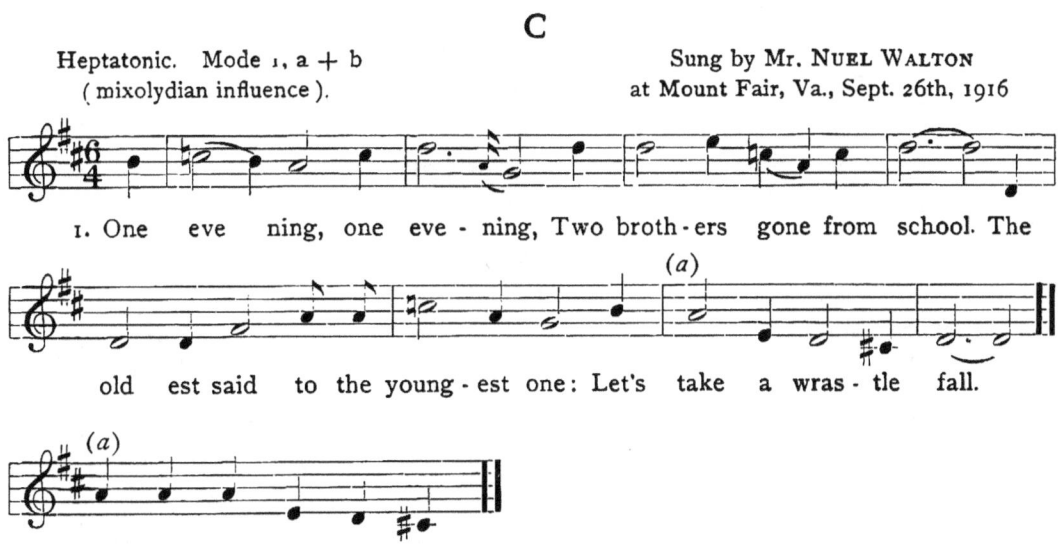

1. One evening, one evening, Two brothers gone from school. The oldest said to the youngest one: Let's take a wrastle fall.

2 The oldest threw the youngest down,
  He threw him to the ground,
  And from his pocket came a penknife
  And give him a deathless wound.

3 Pull off, pull off, your woollen shirt,
  And tear it from gore to gore,
  And wrap it around this deathless wound,
  And that will bleed no more.

4 He pulled off his woollen shirt,
  And tore it from gore to gore,
  And wrapped it around this deathless wound,
  And it did bleed no more.

The Two Brothers

5 It's take me up all on your back
   And carry me to yonder churchyard,
   And dig my grave both wide and deep
   And gentle lie me down.

6 What will you tell your father
   When he calls for his son John?
   You can tell him I'm in some low green woods
   A-learning young hounds to run.

7 What will you tell your mother
   When she calls for her son John?
   You can tell her I'm in some graded school,
   Good scholar to never return.

8 What will you tell your true love
   When she calls for her dear John?
   You can tell her I'm in some lonesome grave,
   My books to carry home.

9 One sweet kiss from your clay, clay lips
   Will bring my day short on.

D

Heptatonic. Mode 1, a + b (mixolydian).

Sung by Mr. Ozzo Keeton
at Mount Fair, Va., Sept. 26th, 1916

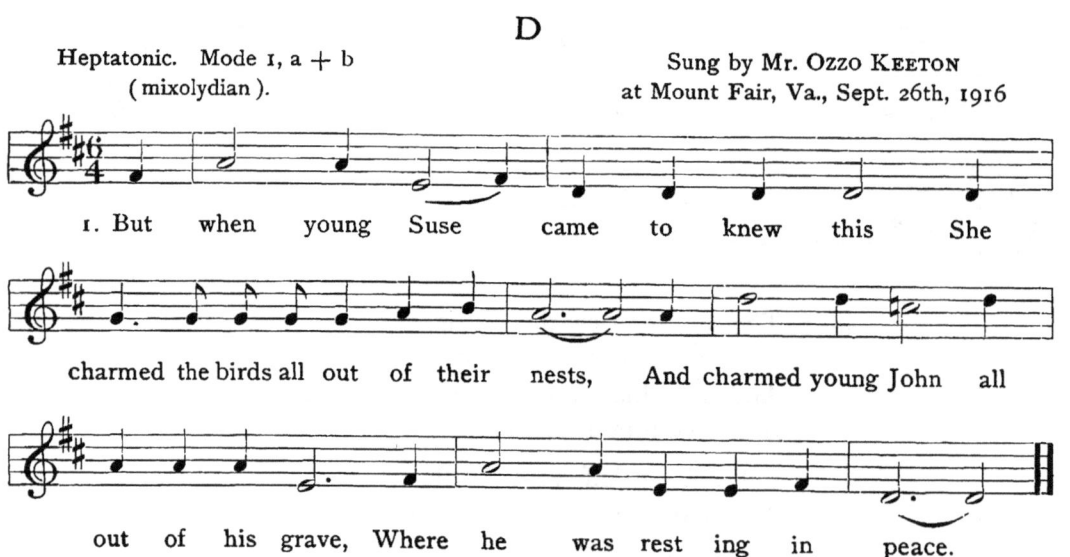

1. But when young Suse came to knew this She charmed the birds all out of their nests, And charmed young John all out of his grave, Where he was resting in peace.

2 O what do you want with me, young Suse,
   O what do you want with me?
   I want one kiss from your sweet lips
   And then I can rest in peace.

The Two Brothers

E

Hexatonic. Mode 3, b.

Sung by Mrs. Carrie Ford
at Black Mountain, N. C., Sept. 18, 1916

1. It's Mon-day morn-ing go to school, Fri day eve-ning home.

Broth-er comb my sweet-heart's hair and wel-come her in home.

F

Heptatonic. Ionian.

Sung by Mrs. Margaret Dunagan
at St. Helen's, Lee Co., Ky., Sept. 5, 1917

1. O bro-ther, can you toss the stone, Or can you play the ball? I am too lit-tle, I am too young, Go, bro-ther, let me a lone.

2 His brother took his little penknife,
   He hung it by his side,
   He put it deeply deathly wound
   As it hung by his side.

3 O brother, take my holland shirt,
   And rip it from gore to gore;
   You tie it around my bleeding wound
   And still it'll bleed no more.

4 His brother took his holland shirt
   And ripped it from gore to gore;
   He tied it around his bleeding wound,
   But still it bled the more.

The Two Brothers

5 O brother, take me on your back,
   Carry me to Chesley Town;
   You dig me a deep and large, wide grave
   And lay me there so sound.

6 You put my bible at my head,
   My solberd (psalter?) at my feet,
   My little bow and arrow by my side,
   And sounder I will sleep.

7 His brother took him on his back,
   He carried him to Chesley Town;
   He dug him a deep and large, wide grave
   And laid him there so sound.

8 He put his bible at his head,
   His solberd at his feet,
   His little bow and arrow at his side,
   So sounder he will sleep.

9 O brother, as you go home at night
   And my mother asks for me,
   You'll tell her I'm along with some schoolboys,
   So merry I'll come home.

10 And if my true love asks for me,
   The truth to her you'll tell;
   You'll tell her I'm dead and in grave laid
   And buried in Chesley Town.

11 With my bible at my head,
   My solberd at my feet,
   My little bow and arrow at my side,
   And sounder I will sleep.

12 And as his brother went home at night,
   His mother asked for him.
   He told he's along with some schoolboys,
   So merry he'll come home.

13 And then his true love asked for him;
   The truth to her he told.
   He told he was dead and in grave laid
   And buried in Chesley Town,

14 With his bible at his head,
   His solberd at his feet,
   His little bow and arrow at his side,
   So sounder he will sleep.

The Two Brothers

15 And then his true love put on small hoppers
   And tied them with silver strings.
   She went hopping all over her true lover's grave
   A twelve-months and a day.

16 She hopped the red fish out of the sea,
   The small birds out of their nests;
   She hopped her true love out of his grave,
   So he can't see no rest.

17 Go home, go home, you rambling reed;
   Don't weep nor mourn for me;
   For if you do for twelve long years,
   No more you'll see of me.

G

Sung by Mrs. Delie Knuckles
at Barbourville, Knox Co., Ky., May 16, 1917

Hexatonic (no 7th).

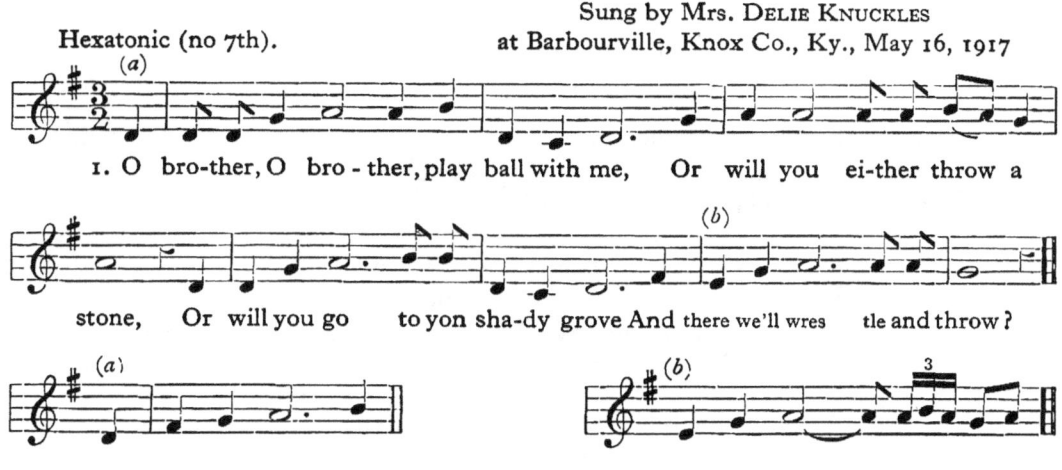

1. O brother, O brother, play ball with me, Or will you either throw a stone, Or will you go to yon shady grove And there we'll wrestle and throw?

2 I'll not play at ball with you,
  Or either will I throw a stone;
  But if you'll go to yon shady grove
  There we will wrestle and throw.

3 O brother, O brother, you've wounded me,
  You've wounded me so bad.
  Go and tear my shirt from off my back
  And tear it from gore to gore,
  And wrap it around my bleeding wound
  That it won't bleed no more.

4 He tore his shirt from off his back,
  And tore it from gore to gore.
  And wrapped it around his bleeding wound
  That it might bleed no more.

The Two Brothers

5 If you meet my father, as you turn round home,
  Enquiring for his son John,
  Go tell him I've gone to Langford's Town
  To bring those new books home.

6 If you meet my mother, as you turn round home,
  Enquiring for her son John,
  Go tell her I'm gone to the cottage gate
  To learn to sing and pray.

7 If you meet my true love, as you turn round home,
  Enquiring for her true love John,
  Go tell her I'm buried in the old churchyard,
  And it's for her sake I'm gone.

8 He met his father, as he turned round home,
  Enquiring for his son John.
  O father, O father, he's gone to Langford's Town
  To bring those new books home.

9 He met his mother, as he turned round home,
  Enquiring for her son John.
  O mother, O mother, he's gone to the cottage gate
  To learn to sing and pray.

10 He met his true love, as he turned round home,
  Enquiring for her true love John.
  O true love, O true love, he's buried in the old churchyard,
  And it's for your sake he's gone.

11 They buried his bible at his head,
  His testament at his feet,
  And on his breast his little hymn-book,
  That with them he might sleep.

H

(No 4th or 6th.)

Sung by Mrs. Sudie Sloan
at Barbourville, Knox Co., Ky., May 6, 1917

Two lit-tle boys were going to school, O ve-ry fine boys were they;

On Sun-day eve ning they come home, On Mon-day they go a-way.

The Two Brothers

There's no little fishes in the brook,
And no little girls to mourn,
But Willie will sigh and mourn for me
When I am dead and gone.

O tell our loving mother,
What a change to see;
Just tell her I'm gone to the golden land
My prayer-books for to learn.

I

Heptatonic. Ionian.

Sung by Mrs. OLLIE HUFF
at Berea, Knox Co., Ky., May 31, 1917

1. There's two lit-tle bro-thers going to school. The old-est to the young-est called: Come go with me to the green sha-dy grove And I'll wres-tle you a fall.

2 They went to the green shady grove,
Where they wrestled up and down.
The oldest to the youngest said:
You've given me a deadly wound.

3 Rip my shirt from off my back,
Rip it from gore to gore,
And then tie up those bleeding wounds,
And they won't bleed no more.

4 He ripped his shirt from off his back,
Ripped it from gore to gore,
And then tied up those bleeding wounds,
And they did bleed no more.

The Two Brothers

5 When you go home tell mother dear,
   If she isn't quarrelling about me,
   Tell her I'm laid at the new church-yard,
   Let be what church it may.

6 She mourned and she mourned,
   She mourned for little Willie,
   She nearly mourned him out of his grave
   To come home and be with her.

J

Sung by Mrs. LUCINDIE FREEMAN
at Marion, N. C., Sept. 3, 1918

Hexatonic (no 4th).

1. Mon-day morn-ing go to school, Fri-day eve-ning home.

Sis - ter, comb my sweet-heart's hair And wel-come her at home

2 It's O brother, O brother, don't play no game of ball,
   Brother don't cast no stone,
   Don't play no other game
   As we go marching home.

3 I won't play no game of ball,
   Nor neither cast no stone,
   I won't play no other game,
   But sister won't let me alone.

4 Brother pulled out his little penknife,
   It was both sharp and keen.
   He pierced his own brother to the heart,
   It made a dreadful wound.

5 O brother, O brother, pull off your little check shirt,
   Stitched from gore to gore,
   And bind it around this dreadful wound
   And it will bleed no more.

6 Brother pulled off his little check shirt,
   Stitched from gore to gore,
   And bound it around his dreadful wound,
   And it did bleed no more.

The Two Brothers

7 O brother, go dig my grave,
   Dig it wide and deep,
   Bury a bible at my head
   And a prayer-book at my feet.

8 He buried his bible at his head,
   His prayer-book at his feet,
   A bow and arrow by his side,
   And now he lies asleep.

K

Sung by Mrs. Virginia Bennett
at Burnsville, N. C., Sept. 13, 1918

Hexatonic (no 3rd).

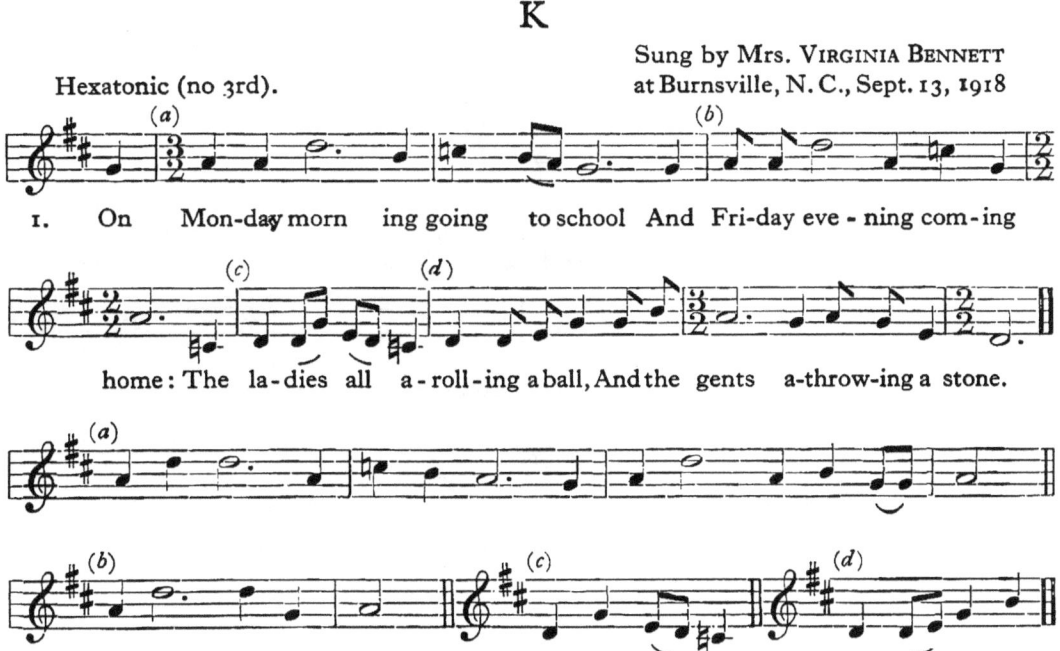

1. On Monday morning going to school And Friday evening coming home: The ladies all a-rolling a ball, And the gents a-throwing a stone.

2 He wrestled him up and he wrestled him down,
   Till he wrestled him to the ground.

3 What will you tell to my father dear
   When he calls for his son John?
   I'll tell that I left you in the Mackintaw woods
   A-learning your hounds to run.

4 What will you tell to your mother dear
   When she calls for her son John?
   I'll tell that I left you in the old school-house
   With a long, long lesson to learn.

The Two Brothers

5 What will you tell to your sister Susan dear
  When she calls for her brother John?
  I'll tell that I left you in the cold grave-yard,
  No more for her to see.

6 She took her banjo in her arms,
  Her harp strung to her back.
  She harped till she harped the fowls from the air
  And the fishes from the sea.

7 She harped till she harped brother John from his grave.
  Sister, what do you want with me?
  One sweet kiss from your sweet ruby lips,
  This world's not long for me.

L

(No 4th or 6th.) Sung by Mr. and Mrs. Jas. A. Maples at Bird's Creek, Sevierville, Tenn., April 17, 1917

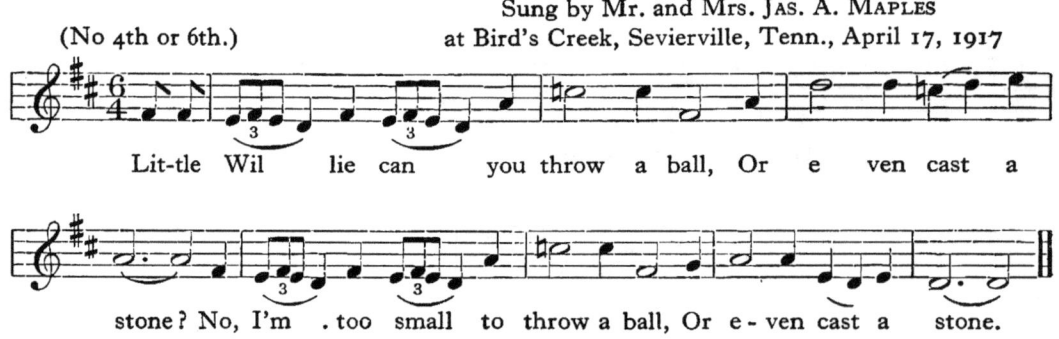

M

Hexatonic (no 6th). Sung by Mrs. Florence FitzGerald at Afton, Va., April 23, 1918

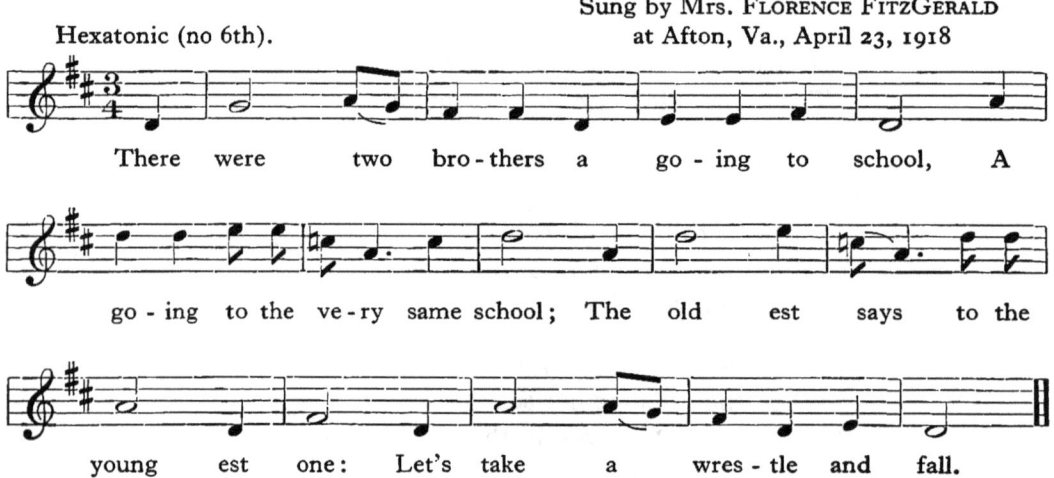

No. 13

Young Beichan
A

Sung by "Granny" BANKS
at White Rock, N. C., July 28, 1916

Mode 1, a (no 6th).

1. Lord Bacon was a noble man, As fine as any you should see; He'd gathered all his silks and rubies, The Turkish land he'd go and see.

2 He first blowed East and then blowed West,
And he blowed down to the Turkish land.
The Turks they got him and so sadly used him,
To leave his life he was quite wearied.

3 They bored a hole in his left shoulder
And nailed him down unto a tree.
They gave him nothing but bread and water,
And bread and water but once a day.

4 The Turks they had but one fair daughter,
As fair a one as you should see.
She stole the keys of the prison strong
  (*or*, She stole the jail keep from her father)
And vowed Lord Bacon she would set free.

5 She said: Have you got any land or living,
Or have you any dwelling free?
Would you give it all to a prince's daughter
If she would set you free?

6 Then he says: I've got a land and living
And I have got a dwelling free,
And I'll give it all to you, (my) pretty creature,
If you will do that thing for me.

7 She went on to her master's cellar
And from her father stole a jail key.
She opened the dungeon both deep and wide,
And vowed Lord Bacon she would set free.

Young Beichan

8 Then she took him to her master's (*or* father's) cellar
   And drawed some of the best port wine,
   And drink a health, you pretty creature,
   I wish, Lord Bacon, you were mine.

9 And then they drawed each other's notes of love
   And seven years they were to stand.
   He vowed he'd marry no other woman
   Unless(*or* Until) she married some other man.

10 Then she took him on to the sea-side
   And left him sailing over the main:
   Fare-ye-well, fare-ye-well, you pretty creature.
   O when shall I see you again?

11 When seven years was passed and gone,
   And seven months and almost three,
   She gathered all her silks and rubies
   And vowed Lord Bacon she'd go and see.

12 When she got to Lord Bacon's hall
   She knocked so far below the ring.
   Who's there, who's there (*or* O yes, O yes), said the bold, proud porter,
   Who knock so hard fain would come in?

13 Is this Lord Bacon's hall, she said,
   Or is there any man within?
   O yes, O yes, said the bold, proud porter,
   This day has fetched him a young bride in.

14 She says: Now you've married some other woman
   And I have married no other man,
   I wish I had my notes of love,
   Straight back I'd go to the Turkish land.

15 She's got a ring on every finger
   And on her middle one she's got three,
   And gold around her neck a-plenty
   To buy all Cumberland of thee.

16 Then up spoke the young bride's mother,
   An angry spoken old thing was she,
   Saying: Would you quit my own fair daughter
   And take up with a Turkish lady?

Young Beichan

17 He said: You may take your daughter home with you,
   For I'm sure she's none the worse of me,
   For the prettiest thing stands there a-waiting
   That ever my two eyes did see.

18 He took her by the lily-white hand
   And took her to her father's cellar,
   And drawed some of the best port wine,
   Saying: Drink a health, you pretty creature,
   Who freed me from such a prison strong.

19 He took her by the lily-white hand
   And gently led her to his hall,
   And changed her name from Pretty Nancy,
   And called her name, it was Noble Jane.

B

Pentatonic. Mode 3. Sung at Hindman School, Knott Co., Ky., 1907

1. There was a man who lived in Eng-land And he was of some high degree; He became uneasy, discontented, Some fair land, some land to see.

2 He sailed East, he sailed West,
  He sailed all over the Turkish shore,
  Till he was caught and put in prison,
  Never to be released any more.

3 The Turk he had but one lone daughter,
  She was of some high degree;
  She stole the keys from her father's dwelling,
  And declared Lord Batesman she'd set free.

4 She led him down to the lower cellar
  And drew him a drink of the strongest wine,
  Every moment seemed an hour.
  O Lord Batesman, if you were mine!

5 Let's make a vow, let's make a promise,
  Let's make a vow, let's make it stand;
  You vow you'll marry no other woman,
  I'll vow I'll marry no other man.

Young Beichan

6 They made a vow, they made a promise,
   They made a vow, they made it stand;
   He vowed he'd marry no other woman,
   She vowed she'd marry no other man.

7 Seven long years had rolled around,
   It seemed as if it were twenty-nine,
   She bundled up her finest clothing,
   And declared Lord Batesman she'd go find.

8 She went till she came to the gate, she tingled,
   It was so loud, but she wouldn't come in,
   Is this your place, she cried, Lord Batesman,
   Or is it that you've let yours, brought your new bride in?

9 Go remember him of a piece of bread,
   Go remember him of a glass of wine,
   Go remember him of the Turkish lady
   Who freed him from the iron, cold bonds.

10 He stamped his foot upon the floor,
   He burst the table in pieces three,
   Saying: I'll forsake both land and dwelling
   For the Turkish lady that set me free.

11 She went till she came to the gate, she tingled,
   It was so loud, but she wouldn't come in,
   She's got more gold on her little finger
   Than your new bride and all your kin.

C

Heptatonic. Mode 1,
a + b (mixolydian).

Sung by Mrs. Zippo Rice
at Big Laurel, N. C., Aug. 15, 1916

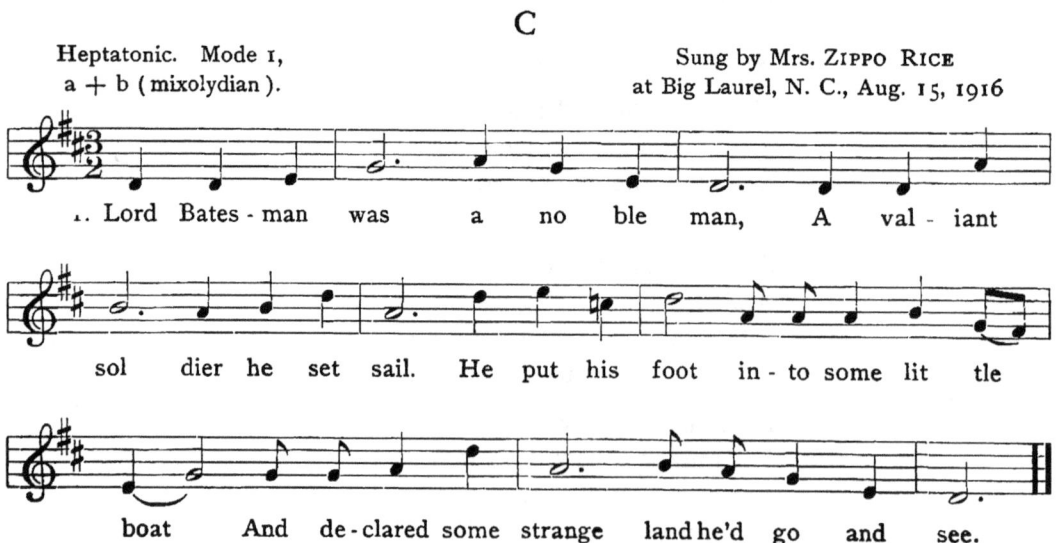

1. Lord Bates-man was a no ble man, A val-iant sol dier he set sail. He put his foot in-to some lit tle boat And de-clared some strange land he'd go and see.

Young Beichan

D

Hexatonic. Mode 1, b.

Sung by Mrs. Tom Rice
at Big Laurel, N. C., Aug. 17, 1916

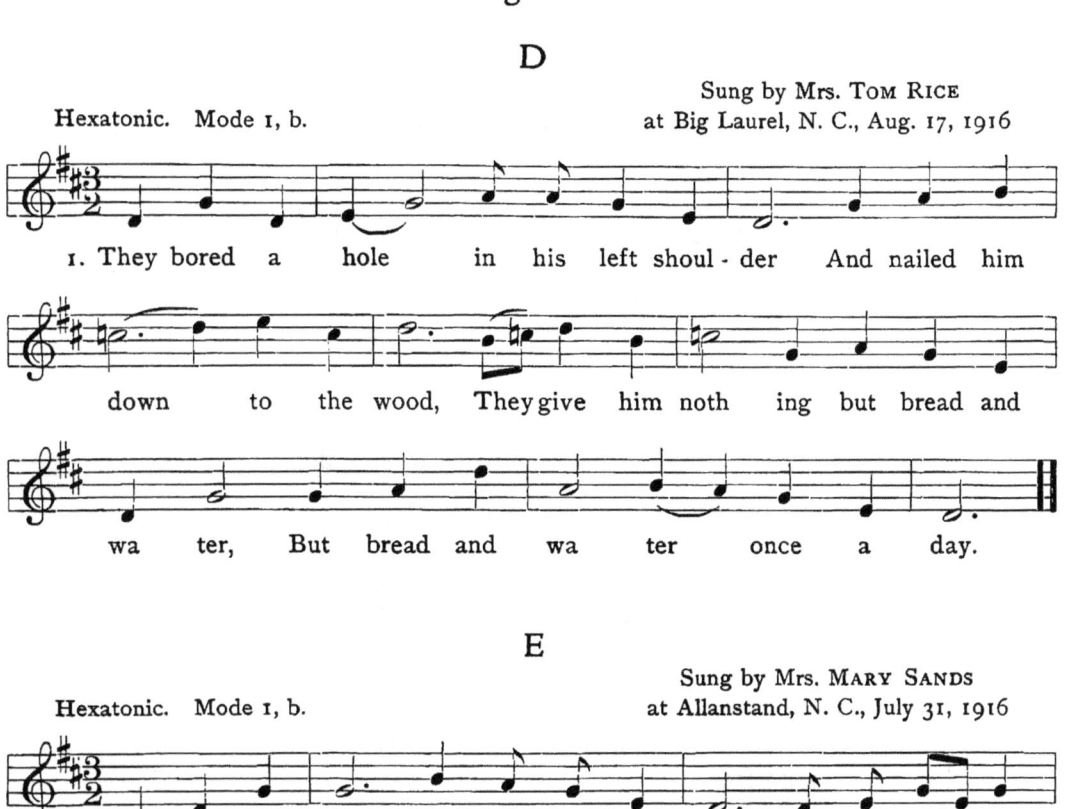

1. They bored a hole in his left shoul-der And nailed him down to the wood, They give him noth-ing but bread and wa-ter, But bread and wa-ter once a day.

E

Hexatonic. Mode 1, b.

Sung by Mrs. Mary Sands
at Allanstand, N. C., July 31, 1916

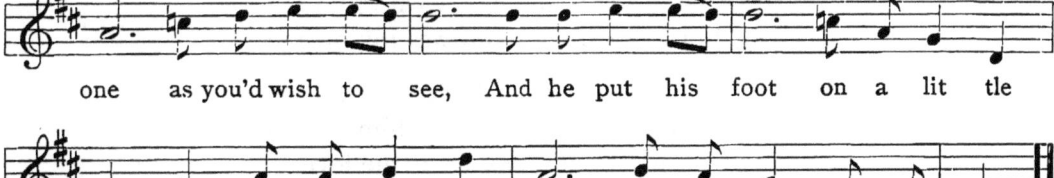

1. Lord Bates-man was a no-ble young man And as fair a one as you'd wish to see, And he put his foot on a lit-tle boat-en, And he vowed some strange land he would go and see.

F

Hexatonic (no 6th).

Sung by Miss May Ray
at Lincoln Memorial University, Harrogate,
Claiborne Co., Tenn., April 25, 1917

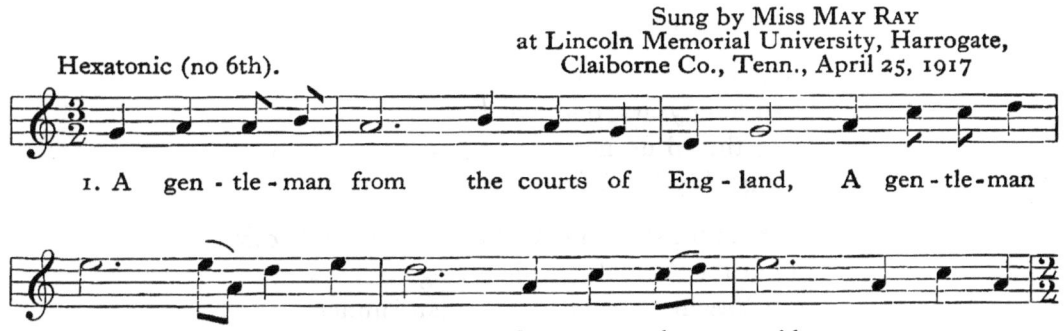

1. A gen-tle-man from the courts of Eng-land, A gen-tle-man of a high de-gree, But yet he could not rest con-

Young Beichan

tent ed Un til he ploughed the ra ging sea.

2 O he rode East and he rode West,
   And he rode till he came to the Turkey shore;
   There he was caught and put in prison,
   No hopes for freedom any more.

3 The Turks they had a beautiful lady,
   And she's as kind as kind could be.
   She stole the keys of her father's castle,
   Saying: My Lord Beechman I'll go and see.

4 O have you house and have you land?
   And are you a man of a high degree?
   And will you will it to any young lady
   Who from this prison will set you free?

5 O I have house and I have land
   And I am a man of a high degree,
   And I will will it to any young lady
   Who from this prison will set me free.

6 She took him up to her father's castle
   And there she ordered wine so strong,
   And every glass that she drank with him:
   I wish, Lord Beechman, you was my own.

7 She took him down to her father's hall,
   And there she ordered a ship for him,
   Saying: Fare you well, my own true love.
   Saying: Fare you well till we meet again.

8 It's seven long years I'll make this bargain,
   It's seven long years give you my hand,
   That you will wed no other woman
   And I will marry no other man.

9 O seven long years had done passed over,
   Seven long years, one, two, or three.
   She gathered up her golden jewelry,
   Saying: My Lord Beechman I'll go see.

10 She rode till she came to Lord Beechman's castle,
   And at the door she made a ring.
   Lord Beechman sent his footman-runner
   To see who might wish to come in.

Young Beichan

11 Pray tell me is this Lord Beechman's castle?
    And is the lord himself at home?
    O yes, this is Lord Beechman's castle.
    He has this day brought a new bride home.

12 Go tell him I want a piece of his bread
    And also a glass of his wine so strong;
    And ask him if he has forgotten the lady
    Who freed him from the prison so long.

13 There stands at your gate the prettiest lady
    That ever my two eyes did see,
    And on her right hand she wears a ring,
    And on her left one, two or three,
    And around her waist the gold and jewelry
    To buy your bride and company.

14 She said she wanted a piece of your bread
    And also a glass of your wine so strong,
    And asked you if you had forgotten the lady
    That freed you from the prison so strong.

15 Lord Beechman rose up from his table,
    And bursted it in splinters three,
    Saying: Here, woman, take back your daughter,
    My dear Susanne has come to me.

16 Saying: Here, woman, take back your daughter,
    I'm sure she's none the worst by me,
    For she came here in a horse and saddle,
    She can go back in two coachmen free.

17 He took Susanne by her lily-white hand
    And led her through rooms two or three.
    Her name was put on the house enrolment,
    Lord Beechman's landlady.

G

Pentatonic. Mode 1. Sung by Mrs. NANNY SMITH and Mrs. POLLY PATRICK at Goose Creek, Manchester, Clay Co., Ky., Aug. 16, 1917

4. The Turks they had one on-ly daugh-ter, The fair est

Young Beichan

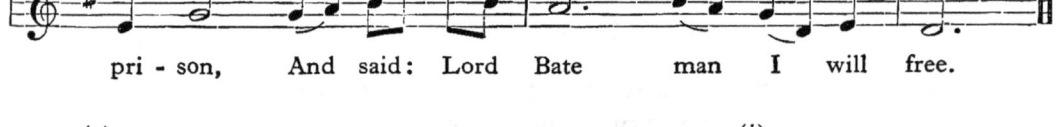

1 There was a noble lord,
   A noble lord was he.
   He shipped himself on board a ship,
   Some foreign country he would see.

2 He sailed East and he sailed West
   Until he came to Turkey,
   And there was he put into prison
   Until his life grew weary.

3 All in this prison there grew a tree
   So very stout and strong,
   And he was fastened to this tree
   Until his life was almost gone.

4 The Turks they had one only daughter,
   The fairest creature eyes ever did see.
   She stole the keys of her father's prison,
   And said: Lord Bateman I will free.

5 Have you houses, have you got land?
   Does Northumberland belong to thee?
   And what will you give to the fair young lady
   That out of prison will set you free?

6 I have houses and I have land,
   Half of Northumberland belongs to me,
   And I'll give it all to the fair young lady
   That out of prison will set me free.

Young Beichan

7 Then she took him to her father's table
And gave to him the best of wine;
And every health she drunk unto him:
O Lord Bateman, I wish that you were mine.

8 Then she led him to her father's harbour
And gave to him a ship of mine.
Farewell, farewell to you, Lord Bateman,
I fear I'll never see you again.

9 With these I'll make a vow,
And seven long years I'll hold it strong.
If you will wed no other woman,
I will wed no other man.

10 Seven long years had come and gone,
Fourteen days well known to thee.
She dressed herself in her fine, gay, gold clothing,
And says: Lord Bateman, I'll go see.

11 And when she come to Lord Bateman's castle
And there she tingled at the bell.
Who's there, who's there? cried the proud young porter.
Who's there, who's there? Unto me tell.

12 Is this Lord Bateman's castle,
And is his lordship here within?
This is Lord Bateman's castle;
He's just now taken a young bride in.

13 Go tell him to send me a slice of cake,
A bottle of the best wine,
And not to forget the fair young lady
That did release him from close confine.

14 Away, away went the proud young porter,
Until Lord Bateman he did see.
What news, what news, my proud young porter?
What news, what news have you brought unto me?

15 There is the fairest young lady
That ever my eyes did see;
She has a ring on every finger,
On one she wears three.

Young Beichan

16 She says for you to bring her a slice of cake,
   A bottle of the best wine,
   And not to forget the fair young lady
   That did release you from close confine.

17 Lord Bateman in a passion flew,
   His sword he broke in pieces three.
   I'll forsake my house and all my living
   If Sophie hasn't crossed the sea.

18 Then up spoke the young bride's mother
   Who was never heard to speak so free:
   O don't forsake my only daughter,
   Although Sophie have crossed the sea.

19 I own I've made a bride of your only daughter;
   She's none the worse by me.
   She come here on her own horse and saddle,
   I'll send her home in a coacheree.

20 O then the wedding was prepared;
   It's both their hearts is full of glee.
   I'll range no more in a foreign country
   So Sophie has crossed the sea.

H

Heptatonic. Ionian.

Sung by Mr. SOLOMON WILLIAMS
at Webb's Creek, Sevier Co., Tenn., April 18, 1917

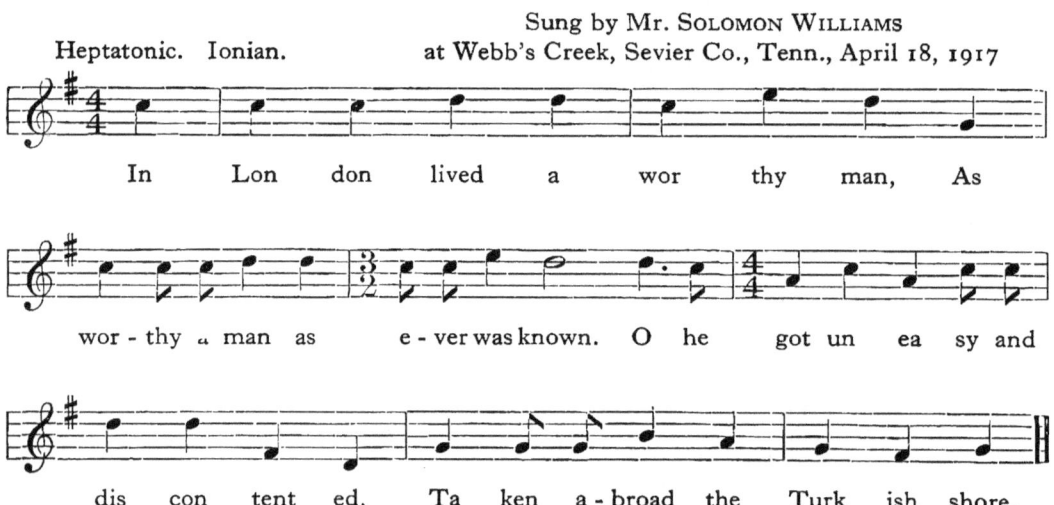

In London lived a worthy man, As worthy a man as ever was known. O he got uneasy and discontented, Taken abroad the Turkish shore.

Young Beichan

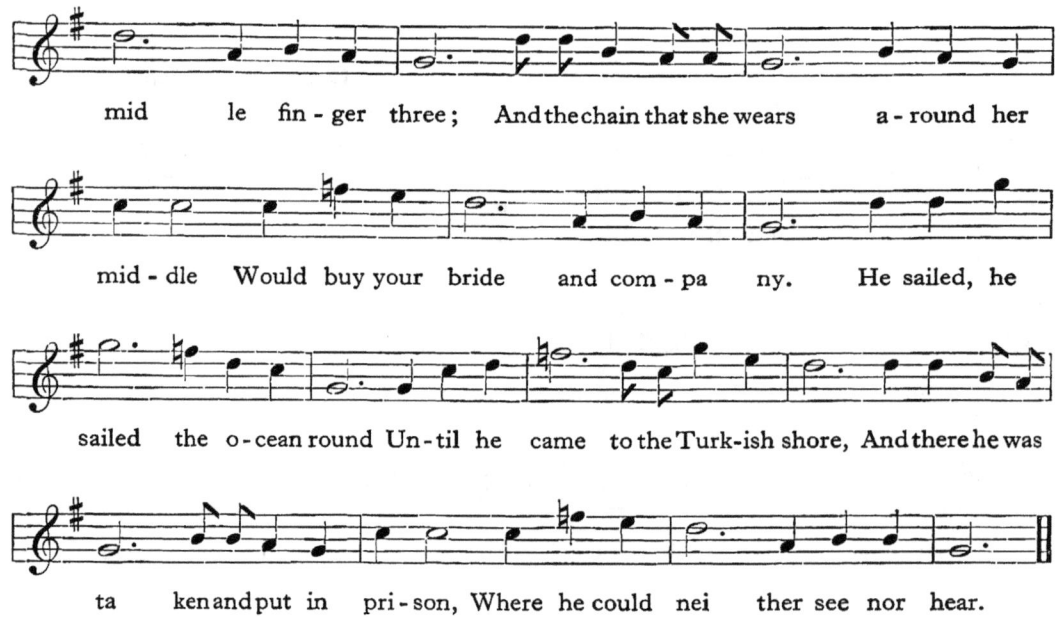

L

Hexatonic (no 7th).

Sung by Mrs. Berry Creech at Greasy Creek,
Pine Mountain, Harlan Co., Ky., Aug. 31, 1917

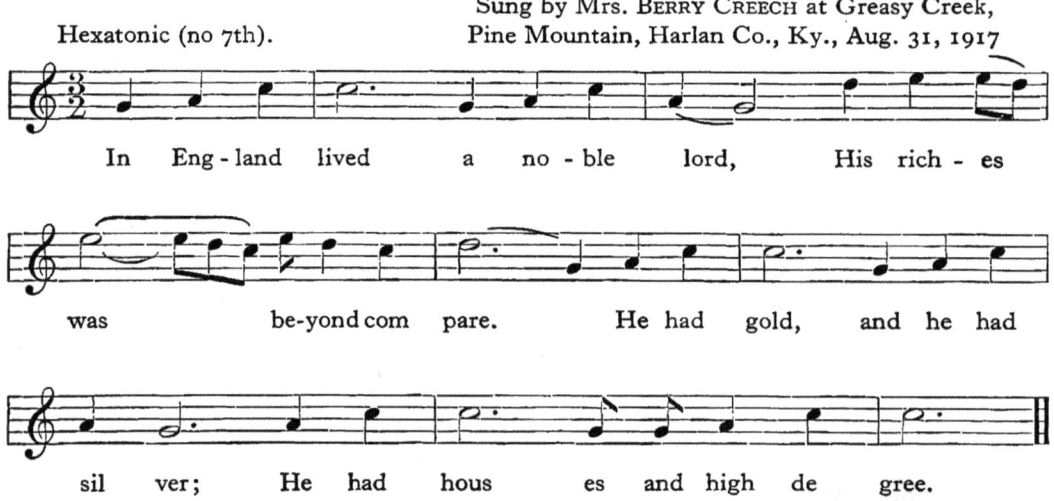

No. 14

Lizzie Wan

Sung by Mr. Ben. J. Finlay
at Manchester, Clay Co., Ky., Aug. 10, 1917

1. Fair Lucy sitting in her father's room, Lamenting and a-making her mourn; And in steps her brother James: O what's fair Lucy done?

2 It is time for you to weep,
  Lamenting and a-making your mourn.
  Here's a babe at my right side,
  And it is both mine and yourn.

3 O what will you do when your father comes home?
  Dear son, come tell to me.
  I'll set my foot into some little ship
  And I'll sail plumb over the sea.

4 O what will you do with your house and land?
  Dear son, come tell to me.
  I'll leave it here, my old, dear mother;
  Be kind to my children three.

5 O what will you do with your pretty, little wife?
  Dear son, come tell to me.
  She can set her foot in another little ship
  And follow after me.

6 Back home, back home will you return?
  Dear son, come tell to me.
  When the sun and moon sets in yon hill,
  And I hope that'll never be.

No. 15

The Cherry-Tree Carol
A

Hexatonic. Mode 1, b.

Sung by Mrs. Tom Rice
at Big Laurel, N. C., Aug. 17, 1916

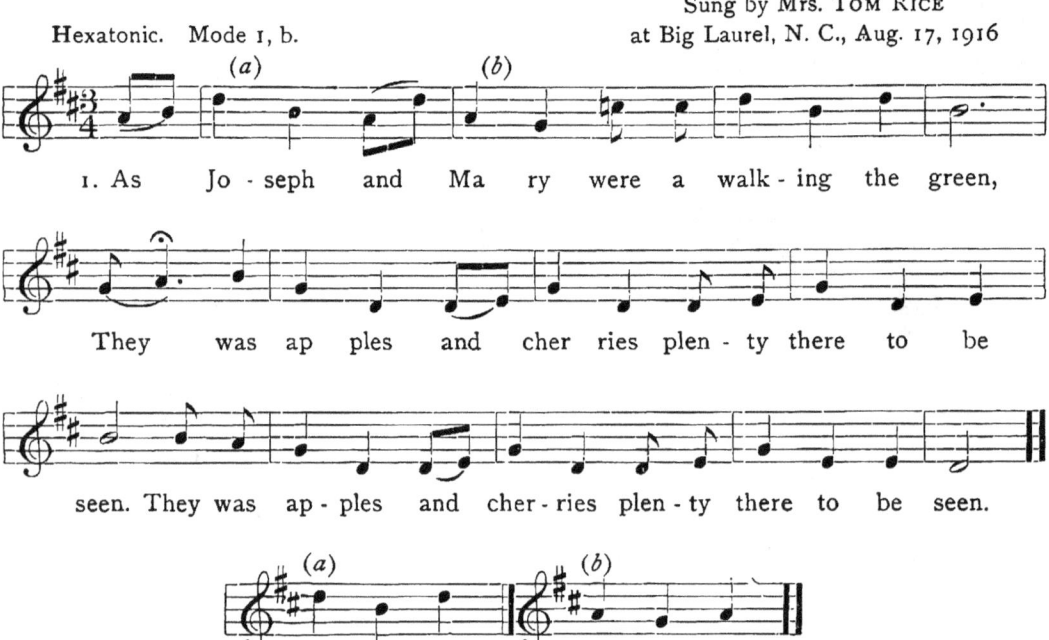

1. As Joseph and Mary were a-walking the green,
They was apples and cherries plenty there to be seen. They was apples and cherries plenty there to be seen.

2 And then Mary said to Joseph so meek and so mild:
Gather me some cherries, Joseph, for I am with child.

3 Then Joseph said to Mary so rough and unkind:
Let the daddy of the baby get the cherries for thine.

4 Then the baby spoke out of its mother's womb:
Bow down you lofty cherry trees, let my mammy have some.

5 Then the cherry tree bent and it bowed like a bow,
So that Mary picked cherries from the uppermost bough.

6 Then Joseph took Mary all on his left knee,
Saying: Lord have mercy on me and what I have done.

7 Then Joseph took Mary all on his right knee,
Saying: O my little Saviour, when your birthday shall be,
The hills and high mountains shall bow unto thee.

8 Then the baby spoke out of its mother's womb:
On old Christmas morning my birthday shall be (*or*, it'll be just before day),
When the hills and high mountains shall bow unto me.

The Cherry-Tree Carol

B

Heptatonic. Mode 3, a+b (ionian).

Sung by Mrs. Jane Gentry
at Hot Springs, N. C., Aug. 24, 1916

1. Joseph were a young man, A young man were he, And he court-ed Vir-gin Ma-ry, The Queen of Gal-li-lee.

2 Mary and Joseph
  Were a-walking one day.
  Here is apples and cherries
  A-plenty to behold.

3 Mary spoke to Joseph
  So meek and so mild:
  Joseph, gather me some cherries,
  For I am with child.

4 Joseph flew in angry,
  In angry he flew,
  Saying: Let the father of your baby
  Gather cherries for you.

5 The Lord spoke down from Heaven,
  These words he did say:
  Bow you low down, you cherry tree,
  While Mary gathers some.

6 The cherry tree bowed down.
  It was low on the ground;
  And Mary gathered cherries
  While Joseph stood around.

7 Then Joseph took Mary
  All on his right knee:
  Pray tell me, little baby,
  When your birthday shall be.

8 On the fifth day of January
  My birthday shall be,
  When the stars and the elements
  Shall tremble with fear.

9 Then Joseph took Mary
  All on his left knee,
  Saying: Lord have mercy upon me
  For what I have done.

The Cherry-Tree Carol

C

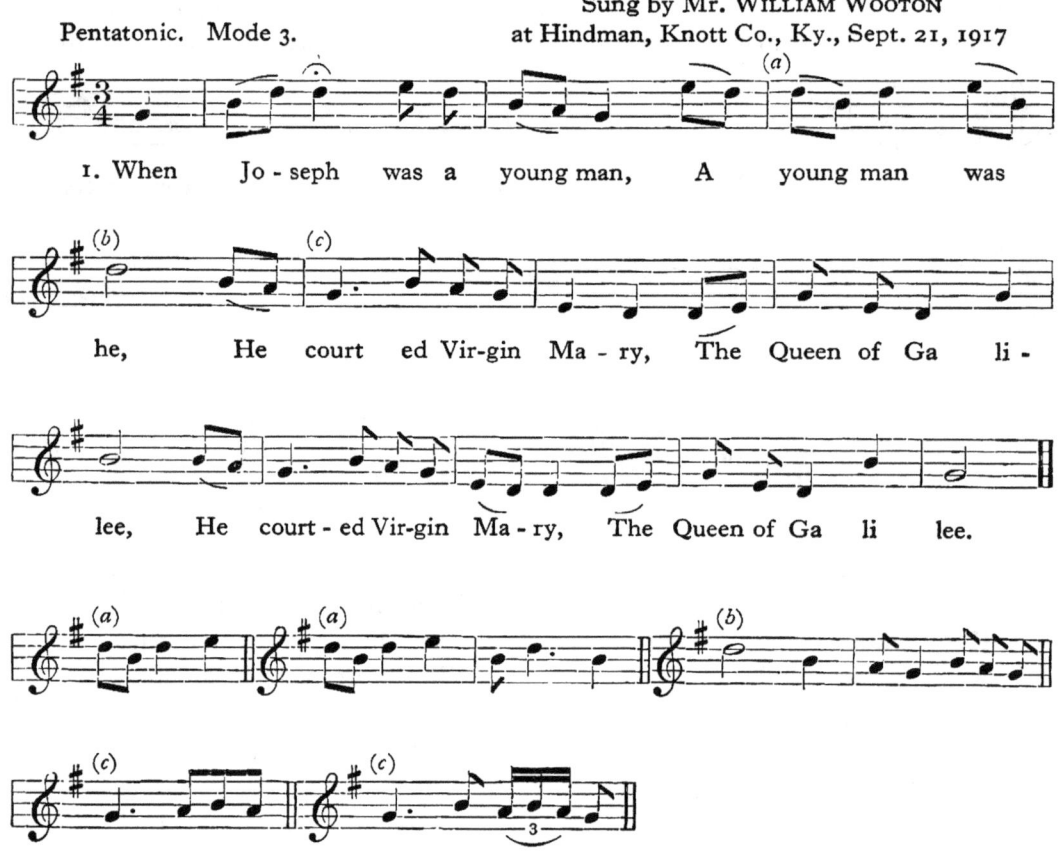

2 As Joseph and Mary
 Were walking one day,
 Here is apples and cherries
 Enough to behold.

3 Then Mary spoke to Joseph
 So neat (meek?) and so mild:
 Joseph, gather me some cherries,
 For I am with child.

4 Then Joseph flew in angry,
 In angry he flew:
 Let the father of the baby
 Gather cherries for you.

The Cherry-Tree Carol

5 Lord Jesus spoke a few words
  All down unto them:
  Bow low down, low down, cherry tree,
  Let the mother have some.

6 The cherry tree bowed low down,
  Low down to the ground,
  And Mary gathered cherries
  While Joseph stood around.

7 Then Joseph took Mary
  All on his right knee.
  He cried: O Lord, have mercy
  For what have I done.

8 And Joseph took Mary
  All on his left knee.
  Pray tell me, little baby,
  When your birthday will be?

9 On the fifth day of January
  My birthday will be,
  When the stars and the elements
  Doth tremble with fear.

D

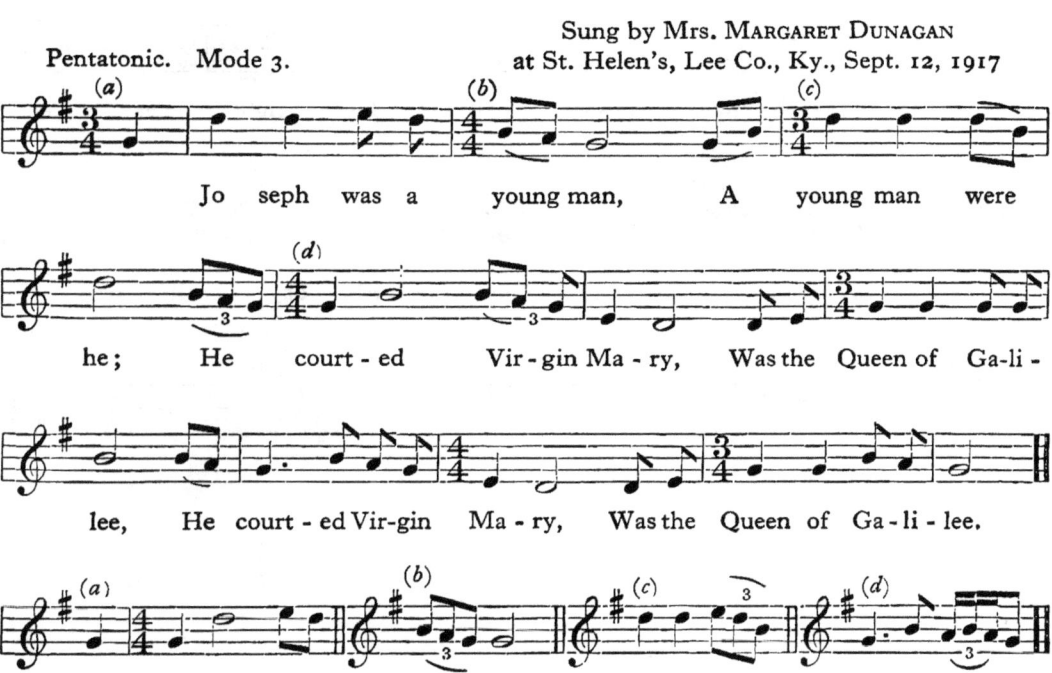

Pentatonic. Mode 3.

Sung by Mrs. Margaret Dunagan
at St. Helen's, Lee Co., Ky., Sept. 12, 1917

No. 16

Fair Annie

Sung by Mrs. Jane Gentry
at Hot Springs, N. C., Aug. 24, 1916

Pentatonic. Mode 3

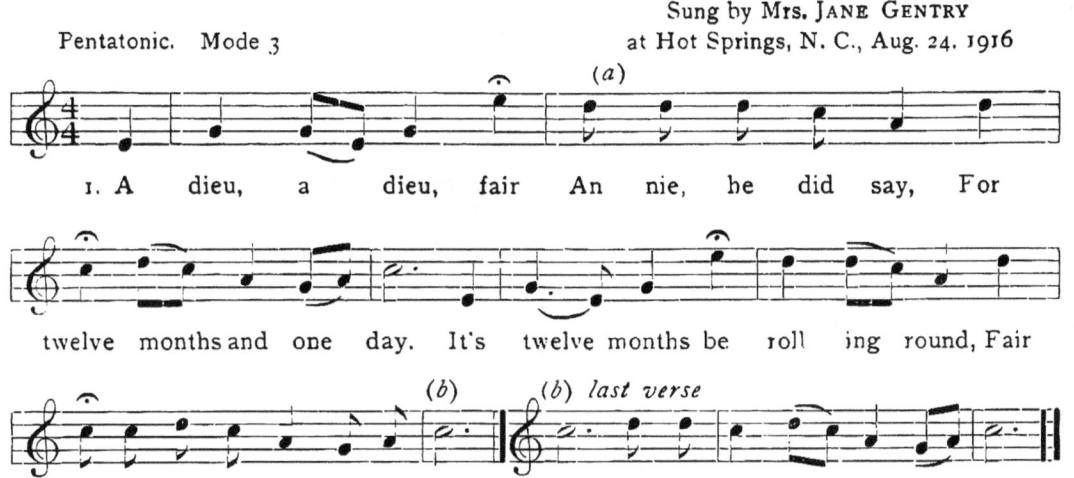

2 She took her spy glass in her hands
And out of doors she went;
She looked to the East, West, both North and South,
And looked all under the sun.

3 She thought she saw Lord Thomas a-coming,
All bringing his new briden home.
She called her own seven sons:
I think I see your father a-coming
And bringing your step-mother home.

4 Come down, come down, dear mother they did say,
Some clothing to put on.
Saying: All of his merry, merry, merry maids
Might as well to come as one.

5 Fair Annie she had a silken towel
Hanging on a silver pin,
And she wiped out her watery eyes
As she walked out and in.

6 The rest of them drunk ale, beer and wine,
But fair Annie she drunk cold well water
To keep her spirits alive.

Fair Annie

7 There is a fair lady in our house,
   Before tomorrow morning she'll be dead,
   We will call to our waiting-maids
   And have her taken out of town.
   A word or two, Lord Thomas, she did say,
   Before I go away.

8 I wish my sons was seven greyhounds
   And I was a fox on the hill,
   And they might have longer (*or* more) breath than I
   That they might worry me down.

9 It's who is your father dear,
   And who is your mother,
   And who is your brother dear
   And who is your sister?

10 It's King Henry he's my father dear,
   Queen Chatry's my own mother,
   Quince* Dudley he's my own brother dear
   And fair Annie she's my own sister.

11 If King Henry he's your own father dear,
   Queen Chatry she's your own mother,
   Quince Dudley your brother dear,
   I'll ensure I'm your own sister.

12 We have seven ships all on the sea,
   They're loaded to the brim,
   And five of them I'll give to you
   And two will carry me home,
   And we'll have Lord Thomas burned.

* Prince?

No. 17

Lady Maisry

A

Hexatonic (no 6th).

Sung by Mrs. Delie Knuckles
at Barbourville, Knox Co., Ky., May 16, 1917

12. Go saddle to me the next speed-horse, Go saddle to me the brown, Go saddle to me the finest horse That ever trod the ground.

1 My Lady Margaret sitting in her own chamber a-weeping,
  Her father and mother's a-gathering wood
  To burn her poor body.

2 I wish I had some pretty little boy,
  Some one to go an errand for me.
  Downstairs came her oldest brother's son,
  He stepped across the floor,
  Saying: A many an errand have I went,
  Lady Margaret, one for you I'll run.

3 Go down, go down to my young lord
  And tell him my mother and father's gathering wood
  To burn my poor body.

4 And here I'll send him my ring,
  In hopes that he might mourn after me,
  But come to my burial.

5 And here I send my glove,
  In hopes that he might mourn after me,
  But seek him another true love.

6 He run, he run, he run and he walked,
  He run till he came to the broad water's side,
  Then he caught his breath and he swum.

Lady Maisry

7 He swum till he came to the other shore,
Then he took to the banks and he run;
And he run till he came to the young lord's gate,
And dingled on the ring.
No one so ready as the young lord himself
For to rise and let him in.

8 What news, what news, my pretty little boy?
Is any of my fiery furnace burned down?
Or is my still over-run?
Or has my pretty, fair Miss brought to me
A daughter or a son?

9 Your fiery furnace is not burned down,
Your stills are neither over-run;
Your pretty, fair Miss's father and mother's gathering wood
To burn her poor body.

10 And here she sends you her ring,
In hopes that you might mourn after her,
But come to her burial.

11 And here she sends you her glove,
In hopes that you might mourn after her,
But seek you another true love.

12 Go saddle to me the next speed-horse,
Go saddle to me the brown,
Go saddle to me the finest horse
That ever trod the ground.

13 He hung his horn bugle round his neck,
His sword went dragging the ground;
As he rode round them all open fields,
He made his bugle sound.

14 O mother, O mother, I fear you not,
I fear you not one straw,
For I hear my young lord,
I heard his bugle sound.

15 They tied her high and fast to the stake,
And rushed the fire around.
As he rode nigh to the place
He mounted on the ground.

16 He tore her body from the stake
And clasped it in his arms.
Says: I'll first kiss her red, rosy cheeks,
Then kiss her cherry chin;
I'll kiss your ruby lips
That'll never kiss mine again.

Lady Maisry

17 He called for a chair he may sit down,
   A pen to write his will.
   He willed her oldest brother's son
   Of all his house and still.

B

Hexatonic. Tonic G (no 7th).

Sung by Mrs. Dan Bishop
at Teges, Clay Co., Aug. 21, 1917

1. Down stepped her old father dear, He stepped over the floor. It's

how do you do, Lady Margrie, said he, Since you became a whore?

2 O dear father, I am no whore,
  Nor never expect to be;
  But I have a child by an English lord,
  And I hope he'll marry me.

3 Down stepped her old mother dear,
  She stepped over the floor.
  It's how do you do, Lady Margrie, said she,
  Since you became a whore?

4 O dear mother, I am no whore,
  Nor never expect to be;
  But I have a child by an English lord,
  And I hope he will marry me.

5 Down stepped her oldest brother dear,
  He stepped over the floor.
  It's how do you do, Lady Margrie, said he,
  Since you became a whore? (*or*, How do you do to-day?)

6 Very bad, very bad, dear brother,
  As you can plainly see,
  For my father and mother is both gathering wood
  To burn my poor body.

7 I wish I had some pretty little one,
  One errand for to run.
  I'd run to my young lord's house
  And tell him I said to come,

Lady Maisry

And to come quickly,
For my father and mother are both gathering wood
To burn my poor body.

8 Down stepped her brother's eldest son,
And stepped down over the floor,
And says: Many a mile that I have run,
And one for you I'll go.

9 I wish him well, for ever well,
And here send him a ring,
In hopes that he may mourn after me
But come to my burying.

10 I wish him well, for ever well,
And here I send him a glove,
In hopes that he might mourn after me,
But seek him another true love.

11 He run and he run till he came to the broad water,
He pitched in and swum;
He swum to the other side
And took to his heels and run.

12 He run to the young lord's gate,
And tingled on the bell;
And no one was so ready to rise and let him in
As the young lord himself.

13 What news, what news, my pretty little page,
What news have you brought to me?

14 Go saddle unto me the make-speed horse,
Go saddle unto me the brown,
Go saddle unto me the fastest horse
That ever run on ground.

15
He got his pistols and sword and bugle,
And threw his bugle around his neck.

16 As he was going round them lone fields
And a-going in full speed,
The ring bursted off his finger
And his nose broke out for to bleed.

17 O dear mother, I value you not one straw,
For my young lord is coming,
I hear his bugle blow.

No. 18

Young Hunting
A

Hexatonic. Mode 2, a.

Sung by Mrs. JANE GENTRY
at Hot Springs, N. C., Aug. 25, 1916

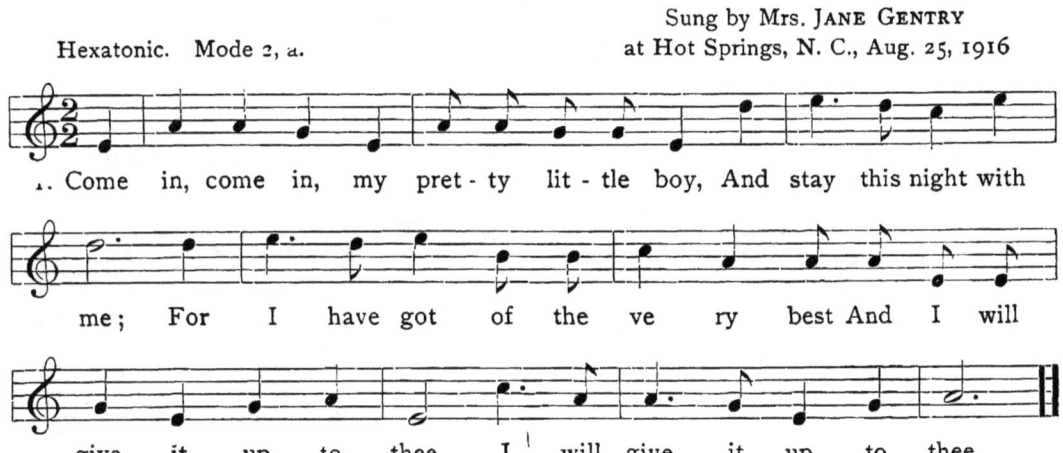

1. Come in, come in, my pret-ty lit-tle boy, And stay this night with me; For I have got of the ve-ry best And I will give it up to thee, I will give it up to thee.

2 I can't come in, I won't come in
And stay this night with thee,
For I have a wife in old Scotchee
This night a-looking for me.

3 She did have a little penknife,
It was both keen and sharp.
She gave him a deathlike blow
And pierced him through the heart.

4 She picked him up all in her arms,
Being very active and strong,
And she throwed him into an old dry well
About sixty feet.

5 One day she was sitting in her father's parlour door,
Thinking of no harm.
She saw a bird and a pretty little bird
All among the leaves so green.

6 Come down, come down, my pretty little bird
And parley on my knee.
I'm afeard you'd rob me of my life
Like you did the poor Scotchee.

7 I wish I had my bow and arrow,
My arrow and my string;
I'd shoot you through your tender little heart,
For you never no more could sing.

Young Hunting

8 I wish you had your bow and arrow,
Your arrow and your string;
I'd fly away to the heavens so high,
Where I could for evermore sing.

B

Sung by Mr. Floyd Chandler
at Alleghany, N. C., Aug. 29, 1916

Hexatonic. Mode 4, b.

1. Come in, come in, my own true love, And stay all night with me. For I have a bed, and a very fine bed, And I'll give it up to thee, And I'll give it up to thee.

2 It's I ain't coming in, nor I can't come in
To stay all night with thee,
For I have a wife in old Scotland
And this night she weeps over me.

3 It's out she drew her little penknife
And stabbed him through his heart.
She cried out with a very loud cry:
There's a dead man in my house.

4 It's she picked him up by the middle so small,
She picked him up by his feet,
She plunged him over in a deep, wide well
Just about eighteen feet, feet,
Just about eighteen feet.

5 And as she was sitting in her parlour door
Thinking of what she had done,
She saw a bird and a very pretty bird
All among the leaves so green, green.

Young Hunting

6 Come here, come here, my pretty little bird
  And perch all on my thumb,
  For I have a cage and a very fine cage
  And I'll give it up to thee.

7 It's I ain't a-coming there and I won't come there
  To perch all on your thumb,
  For I'm afraid you'll rob me of my tender little heart
  Just like a Scotland man, man.

8 It's if I had my bow and arrow,
  My arrow and my bow,
  I'd shoot you right through the tender little heart
  Just like the Scotland man, man.

9 It's if you had your bow and arrow,
  Your arrow and your bow,
  I'd fly away to the heavens above
  And ne'er be seen any more.

C

Heptatonic. Major Mode (mixolydian influence).

Sung by Miss LINNIE LANDERS at Carmen, N. C., Sept. 5, 1916

2 I can't come in, nor I'm not coming in
  To stay all night with thee,
  For I have a wife in the old Scotland,
  This night she waits for me.

(*The remaining stanzas as in B*)

Young Hunting

D

Heptatonic. Major Mode
(mixolydian influence).

Sung by Mrs. ORILLA KEETON,
at Mount Fair, Va., Sept. 26, 1916

1. As Lady Mar-g'ret was a-go-ing to bed, She heard the sound of a mu-si-cal horn, which made her heart feel glad and sad To think that it was her broth-er John, broth-er John, Coming in from his wild hunt. But who should it be but her true love Hen-e-ry, Re-turn-ing from his King, his King, Re-turn-ing from his King.

Subsequent verses sung thus:

2 O light, O light, love Henery,
   And stay all night with me,
   And you shall have the cheers of the cheer (*or* cheery) cold girl,
   The best I can give you.

3 I will not light and I shall not light
   To stay all night with thee,
   For there's a pretty girl in Merry Green Lea
   I love far better than thee.

Young Hunting

4 He bended over her soft pillow
And gave her a kiss so sweet,
But with a penknife in her right hand,
She wounded him in full deep.

5 Woe be, woe be, Lady Marg'ret, he cried,
Woe be, woe be to thee,
For don't you see my own heart's blood
Come twinkling down my knee?

6 She called unto a maid of hers:
Keep a secret, keep a secret on me.
All these fine robes on my body
Shall always be to thee.

7 One takened him by his long yellow hair
And the other one by his feet,
And they threw him into the well waters
Which was so cool and deep.

8 Lie there, lie there, love Henery,
Till the flesh rots off your bones,
And that pretty girl in Merry Green Lea
Thinks long of your coming home.

9 Up spoke, up spoke a pretty little parrot
Exceeding on a willow tree:
There never was a girl in Merry Green Lea
He loved so well as thee.

10 Come down, come down, my pretty little parrot,
And sit upon my knee,
And you shall have a cage of a pure, pure gold
Instead of the willow tree.

11 I won't come down, nor I shan't come down
To sit upon your knee,
For you have murdered your true love Henery,
More sooner you would kill me.

12 If I had my arrow in my hand,
My bow on tuneful string,
I'd shoot a dart that would win your heart,
So you could no longer sing.

13 If you had your arrow in your hand,
Your bow on tuneful string,
I'd take a flight and fly, fly away
And tune my voice to sing.

Young Hunting

E

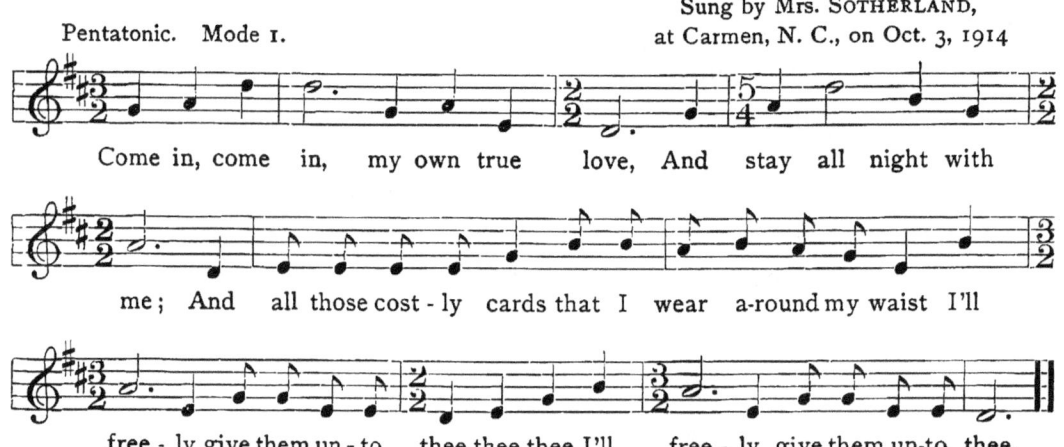

Pentatonic. Mode 1.

Sung by Mrs. SOTHERLAND, at Carmen, N. C., on Oct. 3, 1914

Come in, come in, my own true love, And stay all night with me; And all those cost-ly cards that I wear a-round my waist I'll free-ly give them un-to thee, thee, thee, I'll free-ly give them un-to thee.

2 I won't come in, or I won't sit down,
  Or stay all night with thee,
  For there is another pretty girl in old Scotland
  That I love more better than thee.

3 She had a sharp knife within her right hand,
  She pierced him heartilee.

4 I will come down and I must come down
  And stay all night with thee.
  There is nary nother pretty girl in old Scotland
  That I love more better than thee.

5 O live, Lord Henry, she cried,
  One hour, or two, or three,
  And all these costly cards I wear around my waist
  I'll freely give them unto thee.

6 I can't live, nor I won't live,
  One hour, nor two, nor three,
  And all the costly cards you wear around your waist
  Will do no good for me.

7 She tuk him by his lily-white hand,
  She drug him to the well,
  Which you know was cold and deep.
  She says

8 Lie there, love Henry, she cried,
  Till the flesh all rots off your poor bones
  And all your pretty girls in old Scotland
  Will mourn for your return.

Young Hunting

9 Come down, come down, my pretty parrot bird,
   And sit at my right knee,
   And your cage shall be decked of the yellow beaten gold
   And hung on the ivory.

10 I won't come down, nor I won't come down,
   Nor sit at your right knee,
   For you just now murdered your own true love,
   And soon you'd murder me.

11 I wish I had my bow in flight,
   My arrow keen and sharp,
   I'd pierce a lightning all through your breast
   That you never should sing again.

12 If you had your bow in flight,
   Your arrow keen and sharp,
   My two little wings would carry me away,
   Where you never would see me again.

F

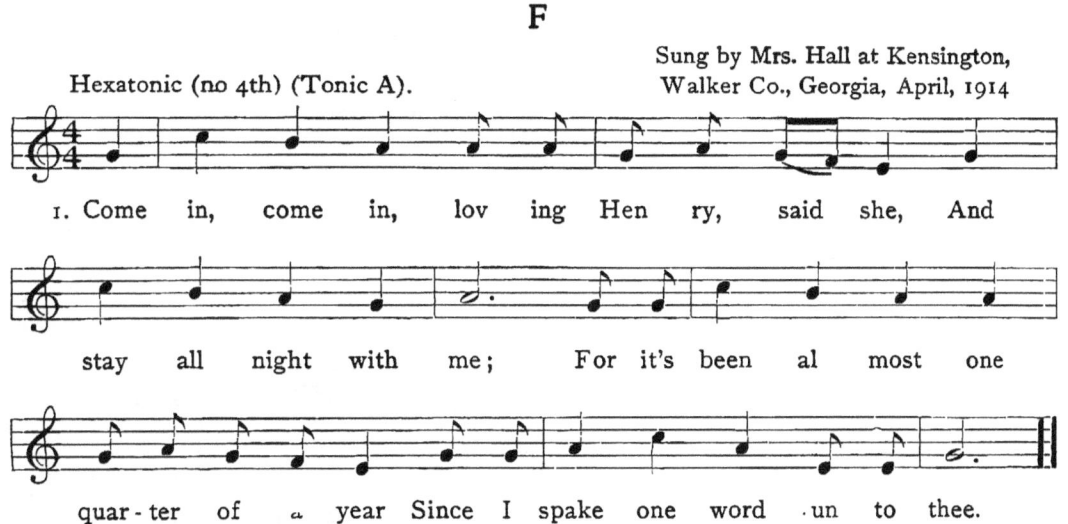

Hexatonic (no 4th) (Tonic A).

Sung by Mrs. Hall at Kensington,
Walker Co., Georgia, April, 1914

1. Come in, come in, loving Henry, said she, And stay all night with me; For it's been almost one quarter of a year Since I spake one word unto thee.

2 I can't come in, Lady Margaret, said he,
  Nor stay all night with thee,
  For the girl that I left in the Arkansas land
  Will think long of my return.

3 Then stooping over the great high fence
  And kissing all so sweet,
  She had a penknife in her hand
  And she plunged it into the deep.

Young Hunting

4 Some taken him by his lily-white hands,
  Some taken him by his feet,
  And they carried him to the broad water side
  And plunged him into the deep.

5 Lay there, lay there, loving Henry, said she,
  Till the meat drops off your bones,
  And the girl you left in the Arkansas land
  Will think long of your return.

6 Come in, come in, pretty parrot, said she,
  And sing all on my knee;
  Your cage shall be made of ivory beaten gold
  And the doors of ivory.

7 I can't come in, Lady Margaret, said he,
  Nor sing all on your knee,
  For you are the girl that killed loving Henry,
  And surely you might kill me.

8 I wish I had a bow and arrow,
  And it all in its prime,
  I'd shoot yon yonders pretty little bird
  That sits on that tall pine.

9 Who cares I for your bow and arrow,
  And it all in its prime,
  I fly away to some lonesome valley
  And 'light on some high pine.

G

Sung by Mrs. Francis Carter
at Beattyville, Lee Co., Ky., Sept. 7, 1917

Hexatonic (no 7th).

1. Light you down, light you down, love Henry, she said, And stay all night with me; For I have a bed and a fire side too, And a candle a-burning bright.

Young Hunting

2 I can't get down, nor I won't get down
 And stay all night with thee,
 For that little girl in the old Declarn
 Would think so hard of me.

3 But he slided down from his saddle skirts
 For to kiss her snowy white cheek.
 She had a sharp knife in her hand,
 And she plunged it in him deep.

4 I will get down and I can get down
 And stay all night with thee,
 For there's no little girl in the old Declarn
 That I love any better than thee.

5 Must I ride to the East, must I ride to the West,
 Or anywhere under the sun,
 To get some good and clever doctor
 For to cure this wounded man?

6 Neither ride to the East, neither ride to the West,
 Nor nowhere under the sun,
 For there's no man but God's own hand
 Can cure this wounded man.

7 She took him by the long, yellow locks
 And also round the feet;
 She plunged him in that doleful well,
 Some sixty fathoms deep.

8 And as she turned round to go home,
 She heard some pretty bird sing:
 Go home, go home, you cruel girl,
 Lament and mourn for him.

9 Fly down, fly down, pretty parrot, she said,
 Fly down and go home with me.
 Your cage shall be decked with beads of gold
 And hung in the willow tree.

10 I won't fly down, nor I can't fly down,
 And I won't go home with thee,
 For you have murdered your own true love,
 And you might murder me.

11 I wish I had my little bow-ben
 And had it with a string;
 I'd surely shoot that cruel bird
 That sits on the briers and sings.

Young Hunting

12 I wish you had your little bow-ben
   And had it with a string;
   I'd surely fly from vine to vine;
   You could always hear me sing.

H

Sung by Mrs. Margaret Dunagan
at St. Helen's, Lee Co., Ky., Sept. 5, 1917

1. She sharpened her knife both sharp and keen, She hung it by her side, As she rode up to the bar-room hall, And passed it by and by.

2 Her true love a-being standing there,
  He looked well and pleased;
  As she stepped on up by his side,
  She pierced it through his heart.

3 All of my friends come to me now
  And see me what I've done.
  Now don't you see my own heart's blood
  Come sprinkling down my knee?

4 Must I ride East, or must I ride West,
  Or must I ride under the shining sun,
  To find that doctor for to come here
  And cure those wounded wounds?

Young Hunting

5 You needn't ride East, you needn't ride West,
   You needn't ride under the shining sun;
   There hain't a doctor but God alone
   Can cure those wounded wounds.

6 This young lady walked out on the street
   For to hear the small birds sing.
   Go home, go home, you mourny little girl,
   And weep and mourn for me.

7 Come to me, my pretty little bird,
   Come and go along with me.
   I've got a cage beside the willow tree
   For you to sit in and sing.

8 I won't come there, and I won't go there,
   For I'll tell you the reason why.
   You've just now killed your own true love,
   Just what might happen to me.

9 I wish I had my bowing little spain,
   And it was bow-end on the string,
   Then surely I'd shoot that pretty little bird
   That sits on the briers and sings.

10 I wish you had your bowing little spain,
   And it was bow-end on the string,
   Then surely I would fly from brier to brier,
   And I'd sing on as I fly.

I

Sung by Mr. Clinton Fitzgerald
at Royal Orchard, Afton, Va., April 28, 1918

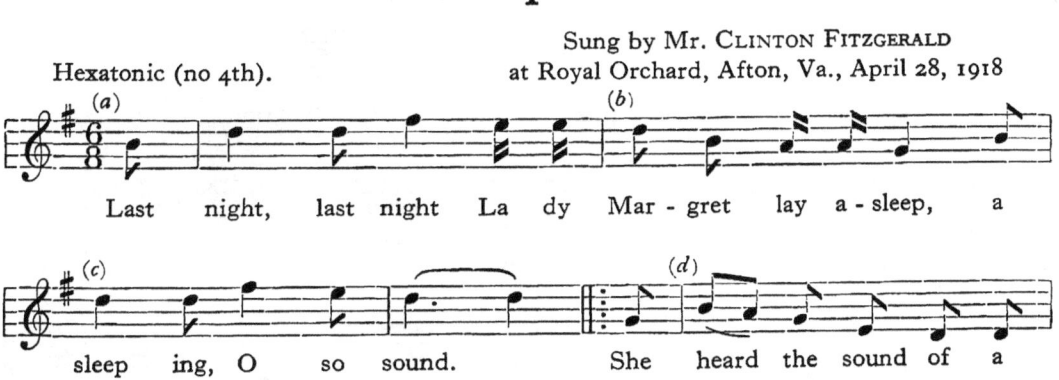

Young Hunting

Young Hunting

2 I can't come in, nor I won't come in
   And stay all night with thee,
   For I have a wife in the old Scotland
   This night a-looking for me.

3 She took her knife all in her hand,
   She pierced him near his heart,
   She cried out all over this town:
   There's a dead man in my house.

4 She was sitting in her parlour door,
   Lamenting what she'd done,
   She saw a bird and a very pretty bird
   All among the leaves so green.

5 I'll go and get my bow and arrow,
   My arrow and my string;
   I'll shoot through your tender little heart
   All among the leaves so green.

6 While you're gone for your bow and arrow,
   Your arrow and your string,
   I'll fly away to the heavens above
   Where I'll never no more be seen.

No. 19

Lord Thomas and Fair Ellinor
A

Pentatonic. Mode 3.

Sung by Mrs. Hester House
at Hot Springs, N. C., Sept. 14, 1916

1. Lord Thom-as he was a brave young man, The keep-ing of bach-e-lor's

hall. Come rid-dle to me, my mo-ther dear, Come rid-dle to me as one.

2 Or shall I marry fair Ellendry now,
Or bring you the brown girl home?
Or shall I marry fair Ellendry now,
Or bring the brown girl home?

3 The brown girl she has house and land,
Fair Ellendry she has none.
My request is to you, my son,
Go bring the brown girl home.

4 Fair Ellendry dressed herself in white,
And trimmed her merry maidens green,
And every town that she rode through
They took her to be some queen.

5 She rode up to Lord Thomas's hall,
And tingled on the ring;
No one so ordel but Lord Thomas himself
For to rise and let her come in.

6 He took her by the lily-white hand,
He led her through the hall,
He sat her down at the head of the table
Amongst those ladies all.

7 Is this your bride?—fair Ellendry she says—
What makes her so wonderful brown?
When you could have married as fair a lady one
As ever the sun shined on.

Lord Thomas and Fair Ellinor

8 Go hold your tongue, you pretty little miss,
And tell no tales on me,
For I love your little finger nail
Better than her whole body.

9 The brown girl had a little penknife
Which just had lately been ground,
She pierced it through fair Ellendry's side,
The blood come tumbling down.

10 He took her by her little hand,
He led her in the room;
He took his sword and cut her head off
And kicked it against the wall.

11 He put the handle against the wall,
The point against his breast.
Here is the ending of three dear lovers.
Pray take their souls to rest.

12 Go dig my grave both wide and deep
And paint my coffin black,
And bury fair Ellendry in my arms,
The brown girl at my back.

13 They dug his grave both wide and deep
And painted his coffin black,
And buried the brown girl in his arms
And fair Ellendry at his back.

B

Heptatonic. Mode 3, a + b (ionian).

Sung by Mrs. MOORE
at Rabun Co., Ga., May 2, 1909

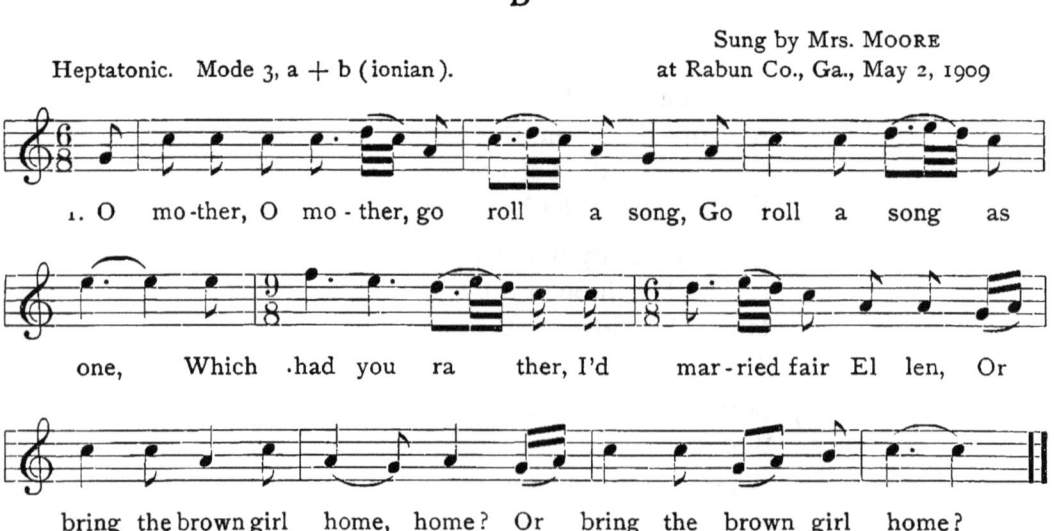

1. O mother, O mother, go roll a song, Go roll a song as one, Which had you rather, I'd married fair El len, Or bring the brown girl home, home? Or bring the brown girl home?

Lord Thomas and Fair Ellinor

2 It's, O my son, I'd advise you at your own blessing
 To bring the brown girl home;
 For she has got both house and land
 And fair Ellender she has none.

3 He dressed himself in the finest he had,
 His image it was broad;
 And every town that he rode round
 They took him to be some lord.

4 He rode up to fair Ellender's gate
 And jangled at the ring—
 No one so ready as fair Ellen herself
 To rise and let him come in.

5 Lord Thomas, Lord Thomas, she replied,
 What news have you brought for me?
 I've come to ask you to my wedding,
 And that's bad news for to hear.

6 O mother, O mother, go roll a song,
 Go roll a song as one,
 Which had you rather, I'd go to Lord Thomas' wedding,
 Or stay and tarry at home?

7 It's, O my daughter, I'd advise you at your own blessing
 To stay and tarry at home.

8 I know I've got a-many a friend,
 Likewise many a foe,
 But if my death coffin was at my door,
 To Lord Thomas' wedding I'd go.

9 She dressed herself in the finest she had,
 Her image it was green;
 And every town that she rode round
 They took her to be some queen.

10 She rode up to Lord Thomas's gate
 And knocked so clear it rung.
 No one so ready as Lord Thomas hisself
 For to rise and let her come in.

11 He took her by her lily-white hand
 And led her in the hall,
 And seated her down by his bright side
 Amongst the ladies all.

Lord Thomas and Fair Ellinor

12 Lord Thomas, Lord Thomas, is this your bride?
    I think she's very brown;
    When you once might have had as fair a lady
    As ever the sun shined on.

13 This brown girl she had a knife in her hand,
    And the blade both keen and sharp.
    'Twixt the long ribs and the short
    She pierced it through fair Ellender's heart.

14 Fair Ellen, fair Ellen, he replied,
    What makes you look so pale?
    Your cheeks were once the rosy red,
    And all your fine color has failed.

15 Lord Thomas, Lord Thomas, she replied,
    Are you blind, or cannot you see?
    Or don't you see my own heart's blood
    Come twinkling down so free?

16 Lord Thomas had a sword hung by his side
    With a blade both keen and sharp.
    He cut this brown girl's head smooth off
    And cleaved the body apart.

17 And then he pointed toward the floor
    With the point toward his heart.
    Did you ever see three own true loves
    Sudden in death to part?

18 Go dig my grave both wide and deep
    And paint my coffin black,
    And put fair Ellender in my arms
    And the brown girl at my back.

C

Pentatonic. Mode 3.

Sung by Mrs. Rosie Hensley
at Carmen, N, C., Aug. 8, 1916

Lord Thomas and Fair Ellinor

D

Hexatonic. Mode 3, b.

Sung by Mrs. MANDY SHELTON
at Carmen, N. C., Aug. 11, 1916

1. Lord Thomas he was a brave young man, A keeping of all king's hall; Fair Ellender was a gay young lady, Lord Thomas he loved her dear.

E

Pentatonic. Mode 1. -

Sung by Mrs. JANE GENTRY
at Hot Springs, N. C., Aug. 24, 1916

1. Come well to me, dear mother, he says. Come well me your design; Whether I marry fair Ellinor dear, Or bring you the brown girl, home, home, home, Or bring you the brown girl home.

* If B♭ be tonic :—Mode 3.

F

Pentatonic. Mode 1. *

Sung by Mrs. ADDY CRANE
at Flag Pond, Tenn., Aug. 31, 1916

1. Lord Thomas, Lord Thomas, is this your bride? I think she's miserable

Lord Thomas and Fair Ellinor

brown; And you could have mar-ried as fair a skinned girl As

ev-er the sun shined on, shined on, As ev-er the sun shined on.

* If G be tonic:—Mode 3.

G

Hexatonic. Mode 3, b.
Sung by Mrs. Noah Shelton
at Alleghany, N. C., July 29, 1916

H

Hexatonic. Mode 1, a. *
Sung by Mrs. Kate Campbell
at Woodridge, Va., Sept. 21, 1916

1. O moth-er, O moth-er, O moth-er, says he, Pray tell your wil-ling mind,

Wheth-er I must mar-ry fair El-ling-ton, Or bring the brown girl home.

* If B♭ be tonic:—Mode 3 a.

Lord Thomas and Fair Ellinor

I

Pentatonic. Mode 3.

Sung by Mrs. MARY SANDS
at Allanstand, N. C., Aug. 5, 1916

1. I'll rid dle to you, my youn ger son, And ad vise you all as one The brown girl she's got house and home, Fair El lin der she's got none, Fair El-len-der she's got none.

J

Hexatonic. Mode 3, b.

Sung by Miss DELLA MOORE
at Rabun Co., Ga.

O mo-ther, O mo-ther, go roll a song, go roll a song as one. Which had you ra-ther, I'd mar-ried fair El-len, Or bring the brown girl home? The brown girl she has house and land, Fair El-len-der she has none; There-fore I warn you at your own ad-bles-sing To bring the brown girl home.

K

Hexatonic. Mode 3, a.

Sung by Mrs. ISABEL A. DAME
(Mass.), in 1914

1. Lord Thom-as he was a bold for-est-er, A hunts-man of the King's deer; La-dy He-len she was a fair la-dy, Lord Thomas he loved her dear.

Lord Thomas and Fair Ellinor

L

Sung by Miss Alice Parsons
at Lincoln Memorial University, Harrogate,
Claiborne Co., Tenn., April 27, 1917

Pentatonic. Mode 3.

1. Mother, O mother, come riddle my sport, Come riddle us both in one. Must I go marry fair Ellender, Or bring the brown girl home?

2 The brown girl has both houses and lands,
Fair Ellender has none,
And my advice would be for you
To bring the brown girl home.

3 Mother, O mother, go saddle my steed,
Go catch him up for me,
For I must invite fair Ellender
Unto my wedding day.

4 He dressed himself in scarlet red,
And wore a robe of green,
And every town that he passed through
They took him to be some king.

5 He rode up to fair Ellender's gate,
He jingled, he jingled the ring,
And none were so ready as fair Ellender
To rise and let him in.

6 What news, what news, Lord Thomas? she cried,
What news you bring to me?
O I have come to invite you
Unto my wedding day.

7 Mother, O mother, come riddle my sport,
Come riddle us both in one.
Must I go to Lord Thomas's wedding,
Or stay at home and mourn.

Lord Thomas and Fair Ellinor

8 There may be many of your friends,
   And many more of your foes,
   But my advice would be for you
   To tarry this day at home.

9 There may be many of foes,
   And many more of my friends,
   But I'll go to Lord Thomas's wedding,
   If I never return again.

10 She dressed herself in scarlet so fine
   And wore a belt of green,
   And every town that she rode through
   They took her to be some queen.

11 She rode up to Lord Thomas's gate,
   She jingled, she jingled the ring;
   None were so ready as Lord Thomas himself
   To rise and let her in.

12 He took her by her lily-white hand
   And led her across the hall,
   And sat her down in a golden chair
   Which leaned against the wall.

13 Is this your bride, Lord Thomas? she cried,
   I see she is quite brown.
   Once you could have married as fair a young lady
   As ever the sun shone round.

14 The brown girl had a little penknife
   Which was both keen and sharp;
   She placed it on poor Ellender's fair body
   And pierced it to the heart.

15 What's the matter, what's the matter? Lord Thomas he cried.
   What's the matter? again cried he.
   O now you see my own heart's blood
   Come tinkling down so free.

16 He took the brown girl by the hand,
   And led her across the hall,
   And drew his sword and cut her head off
   And threw it against the wall.

17 He placed the handle against the wall,
   The point against his breast.
   Here ends the life of three true lovers.
   Lord, take them home to rest.

Lord Thomas and Fair Ellinor

18 Mother, O mother, go dig my grave,
   Go dig it both wide and deep,
   And place fair Ellender in my arms
   And the brown girl at my feet.

Lord Thomas and Fair Ellinor

125

Lord Thomas and Fair Ellinor

S

Pentatonic. Mode 2.

Sung by Mrs. SINDA WALKER
at Hyden, Leslie Co., Ky., Oct. 3, 1917

Lord Thomas and Fair Ellinor

Lord Thomas and Fair Ellinor

A a

Sung by Mrs. MOLLY AGEE
at Peaks of Otter, Bedford Co., Va., July 24, 1918

Heptatonic. Mixolydian.

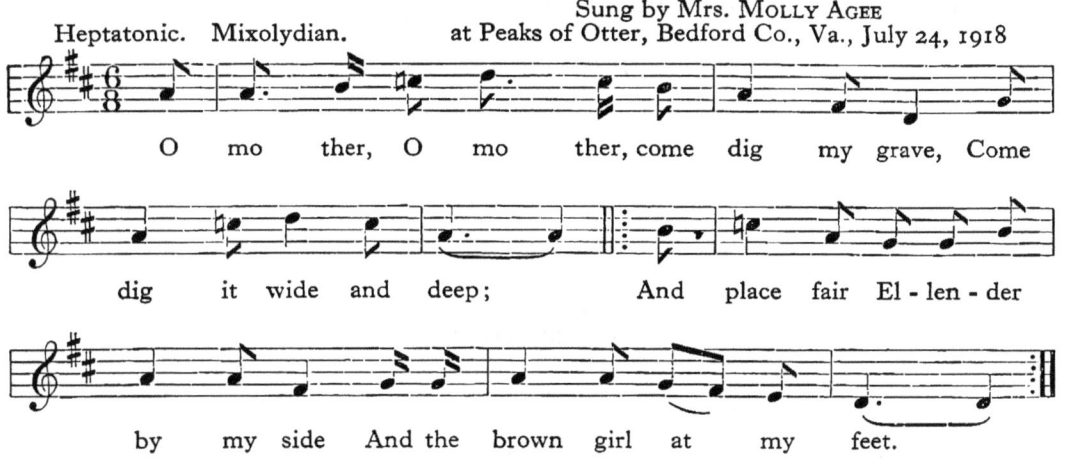

O mother, O mother, come dig my grave, Come dig it wide and deep; And place fair El-len-der by my side And the brown girl at my feet.

B b

Sung by Mrs. EMILY JOSEPHINE SNIPES
at Marion, N. C., Sept. 5, 1918

Heptatonic. Ionian.

1. Lord Tho-mas was a bold for-est-er, A hunt-er of the king's deer. Fair El-len was a fair la-dy, Lord Thom-as he loved her dear.

2 There's hundreds are my friends, mother,
  And thousands are my foes;
  Betide my life, betide my death,
  To Lord Thomas's wedding I'll go.

3 Depise her not, Lord Thomas says,
  Despise her not unto me,
  For I like the tip of your little finger
  More than her whole body.

4 Fair Ellinor, fair Ellinor, Lord Thomas said,
  What makes you look so dun?
  You used to wear as good a colour
  As ever the sun shone on.

5 Lord Thomas, Lord Thomas, fair Ellinor cries,
  Can you not plainly see
  My own heart's blood streaming from my side?
  Look what she's done to me.

Lord Thomas and Fair Ellinor

6 He had a sword by his side
  As he walked through the hall,
  And he cut off the brown girl's head
  And kicked it against the wall.

7 He called for his grave to be dug,
  Go dig it wide and deep,
  And bury fair Ellinor in my arms
  And the brown girl at my feet.

8 He put the butt against the floor,
  The point against his heart.
  There never was three lovers, sure,
  So soon they did depart.

C c

Sung by Mrs. Ef Chrisom
at Cane Branch, Burnsville, N. C., Oct. 3, 1918

Pentatonic. Mode 1.*

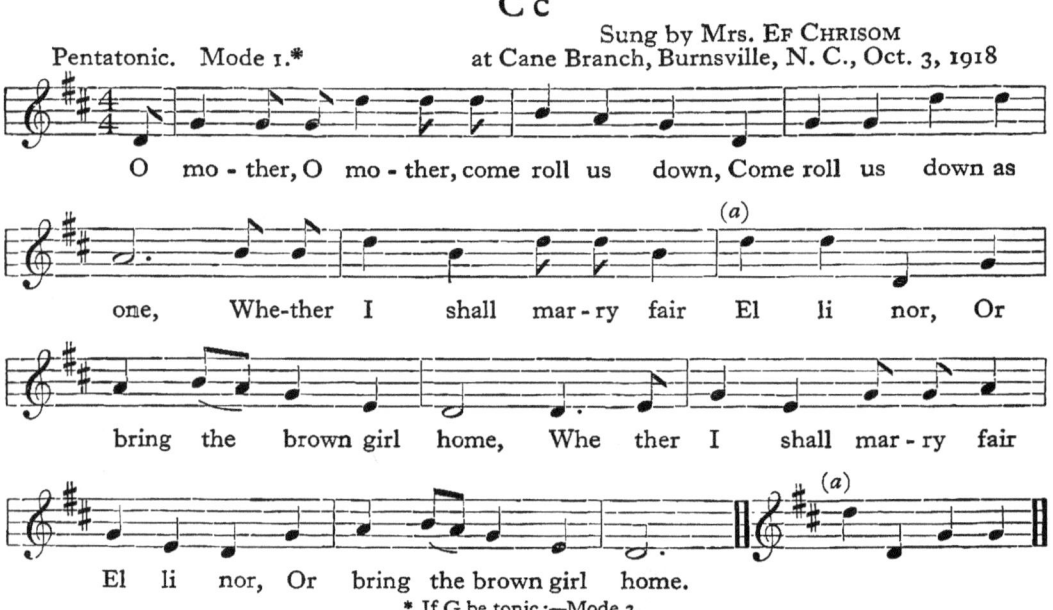

O mo-ther, O mo-ther, come roll us down, Come roll us down as one, Whe-ther I shall mar-ry fair El li nor, Or bring the brown girl home, Whe ther I shall mar-ry fair El li nor, Or bring the brown girl home.

* If G be tonic :—Mode 3.

2 He took her by her lily-white hand,
  He led her to the hall;
  There were four and twenty gay ladies there,
  And she was the flower of them all.

3 Lord Thomas, Lord Thomas, are you blind,
  Or can't you not well see?
  O don't you see my own heart's blood
  Come trinkling to my knee?

4 Go bury the brown girl at my head,
  Fair Ellender by my side.
  If we all had lived to have seen that day,
  Fair Ellender'd a-been my bride.

No. 20

Fair Margaret and Sweet William
A

Hexatonic. Mode 3, b.

Sung by Mr. Jeff Stockton
at Flag Pond, Tenn., Sept. 4, 1916

1. Sweet William he rose in the month of May, He a decked himself in blue, Saying: I long to know that long, long love has been Betwixt Lady Marget and me.

2. No harm, no harm of Lady Marget,
   Nor she knows none by me,
   But before tomorrow morning at eight o'clock
   Lady Marget a bride shall see.

3. Lady Marget was a-sitting in her bowing room
   Combing back her yellow hair,
   And she saw Sweet William and his new wedded bride,
   To church they did draw nigh.

Fair Margaret and Sweet William

4 And it's down she stood her ivory comb
   And back she threw her hair.
   And it's you may suppose and be very well assured
   Lady Marget was heard no more.

5 The time has passed away and gone
   For all men to be asleep,
   And something appeared to Sweet William and his new wedded bride
   And stood up at their bed feet.

6 Saying: How do you like your bed making?
   Or how do you like your sheets?
   Or how do you like that new wedded bride
   That lies in your arms and sleeps?

7 Very well do I like my bed making,
   Much better do I like my sheets;
   But the best of all is the gay lady
   That stands at my bed feet.

8 The time was passed away and gone
   For all men to be awake.
   Sweet William he said he was troubled in his head
   By the dreams that he dreamed last night.

9 Such dreams, such dreams cannot be true,
   I'm afraid they're of no good,
   For I dreamed that my chamber was full of wild swine
   And my bride's bed a-floating in blood.

10 He called down his waiting-men,
    One, by two, by three,
    Saying: Go and ask leave of my new wedded bride
    If Lady Marget I mayn't go and see.

11 It's he rode up to Lady Marget's own bowing room,
    And he knocked so clear at the ring;
    And who was so ready as her own born brother
    For to rise and let him in.

12 Is Lady Marget in her own bowing room?
    Or is she in her hall?
    Or is she high in her chambry
    Amongst her merry maids all?

13 Lady Marget's not in her bowing room,
    Nor neither is she in her hall;
    But she is in her long coffin,
    Lies pale against yon wall.

Fair Margaret and Sweet William

14 Unroll, unroll the winding-sheets,
   Although they're very fine,
   And let me kiss them cold pale lips
   Just as often as they've kissed mine.

15 Three times he kissed her ivory cheeks,
   And then he kissed her chin,
   And when he kissed them cold pale lips
   There was no breath within.

16 Lady Marget she died like it might be to-day,
   Sweet William he died on tomorrow;
   Lady Marget she died for pure, true love,
   Sweet William he died for sorrow.

17 Lady Marget were buried in yons churchyard,
   Sweet William was buried by her;
   From her there sprung a red, red rose,
   From his there sprung a briar.

18 They both growed up the old church wall
   Till, of course, could grow no higher,
   And they met and they tied in a true love's knot,
   For the rose rolled round the briar.

B

Sung by Mrs. LOUISA HENSLEY
at Clay Co., Ky., 1910

Heptatonic. Mode 4, a + b (dorian)*.

1. La-dy Mar-gret was sit-ting in the new church door, A-comb-ing her yel-low

hair And down she threw her high-row comb, And out of the door she sprung.

2 O mother, O mother, I saw a sight
  Which I never shall see any more.
  She dies, she never drew another breath,
  And she never lived any longer.

3 Willy rode on home that night
  And quickly fell asleep,
  Bothered and pestered all night
  In a dream he dreamed before.

*i.e with tonic D. If C be tonic, Mode 1, a + b (ionian).

Fair Margaret and Sweet William

4 Early, early he rose up,
  Dressed himself in blue;
  Asked of his new wedded wife
  To ride one mile or two.

5 They rode on till they got to Lady Margret's gate,
  Tingled at the wire;
  There was none so ready to let them in
  But Lady Margret's mother dear.

6 Is she in her sewing-room?
  Nor in her chamber asleep?
  Or is she in her dining-room,
  A lady before them all?

7 She is not in her sewing-room,
  Nor in her chamber asleep;
  Although she's in her dying-room,
  A lady before them all.

8 Her father opened the coffin lid,
  Her brother unwrapped the sheet;
  He kneeled and kissed her cold clay lips
  And died all at her feet.

9 They buried Lady Margret in the new church-yard,
  And Willy close by her side;
  And out of her heart sprang a red rose,
  And out of his a green briar.

10 They grew and grew so very high,
   Uhtil they couldn't grow any higher;
   They looped and tied in a true love knot
   The red rose and green briar.

C

Sung by Mrs. MARY SANDS
at Allanstand, N. C., July 31, 1916

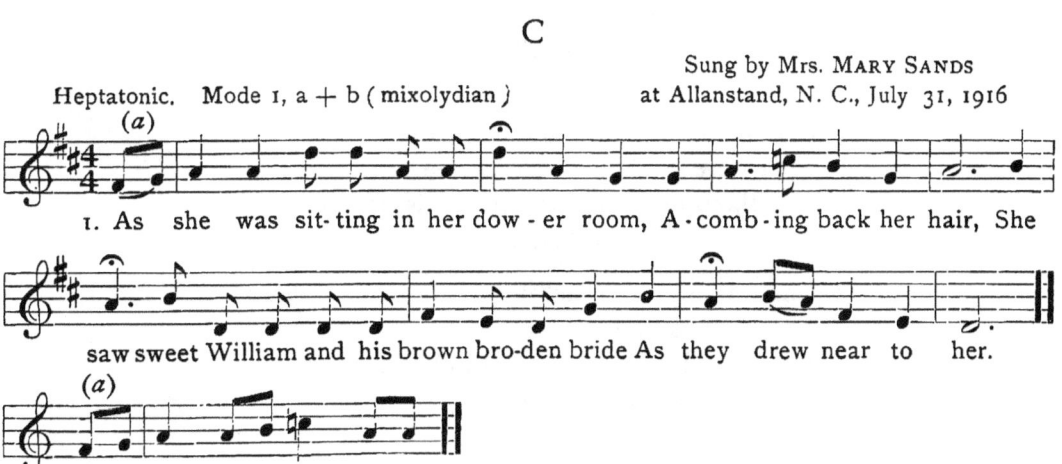

Heptatonic. Mode 1, a + b (mixolydian)

1. As she was sitting in her dow-er room, A-comb-ing back her hair, She saw sweet William and his brown bro-den bride As they drew near to her.

Fair Margaret and Sweet William

2 Lady Marget she rose in the dead hour of night
When they'se all a-lying at sleep,
Lady Marget she rose in the dead hour of night
And stood at his bed feet.

3 Says, how do you like your bed? she says,
And how do you like your sheet?
Or how do you like your brown broden bride
That lays in your arms at sleep?

4 Very well, very well do I like my bed,
But better do I like my sheet,
But better do I like a lady gay
Who stands at my bed feet.

5 Sweet William arose at the dead hour of night
When they was all a-lying at sleep,
Sweet William arose at the dead hour of night
And tingled on the ring.
There was none so ready as her seven brothers
To rise and let him come in.

6 O where is Lady Marget, Lady Marget? he cries,
O where is Lady Marget? says he;
For she's a girl I always did adore
And she stole my heart from me.

7 Is she in her dower room?
Or is she in the hall?
Or is she in her bed chambry
Along with the merry maids all?

8 She is not in her dower room,
Nor neither in the hall,
But she is in her cold, cold coffin
With her pale face toward the wall.

9 And when he pulled the milk-white sheets
That were made of satin so fine:
Ten thousand times you have kissed my lips
And now, love, I'll kiss thine.

10 Three times he kissed her snowy white breast,
Three times he kissed her cheek,
But when he kissed her cold clay lips
His heart was broke within.

Fair Margaret and Sweet William

11 What will you have at Lady Marget's burying?
   Will you have bread and wine?
   Tomorrow morning at eight o'clock
   The same shall be had at mine.

12 They buried Lady Marget in our church-yard,
   And buried Sweet William by her;
   And out of Sweet William's breast sprung a blood-red rose,
   And out of Lady Marget's a briar.

13 They grew and grew to the top of the church,
   And they could grow no higher,
   And they tied a true love's knot
   And lived and died together.

D

Sung by Mrs. Rosie Hensley
at Carmen, N. C., Aug. 8, 1916

Hexatonic. Mode 3, b.

1. Sweet Wil-liam he rose one morn-ing in May, He dressed him-self in blue. And

pray will you tell me that long, long love Be-tween La-dy Mar-gret and you.

2 I know nothing of Lady Margret, he says,
  Lady Margret knows nothing of me.
  To-morrow morning about eight o'clock
  Lady Margret my bride shall see.

3 Lady Margret was in her dowel room,
  Combing back her yellow hair.
  She saw Sweet William and his new wedded wife
  As they drew near to her.

4 O down she threw her ivory comb,
  And back she threw her hair,
  And running to her bed-chamber
  To never no more appear.

5 The very same night they were all in the bed,
  They were all in the bed asleep,
  Lady Margret she rose and stood all alone
  And sung at Sweet William's bed feet.

Fair Margaret and Sweet William

6 Saying: How do you like your bed, Sweet William?
  Or how do you like your sheet?
  Or how do you like your new wedded wife
  That lies in your arms and sleeps?

7 Very well, very well I like my bed,
  Very well I like my sheet,
  But ten thousand times better do I like the lady gay
  That stands at my bed-feet.

8 Sweet William he rose and stood all alone,
  He tingled at the ring.
  There was none so ready as her dear old mother
  To rise and let him come in.

9 O where's Lady Margret? he says,
  O where's Lady Margret? he cries.
  Lady Margret is a girl I always adored,
  She hath stole my heart away.

10 Or is she in her dowel room?
   Or is she in her hall?
   Or is she in her bed-chamber
   Among her merry maids all?

11 She's neither in her dowel room,
   Nor neither in her hall;
   Lady Margret she's in her cold coffin
   With her pale face all to the wall.

12 O down he pulled the milk-white sheets
   That was made of satin so fine.
   Ten thousand times she has kissed my lips,
   So lovely I'll kiss thine.

13 Three times he kissed her cherry, cherry cheeks,
   Three times he kissed her chin,
   And when he kissed her clay cold lips
   His heart it broke within.

14 Saying: What will you have at Lady Margret's burying?
   Will you have some bread and wine?
   To-morrow morning about eight o'clock,
   The same may be had at mine.

15 They buried Lady Margret in the old church-yard,
   They buried Sweet William by her;
   Out of Lady Margret's grave sprung a deep-red rose,
   And out of William's a briar.

Fair Margaret and Sweet William

16 They grew to the top of the old church house,
They could not grow any higher,
And met and tied in a true love's knot,
And the rose hung on the briar.

E
Hexatonic. Mode 3, b.

Sung by Miss Wonnie Shelton
at Carmen, N. C., Aug. 11, 1916

1. Lady Margret was sitting in her dower room, A combing back her hair; She saw Sweet William and his new wedded wife As they drew near to her.

F
Pentatonic. Mode 3 (Tonic G).

Sung by Mrs. Orilla Keeton
at Mount Fair, Va., Sept. 26, 1916

O down she threw her ivory comb, And back she toss'd her hair; And a-down she fell from that high, high window And never was more seen there, seen there, And never was more seen there.

G
Heptatonic. Mode 1, a + b (mixolydian).

Sung by Mr. N. B. Chisholm
at Woodridge, Va., Sept. 23, 1916

When the night was spent and the day coming in And the

Fair Margaret and Sweet William

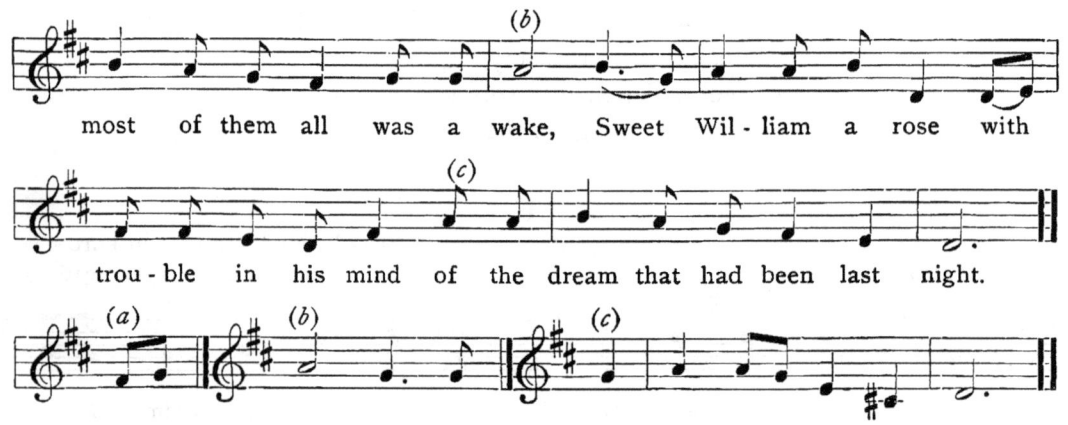

most of them all was a wake, Sweet Wil-liam a rose with
trou-ble in his mind of the dream that had been last night.

H

Pentatonic. Mode 1.

Sung by Miss May Ray at Lincoln Memorial University, Harrogate, Claiborne Co., Tenn., April 29, 1917

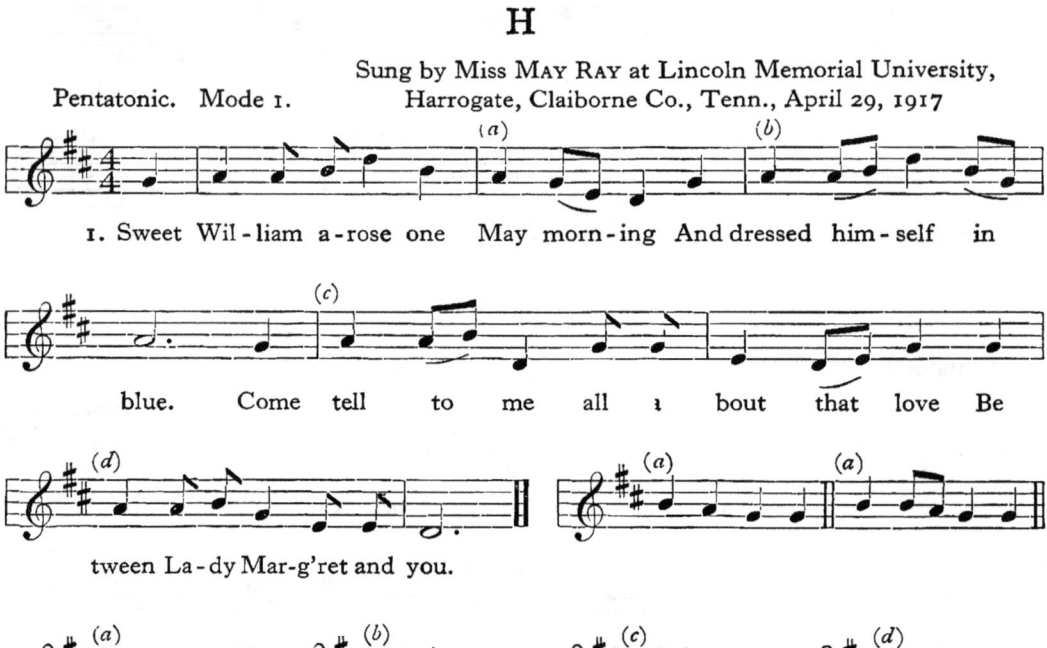

1. Sweet Wil-liam a-rose one May morn-ing And dressed him-self in blue. Come tell to me all a bout that love Be-tween La-dy Mar-g'ret and you.

2 I know nothing of Lady Margaret's love,
   But I know that she don't love me,
   And in the morning at half-past eight
   Lady Margaret my bride shall see.

3 Lady Margaret was standing in her own room door,
   A-combing back her hair,
   When who did she spy but Sweet William and his bride
   As to the church they drew nigh.

Fair Margaret and Sweet William

4 Then down she threw her ivory comb,
   In silk bound up her hair,
   And out of the room this lady ran;
   She was never any more seen there.

5 The day passed away and night a-coming on
   And the most of the men were asleep,
   Sweet William he espied Lady Margaret's ghost
   A-standing at his bed-feet.

6 O how do you like your bed?
   And how do you like your sheet?
   And how do you like the fair young bride
   That's lying in your arms at sleep?

7 Very well do I like my bed,
   Much better do I like my sheet,
   But best of all that fair young girl
   That's standing at my bed-feet.

8 The night passed away and the day coming on
   And most of all the men were awake.
   Sweet William said: I am troubled in my head
   By the dream that I dreamed last night.

9 Such dreams, such dreams as these,
   I know they mean no good.
   I dreamed last night that my room was full of swine
   And my bride was floating in blood.

10 He called his servants all to him,
   By one, by two, by three,
   And the last he called was his own new-made bride,
   That he Lady Margaret might see.

11 O what will you do with Lady Margaret's love,
   And what will you do with me?
   He said: I'll go and Lady Margaret see,
   And I'll return unto thee.

12 He rode till he came to Lady Margaret's door
   And dingled at the ring;
   And who was so ready as her seventh lonely brother
   But to rise and let him in.

Fair Margaret and Sweet William

13 O is she in her kitchen-room?
    Or is she in her hall?
    Or is she in her dining-room
    Among her merry maids all?

14 She's neither in her kitchen-room,
    Nor neither in her hall;
    But she lies both dead and cold,
    Stretched out against the wall.

15 You go fold up those snow-white sheets
    That are made of linen so fine;
    To-day they're hanging over Lady Margaret's corpse,
    To-morrow they'll hang over mine.

16 Lady Margaret was buried in the old church-yard,
    Sweet William was buried close by,
    And out of her grave there sprung a red rose,
    And out of his a brier.

17 They grew so tall and they grew so high
    That they scarcely could grow any higher.
    The brier ran around the corner of the church,
    And the rose ran around the brier.

I

Sung by Mrs. MOLLIE BROGHTON
at Barbourville, Knox Co., May 9, 1917

Heptatonic. Mixolydian.

Sweet Wil-liam a-rose one May morn ing, He dressed him-self in

blue. He ask-ed leave of his own true love La-dy Mar-gret to go and see.

Fair Margaret and Sweet William

J

(No 6th or 7th.) Sung by Mrs. Talithah Powell at Berea, Madison Co., Ky., May 28, 1917

Sweet William rose one morning in May, And dressed himself in blue. Come tell unto me what the long, long love Lies between Margret and you.

K

Heptatonic. Mixolydian. Sung by Mrs. Lizzie Gibson at Crozet, Va., April 26, 1918

Sweet William he a-rose one merry morning, And he trimmed himself in blue. Pray tell unto me of your long, long love O Betwixt Lady Margret and you, Pray tell unto me of your long, long love O Betwixt Lady Margret and you.

L

Hexatonic (no 6th). Sung by Mrs. Margaret Jack Dodd at Beechgrove, Va., May 24, 1918

Sweet William's bride rose one merry morning, He

Fair Margaret and Sweet William

dressed himself in blue. Pray tell to me that long, long love Betwixt Lady Margret and you.

M

Sung by Mrs. LAURA DONALD
at Dewey, Va., June 6, 1918

Hexatonic (no 7th).

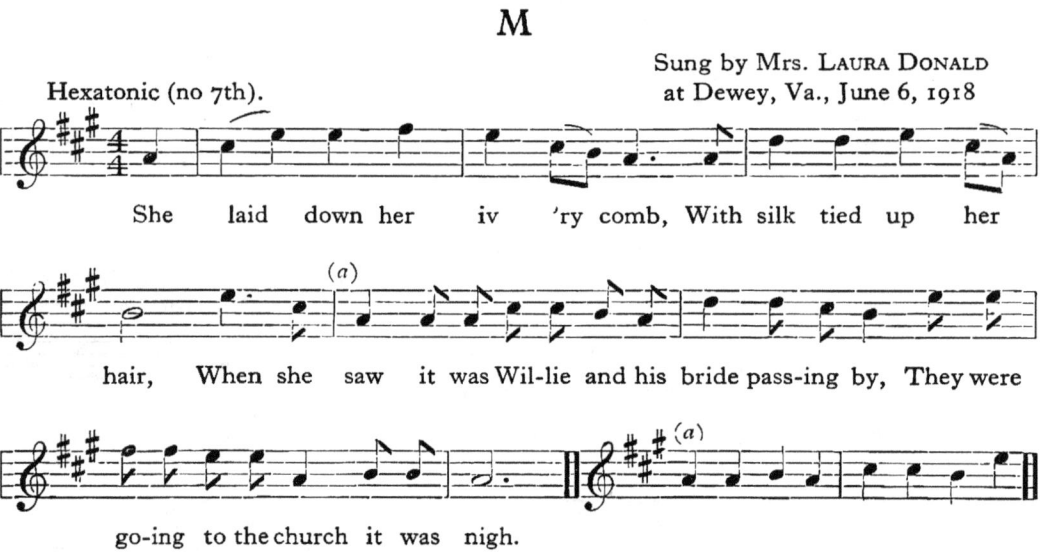

She laid down her iv'ry comb, With silk tied up her hair, When she saw it was Willie and his bride passing by, They were going to the church it was nigh.

N

Sung by Mr. BOB BRADLEY
at Blue Ridge Springs, Va., June 9, 1918

Hexatonic (no 7th).

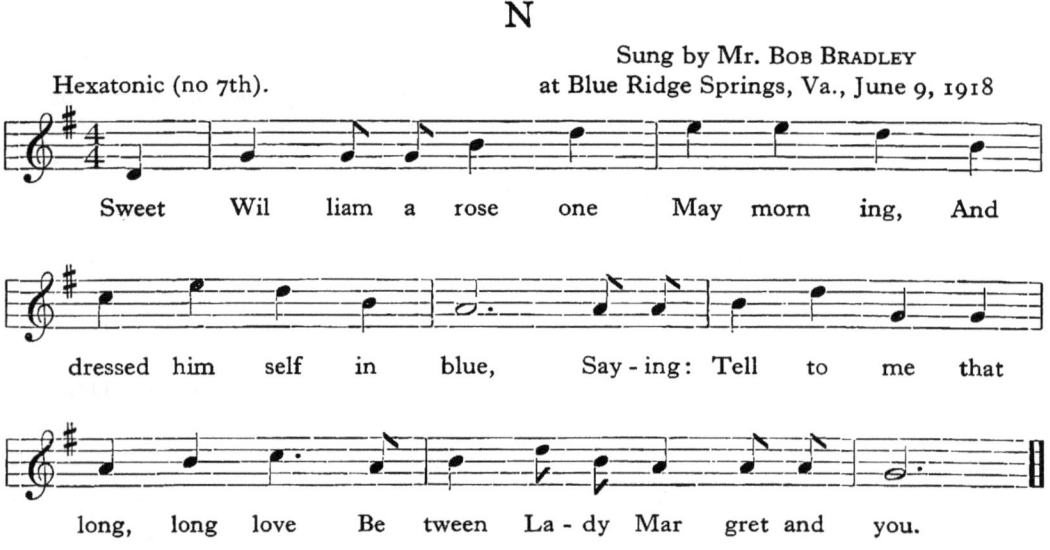

Sweet William arose one May morning, And dressed himself in blue, Saying: Tell to me that long, long love Between Lady Margret and you.

Fair Margaret and Sweet William

No. 21
Lord Lovel
A

Pentatonic. Mode 3.

Sung by Mrs. MARY SANDS
at Allanstand, N. C., Aug. 3, 1916

1. Lord Lov-el was at his gate side, A cur-ry-ing his milk-white

steed; Miss Nan-cy Bell come ri-ding by, A-wish-ing Lord Lov-el good

speed, good speed, A wish-ing Lord Lov el good speed.

2 Where are you going, Lord Lovel? she says,
  Where are you going? says she.
  I'm going to ride my milk-white steed
  Some foreign country to see.

3 How long will you be gone, Lord Lovel? she says,
  How long will you be gone? says she.
  One year, or two, or two, or three,
  Then 'turn to my Lady Nancy.

4 He had not been gone but one year and one day,
  Strange thoughts rolled through his mind

  About his Lady Nancy.

5 And so he mounted his milk-white steed
  And rode to London town,
  And there he heard the death-bells ringing
  And the people a-mourning all round.

6 Who is dead? Lord Lovel he said,
  Who is dead? says he.
  Miss Nancy Bell from London town
  That is called your Lady Nancy.

Lord Lovel

7 Go open her coffin, Lord Lovel he said,
  Pull down her shroud, says he,
  And let me kiss her cold, cold lips—
  And the tears come trinkling down.

8 Go dig my grave, Lord Lovel he said,
  Go dig my grave, says he,
  For I have no longer in this world to stay
  For the loss of my Lady Nancy.

B

Sung by Mr. PHILANDER FITZGERALD
at Nash, Va., May 7, 1918

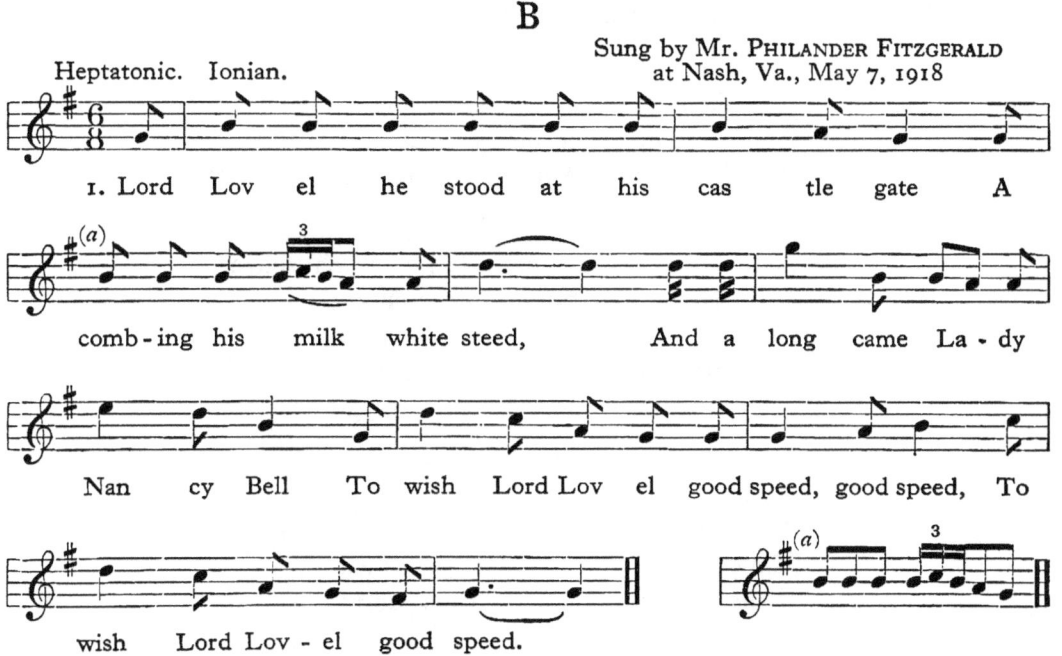

1. Lord Lovel he stood at his castle gate A-combing his milk white steed, And a long came Lady Nancy Bell To wish Lord Lovel good speed, good speed, To wish Lord Lov-el good speed.

2 A where are you going, Lord Lovel? she said.
  O where are you going? said she.
  I'm going, Lady Nancy Bell,
  Strange countries for to see, to see,
  Strange countries for to see.

3 When will you be back, Lord Lovel? she said.
  When will you be back? said she.
  A year or two or three at most,
  I'll return to my Lady Nancy, cy, cy,
  I'll return to my Lady Nancy.

4 He had not been gone twelve months and a day,
  Strange thoughts come in his head,
  That Lady Nancy he would see,
  Fearing that she was dead, was dead,
  Fearing that she was dead.

Lord Lovel

5 He mounted on his milk-white steed,
   And he rode to London town,
   And there he heard those bells a-mourn,
   A-mourning round and round and round,
   A-mourning round and round.

6 O what is the matter? Lord Lovel he cried.
   O what is the matter? cried he
   A lady is dead, a woman replied,
   Some called her Lady Nancy, cy, cy,
   Some called her Lady Nancy.

7 He ordered the coffin to be opened wide,
   And the shroud he turn-ed down,
   And there he kissed her cold, clay lips
   Till the tears come trinkling down, down, down,
   Till the tears come trinkling down.

8 Lord Lovel was buried in the green churchyard,
   Lady Nancy was buried in the choir;
   And out of his grave grew a red rose,
   And out of her a brier, brier, brier,
   And out of her a brier.

9 They grew up to the church steeple top
   To the admiration of the town;
   And they would have been there until now
   If the sexton had not cut them down, down,
   If the sexton had not cut them down.

C

Sung by Miss VIOLET HENRY
at Berea, Madison Co., Ky., May 21, 1917

Hexatonic (no 7th).

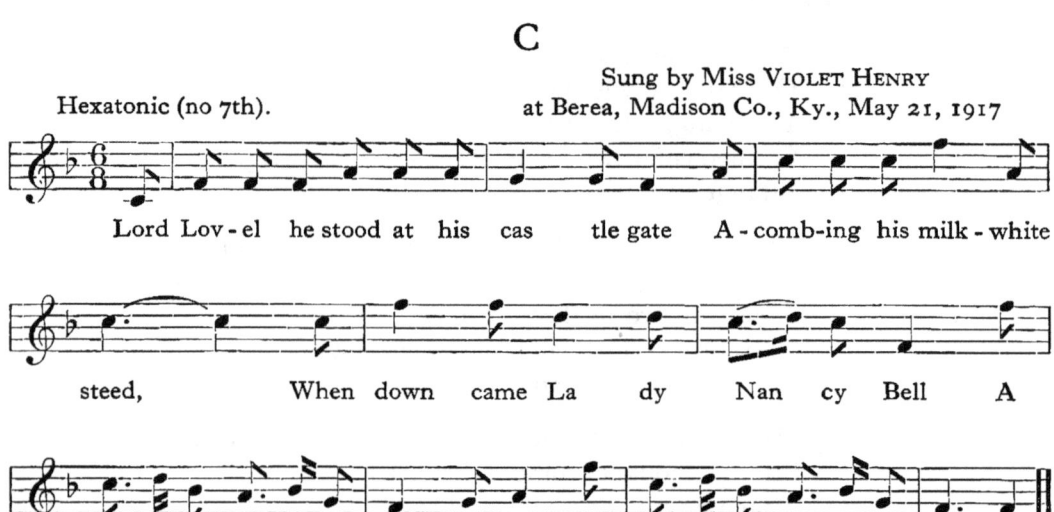

Lord Lov-el he stood at his cas-tle gate A-comb-ing his milk-white steed, When down came La-dy Nan-cy Bell A wish-ing her lov-er good speed, speed, speed, A-wish-ing her lov-er good speed.

Lord Lovel

D

Heptatonic. Ionian.

Sung by Mrs. WILLIE ROBERTS
at Nellysford, Va., May 23, 1918

Where are you go-ing, Lord Lov-el, she said, O where are you go-ing? said she. I am go-ing, my la-dy Nan-cy Bell, Strange coun-tries for to see.

E

Hexatonic (no 7th).

Sung by Mrs. SINA BOONE
at Shoal Creek, Burnsville, N. C., Sept. 28, 1918

1. Lord Lov-er stands by his dest cas-tle gate A-comb-ing his milk-white horse, And out comes La-dy Nan-cy Bell To wish her lov-er good speed, speed, speed, To wish her lov-er good speed.

1 Lord Lover stands by his des (*sic*) castle gate
  A-combing his milk-white horse,
  And out comes Lady Nancy Bell
  To wish her lover good speed, speed, speed,
  To wish her lover good speed.

2 Some people called her Nancy Bell,
  Some called her Lady Nancy.
  He ordered the lid to be opened wide
  And the winding sheet laid back.

3 They grew and they grew to the top of the church,
  They could not grow much higher.
  They twittered and they tied in a true love's knot
  For all true lovers to admire.

No. 22

The Wife of Usher's Well
A

Sung by Mr. Sol. and Miss Virginia Shelton
at Alleghany, N. C., July 29, 1916

Pentatonic. Mode 2.

1. She hadn't been married but a very short time
Until children she had three;
She sent them out to the north countree
To learn the grammaree.

2 They hadn't been there before a very short time,
Scarcely six weeks and three days,
Till sickness came into that old town
And swept her three babes away.

3 She dreamed a dream when the nights were long,
When the nights were long and cold;
She dreamed she saw her three little babes
Come walking down to their home.

4 She spread them a table all on a white cloth,
And on it she put bread and wines.
Come and eat, come and eat, my three little babes,
Come and eat and drink those wines.

5 Take it off, take it off, mother dear, cried they,
For we can no longer stay,
For yonder stands one, our Saviour dear,
To take us in his arms.

6 She spread them a bed in the backside room,
And on it she put three sheets,
And one of the three was a golden sheet,
For the youngest one might sleep.

7 Take it off, take it off, mother dear, cried they,
For we can no longer stay,
For yonder stands one, our Saviour dear,
To take us in his arms.

The Wife of Usher's Well

8 Dear mother, it is the fruits of your own pride heart
That has caused us to lie in the clay.
Cold clods at our head, green grass at our feet,
We are wrapped in our winding-sheets.

B

Sung by Miss LINNIE LANDERS
at Carmen, N. C., Sept. 5, 1916

Pentatonic. Mode 2.

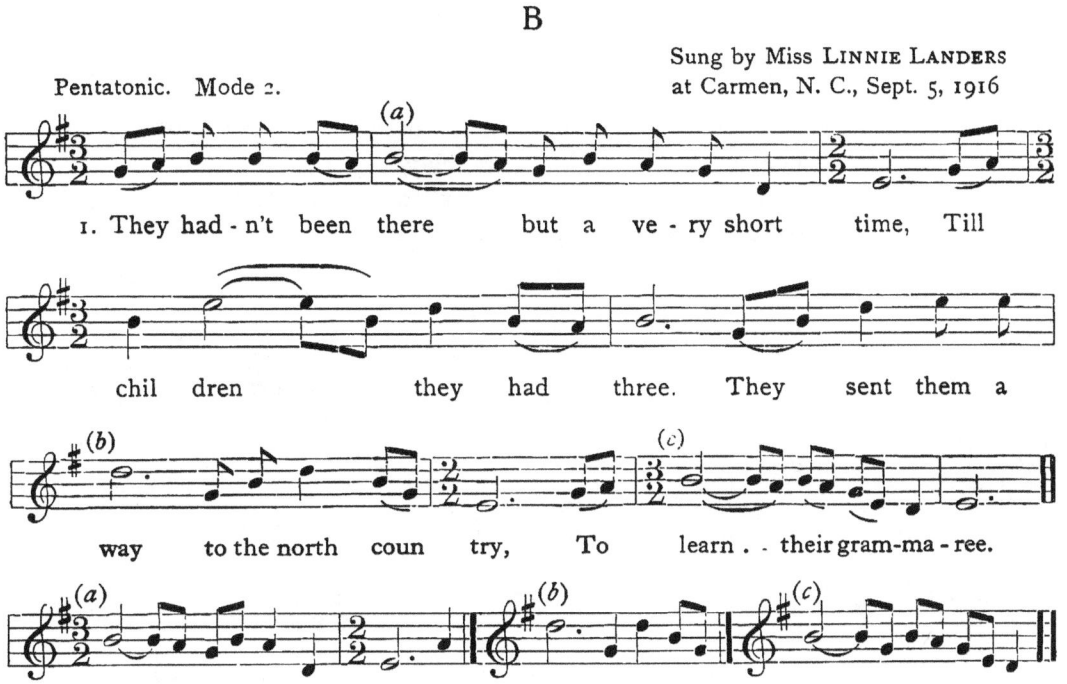

1. They hadn't been there but a very short time, Till children they had three. They sent them away to the north country, To learn their grammaree.

2 They hadn't been there but a very short time,
Scarcely six weeks and three days,
Till sickness came into that whole town
And swept her babes away.

3 She dreamed a dream when the nights were long,
When the nights were long and cold.
She dreamed she saw her three little babes
Come walking down to their home.

4 She spread them a table on a milk-white cloth
And on it she put cake and wine.
Come and eat, come and eat, my three little babes,
Come and eat and drink of mine.

5 No mother, no mother, don't want your cakes,
Nor neither drink your wine,
For yonder stands our Saviour dear
To take us in his arms.

The Wife of Usher's Well

6 She fixed them a bed all in the back side room
  And on it she put three sheets,
  And one of the three were a golden sheet,
  Under it that the youngest might sleep.

7 Take it off, take it off, dear mother, they said,
  For we haven't got long to stay,
  For yonder stands our Saviour dear,
  Where we must shortly be.

8 Dear mother, dear mother, it's the fruit of your poor pride heart
  That caused us to lie in the clay.
  Cold clods at our heads, green grass at our feet
  We are wrapped in our winding-sheet.

C

Mode 4, b (no 2nd).

Sung by Mr. T. Jeff. Stockton
at Flag Pond, Tenn., Sept. 4, 1916

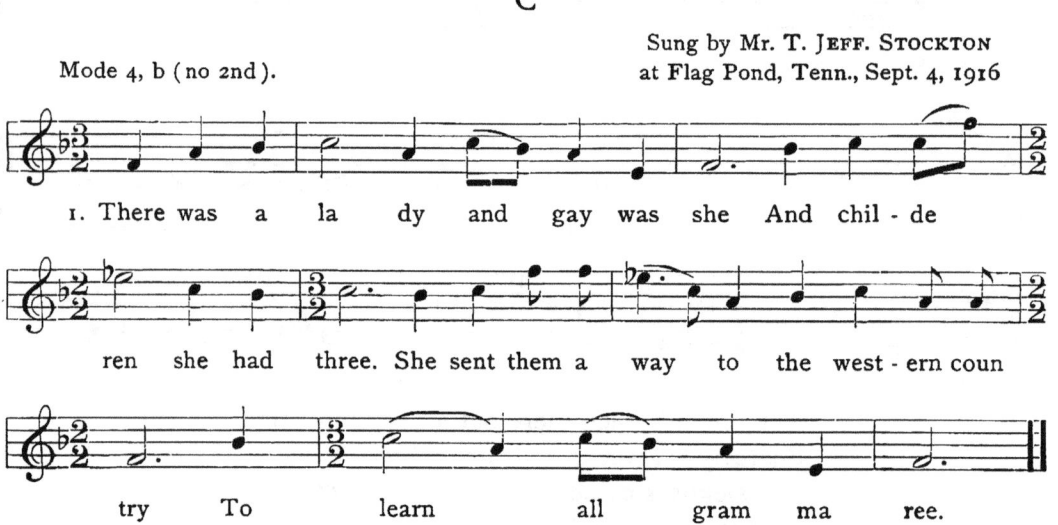

1. There was a lady and gay was she And children she had three. She sent them away to the western country To learn all grammaree.

2 They hadn't been gone but a very short time,
  Scarcely three weeks and a day,
  Till death came along through them dark woods
  And swept them all away.

3 There is a King in the Heavens all bright,
  He used to wear a crown.
  I hope he'll send me my three babes to-night
  Or in the morning soon.

4 The beds was fixed in the back wall room,
  Spread over with clean sheets,
  And on the top was a golden cloth
  That they might rest and sleep.

The Wife of Usher's Well

5 The table was set in the dining-room,
   Spread over with cakes and wine.
   Go sit down, my three little babes,
   And eat and drink of mine.

6 Take it off, take it off, dear mother, said they,
   Take it off, I say again,
   For we'll not be here till the break of day;
   My Saviour will call us away.

7 Rise up, rise up, said the oldest one,
   I think it's almost day.
   See my Saviour standing by
   To welcome us three home.

D

Pentatonic. Mode 2.

Sung by Mrs. Dora Shelton
at Allanstand, N. C., Aug. 15, 1916

Pret-ty Pol-ly had-n't been mar-ried but a ve-ry short time, When she had her three lit-tle babes; She sent them a way to the North coun-try To learn their gram-ma-ree.

E

Hexatonic. Mode 2, a.

Sung by Mrs. Gentry
at Hot Springs, N. C., Aug. 24, 1916

1. Come in, come in, my two lit-tle babes And eat and drink with me; We will nei-ther eat, sweet Mo-ther dear, Nor nei-ther drink of wine, For yon-der stands our Sa-viour dear, And

The Wife of Usher's Well

The Wife of Usher's Well

I

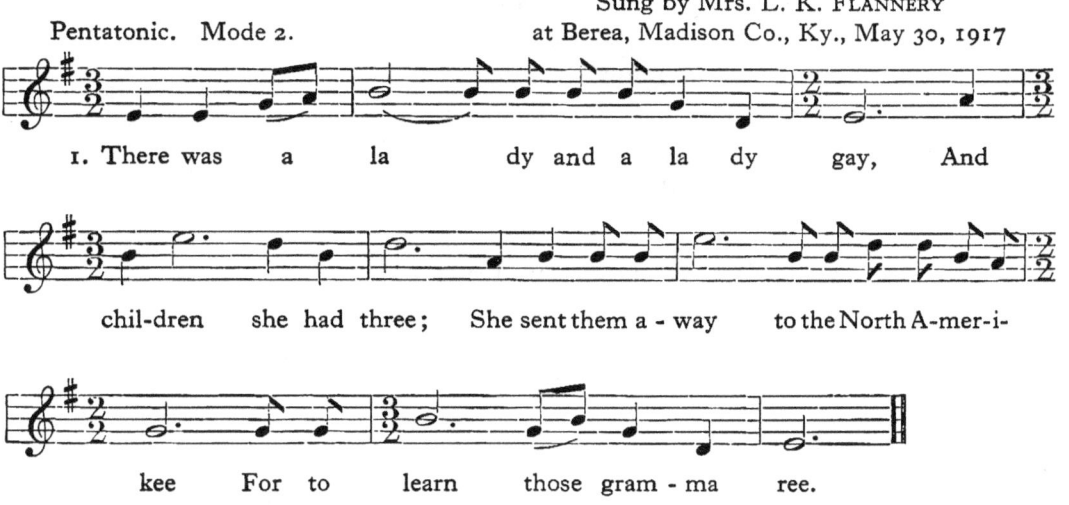

Pentatonic. Mode 2.　　Sung by Mrs. L. K. Flannery at Berea, Madison Co., Ky., May 30, 1917

1. There was a lady and a lady gay, And children she had three; She sent them away to the North A-mer-i-kee For to learn those gram-ma-ree.

2 They hadn't been there very long,
Scarce three months and a day,
When death, sweet death came hastening along
And took those babes away.

3 The lady dreamed a dream by night,
All in a backward room.
She dreamed that she saw her sweet little babes
Come walking in the light of the moon.

4 She spread her table broad and wide,
On it put bread and wine.
Come eat, come drink, my sweet little babes,
Come eat, come drink of mine.

5 We cannot eat your bread, mother,
Neither can we drink your wine,
For yonder stands our Saviour so dear.
Come eat, come drink of mine.

6 It was about old Christmas time,
The nights being long and cold,
When the lady spied her three little babes
Come walking into the room.

7 Let's go, says the oldest one,
For the chickens are crowing for day,
And yonder stands our Saviour so dear,
And we must fly away.

The Wife of Usher's Well

8 She spread her bed in the backward room,
  And on it she put white sheets,
  On top of that a golden spread
  That they might the better sleep.

9 We cannot rest on your bed, mother,
  We cannot sleep on your sheets,
  For yonder stands our Saviour so dear,
  And we must rest at his feet.

10 Marble stones at our heads, mother,
   Cold clay upon our feet;
   The tears that was shed over us last night
   Would have wet our winding sheet.

J

Hexatonic (no 6th). Sung by Mrs. MINNIE POPE at Clear Creek, Wasioto, Bell Co., Ky., May 1, 1917

There was a lady, a lady gay, Three babes, she has three, She sent them off to the for-eign coun-tree, For to learn both gram-ma-ree.

K

Hexatonic (no 6th). Sung by Mrs. VESTIE THOMPSON at Pineville, Bell Co., Ky., June 2, 1917

There was a lady, and a lady gay, And chil-dren she had three; She sent them a-way to the north-ern coun-tree To learn those gram-ma-ree.

The Wife of Usher's Well

L

Sung by Mr. George W. Gilison
at Oneida, Clay Co., Ky., Aug. 21, 1917

Hexatonic (no 6th).

There was a lady, and a lady gay, And children she had three; O she sent them off to the northern school For to learn their grammaree.

M

Sung by Mr. Napoleon Fitzgerald
at Beechgrove, Va., May 24, 1918

Pentatonic. Mode 2.

O there was a lady, gay And children she had three. She sent them away to the north countree To learn their grammaree.

The Wife of Usher's Well
N

Pentatonic. Mode 2.

Sung by Mrs. Virginia Reynolds
at Meadows of Dan, Va., Aug. 29, 1918

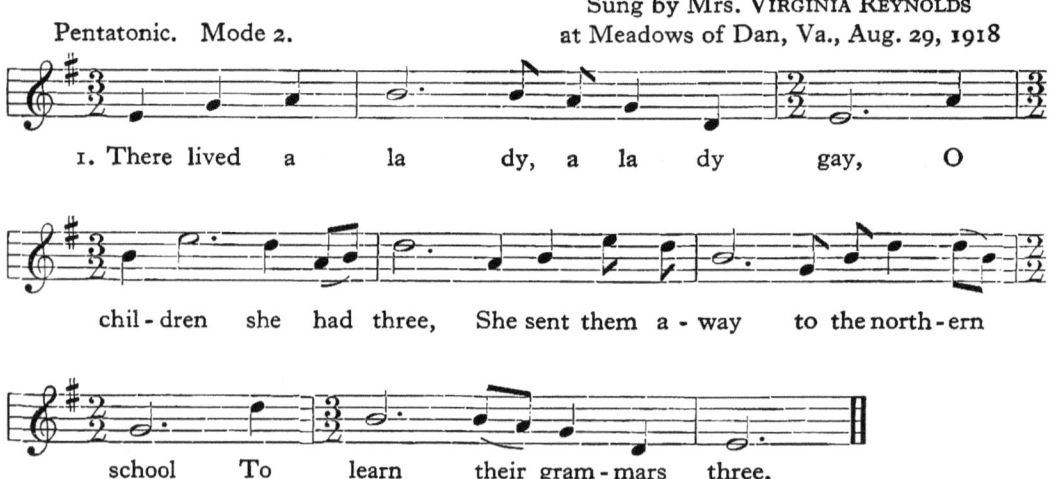

1. There lived a lady, a lady gay, O children she had three, She sent them away to the northern school To learn their grammars three.

2 They hadn't been gone but a very short time,
  Scarcely three weeks and a day,
  Till death, sweet death come hastening along
  And stole those babes away.

3 There is a king in heaven, cried she,
  A king of the third degree.
  Send back, send back my three little babes,
  This night send them back to me.

4 She made them a bed in the backward room,
  And on it put a neat white sheet,
  And over the top a golden spread,
  Much better that they might sleep.

5 Take it off, take it off, cried the oldest one,
  Take it off, take it off, cried he,
  For what's to become of this wide wicked world
  Since sin has first begun.

6 She spread them a table of bread and wine,
  As neat as neat could be,
  Come eat, come drink, my three little babes,
  Come eat, come drink with me.

The Wife of Usher's Well

7 I cannot eat your bread, says one,
  Neither can I drink your wine,
  For my Saviour dear is standing near,
  To him we must resign.

8 Cold clay, cold clay hangs over my head,
  Green grass grows over my feet;
  And every tear that you shed for me
  Doth wet my winding sheet.

O

Sung by Mrs. Effie Mitchell
at Burnsville, N. C., Sept. 12, 1918

Hexatonic (no 6th).

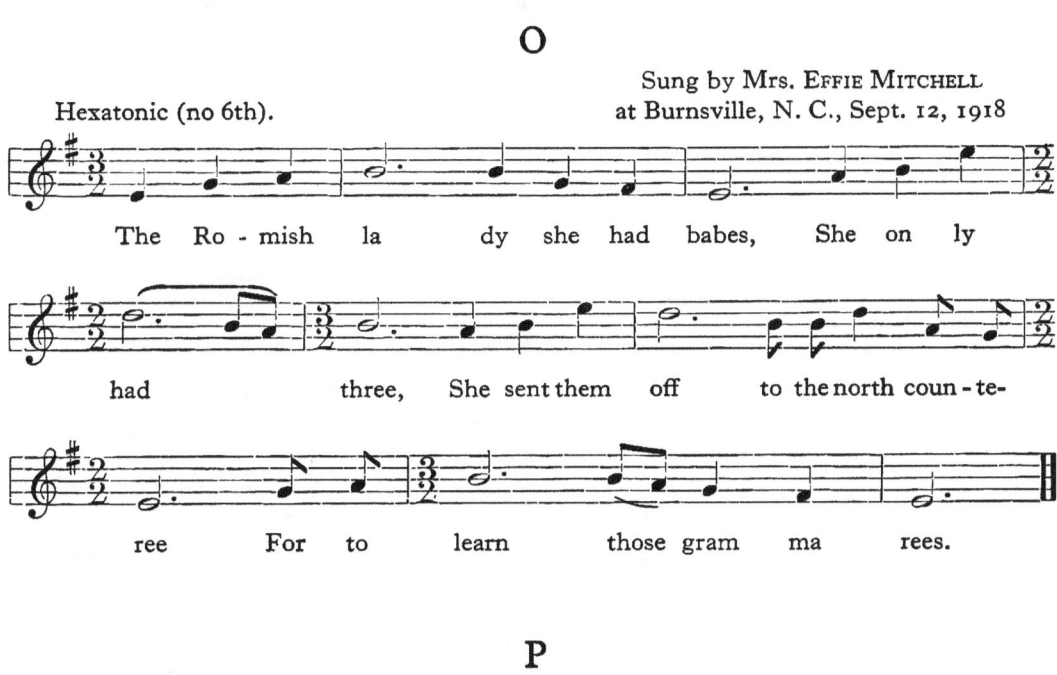

The Ro-mish la dy she had babes, She on ly had three, She sent them off to the north coun-te-ree For to learn those gram ma rees.

P

Sung by Mrs. Lucy Penland
at Bolden's Creek, Burnsville, N. C., Sept. 10, 1918

Pentatonic. Mode 2.

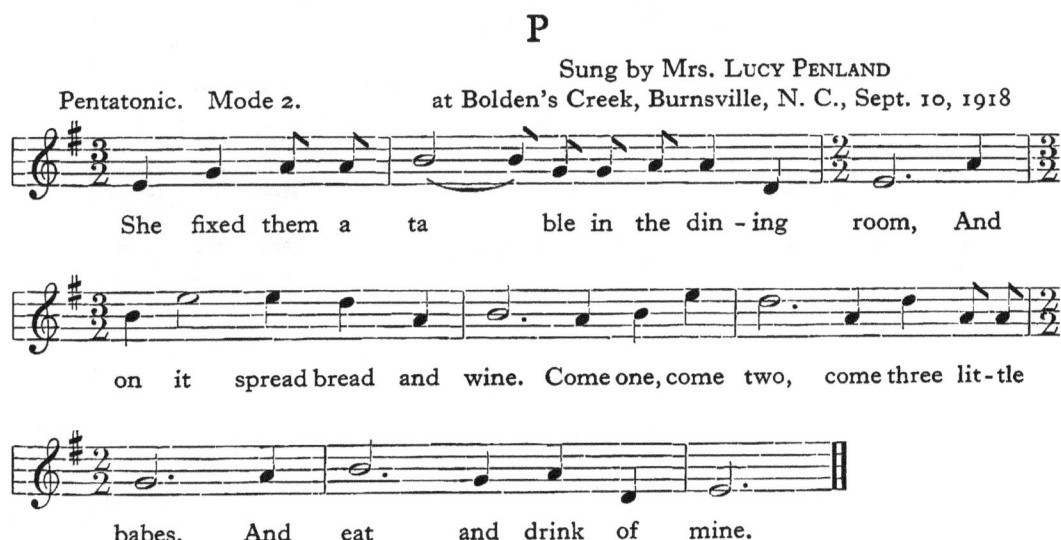

She fixed them a ta ble in the din-ing room, And on it spread bread and wine. Come one, come two, come three lit-tle babes, And eat and drink of mine.

The Wife of Usher's Well

Q

Sung by Mr. Sam Rathbone
at Shoal Creek, Burnsville, N. C., Oct. 1, 1918

(No 2nd or 6th.)

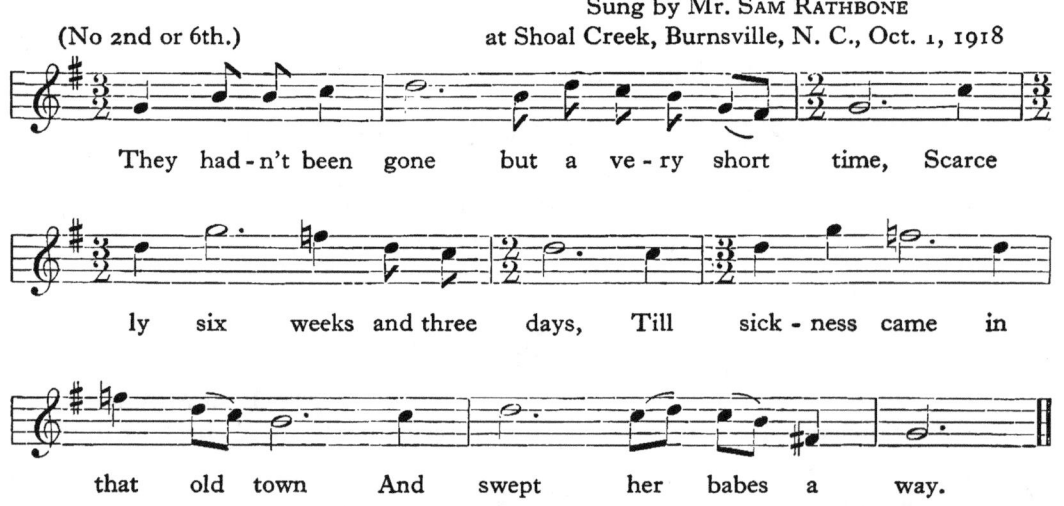

They had-n't been gone but a ve-ry short time, Scarce-ly six weeks and three days, Till sick-ness came in that old town And swept her babes a-way.

R

Sung by Mrs. King
at Bird's Creek, Sevier Co., Tenn., April 19, 1917

Pentatonic. Mode 2.

There were young and la-dy bright, And chil-dren she had three; She sent them a-way to the north-est coun-try To learn those gram-mar free.

No. 23

Little Musgrave and Lady Barnard
A

Pentatonic. Mode 3.

Sung by Mrs. Becky Griffin
at Big Laurel, N. C. Aug. 17, 1916

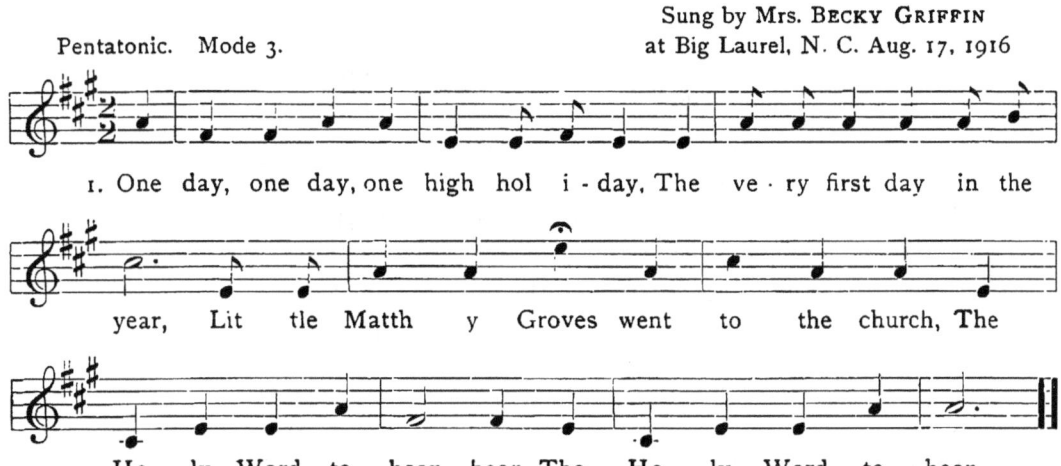

1. One day, one day, one high hol-i-day, The ve-ry first day in the year, Lit-tle Matth-y Groves went to the church, The Ho-ly Word to hear, hear, The Ho-ly Word to hear.

2 Lord Dannel's wife was standing by,
  She cast her eye on him.
  Go home with me, little Matthy Groves,
  A wedded wife to be.

3 Hark, hark, hark, hark, said little Matthy Groves,
  I cannot spare my life,
  I know by the rings you wear on your fingers,
  You are Lord Dannel's wife.

4 It's if I am Lord Dannel's wife,
  It is nothing to you.
  Lord Dannel's gone to Kentucky
  King Georgie for to view.

5 Rise, up, rise up, little Matthy Groves,
  And men's clothing put on.
  It never shall be said in the old Scotland
  I slewed a naked man.

6 Hark, hark, hark, hark says little Matthy Groves
  I cannot spare my life,
  It's you have swords by your side
  And I have ne'er a knife.

7 It's I've got swords by my side,
  They cost me from my purse,
  And you can have the very best
  And I will have the worst.

Little Musgrave and Lady Barnard

8 The very first lick Lord Dannel struck,
   He wound little Matthy deep;
   And the very next lick Lord Dannel struck
   Little Matthy fell at his feet.

9 He took his lady by the right hand,
   He set her on his knee.
   Tell to me which you love best,
   Little Matthy Groves or me.

10 Very well I like your red rosy cheeks,
   Very well I like your chin,
   But better I like little Matthy Groves
   Than Lord Dannel and all his kin.

B

Sung by Mrs. Jane Gentry
at Hot Springs, N. C., Aug. 24, 1916

Pentatonic. Mode 3.

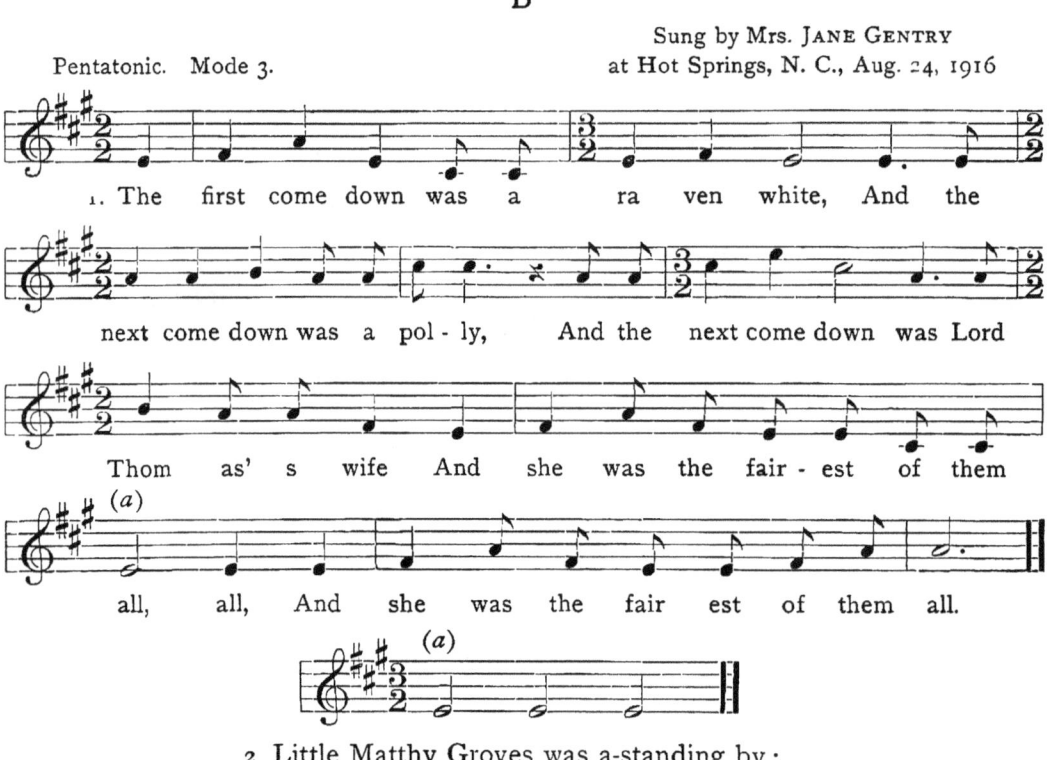

1. The first come down was a raven white, And the next come down was a pol-ly, And the next come down was Lord Thomas's wife And she was the fair-est of them all, all, And she was the fair est of them all.

2 Little Matthy Groves was a-standing by;
   She placed her eyes on him,
   Saying: You're the darling of my heart
   And the darling of my life.

3 It's you no home, no place to lie,
   Go home with me this night.
   I think by the rings you wear on your fingers
   You are Lord Thomas's wife.

Little Musgrave and Lady Barnard

4 True, I am Lord Thomas's wife
Lord Thomas is not at home.
The little foot-page was a-standing by,
These words heareth he,
And he licked to his heels and run.

5 He run, he run to the broken-down bridge,
He bent to his breast and swum;
He swum, he swum to the other, other side,
And he buckled up his shoes and he run.

6 He run, he run to Lord Thomas's gate
And he dingled at the ring and it rung,
And he dingled at the ring and it rung.
What news, what news, my little foot-page?
What news you've brought to me?
Little Matthy Groves is at your house
In the bed with the gay lady.

7 If that be a lie you've brought to me
And a lie I expect it to be,
If there is e'er a green tree in these whole worlds
A hangman you shall be.

8 If that be the truth you've brought to me,
And the truth I don't expect it to be,
You may wed my youngest daughter
And you may have all I've got.

9 Lord Thomas's wife raised up about half a doze asleep.
Lay still, lay still, little Matthy Groves says,
Lay still I tell to thee,
For it's nothing, but your father's little shepherd boy
A-driving the wolves from the sheep.

10 When little Matthy Groves did wake
Lord Thomas was at his feet.
Rise up, rise up, Lord Thomas he says,
And put your clothing on,
For it never shall be known in old England
That I slew a naked man.

11 How can I rise up, he says,
When I am afeard of my life?
For you have two good broad-edged swords
And I have not so much as a knife.

Little Musgrave and Lady Barnard

12 True, I have two good broad swords
   They cost me deep in the purse.
   But you may have the very best one
   And you may have the first lick.

13 The very first lick little Matty Groves struck,
   He struck him across the head,
   And the very next lick Lord Thomas he struck,
   And it killed little Matty Groves dead.

14 He took his gay lady by the hand,
   And he led her up and down.
   He says: How do you like my blankets
   And how do you like my sheets?

15 Well enough your blankets
   And well enough your sheets,
   But much better do I love little Matty Groves
   Within my arms asleep.

16 He took his gay lady by the hand
   And he pulled her on his knee,
   And the very best sword that he did have
   He split her head into twine (twain).

C

Sung by Mr. DAVID NORTON
at Rocky Fork, Tenn., Aug. 31, 1916

Hexatonic. Mode 3. b

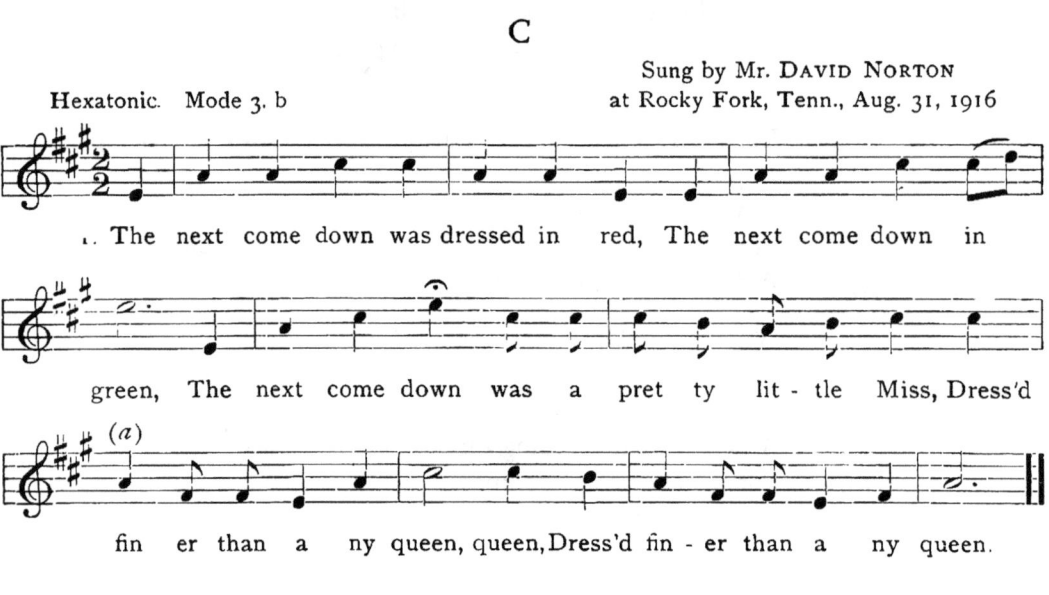

1. The next come down was dressed in red, The next come down in green, The next come down was a pretty little Miss, Dress'd finer than any queen, queen, Dress'd finer than any queen.

Little Musgrave and Lady Barnard

2 She stepped up to little Matthy Groves
And says: Come and go with me.
I know by the rings that is on your hand
You are Lord Dannel's wife,
That you are Lord Dannel's wife.

3 It makes no difference by the rings on my hand,
Nor whose wife I am.
My husband he's not at home,
He's in some foreign land.

4 Little foot Dannel (page?) was standing by,
And he heard every word they were saying.
If I live till broad daylight
Lord Dannel shall know of this.

5 He had about fifteen miles to go
And ten of them he run;
He run till he came to the river
And he held his breath and swum.

6 He swum till he came to the grassy green grove,
He sprang to his feet and he run;
He run till he came to Lord Dannel's gate
And he rang his bells and rung.

7 Is my castle burning down,
Or what is a-going to be done?
No, your wife's with another man
And both of their hearts are one.

8 He gathered him up about fifty good men,
And done it with a good will.
He put his bugle to his mouth
And blowed it with a shrill.

9 How do you like my pillow, sir,
How do you like my sheet,
And how do you like the pretty little girl
That lies in your arms asleep?

10 Very well do I like your pillow, sir,
Very well do I like your sheet,
But very much better do I like the pretty little girl
That lies in my arms asleep.

11 Little Matthy Groves struck the very first lick,
Which made Lord Dannel sore.
Lord Dannel struck the very next lick
And killed little Matthy on the floor.

Little Musgrave and Lady Barnard

12 He took his wife by the lily-white hand
    And he sat her upon his knee.
    Said: Which one do you love best,
    Little Matthy Groves or me?

13 He took his wife by the lily-white hand
    And he led her through the hall.
    He jobbed the pistol in her breast
    And she fell with a special ball.

14 Go bury me on yonder church hill
    With Matthy in my arms asleep.

    And bury Lord Dannel at my feet.

D

Hexatonic. Mode 3, b.

Sung by Mr. HILLIARD SMITH
at Hindman, Ky., Aug. 10, 1909

1. The first came in were li-ly white, The next were pink and blue, The next came in Lord Van-ner's wife, The flow-er of the view.

2 This young Magrove a-being there,
   Fair as the morning sun,
   She looked at him and he looked at her,
   The like was never known.

3 She stepped up to him and says: Kind Sir,
   Won't you take a ride with me?

4 I dare not to, I dare not to,
   I dare not to for my life;
   From the ring that you wear on your finger,
   You are Lord Vanner's wife.

5 Well, if I am Lord Vanner's wife,
   Lord Vanner is not at home,
   Lord Vanner is to redemption gone,
   To King McHenry's throne.

6 This little foot-page a-being by,
   Hearing every word they said,
   He swore Lord Vanner should have the news
   Before the rising sun.

Little Musgrave and Lady Barnard

7 He run till he came to the river side,
And he jumped in and swam,
He swam and he swam to the other side,
And he rose and run.

8 He run till he came to McHenry's throne,
He dingled so loud with the ring,
There's none so ready as Lord Vanner himself
To arise and let him in.

9 What news, what news? my little foot-page,
What news have you brought to me?
Has any of casten walls fell down,
Or any of my men false be?

10 There's none of your casten walls fell down,
Nor none of your men false be.
This young Magrove is in fair Scotland
In bed with your lady.

11 If this be lie you bring to me,
As I believe it to be,
I'll build a gallow just for you,
And hangen you shall be.

12 If this be lie I bring to you
As you believe it to be,
You needn't build any gallows for me,
Just hang me on a tree.

13 Lord Vanner calling up his best men,
By one, by two, by three,
Saying: Let's take a trip to fair Scotland,
This happy couple for to see.

14 They rolled and they rolled all over the bed
Till they fell fast asleep,
And when they woke Lord Vanner was there
A-standing at their bed feet.

15 It's how do you like my blanket, sir?
It's how do you like my sheet?
How do you like that fair lady,
That lies in your arms asleep.

16 Very well I like your blanket, sir,
Very well I like your sheet,
Ten thousand times better I like this fair lady
Lies in my arms asleep.

Little Musgrave and Lady Barnard

17 Get up, get up, put on your clothes,
And fight me like a man;
Never should have been said in fair Scotland
I killed a naked man.

E

Hexatonic. Mode 2, a.

Sung by Mr. JEFF STOCKTON
at Flag Pond, Tenn., Sept. 4, 1916

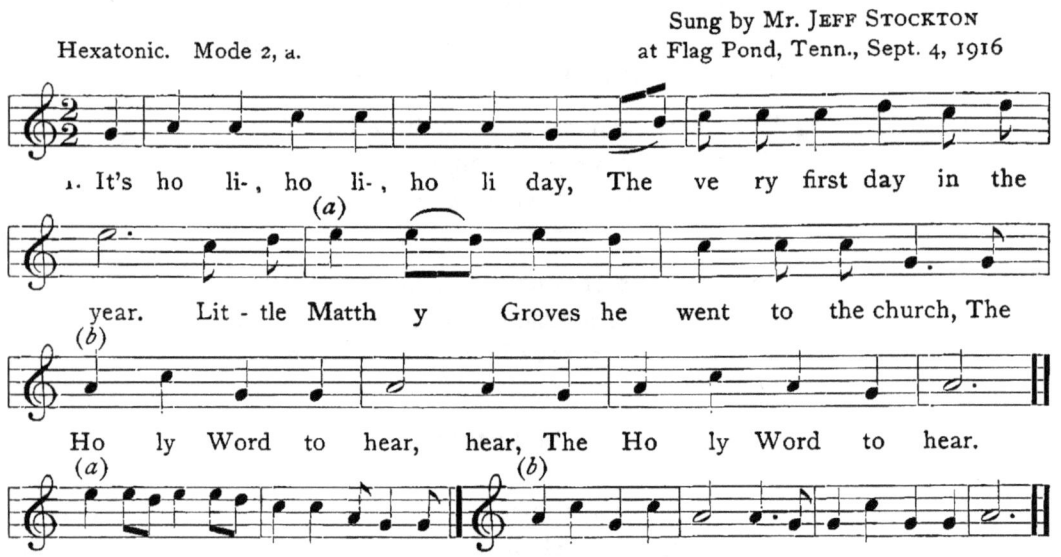

1. It's ho li-, ho li-, ho li day, The very first day in the year. Little Matthy Groves he went to the church, The Holy Word to hear, hear, The Holy Word to hear.

2 If I am Lord Thomas's wife,
Lord Thomas is not at home.
He's gone away to his false taverin
His prentiss for to see.

F

Hexatonic. Mode 3, a.

Sung by Mrs. CARRIE FORD
at Black Mountain, N. C., Sept. 18, 1916

.. Well, if I am Lord Dan-nel's wife, Lord Dan-nel is not at home; He's gone over yonder to yon bright church The Holy Word to hear, The Holy Word to hear.

Little Musgrave and Lady Barnard

1 Go home with me, little Matthy Groves,
   And keep me from the cold.
   I wouldn't go home with you to-night
   If I know'd it would save your life,
   For I can tell by the rings on your fingers
   That you're Lord Dannel's wife.

2 Well, if I am Lord Dannel's wife,
   Lord Dannel is not at home;
   He's gone over yonder to yon bright church
   The Holy Word to hear.

3 His little foot-page was standing by,
   He took to his heels and run;
   He run till he came to the broken bridge,
   And he laid upon his breast and swum.

4 O Lord Dannel, you'd better go home.
   Little Matty Groves in bed with your wife
   Keeping her from the cold.

5 I heard Lord Dannel's bugle blow.
   Lay still, lay still, little Matthy Groves,
   And keep me from the cold,
   For it's only my father's shepherd boy
   Driving the sheep from the fold.

6 O how do you like my fine feather bed?
   And how do you like my sheet?
   And how do you like my pretty little wife,
   That lies in your arms asleep?

7 Very well do I like your fine feather bed,
   Very well do I like your sheet;
   Much better do I like your sweet little wife
   That lay in my arms asleep.

8 Get up from there, little Matthy Groves,
   And put you on your clothes.
   I wouldn't have it known in this native land
   I'd slain a naked man.

9 I'll get up, put on my clothes,
   I'll fight you for my life.
   Your two bright swords hang by your side,
   And me not even a knife.

Little Musgrave and Lady Barnard

10 My two bright swords hang by my side,
    They cost me in my purse,
    But you shall have the best of them
    And I will have the worst.

11 You shall have the very first lick,
    You strike it like a man,
    And I will take the very next lick,
    I'll kill you if I can.

12 Little Matthy had the very first lick,
    He struck and hit the floor.
    Lord Dannel had the very next lick,
    Little Matthy struck no more.

13 He took her by the lily-white hand,
    He laid her on his knee.
    Which do you like the best of the two,
    Little Matthy Groves or me?

14 Very well do I like your red rosy cheeks,
    Also your dimpling chin,
    Much better do I like little Matthy Groves
    Than any of your kin.

15 He took her by the lily-white hand,
    He led her in the hall.
    He drew his sword, cut off her head
    And kicked it against the wall.

G

Pentatonic. Mode 2.

Sung by Miss LAURA BREWER,
Clay Co., Ky., in 1909.

1. Ho li-, ho li-, ho li day, On the ve-ry first day of the year, Lit tle Matth y Grove went to the church The Ho ly Word to hear, hear, The Ho ly Word to hear.

Little Musgrave and Lady Barnard

2 First came down was the lady gay,
   The next came down was a girl,
   The next came down was Lord Donald's wife,
   The flowers of the world.

3 She placed her arm on little Matthy Grove,
   Says: Matthy, go home with me,
   This night, this night,
   This livelong night to sleep.

4 I am darsing of my life,
   I can't go home with you.
   I know you by your finger rings,
   You are Lord Donald's wife.

5 If I am Lord Donald's wife,
   Lord Donald is gone from home.
   He's gone across the water side,
   He's gone over there to stay.

6 Little Speedfoot was standing by
   To see what he could hear,
   And as he saw them both walk off,
   He picked up his heels and run.

7 He ran till he came to the river side,
   He bent his breast and swam,
   Swam till he came to the other side
   And he picked up his heels and ran.

8 He ran till he came to the high King Gate;
   He rattled the bell and it rung.
   What news, what news, little Speedfoot, he says,
   What news do you bring me?

9 Is my old scaffold burned down?
   Or is my tavern run?
   Or is my lady gay put to bed,
   With a daughter or a son?

10 No, your scaffold's not burned down,
    Nor your tavern's not run;
    Nor your lady gay is not put to bed
    With a daughter or a son.
    But little Matthy Grove is at your own house
    In bed with your lady gay.

Little Musgrave and Lady Barnard

11 Little Donald he had two bright, keen swords,
Little Matthy he had none.
Lord Donald said to get up and put on his clothes
And fight him like a man—
That he couldn't fight a naked man.

12 Put on your clothes and fight me for your life.
How can I fight you and me not even a knife?

H

Pentatonic. Mode 3.

Sung by Mrs. Jas. Gabriel Coates
at Flag Pond, Sept. 1, 1916

1. One ho li - day, one right- eous day, One hol - i - day in the year, Lit - tle Matthy Groves went out to church, The righteous word to hear, The righteous word to hear.

I

Pentatonic. Mode 3.

Sung by Mrs. Doc. Pratt
at Hindman, Knott Co., Ky., Sept. 22, 1917

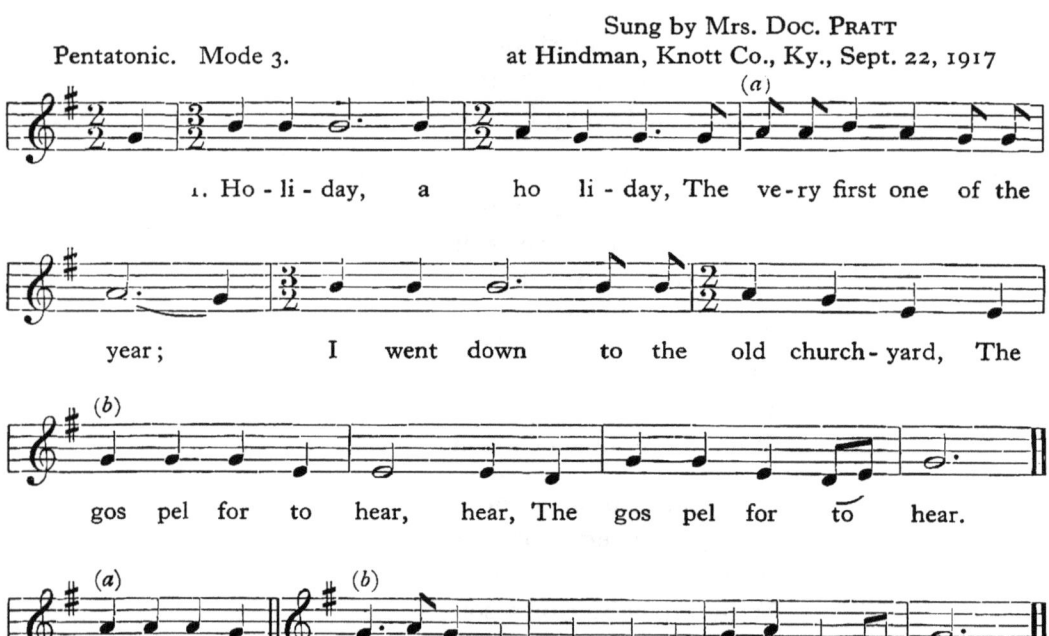

1. Ho - li - day, a ho li - day, The ve - ry first one of the year; I went down to the old church- yard, The gos pel for to hear, hear, The gos pel for to hear.

Little Musgrave and Lady Barnard

2 The first come was young ladies very fair,
The next come was Lord Darnel's wife,
The flower amongst the few.

3 After the meeting was over
She cast her eyes around;
Who did she spy but little Matty Groves
As he passed through the town.

4 Come go home with me, little Matty Groves,
Come go home with me to-night,
Come go home with me, little Matty Groves,
And sleep with me till light.

5 I can't go, I can't go,
I can't go for my life,
For I know you are Lord Darnel's wife
By the rings that wear on your fingers.

6 If I am Lord Darnel's wife,
Lord Darnel's not at home;
He has gone down to the high toll-gate
To call his hirelings home.

7 Little foot-page a-standing by
A-hearing what was said,
He swore Lord Darnel should hear
Before the sun did set.

8 And in the hurry to carry the news,
He buckled his shoes and he run.
He run till he came to the river-side,
Being deep and muddy.
In his hurry to carry the news,
He bowed (*pronounced* ' bode ') his breast and swum.

9 He called out on the other side,
A-being wet and muddy.
In a hurry to carry the news,
He buckled his shoes as he run.

10 He run till he came to Lord Darnel's hall,
He jingled so loud at the rung.
No one at all so ready as he was
To rise and let him in.

11 What news, what news, little foot-page?
What news do you bring to me?
Is my castle fell,
Or is my lady dead?

Little Musgrave and Lady Barnard

12 Your castle has not fell,
    Neither is your lady dead,
    But little Matthy Groves sleeps this night
    In the arms of your lady gay.

13 If this be a lie, little foot-page,
    If this be a lie, said he,
    I won't take time to make a gallows,
    I'll hang you to a tree.

14 But if this be true, little foot-page,
    If this be true, said he,
    I'll give you all of the wee gay gold
    That your horse can carry away.

15 He called all his men around,
    And he counted two by three.
    Then he gave command
    That ne'er a horn should blow.

16 When they got all on the top of the mountain,
    Being one man in the crowd that meaned little Matthy to know,
    He put his horn up to his mouth,
    And loudly he did blow.

17 Little Matthy he rose up in bed,
    Saying: I must go, I must go,
    For I hear Lord Darnel blowing.

18 Lie down, lie down, you foolish boy,
    Lie down and keep me warm;
    It's just my uncle's negroes
    Herding my sheep to the barn.

19 Little Matthy he lie down
    And took a nap of sleep;
    But when he awoke, Lord Darnel's men
    Were standing at his feet.

20 Saying: How do you like my feather bed?
    And how do you like my sheets?
    And how do you like my lady gay
    That lies in your arms to sleep?

21 Very well I like your feather bed,
    Very well I like your sheets,
    Much better I like your lady gay
    That lies in my arms to sleep.

Little Musgrave and Lady Barnard

22 Get up, little Matthy, and put on your clothes,
  Get up, little Matthy, said he,
  For it never shall be alleged to me
  That I slew a naked man.

23 I can't get up, I can't get up,
  I can't get up for my life,
  For you have two long bitteren swords,
  And me not a pocket-knife.

24 I know I have two long bitteren swords,
  And they cost me deep in my purse;
  But you may take the very best,
  And I will take the worst.

25 You may strike the very first lick,
  You must strike it like a man;
  I will strike the very next lick;
  I'll kill you if I can.

26 Little Matthy struck the very first lick,
  He wounded deep and sore.
  Lord Darnel struck the very next lick;
  Little Matthy struck no more.

27 He took his lady by the hand,
  He set her on his knee.
  Now, which do you like best,
  Little Matthy Groves or me?
  I'd rather have a kiss from little Matthy's lips
  Than you and all your money.

28 He pulled out his long bitteren sword
  And slung it around and around;
  And with the edge he chopped off her head
  And stove it against the ground.

J

Sung by Mrs. DELIE KNUCKLES
at Barbourville, Knox Co., Ky., May 16, 1917

Pentatonic. Mode 3 (Tonic G).

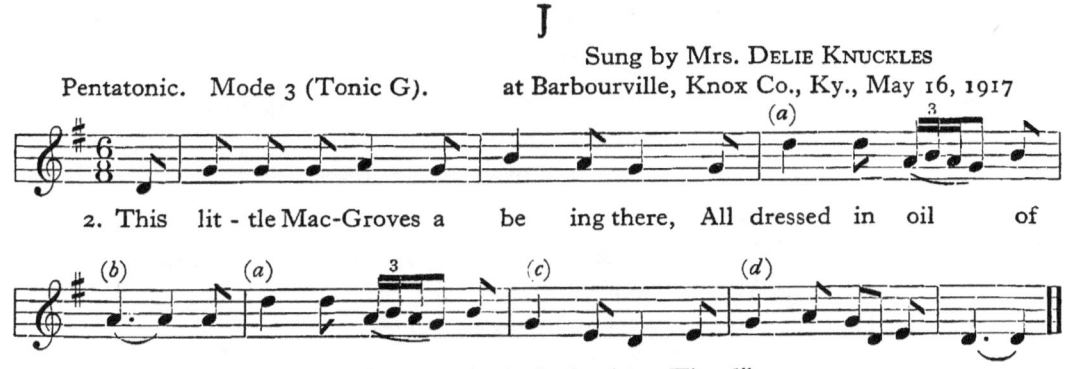

Little Musgrave and Lady Barnard

1. There was four and twenty ladies there
   A-dancing at the ball.
   The first came in was a lily-white robe,
   The next came pink and blue,
   The third came in was Lord Banner's wife,
   The flower of the view.

2. This little MacGroves a-being there,
   All dressed in oil of green,
   He looked at her, she looked at him,
   The like was never seen.

3. She said to him: My sweet MacGroves,
   Go home with me to-night;
   There's waiting-boys plenty there,
   And I'll ride by your side.

4. O no, O no, I dare not go,
   I dare not for my life;
   I know by the ring you wear
   You are Lord Banner's wife.

5. O if I am Lord Banner's wife,
   Lord Banner's hain't at home;
   Lord Banner he's Redemption gone,
   He's on Queen Anna's throne.

6. This little foot-page a-being there,
   Determined Lord Banner should know.
   He turned his course to Lord Banner's hall
   And dingled on the ring.

7. What news, what news, my little foot-page?
   What news are you bringing to me?
   Is any of my fine brick castles blown down,
   Or any of my men false been?

8. There's none of your fine brick castles blown down,
   Nor none of your men false been,
   But little MacGroves in fair Scotland
   In bed with your lady.

Little Musgrave and Lady Barnard

9 O if this be a lie your telling to me,
   As O I take it to be,
   I'll build me a gallows in fair Scotland,
   And hanged you shall be.

10 If this be a lie I'm telling to you,
   As O you take it to be,
   You need not build no gallows at all,
   Just hang me on a tree.

11 In calling all his merry men,
   By one, by two, by threes,
   Saying: Let's all go to fair Scotland
   This young MacGroves to slay.

12 Then one of Lord Banner's foremost men
   Who wished MacGroves no ill,
   He drew his horn and he blew it loud,
   He blew it loud and thrill.

13 What's this I hear, says little MacGroves,
   It blew so loud and clear.
   I think it's Lord Banner's horn.
   O him how do I fear.

14 Lie down, lie down, my sweet MacGroves,
   And keep me from the cold;
   It's nothing but my father's horn
   Calling the sheep to the fold.

15 They lay and slept, they slumbered and slept,
   So sweetly they did sleep;
   But when they woke who did they spy,
   Lord Banner's at their feet.

16 Says: How do you like my own bedside?
   Or how do you like my sheet?
   Or how do you like my gay young wife
   Lies in your arms asleep?

17 Very well I like your own bedside,
   Much better I like your sheet,
   But the best of all's your gay young wife
   Lies in my arms asleep.

18 Rise up, rise up, you young MacGroves,
   Rise up, draw on your clothes.
   It shall never be said in the fair Scotland
   I slain a naked man.

Little Musgrave and Lady Barnard

19 O no, O no, I dare not rise,
   I dare not for my life,
   For you have two big, new, keen swords,
   I have ne'er a knife.

20 O if I have two new, keen swords,
   They cost deep in purse,
   And you can take the best of them
   And I will take the worst.

21 You can strike the very first blow,
   But strike it like a man;
   And I will strike the second blow;
   I'll kill you if I can.

22 The very first lick that MacGroves struck,
   He wounded Lord Banner full sore;
   The second lick Lord Banner struck,
   MacGrove he spoke no more.

23 Rise up, rise up, my gay young wife,
   Rise up, draw on your clothes,
   And tell to me which you like best,
   I or this young MacGroves.

24 If you lay struggling in your blood
   As MacGroves he does now,
   I'd kiss the lips of sweet MacGroves,
   But I never would kiss yours.

K

Pentatonic. Mode 3.

Sung by Mrs. SUDIE SLOAN
at Barbourville, Knox Co., Ky., May 6, 1917

1. One day, one day, one ho-li, whole day, The ve-ry first day in the year, Lord Dan nel's wife went to church that day, She went both ho ly to hear, She went both ho ly to hear.

(Several times, in irregular stanzas.)

Little Musgrave and Lady Barnard

2 The very first man she saw that day
 Was little Matthy Grove.
 Rise up, rise up, little Matthy Grove
 And you go home with me.

3 Hark from the gold that's on your fingers
 And from your golden cage,
 Hark from the milk-white horses you have,
 You are Lord Dannel's new wedding wife.

4 Now if I am Lord Dannel's wife,
 Which you suppose me to be,
 Lord Dannel's gone to the ship
 For to sail upon the sea.

5 This little footy-page was a-standing around,
 And he heard this bargain made.
 He wheeled, he wheeled all around and around,
 Fell to his feet and he run.

6 He run till he came to the broken-down bridge,
 He leaned to his breast and he swum,
 He swum unto the other side,
 And he fell to his feet and he run.

7 He swum unto the other side,
 He rattled that bell and it rung.
 It rung, it rung both south and west,
 And it rung both north and east.

8 What news, what news, my little footy-page?
 What news have you brought to me?
 There is a man in old England town
 In the bed with your new wedded wife.

9 Now if this a lie, my little footy-page,
 Which I expose it to be,
 I have a gallows in old England town;
 A-hanged you shall be.

10 Now if this the truth, my little footy-page,
 Which I expect it to be,
 I have a daughter in old England town,
 Your new wedded wife shall be.

11 He called up his army of men
 And told them for to go,
 No narey word to speak,
 Nor narey horn to blow.

Little Musgrave and Lady Barnard

12 Little Matthy had one friend in the flock,
    He gave his horn a blow.
    Then up spoke little Matthy Grove:
    It's I must arise and go.

13 Lie still, lie still, little Matthy Grove,
    And go to sleep with me,
    It is just my father's shepherd
    A-driving his sheep to fold.

14 Then they fell to hugging and kissing,
    And then they fell to sleep.
    The very next thing little Matthy knowed
    Lord Dannel stood at his feet.

15 Says: How do you like my new feather-bed?
    And how do you like my sheet?
    And how do you like my new wedded wife
    Lies in your arms asleep?

16 Very well I like your new feather-bed,
    Very well I like your sheet,
    Much better I like your new wedded wife
    Lies in my arms asleep.

17 Rise up, rise up, little Matthy Grove,
    And put your clothing on.
    It shan't be said in old England town,
    I slew a naked man.

18 Now I have two mighty sharp swords;
    You may have the sharpest of them all;
    You may have the very first lick
    And I will take the next.

19 The very first lick little Matthy struck,
    He hit a wounded blow;
    The very next lick Lord Dannel hit,
    Little Matthy hit to the floor;
    Little Matthy can't hit no more.

Little Musgrave and Lady Barnard

L

Pentatonic. Mode 3. Sung by Mrs. LEANNA TAYLOR at Clear Creek, Wasioto, Bell Co., Ky., May 1, 1917

One day, one day, one ho-li-day, One ho-li-day in the year, Lit-tle Matth-y Grove he come to church This ho-ly word for to hear, hear, This ho-ly word for to hear.

M

Pentatonic. Mode 3. Sung by Mrs. CIS JONES at Goose Creek, Manchester, Clay Co., Ky., Aug. 24, 1917

I will not go, nor I shall not go, Not for my ve-ry life, For I know by the rings on your left hand That you are Lord Ri-ner's wife.

N

Pentatonic. Mode 3. Sung by Mrs. BERRY CREECH at Pine Mountain, Harlan Co., Ky., Aug. 29, 1917

One day, one day, one high ho-li-day, The high-est day in the year, Lit-tle Matth-y Groves went to the church The ho-ly word to hear, hear, The ho-ly word to hear.

No. 24

Barbara Allen

A

Pentatonic. Mode 3.

Sung by Miss Lula McCoy
at Chicopee Co., Ga., 1914

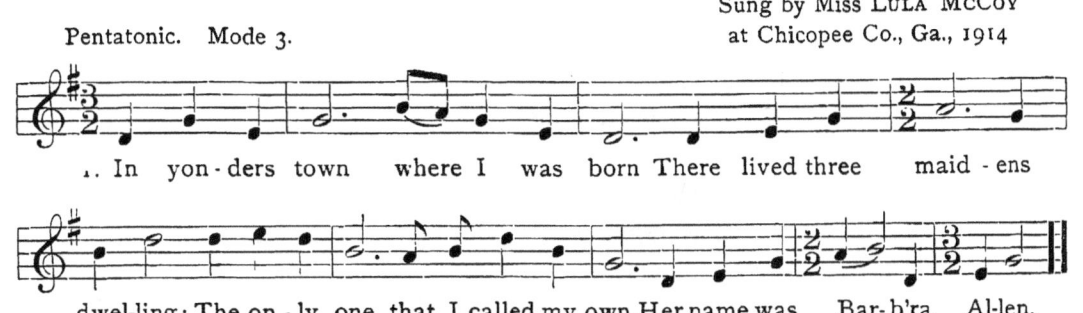

1. In yon-ders town where I was born There lived three maid-ens dwel-ling; The on-ly one that I called my own, Her name was Bar-b'ra Al-len.

    2 I was taken sick, so very sick,
      Death on my brows were dwelling.
      I sent for the only one I loved,
      Her name was Barbara Allen.

    3 I am sick, so very sick,
      Death on my brows are dwelling,
      And none of the better will I ever be
      Till I get Barbara Allen.

    4 You remember the day, the bright groom day,
      When you passed your dranks so willing?
      You gave your dranks to the ladies all,
      But you slighted Barbara Allen.

    5 I remember the day, the bright groom day,
      When I passed my dranks so willing.
      I gave my dranks to the ladies all,
      And my love to Barbara Allen.

    6 He turned his pale face to the wall
      And bursted out to crying.
      She turned her back on Sweet Willie's bed
      And tipped downstairs a-smiling.

    7 I had not got but a mile from the place
      Till I heard his death-bells ringing,
      And as they rung they seemed to say:
      Hard-hearted Barbara Allen.

    8 I looked to the East, I looked to the West,
      I saw his coffin coming.
      Lay down, lay down his cold, clay corpse
      And let me gaze upon him.

Barbara Allen

9 I went right home to my mother dear,
   Says: Make my death bed long and narrow.
   Sweet Willie has died for me to-day,
   I'll die for him tomorrow.

10 Sweet Willie he died like as to-day,
   And Barbara as tomorrow;
   Sweet Willie died with the purest love,
   And Barbara died with sorrow.

11 Sweet Willie was buried in one churchyard,
   And Barbara in another.
   A rose bud sprang from Willie's grave,
   And a briar from Barbara Allen's.

12 They grew and they grew to the tall church door;
   They could not grow any higher.
   They linked and tied in a true love's knot
   And the rose wrapped around the briar.

B

Pentatonic. Mode 3.

Sung by Miss FLORENCE MacKINNEY
at Habersham Co., Ga., May 28, 1910

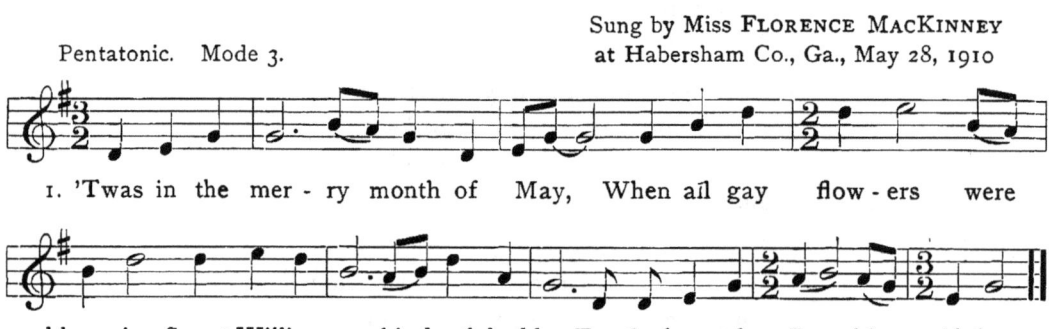

1. 'Twas in the mer-ry month of May, When all gay flow-ers were bloom-ing, Sweet William on his death-bed lay, For the love of Bar-b'ra Al-len.

2 He sent his servant to the town,
  He sent him to her dwelling,
  Saying: Master's sick and very sick,
  And for your sake he's dying.

3 Slowly, slowly, she gets up,
  And to his bedside going,
  She drew the curtains to one side
  And says: Young man, you're dying.

4 He reached out his pale, white hands
  Intending for to touch her.
  She jumped, she skipped all over the room,
  And says: Young man, I won't have you.

Barbara Allen

5 He turned his pale face to the wall
  And bursted out a-crying,
  Saying: Adieu to thee, adieu to all,
  Adieu to Barbara Allen.

6 She had not more than reached the town,
  She heard the death bells tolling.
  She looked to the east, she looked to the west,
  And saw his pale face coming.

7 Hand down, hand down that corpse of clay
  And let me gaze upon him.
  The more she gazed, the more she grieved,
  And she bursted out a-crying.

8 Cursed, cursed, be my name,
  And cursed be my nature,
  For this man's life I might have saved
  If I had done my duty.

9 O mother, O mother, go make my bed,
  And make it long and narrow.
  Sweet William died for me to-day,
  And I'll die for him tomorrow.

10 Sweet William died on Saturday night,
   Miss Barbara died on Sunday,
   The old lady died for the love of both,
   She died on Easter Monday.

11 Sweet William was carried to one churchyard,
   Miss Barbara to another.
   A briar grew out of one of their graves,
   A rose tree out of the other.

12 They grew as high as the old church top,
   They could not grow any higher.
   They bound and tied in a true love's knot,
   For all true lovers to admire.

C

Hexatonic. Mode 3, b.

Sung by Miss ROXIE GAY
at Chicopee Co., Ga., Feb. 1914

1. One cold and cloud-y day in the month of May, When the ros-es was a bud-ding, A young man lay on his death-bed In love with Bar-b'ra El-len.

Barbara Allen

2 He sent his servants after her
  And for his sake he sent them:
  My master's sick and about to die
  And for your sake he's dying.

3 Slowly, slowly, she got up,
  And went away unto him,
  Saying: Kind Sir,
  You are pale looking.

4 O yes, my love, I'm mighty sick,
  A kiss or two
  From your sweet lips
  Would save me from this dying.

5 He turned his pale cheeks toward the wall;
  She turned her back upon him,
  Saying: Kind sir, you're none the better of me,
  If your heart's blood was a-spilling.

6 Slowly, slowly she gets up
  And goes away and leaves him.
  She hadn't rode but a mile in town,
  She heard his death bells ringing.

7 They rung so clear unto her ear
  That she commence lamenting.
  She looked to the East and she looked to the West,
  She saw his cold corpse coming.

8 Go bring him here as cold as clay
  And let me look upon him.

9 Go and tell to my parents most dear,
  Who would not let me have him.
  Go and tell to the rest of my kin folk,
  Who caused me to forsake him.

10 Sweet Willie was buried on Saturday night,
   Barbara was buried on Sunday.
   Both of the mothers died for them,
   Was buried on Easter Monday.

11 Sweet Willie was buried in the new churchyard,
   Barbara was buried close beside him.
   A red rose grew from sweet Willie's breast,
   A briar grew from her feet.

Barbara Allen

12 They grew as high as the new church house,
   They could not grow any higher;
   They grew and tied in a true love knot,
   A rose grew on the briar.

D

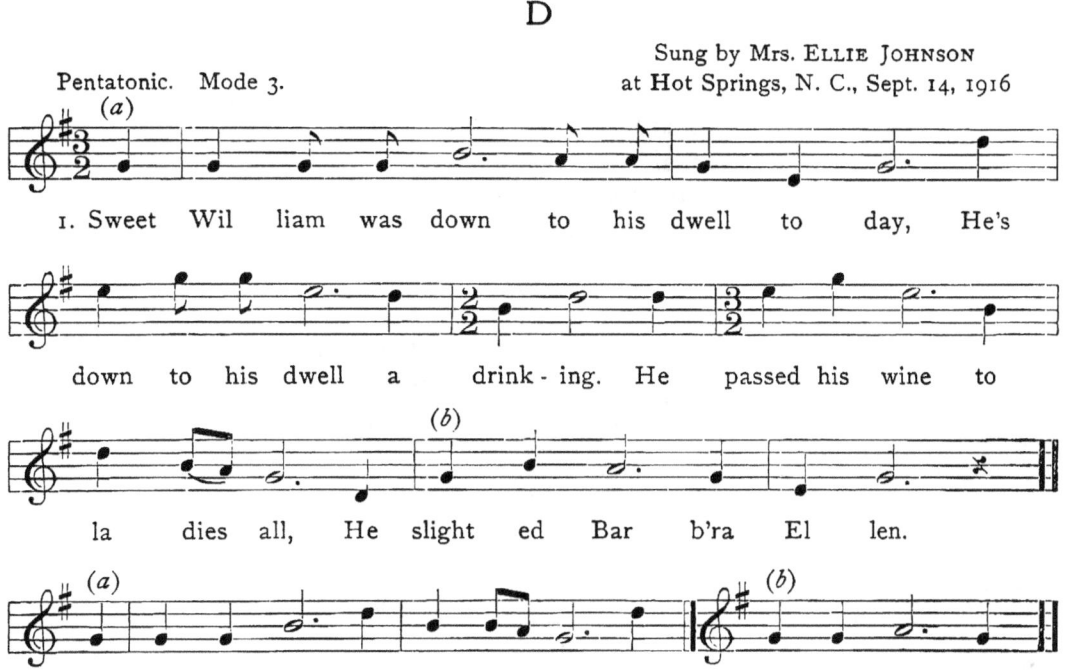

Pentatonic. Mode 3.

Sung by Mrs. ELLIE JOHNSON at Hot Springs, N. C., Sept. 14, 1916

1. Sweet William was down to his dwell to day, He's down to his dwell a drink-ing. He passed his wine to la dies all, He slight ed Bar b'ra El len.

2 There stands three young ladies so fair,
   They're dressed in every colour.
   There's not but one that I call my own
   And that is Barbara Ellen.

3 It wasn't very long before William taken sick,
   Death was all he dreaded.
   Sent his love for Barbara to come,
   She come, she come a-running.

4 And all she said when she got there:
   Young man, I think you're dying.
   O yes, I'm sick, I'm very sick
   And never be no better.

5 It wasn't very long till Barbara started home.
   She heard the corpse bells ringing.
   She looked East, she looked West
   And saw the pale corpse coming.

Barbara Allen

6 Unfold, unfold those lily-white sheets
 And let me look upon him.
 Sweet William died for me to-day,
 I'll die for him tomorrow.

7 Sweet William died on Saturday night,
 And Barbara on Sunday.
 The old woman died for the love of both,
 She died on Easter Monday.

8 On William's grave a turtle dove,
 On Barbara's grave a sparrow.
 The turtle dove is the sign of love,
 The sparrow was for sorrow.

E

Sung by Mr. ALFRED H. NORTON
at Rocky Fork, Tenn., Sept. 2, 1916

Hexatonic. Mode 4, b.

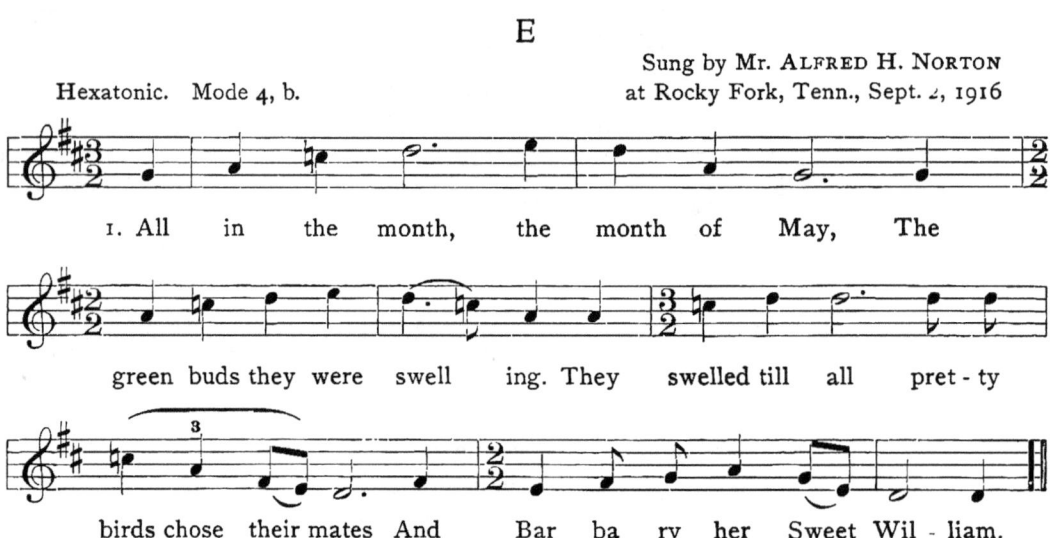

1. All in the month, the month of May, The green buds they were swell-ing. They swelled till all pret-ty birds chose their mates And Bar-ba-ry her Sweet Wil-liam.

2 He sent a letter through the town
 To Barbary Allen's dwelling,
 Saying: Here's a young man sick and he sends for you,
 For you to come and see him.

3 She walked in, she walked in,
 She placed her eyes upon him.
 The very first word that she said to him:
 Young man, I think you're dying.

4 I know I'm sick and very sick,
 And sorrow it is dwelling with me.
 No better, no better I never will be
 Until I get Barbary Allen.

Barbara Allen

5 I know you're sick and very sick,
And sorrow it is dwelling with you.
No better, no better you never will be,
For you'll never get Barbary Allen.

6 He turned his pale face to the wall,
He burst out a-crying,
Saying: Adieu, adieu to the ladies all around,
Farewell to Barbary Allen.

7 Don't you remember last Saturday night
When I were at your tavern,
You swang you treated the ladies all around,
You slighted Barbary Allen.

8 She rode, she rode a mile from town
The small birds they were singing,
They sung so loud, they sung so swift,
Hard-hearted Barbary Allen.

9 She looked East, she looked West,
She saw the cold corpse coming,
Saying: Lay him down on this cold ground
And let me look upon him.

10 The more she looked the more she mourned
Till she burst out a-crying,
Saying: I could have saved this young man's life
If I'd a-tried my true endeavour.

11 O mother, O mother, O fix my bed,
Go fix it long and narrow.
Sweet William he died for me to-day,
And I'll die for him tomorrow.

12 O father, O father, go dig my grave,
Go dig it deep and narrow.
Sweet William he died for me to-day,
And I'll die for him tomorrow.

13 They buried Sweet William in the old churchyard
And Barbary close by the side of him.
At the head of Sweet William's grave there sprung a red rose
And Barbary Allen's was a briar.

14 They grew, they grew to the top of the church
And they could not grow any higher.
They leaned and tied in a true lover's knot
And the rose hanged on to the briar.

Barbara Allen

F

Pentatonic. Mode 4.

Sung by Miss ADA B. SMITH
at Knott Co., Ky., Dec. 16, 1907

1. 'Twas in the merry month of May, The green buds were swel-ling, Poor

Wil-liam Green on his death-bed lay For the love of Bar-b'ra El-len.

2 He sent his servant to the town
  To the place where she was dwelling,
  Saying: Love, there is a call for you,
  If your name is Barbara Ellen.

3 She was very slowly getting up
  And very slowly going,
  And all she said when there she come:
  Young man, I believe you're dying.

4 O yes, I know I'm very bad,
  And never will be any better
  Until I have the love of one,
  The love of Barbara Ellen.

5 He turned his pale face toward the wall,
  And death was in him dwelling.
  Adieu, adieu, adieu to my dear friends.
  Be kind to Barbara Ellen.

6 When she got in about two miles of town,
  She heard the death bells ringing.
  She says: Come around, you nice young men,
  And let me look upon you.

7 O mother, O mother, come make my bed,
  Come make it both soft and narrow
  For Sweet William died to-day,
  And I will die tomorrow.

8 O father, O father, come dig my grave,
  Come dig it both deep and narrow,
  For sweet William died in love,
  And I will die in sorrow.

Barbara Allen

9 Sweet William was buried in the old church tomb,
  Barbara Ellen was buried in the yard.
  Out of sweet William's grave grew a green, red rose,
  Out of Barbara Ellen's a briar.

10 They grew and grew to the old church top
   And still they couldn't grow any higher,
   And at the end tied a true love-knot,
   The rose wrapped around the briar.

G

Pentatonic. Mode 4.

Sung by Miss EMMA HENSLEY
at Carmen, N. C., Aug. 8, 1916

1. All in the mer-ry month of May, When green buds they were swel-ling, Young Jem-my Grove on his death-bed lay For love of Bar-b'ra El len.

H

Hexatonic. Mode 4, b.

Sung by Mr. N. B. CHISHOLM
at Woodridge, Va., Sept. 21, 1916

I

Pentatonic. Mode 3.

Sung by Miss WONNIE SHELTON
at Carmen, N. C., Aug. 11, 1916

Barbara Allen

* The last phrase repeated in stanzas 9 and 10 only.

2 He courted her for seven long years,
  She said she would not have him.
  Pretty William went home and took down sick
  And sent for Barbara Ellen.

3 He wrote her a letter on his death-bed;
  He wrote it slow and moving.
  Go take this to my pretty little love,
  And tell her I am dying.

4 They took it to his pretty little love;
  She read it slow and mourning.
  Go take this to my pretty little love,
  And tell him I am coming.

Barbara Allen

5 As she walked on to his bed-side,
  Says: Young man, young man, you're dying.
  He turned his pale face toward the wall
  And bursted out a-crying.

6 He reached his lily-white hand to her.
  O come and tell me 'howdey'
  O no, O no, O no, says she,
  And she would not go about him.

7 Do you remember last Saturday night
  Down at my father's dwelling?
  You passed the drink to the ladies all around
  And slighted Barbara Ellen.

8 Yes, I remember last Saturday night
  Down at your father's dwelling,
  I passed the drink to the ladies all around,
  My heart to Barbara Ellen.

9 As she walked down those long stair-steps,
  She heard some death-bells ringing,
  And every bell it seemed to say:
  Hard-hearted Barbara Ellen,
  Hard-hearted Barbara Ellen.

10 As she walked down that shady grove,
   She heard some birds a-singing,
   And every bird it seemed to say:
   Hard-hearted Barbara Ellen,
   Hard-hearted Barbara Ellen.

11 As she walked out the very next day,
   She saw his corpse a-coming.
   O lay him down, O lay him down,
   And let me look upon him.

12 The more she looked the worse she felt,
   Till she bursted out a-crying:
   I once could have saved pretty William's life,
   But I would not go about him.

13 O mother, O mother, go make my bed,
   Go make it soft and narrow;
   Pretty William has died for pure, pure love,
   And I shall die for sorrow.

14 O father, O father, go dig my grave,
   Go dig it deep and narrow;
   Pretty William has died for me to-day,
   And I shall die to-morrow.

Barbara Allen

15 A rose grew up from William's grave,
   From Barbara Ellen's a brier.
   They grew and they grew to the top of the church-house
   Till they could not grow any higher.

16 They grew and they grew to the top of the church-house
   Till they could not grow any higher,
   And there they tied in a true love's knot,
   And the rose wrapped round the brier.

L

Sung by MRS. ALICE SLOAN
at Barbourville, Knox Co., Ky., May 6, 1917

Hexatonic (no 6th).

All in, all in the month of May, When the flow-ers they were bloom-ing, When this young man was a ta-ken sick For the love of Bar b'ra El-len.

M

Sung by MR. BIN. HENSON
at Barbourville, Knox Co., Ky., May 9, 1917

Pentatonic. Mode 2.

One day, one day, in the month of May, When the red-buds they were swell-in' I fell in love with a ret-ty, lit-tle girl; And her name be Ma ry El-len.

Barbara Allen

No. 25

Giles Collins
A

Mode 3, b (no 6th).

Sung by Mrs. Dora Shelton
at Allanstand, N. C., Aug. 2, 1916

1. George Collins come home last Friday night, And there he take sick and died; And when Mrs. Collins heard George was dead, She wrung her hands and cried.

2 Mary in the hallway, sewing her silk,
   She's sewing her silk so fine,
   And when she heard that George were dead,
   She threw her sewing aside.

3 She followed him up, she followed him down,
   She followed him to his grave,
   And there all on her bended knee
   She wept, she mourned, she prayed.

4 Hush up, dear daughter, don't take it so hard,
   There's more pretty boys than George.
   There's more pretty boys all standing around,
   But none so dear as George.

5 Look away, look away, that lonesome dove
   That sails from pine to pine;
   It's mourning for its own true love
   Just like I mourn for mine.

6 Set down the coffin, lift up the lid,
   And give me a comb so fine,
   And let me comb his cold, wavy hair,
   For I know he'll never comb mine.

7 Set down the coffin, lift up the lid,
   Lay back the sheetings so fine,
   And let me kiss his cold, sweet lips,
   For I know he'll never kiss mine.

Giles Collins

B

Mode 3, a + b (no 6th).

Sung by Mrs. HESTER HOUSE
at Hot Springs, N. C., Sept. 16, 1916

1. George Collins came home last Friday night And then took sick and died. His girl sat in the next door side A sewing her silk so fine.

2 And when she heard George Collins was dead
   She laid her silk aside,
   And fell down on her trembling knee
   And wept and mourned and cried.

3 O Mary, O Mary, what makes you weep,
   What makes you weep and mourn,
   What makes you weep when you ought to be asleep?
   O Lord, I've lost a friend.

4 God bless the dove that mourns for love
   And flies from pine to pine.
   It mourns for the loss of its own true love.
   O why not me for mine?

5 I followed George Collins by day, by day,
   I followed him to his grave.
   Lay off, lay off those coffin lids
   And spread the sheets so fine.

6 Lay off, lay off, those coffin lids
   And spread the sheets so fine,
   And let me kiss his cold, clay lips.
   O Lord, he'll never kiss mine.

C

Mode 3, b (no 6th).

Sung by Miss MARY McKINNEY
at Henderson Co., N. C., 1914

1. George Collins came home last Wednesday night And there took sick and died; And when Mrs. Collins

Giles Collins

heard George was dead, She bowed her head and died.

2 His own little bride was in the hall,
   Sewing her silk so fine,
   And she heard that George was dead,
   She threw it all aside.

3 She followed him up, she followed him down,
   She followed him to his grave,
   And there upon her bended knees,
   She wept, she mourned, she prayed.

4 O daughter, O daughter, the mother then said,
   There is more young men than George;
   There is more young men standing round
   To hear you weep and mourn.

5 O mother, O mother, the daughter then said,
   There is more young men than George;
   There is more young men standing round,
   But none so dear as he.

6 Sit down the casket, take off the lid,
   Fold back the sheets so fine,
   And let me kiss his cold, sweet lips,
   I'm sure he'll never kiss mine.

7 Look away over yonder at the lonesome dove,
   It flies from pine to pine,
   Mourning for its own true love.
   Why shouldn't I mourn for mine?

D

Sung by Mr. Dana Norton
at Flag Pond, Tenn., Aug. 31, 1916

Hexatonic. Mode 3, a.

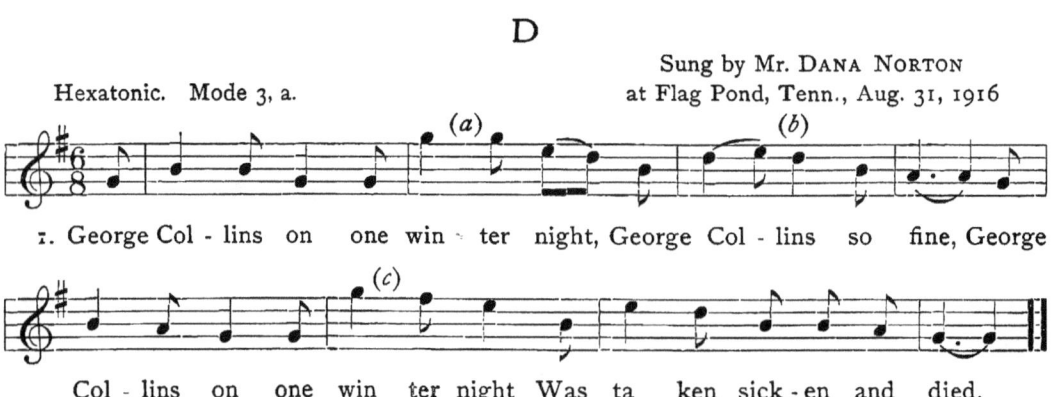

1. George Collins on one winter night, George Collins so fine, George Collins on one winter night Was taken sick-en and died.

Giles Collins

E

Hexatonic. Mode 3, b.

Sung by Miss Viney Norton
at Big Laurel, N. C., Aug. 16, 1916

1. Go hand me down my look-ing glass, Go hand me down my comb, And

let me comb lit-tle George's hair For I know he'll nev-er comb mine.

F

Heptatonic. Mixolydian.

Sung by Mrs. Anna Bailey
at Mine Fork, Burnsville, N. C., Sept. 19, 1918

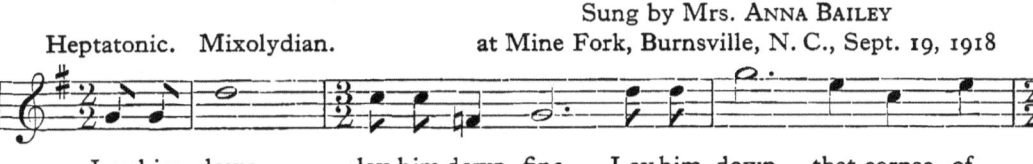

1. Lay him down, lay him down fine, Lay him down, that corpse of

mine. Let me kiss Charles Col-lin's lips, I'm

sure that he'll nev er kiss mine.

2 To-day read over Charles Collin's corpse,
To-morrow read over mine.

3 Haul me over to fair London town
All in fair Ellender's bown.

No. 26

The Lowlands of Holland

Sung by Mr. Philander FitzGerald
at Nash, Va., May 9, 1918

2 O Holland is a pretty place
   All strewed with the lasses round.

3 No candlelight nor fire bright
   Shall in my chamber be
   Since the lowlands of Holland
   Has parted my love and me.

Lamkin

A

Sung by Mrs. Jane Gentry
at Hot Springs, N. C., Sept. 12, 1916

Pentatonic. Mode 3 (Tonic A).

1. Bold Dunkins was as fine a mason As ever was under the sun, And he built a fine castle And pay he got none.

2 But bold Dunkins crept in
   By the way of the back door,
   And persuaded the nurse
   To help him get her down.

3 We'll pick her baby Johnny
   With the silver spade.
   And the blood from the head
   To the foot-board did run.

4 Bewore, ye fair lady,
   You must come to your dearest one.
   How can I get to him
   At this time of night
   When there's no fire burning,
   Nor no candle alight?

5 You've got five golden mantles
   As bright as the sun.
   Bewore, ye fair lady,
   You must come by the light of one.

6 She was a-coming downstairs
   A-thinking no harm,
   When bold Dunkins was ready
   To take her in his arms.

Lamkin

7 O spare my life, Dunkins,
Just one half of an hour,
And you may have as much gold and silver
As endel in the streets.

B

Sung by Mrs. Cis Jones at Goose Creek,
Manchester, Clay Co., Ky., Aug. 16, 1917

2 What cares I for the Lamkin,
Or any other man,
When my doors are fast bolted,
My windows pinned down?

3 The Lamkin he came
By bed-time at night.
He knocked at the door,
And the false nurse let him in.

4 He says: Where is that noble lady?
I want to see her.
She's in her chambery
In the gallerays so high.

5 He says to the false nurse:
How can we get her down?
Pierce the little baby's heart
And the screams will bring her down.

6 She says: Nursie,
Don't let little baby cry.
Go feed it on breast-milk,
Go feed it on pie.

7 I fed it on breast-milk,
I fed it on pie.
Go put on one of those gowns
And light yourself down.

Lamkin

8 How can I go below stairs
   By bed-time at night,
   No fires a-burning,
   No candle alight?

9 You've three as nice gowns
   As ever the sun shined on.
   Go put on one of those
   And light yourself down.

10 As she was a-walking
   In the gallerays so high,
   The Lamkin he caught her
   Right fast in his arms.

11 O spare me my life, sir,
   While's ten o'clock in the night;
   You may have as many guineas
   As there's sand in the sea.

12 I don't want none of your guineas
   As there's sand in the sea,
   To hinder my new sword
   From your lily-white neck.

13 O spare me my life, sir,
   While's eleven o'clock in the night;
   I'll give you my daughter Betsy
   And a hundred fine things.

14 I don't want your daughter Betsy
   And a hundred fine things
   To hinder my new sword
   From your lily-white neck.

15 She sent her daughter Betsy
   In the gallerays so high
   To get a silver basin
   To catch her heart's blood.

16 As she were a-walking
   In the gallerays so high,
   She saw her noble father
   Come riding close by.

17 She says: O father,
   O father, you see,
   The false nurse and the Lamkin
   Has killed your lady.

Lamkin

18 If this be true you tell to me,
    If this be true you see,
    The false nurse shall be hung
    In the gallerays so high,
    And the Lamkin shall be burn-ed
    In the furnace close by.

C

Sung by Mrs. FRANCIS CARTER
at Beattyville, Lee Co., Ky., Sept. 8, 1917

Pentatonic. Mode 3 (Tonic B♭).

1. Old Lam-kin was as good a ma son As e ver laid a stone. He built the fin est cas tle, And pay ment he had none.

2 Then at such an hour
   The king rode from home,
   Saying: Beware of old Lamkin,
   He'll be here at noon.

3 What cares I for Lamkin,
   Or any other man?
   My doors are all locked
   And my windows pinned down.

4 At twelve o'clock at night
   Old Lamkin come,
   And no one so ready
   As the false nurse to let him in.

5 How could we get her downstairs
   On such a dark night?
   Why, we'll stick her little baby
   Full of needles and pins.

6 What a pity, what a pity,
   Cried old Lamkin.
   No pity, no pity,
   Cried the false nurse to him.

Lamkin

7 Pretty Betsy coming downstairs
   Not thinking any harm,
   And there stood old Lamkin
   To catch her in his arms.

8 O spare my life, Lamkin,
   O spare it, I pray.
   You shall have as much gay gold
   As my horse can carry away.

9 What cares I for your gay gold,
   Or any other thing?
   I have got my desire,
   That's all I do crave.

10 O spare my life, Lamkin,
    O spare it, I pray.
    You shall have my daughter Betsy,
    My own blooming flower.

11 Keep your daughter Betsy
    To wade through the blood
    And scour the silver basin
    That catched your own heart's blood.

D

Pentatonic. Mode 3.

Sung by Mrs. MOLLIE BROGHTON
at Barbourville, Knox Co., Ky., May 8, 1917

1. Where is the land-lord? O is he at home? He's gone to Cal i for nia To vi sit his son.

2 Where is the landlady?
   Is she at home?
   She's up in her chamber
   A-sleeping above.

Lamkin

3 How can we get her down here
 This lonesome long night?
 We'll stick her little baby
 With needles and pins.

4 Go feed it on breast-milk,
 Go feed it on pie (*sometimes* pap),
 Go rock it in the cradle
 And then it won't cry.

5 I fed it on breast-milk,
 I fed it on pie,
 I've rocked it in the cradle,
 And yet it will cry.

6 She come running downstairs,
 Not thinking any harm,
 And just as she run downstairs,
 He grabbed her in his arms.

7 Bold Lantern, bold Lantern,
 Spare my life one hour;
 You shall have my daughter Betsy,
 The branch of all flowers.

8 O keep your daughter Betsy
 And send her to Ford,
 For to carry the silver basin
 That catched your heart's blood.

9 Bold Lantern, bold Lantern,
 Spare my sweet life;
 You shall have all the gold
 Your horse shall carry down.

10 O keep your gold
 And send it to Ford,
 To carry your heart's blood;
 It shall overflow.

Lamkin

E

Pentatonic. Mode 3.

Sung by Mrs. Doc. Pratt
at Hindman, Knott Co., Ky., Sept. 22, 1917

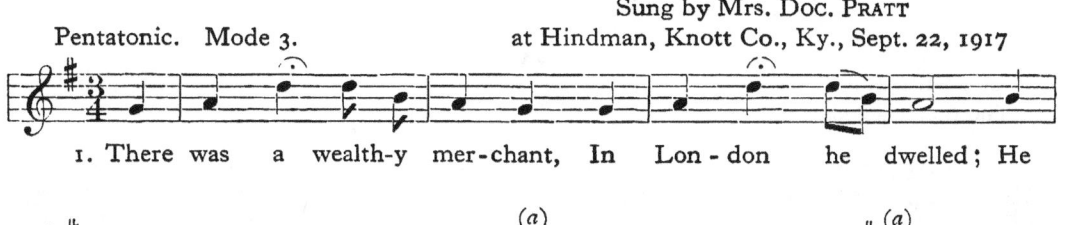
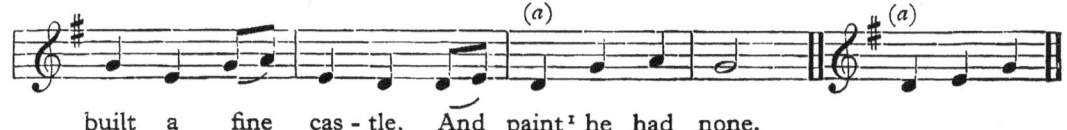

1. There was a wealthy merchant, In London he dwelled; He built a fine castle, And paint[1] he had none.

2 He started to England
To buy his wife a ring.
He called back to her:
Bewore of the Lamkins;
He'll be here at noon.

3 What cares I for the Lamkins?
What cares I? said she.
My doors are all locked
And my windows pinned in.

4 Says the Lamkins to the captain (*or* false nurse):
What'll bring her downstairs?
We'll stick her little infant
Full of needles and pins.

5 What a pity, what a pity,
What a pity it would be
To stick her little infant
Full of needles and pins.

6 O spare my life, Lamkins,
O spare my life, do.
Just listen how pitiful
My little infant does cry.

7 I'll give you my daughter Betsy
And all of the gold
That your horse can carry away.

8 You'd better keep your daughter Betsy
To wade the blood,
And to scour the silver basin
To catch your heart's blood.

9 Last night I killed the king's wife,
To-night I'll kill you.
They won't take time to make a gallows,
They'll hang you on a tree.

[1] Payment?

No. 28

The Maid Freed from the Gallows
A

Mode 1, a + b
(no 6th, mixolydian influence).

Sung by Mr. T. Jeff Stockton
at Flag Pond, Tenn., Sept. 4, 1916

1. Hold up your hands and Josh-u-a, he cries, And wait a lit-tle while and

see. I think I hear my fa ther dear Come lum-ber-ing here for to see.

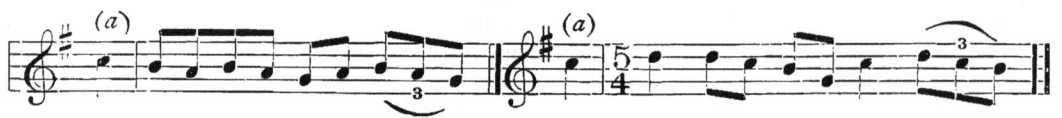

   2 O father, O father, have you got any gold for me?
      Or silver to pay my fee?
      They say I've stoled a silver cup
      And hanged I must be.

   3 No, daughter, I have got no gold for thee,
      Nor silver to pay your fee;
      But I've come here to see you hang
      On yon high gallows tree.

In subsequent verses, " mother," " brother," " sister," and finally " true love " are substituted for " father."
The last verse runs thus:—

      Yes, true love, I have gold for you
      And silver to pay your fee.
      I've come here to win your neck
      From yon high gallows tree.

B

Heptatonic. Mode 1, a + b
(mixolydian influence).

Sung by Mrs. Sarah Buckner
at Black Mountain, N. C., Sept. 19, 1916

1. Hold up your hand, O Josh u ay, she cried, Wait a

The Maid Freed from the Gallows

2 O father, have you any gold for me?
  Any silver to pay my fee?
  For I have stoled a golden cup
  And hanging it will be.

3 No, daughter, no, I have no gold for thee
  Nor silver to pay your fee;
  For I have come for to see you hang
  All on that willow tree.

Yes, true love, I have some gold for you
And silver to pay your fee,
For I have come for to pay your fee
And take you home with me.

C

2 Father, father, have you gold,
  The gold to set me free,
  Or have you come to see me hung
  Beneath the willow tree?

The Maid Freed from the Gallows

3 Daughter, daughter, I have no gold,
  Gold to set you free,
  But I have come to see you hung
  Beneath the willow tree.

True love, true love, I have the gold,
Gold to set you free,
And I shan't come to see you hung
Beneath the willow tree.

D

Pentatonic. Mode 3.

Sung by Mr. N. B. CHISHOLM and Mrs. BETTY SMITH at Woodridge, Va., Sept. 27, 1916

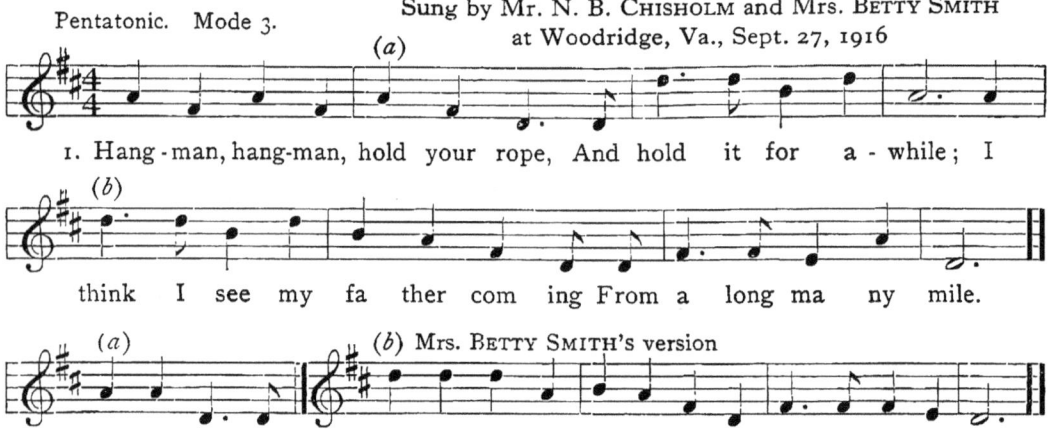

1. Hang-man, hang-man, hold your rope, And hold it for a-while; I think I see my father coming From a long many mile.

(b) Mrs. BETTY SMITH's version

2 Father, father, have you any gold?
  Gold for to set me free?
  Or have you come to see me hung
  Beneath the gallows tree?

3 Son, O son, I have no gold,
  Gold to set you free;
  I've only come to see you hung
  Beneath the gallows tree.

Sweetheart, sweetheart, I have gold,
Gold to set you free,
And I have not come to see you hung
Beneath the gallows tree.

The Maid Freed from the Gallows

E

(No 6th or 7th.) Sung by Mrs. Mary Anne Short
at Pine Mountain, Harlan Co., Ky., Aug. 29, 1917

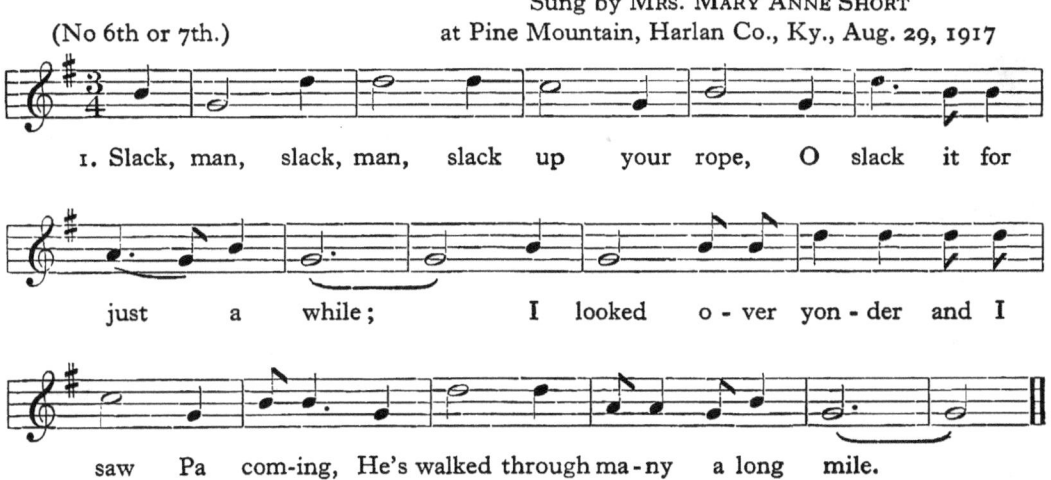

1. Slack, man, slack, man, slack up your rope, O slack it for just a while; I looked o-ver yon-der and I saw Pa com-ing, He's walked through ma-ny a long mile.

2 Say, Pa, say, Pa, have you brought me any gold,
   Any gold to pay on my fine?
   Or have you come over for to see me hung,
   Hung on the gallows line?

3 No, sir, no, sir, I've brought you no gold,
   No gold to pay on your fine,
   But I've come over for to see you hung,
   Hung on the gallows line.

4 It's you won't love, it's hard to love,
   It's hard to make up your mind.
   You've broke the heart of a many poor girl,
   True love, but you can't break mine.

In subsequent verses, 'mother', 'brother', etc., and finally 'true love' are substituted for 'father' The penultimate verse runs thus:—

Yes, sir, yes, sir, I've brought you some gold,
Some gold to pay on your fine,
And I have come for to take you home
Down off the gallows line.

The Maid Freed from the Gallows

2 O mother, have you brought me money?
  Have you come to pay my fee?
  But have you come for to see me hanging
  On this old gallows-tree?

3 I've neither come for to bring you money,
  Nor neither for to pay your fee,
  But I have come to see you hanging
  On this old gallows-tree.

Last verse (after the true-love has appeared).
  I have come for to bring you money,
  And money for to pay your fee,
  And to keep you now from hanging
  On this old gallows-tree.

The Maid Freed from the Gallows

The Maid Freed from the Gallows

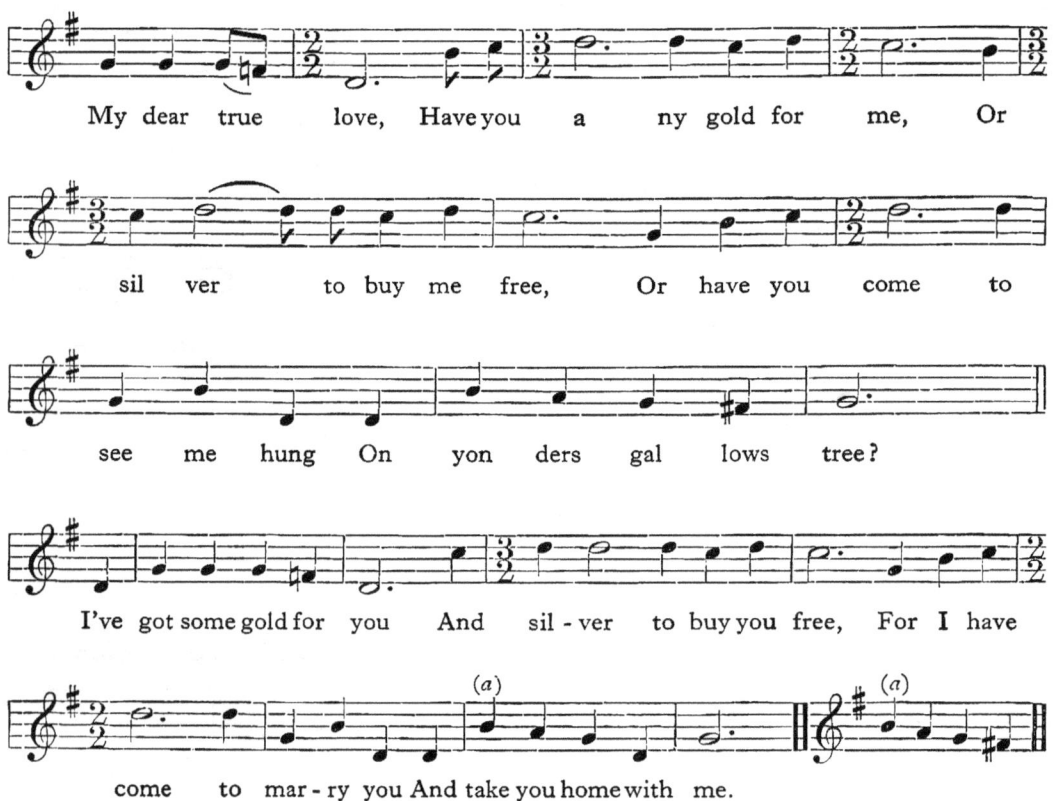

K

Hexatonic (no 6th).

Sung by Mrs. Molly E. Bowyer
at Villamont, Va., June 10, 1918

No. 29

Johnie Scot

A

Pentatonic. Mode 3.

Sung by Mrs. JANE GENTRY
at Hot Springs, N. C., Aug. 25, 1916

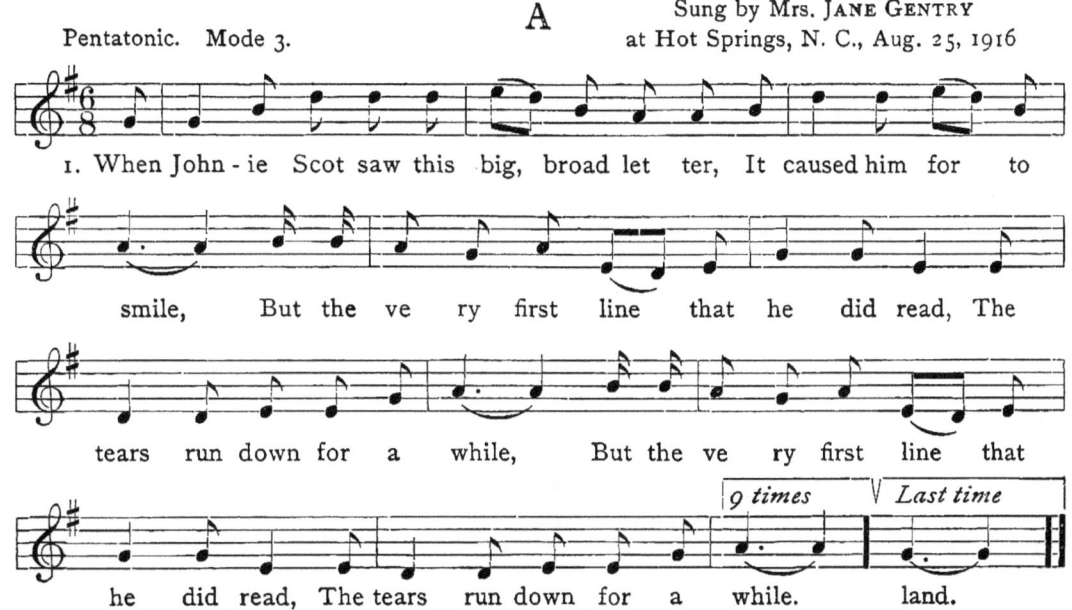

1. When Johnie Scot saw this big, broad letter, It caused him for to smile, But the very first line that he did read, The tears run down for a while, But the very first line that he did read, The tears run down for a while. *(9 times)* land. *(Last time)*

2 Away to old England I must go,
   King Edwards has sent for me.
   Up spoke young Jimmy Scot himself
   As he sat by his knees :
   Five hundred of my best brave men
   Shall bear you company.

3 The very first town that they rode through,
   The drums, the fifes, they played;
   The very next town that they rode through,
   The drums they beat all around.

4 They rode, they rode to King Edwards's gate,
   They dingled at the ring;
   But who did he spy but his own sweetheart
   And her footspade (footpage) a-peeping down.

5 I can't come down, dear Johnny, she says,
   For Poppy has scolded me.
   I'm forced to wear a ball and chain
   Instead of the ivory.

6 Is this young Jimmy Scot himself,
   Or Jimmy Scotland's king?
   Or is the father of that bastard child
   From Scotland just come in?

Johnie Scot

7 I'm not young Jimmy Scot,
   Nor Jimmy Scotland's king;
   But I am young Johnie Scot himself
   From Scotland just come in.

8 There is a taveren in our town
   That's killed more lords than one,
   And before the sun rises tomorrow morning
   A dead man you shall be.

9 The taveren flew over young Johnie's head
   As swift as any bird;
   He pierced the taveren to the heart
   With the point of his broad sword.

10 He whipped King Edwards and all his men,
   And the king he liked to have swung.
   I'll make your girl my gay lady
   And her child the heir of my land.

B

Sung by Mrs. NANCY ALICE HENSLEY
at Oneida, Clay Co., Ky., Aug. 17, 1917

Pentatonic. Mode 2.

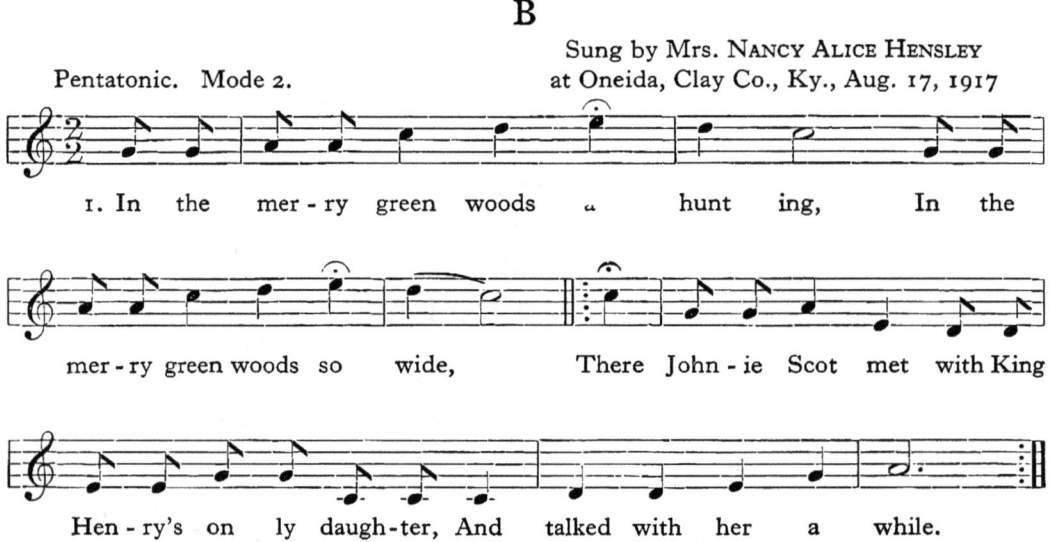

1. In the merry green woods a hunting, In the merry green woods so wide, There Johnie Scot met with King Henry's only daughter, And talked with her a while.

2 The news unto old Ingram's (house),
   Old Ingram being gone;
   The news unto the kitchen house;
   O that's the worst of all.

3 She wrote young Johnie a letter
   That seemed to make him smile;
   Before he read it one half way through,
   He wept like any child.

Johnie Scot

4 I'll go fight for that lady fair
  That lay last by my side.
  Up spoke his old father who was sitting in his chair,
  Saying: If you do to old King Henry go,
  You'll never come back here.

5 Up spoke his oldest brother,
  An angry man was he:
  Here's me and five hundred of my life-guards
  Will bear your company.

6 They all mounted horse-back,
  And as they went on the road,
  The hair hung down young Johnie's back,
  Looked like the links of gold.

7 They rode on to Solver Town,
  They rode it all around.
  No one could see but his own true love
  In a windows looking round.

8 Come down, come down, my own true love,
  Come low-lie unto me;
  Where I will swear before I go,
  I'll ride in your company.

9 I can't come down, I can't come down,
  I can't come unto you.
  My stockings once they was of silk,
  My shoe-buckles of gold;
  But now my feet's in some hard iron band.
  O lor! my feet they're cold.

10 They went a-fighting at two o'clock in the morning,
   They fit till two past noon,
   A-sweating blood lap in the ground
   Like dew upon the grass.
   He killed old King Henry and all his life-guards
   And got his love at last.

Johnie Scot
C

(No 2nd or 6th).

Sung by Mrs. Margaret Dunagan
at St. Helen's, Lee Co., Ky., Sept. 6, 1917

1. Young Johnie, young Johnie, in the green woods,
A hunting so wise, He came across King
Henry's fair daughter, And got in her a child.

2 King Henry he wrote for Johnie to come
And sealed it with a ring.
When he got there King Henry was gone,
And that was worse than all.

3 Thus said his brother James,
An English man were he:
Me and five hundred of my life-guards
Will bear you company.

4 They all mounted horse-back.
That was a sight to be seen.
The hair it hung down young Johnie's back,
It looked like the links of gold.

5 As they rode up, as they rode down,
As they rode over through Lillus Town,
Nothing did he spy but his own true love
Was a-looking from the window down.

6 Come down, come down, my own true love,
Come down, come down and talk with me.
I can't come down, for I am dyings bound (in irons bound?),
And the keys they're turned on me.

7 My stockings used to be of silk.
My shoe-buckles of gold;
But now I am dyings bound,
My feet they are cold.

No. 30

The Bailiff's Daughter of Islington

A

Sung by Mrs. Talithah Powell
at Berea, Madison Co., Ky., May 28, 1917

Heptatonic. Ionian.

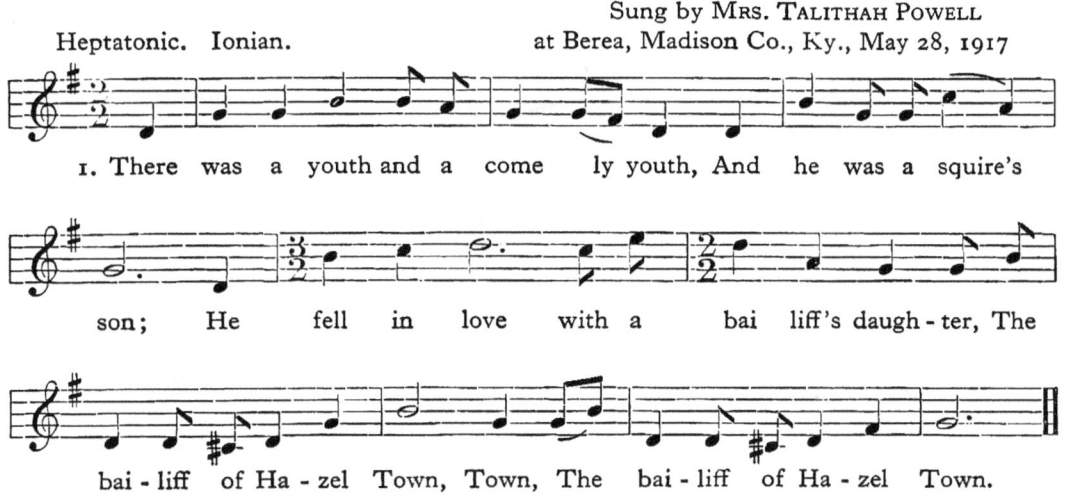

1. There was a youth and a comely youth, And he was a squire's son; He fell in love with a bailiff's daughter, The bailiff of Hazel Town, Town, The bailiff of Hazel Town.

2 *It was about the middle of summer,*
The girls went out to play,
The bailiff's daughter stayed at home,
And so cunningly she stole away.

3 And she pulled off her gown of green
And dressed in ragged attire,
And went to fair London town,
Her true love to enquire.

4 *She met a stranger on the way,*
O where do you reside?
In Hazel Town, kind sir, she said,
Where many a sport's been played.

5
One penny, one penny, kind sir, she said,
Will ease me of my pain.

6 Before I give you one penny, sweetheart,
Pray tell me where you were born.
In Hazel Town, kind sir, she said,
Where I have had many a scorn.

7 If you are from Hazel Town,
Surely I know you.
What has become of the bailiff's daughter?
She is dead, sir, long ago.

219

The Bailiff's Daughter of Islington

8 If she be dead, here take my horse,
My saddle and bridle also,
And I'll go to some far country
Where no man shall me know.

or

If she be dead and me yet alive,
All in this wilderness of woe,
Go bring to me my milk-white steed,
My fiddle and my bow.

9 O no, O no, thou goodly youth,
She's standing by thy side.
She is not dead, she is yet alive,
And ready to be thy bride.

The italicized stanzas are from a version in Professor Raine's collection which he believes was noted down from the same singer.

B

Sung by Mrs. Eliza Pace
at Hyden, Leslie Co., Ky., Oct. 3, 1917

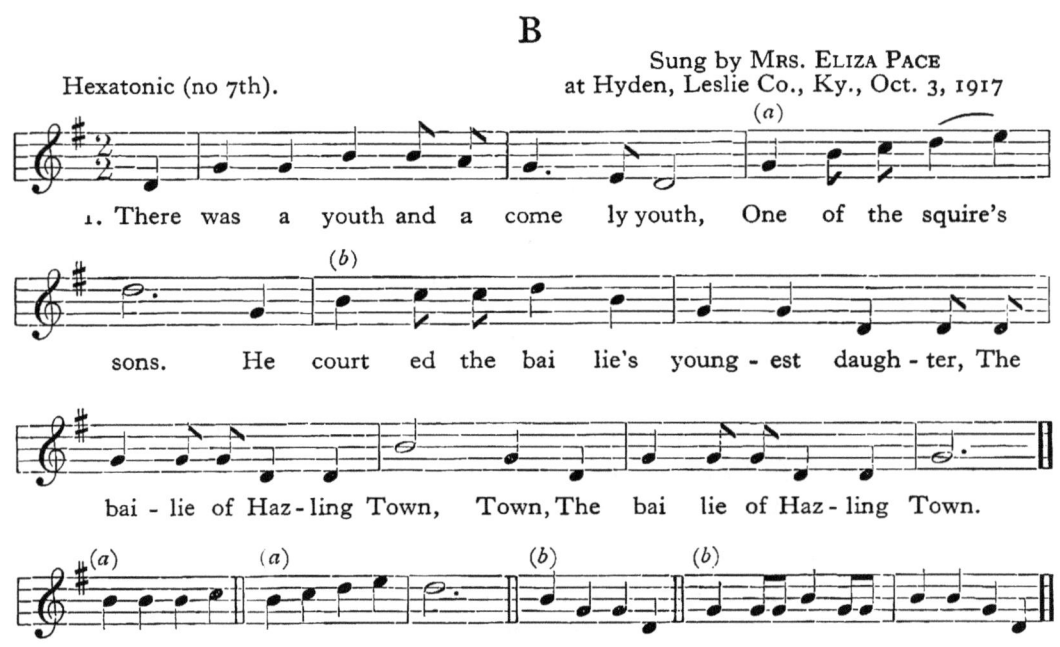

1. There was a youth and a comely youth, One of the squire's sons. He courted the bailie's youngest daughter, The bailie of Hazling Town, Town, The bailie of Hazling Town.

2 And when his old father come for to know
How foolish his son had inclined,
He sent him away to the London city,
And a prencess he did bind.

3 There to read and study law,
Leave his true love behind.
Never, never think of her always,
For she's always in my mind.

The Bailiff's Daughter of Islington

4 One day about the middle of the summer,
　The girls went out to play;
　All but the Bailie's youngest daughter,
　So cunningly stole away.

5 She travelled on one livelong year,
　One livelong year and a day;
　Whom did she meet but her own true love
　A-riding there away.

6 Where are you from, my pretty little Miss?
　Where are you from, I pray?
　I am just from the Hazling city
　Where many a sport's been played.

7 If you are just from Hazling city,
　Surely you must know
　What's become of Bailie's youngest daughter.
　She's dead long ago.

8 If she is dead long ago,
　Her body lies so low.
　You have met with her milk-white steed,
　Her saddle and her bridle and her bow.

9 Stay, kind sir, she is not dead,
　She is yet alive,
　Standing by her true love's side,
　Just ready for to be his bride.

10 Farewell sin and welcome sorrow,
　O welcome unto me;
　I have met with my own true love,
　Whom I never expected to see.

No. 31
Sir Hugh

A

Pentatonic. Mode 3 (no 6th).

Sung by Mrs. Swan Sawyer
at Black Mountain, N. C., Sept. 19, 1916

3. Bury my bible at my head, My prayer-book at my feet. When the scholars calls for me, Pray tell 'em I'm asleep, Pray tell 'em I'm asleep.

1. All the scholars in the school
   As they are a-playing ball,
   They knocked it high, they knocked it through,
   Through the Jew's garden it flew.

2. She took him by his lily-white hand
   And she drug him from wall to wall,
   She drug him to a great, deep well,
   Where none could hear his call.
   She placed a penknife to his heart,
   The red blood it did fall.

B

Pentatonic. Mode 3 (no 6th).

Sung by Mr. Luther Campbell
at Bird's Creek, Sevier Co., Tenn.,
April 19, 1917

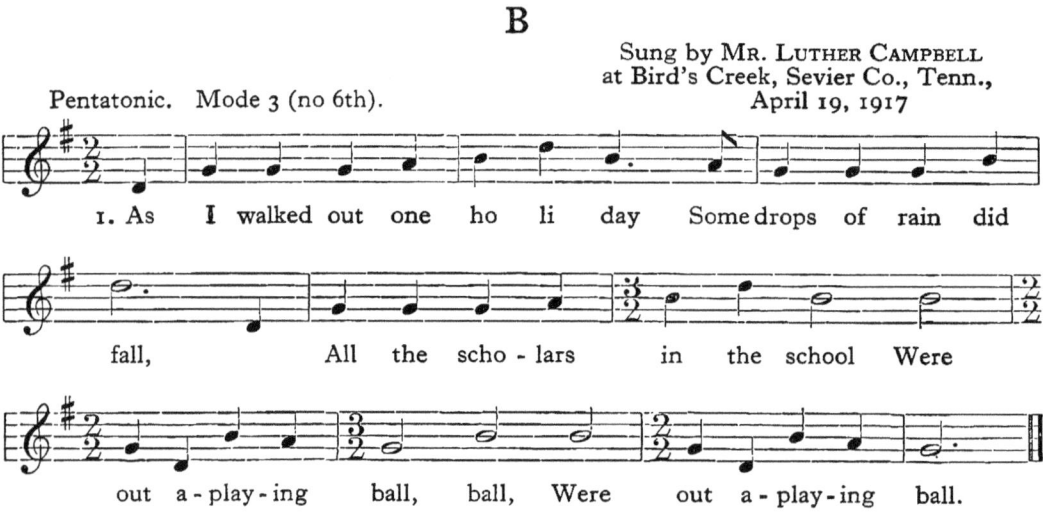

1. As I walked out one holiday Some drops of rain did fall, All the scholars in the school Were out a-playing ball, ball, Were out a-playing ball.

Sir Hugh

2 They tossed the ball both to and fro,
   To the Jews's garden it flew;
   No one was so ready to bring it out
   But our little son Hugh, etc.

3 The Jews's daughter come stepping out
   With apples in her hand:
   Little son Hugh, come go with me
   And I will give you them.

4 I cannot go, I will not go,
   I cannot go at all,
   For if my mother were to know
   The red buds* she'd make fall.

5 His mother broke a birch-rod in her hand;
   She walked all through the town,
   Saying: If I find my little son Hugh,
   O I will whip him home.

6 She walked up to the Jews's gate,
   And they were all asleep,
   And there she spied a great big well
   Which was fifty fathoms deep.

7 Little son Hugh, O are you here,
   Which I suppose you to be?
   Yes, dear mother, I am here
   Who stand in the need of thee.

8 Go bury my bible at my head,
   My prayer-book at my feet,
   If any of the scholars ask about me,
   Pray tell them I'm asleep.

* blood?

C

Pentatonic. Mode 3 (no 6th).

Sung by Mr. W. M. Maples
at Sevierville, Sevier Co., Tenn., April 20, 1917

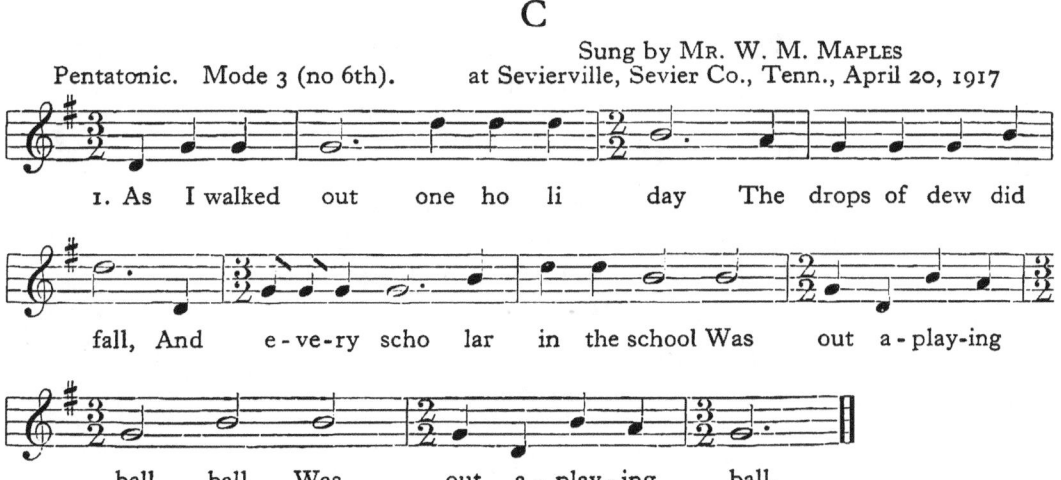

1. As I walked out one ho-li-day The drops of dew did fall, And e-ve-ry scho-lar in the school Was out a-play-ing ball, ball, Was out a-play-ing ball.

Sir Hugh

2 They tossed the ball both to and fro;
In the Jews's garden it did go;
There was no one so ready to get it out,
There stood little son Hugh, etc.

3 The Jews's daughter come stepping along
With some apples in her hand,
Saying: Little son Hugh, come go with me
And I will give you them.

4 I cannot go, I will not go,
I cannot go at all,
For if my mamma she knew it,
The red blood she'd make fall.

5 She took him by the lily-white hand,
She drug him from hall to hall,
And took him to a great stone wall
Where none could hear his call.

6 She set him down in a little arm-chair
And pierced his heart within.
She had a little silver bowl,
His heart blood she let in.

7 She took him into the Jews's garden,
The Jews was all asleep,
And she threw him into a great deep well
Was fifty fathoms deep.

8 His mother then she started out
With a birch-rod in her hand;
Walked the streets through and through.
If I find little son Hugh,
I'd avowed she'd whip him home.

9 When she come to the Jews's gate,
The Jews was all asleep.
She walked on to a great deep well
Was fifty fathoms deep.

10 Saying: Little son Hugh, if you be,
As I suppose you to be.
Dear mother, I am here
And stand in the need of thee.

11 With a little penknife pierced through my heart
And the red blood running so free.
Mother, O mother, dig my grave,
Dig it long, wide and deep.

Sir Hugh

12 And bury my bible at my head,
My prayer-book at my feet.
And if any of the scholars ask for me,
Pray tell them I'm asleep.

D

Sung by Mrs. Mollie Broghton
at Barbourville, Knox Co., Ky., May 8, 1917

Hexatonic (no 7th).

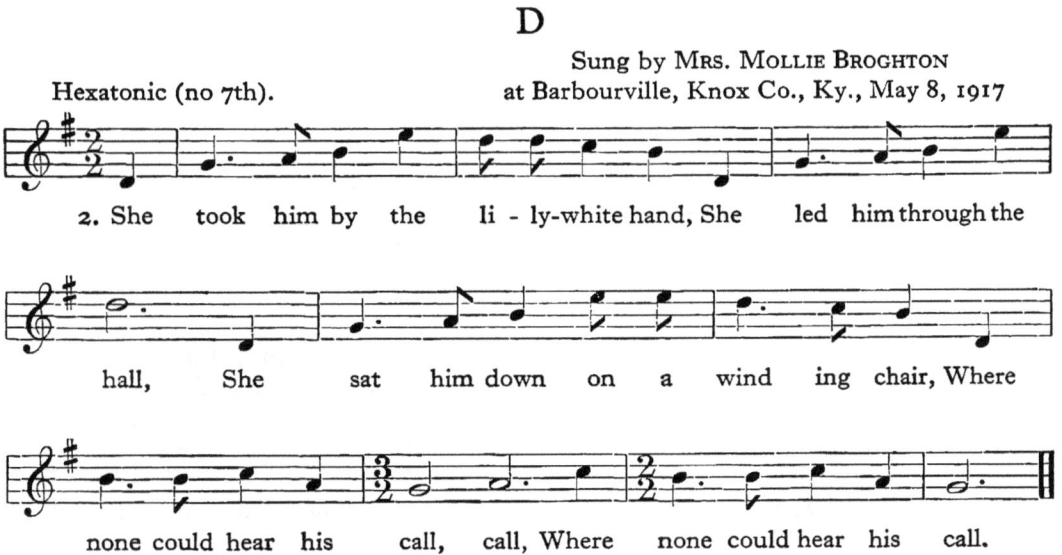

2. She took him by the li-ly-white hand, She led him through the hall, She sat him down on a wind-ing chair, Where none could hear his call, call, Where none could hear his call.

1 Dark and dark some drizzling day,
Some apples in her hand,
The Jewish lady in the town
Walked out with apples in her hand.
Come here, come here, my little son Hugh,
Some apples you may have, have,
Some apples you may have.

2 She took him by the lily-white hand,
She led him through the hall,
She sat him down on a winding chair,
Where none could hear his call, call,
Where none could hear his call.

3 She held a basin in her hand
That catched his own heart's blood,
She picked him up in a winding sheet,
She walked with him for a while,
She took him down to the deepest well
And there she splunged him in, etc.

Sir Hugh

4 She went to the well next day
To see what she could see;
And there she saw her little son Hugh
Come swimming around to thee.

5 O take me out of this deep well,
O take me out, says he,
O take me out of this deep well
And bury me in yonders yard.

6 Sink, O sink, my little son Hugh,
Sink, O sink, said she.
Sink, O sink, and don't you swim,
You are an injury to me and my kin.

E

Sung by MR. BEN. J. FINLAY
at Manchester, Clay Co., Ky., Aug. 10, 1917

Pentatonic. Mode 3.

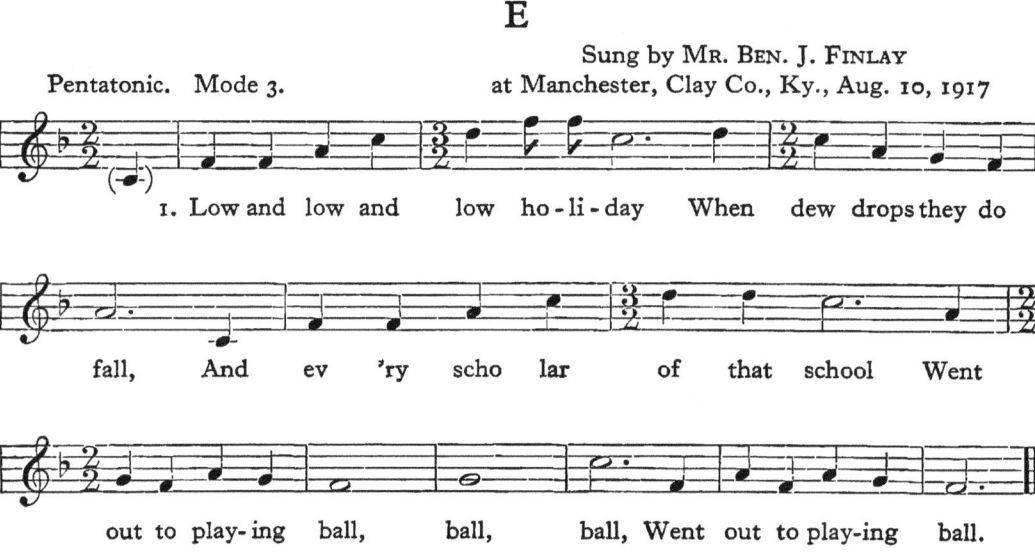

1. Low and low and low ho-li-day When dew drops they do fall, And ev'ry scho lar of that school Went out to play-ing ball, ball, ball, Went out to play-ing ball.

2 Along comes the Jewress lady gay
With some apples in her hand.
She says: Come along, my littly son 'Ugh-ey
And one of these shall ha'.

3 I'm not a-going to come,
Nor I won't a-come,
For if my parents knew,
It would make my red blood run.

4 She took him by his little white hand,
She led him for a while;
She led him down to that cold well
Where it was so cold and deep.

Sir Hugh

5 Sink, O sink, my little son 'Ugh-ey,
   And don't you never swim.
   If you do it'll be a scandal
   To me and all my kin.

6 The day passed off and the night come on,
   The parents went to seek their son;
   And every parent had a son,
   But Urie's she had none.

F

Sung by Mr. Dol Small
at Nellysford, Va., May 22, 1918

(No 4th or 6th).

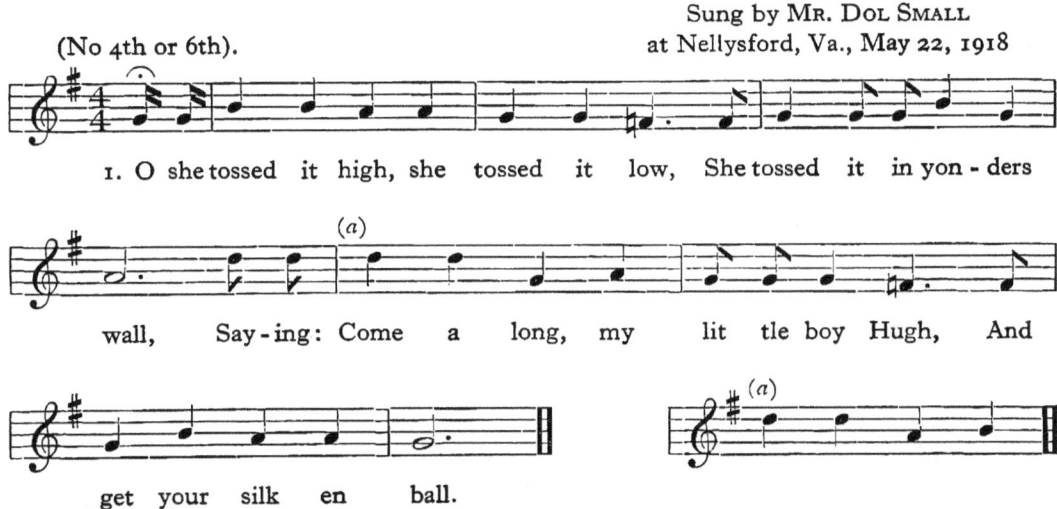

1. O she tossed it high, she tossed it low, She tossed it in yonders wall, Saying: Come along, my little boy Hugh, And get your silken ball.

2 I can't come in, I daren't come in
   To get my silken ball,
   For if my master knew it all
   He'd let my life's blood fall.

3 She took him by his lily-white hand,
   She led him through the hall,
   And in that silver basin clear
   She let his life's blood fall.

4 She wound him up in a lily-white sheet,
   Three or four times four,
   And tossed him in her draw-well,
   It were both deep and cold.

5 The day had passed and the evening come,
   The scholars going home,
   Every mother had a son,
   Little Hugh's had none.

Sir Hugh

6 She broke a switch all off that birch,
  And through the town she run,
  Saying: I'm going to meet my little boy Hugh,
  I'm sure for to whip him home.

7 She run till she came to the old Jew's gate,
  The old Jews all do sleep.
  She heard a voice in that draw-well,
  It were both cold and deep.

8 Cheer up, dear mother, it's here I've lain,
  It's here I've lain so long,
  With a little penknife pierced through my heart,
  The stream do run so strong.

9 Go take me out of this draw-well
  And make me a coffin of birch;
  O take me out of this draw-well
  And bury me at yonders church.

G

Sung by Mrs. Dan Bishop
at Teges, Clay Co., Ky., Aug. 21, 1917

Pentatonic. Mode 3.

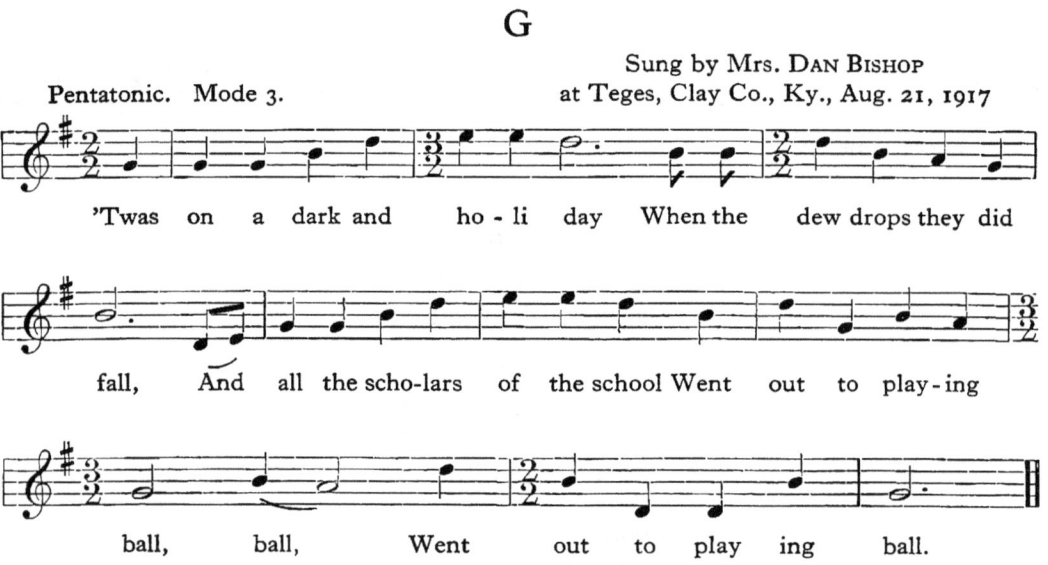

'Twas on a dark and ho-li day When the dew drops they did fall, And all the scho-lars of the school Went out to play-ing ball, ball, Went out to play ing ball.

4 She took him by his lily-white hand,
  She led him from porch to hall,
  She locked him up in a tight little room
  Where no one could hear his call.

Sir Hugh

H
Pentatonic. Mode 3.
Sung by MRS. SOPHIE ANNIE HENSLEY
at Oneida, Clay Co., Ky., Aug. 17, 1917

Up in a dark hol-low, Where the dew drops ne-ver fall, Ev'ry scho-lar in that school Went out to play-ing ball, ball, Went out to play-ing ball.

I
Pentatonic. Mode 3 (Tonic G).
Sung by MRS. NANCY ALICE HENSLEY
at Oneida, Clay Co., Ky., Aug. 17, 1917

Up in a dark hol low, Where the dew drops ne ver fall, Ev e ry scho lar in that school Went out to play-ing ball, ball, Went out to play-ing ball.

J
Pentatonic. Mode 3 (no 6th).
Sung by MRS. BERRY CREECH
at Pine Mountain, Harlan Co., Ky., Aug. 29, 1917

She picked him up all in her arms, And car-ried him to her hall, She set him down in a big arm-chair And scratched him with a pin, pin, pin, And scratched him with a pin.

Last verse. Here I am in this cold place,
Where it is both cold, winding deep.
My soul is high up in Heaven above,
While hers is low down in hell.

The Death of Queen Jane

A

Sung by Mrs. Kate Thomas
at St. Helen's, Lee Co., Ky., Sept. 6, 1917

Pentatonic. Mode 3.

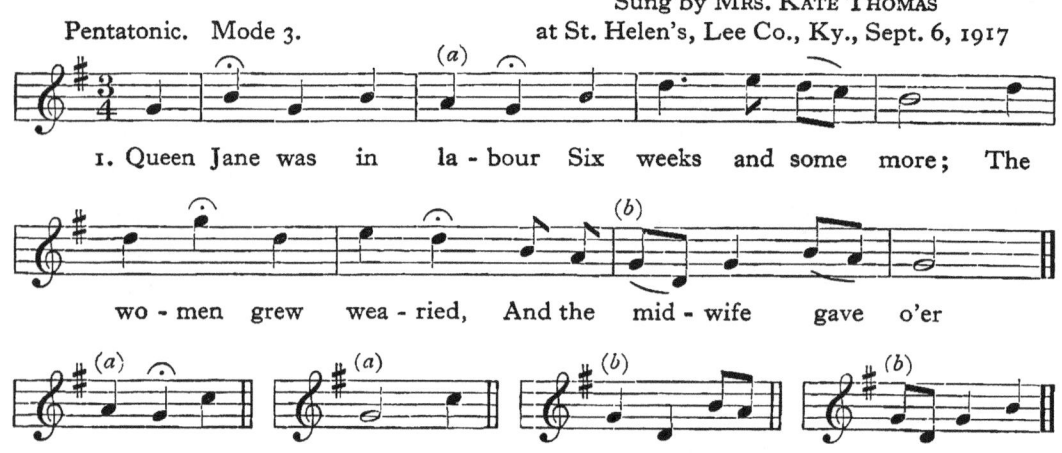

1. Queen Jane was in labour Six weeks and some more; The women grew wearied, And the midwife gave o'er

2 O women, kind women,
  I take you to be,
  Just pierce my right side open
  And save my baby.

3 O no, said the women,
  That never could be;
  I'll send for King Henry
  In the time of your need.

4 King Henry was sent for
  On horse-back and speed;
  King Henry he reached her
  In the hour of her need.

5 King Henry he come
  And he bent o'er the bed:
  What's the matter with my flower
  Makes her eyes look so red?

6 O Henry, kind Henry,
  Pray listen to me,
  And pierce my right side open
  And save my baby.

7 O no, said King Henry,
  That never could be,
  I would lose my sweet flower
  To save my baby.

The Death of Queen Jane

8 Queen Jane she turned over
And fell in a swound,
And her side was pierced open
And the baby was found.

9 The baby were christened
All on the next day;
But it's mother's poor body
Lay cold as the clay.

10 So black was the mourning,
So yellow was the bed,
So costly was the white robe
Queen Jane was wrapped in.

11 Six men wore their robes,
Four carrying her along;
King Henry followed after
With his black mourning on.

12 King Henry he wept
Till his hands was wrung sore.
The flower of England
Will flourish no more.

13 And the baby were christened
All on the next day,
And it's mother's poor body
Lying mouldering away.

B

Sung by Mrs. Margaret Dunagan
at St. Helen's, Lee Co., Ky., Oct. 12, 1917

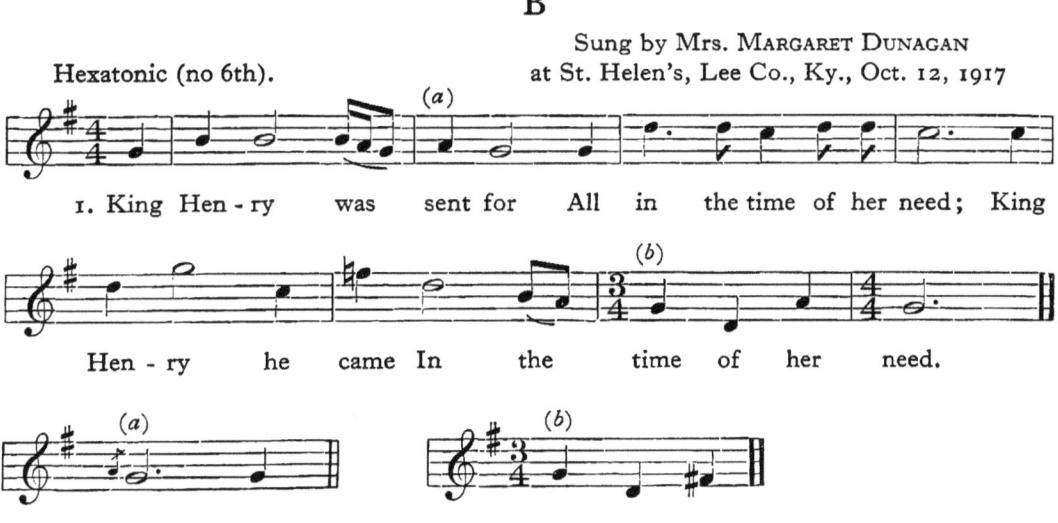

1. King Henry was sent for All in the time of her need; King Henry he came In the time of her need.

The Death of Queen Jane

2 King Henry he stooped
   And kissed her on the lips.
   What's the matter with my flower,
   Makes her eyes look so red?

3 King Henry, King Henry,
   Will you take me to be,
   To pierce my side open
   And save my baby?

4 O no, Queen Jane,
   Such thing never shall be,
   To lose my sweet flower
   For to save my baby.

5 Queen Jane she turned over
   And fell in a swound;
   Her side were pierced
   And her baby was found.

6 How bright was the mourning,
   How yellow were the bed,
   How costly was the shroud
   Queen Jane were wrapped in.

7 There's six followed after
   And six carried her along;
   King Henry he followed
   With his black mourning on.

8 King Henry he wept
   And wrung his hands till they're sore.
   The flower of England
   Shall never be no more.

No. 33

The Gypsy Laddie

A

Heptatonic. Mode 1, a + b (mixolydian).

Sung by Mrs. J. Gabriel Coates
at Flag Pond, Tenn., Sept. 1, 1916

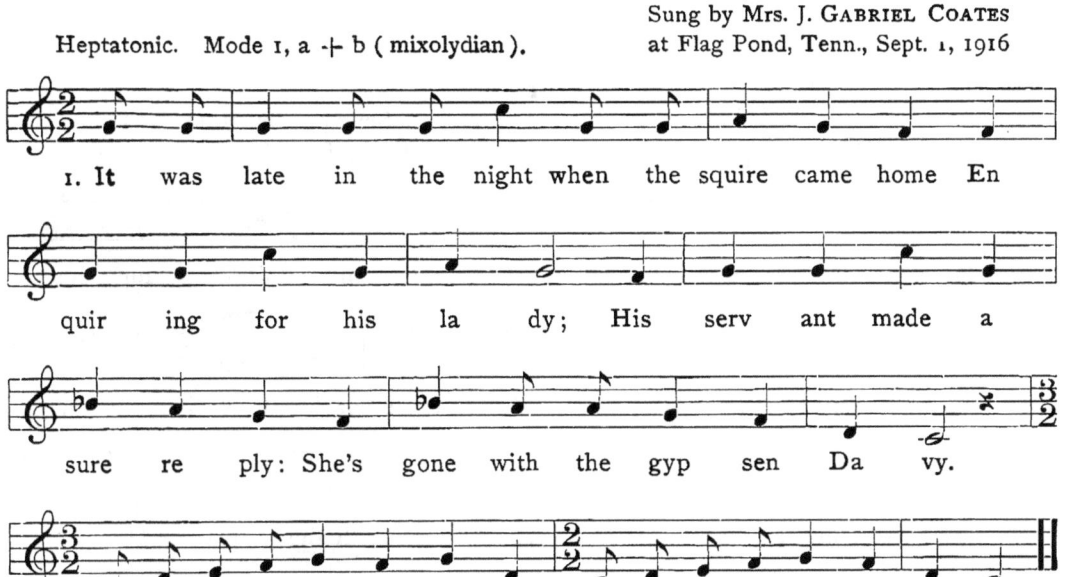

1. It was late in the night when the squire came home Enquiring for his lady; His servant made a sure reply: She's gone with the gypsen Davy. Rattle tum a-gypsen, gypsen, Rattle tum a-gypsen Davy.

2 O go catch up my milk-white steed,
   He's black and then he's speedy.
   I'll ride all night till broad daylight,
   Or overtake my lady.

3 He rode and he rode till he came to the town,
   And he rode till he came to Barley.
   The tears came rolling down his cheeks
   And there he spied his lady.

4 O come, go back, my own true love,
   O come, go back, my honey.
   I'll look you up in the chamber so high
   Where the gypsens can't come round you.

5 I won't come back, your own true love,
   Nor I won't come back, your honey.
   I wouldn't give a kiss from gypsen's lips
   For all your land and money.

6 She soon run through her gay clothing,
   Her velvet shoes and stockings;
   Her gold ring off her finger was gone
   And the gold plate off her bosom.

The Gypsy Laddie

7 O once I had a house and land,
  Feather-bed and money,
  But now I've come to an old straw pad
  With the gypsens all around me.

B

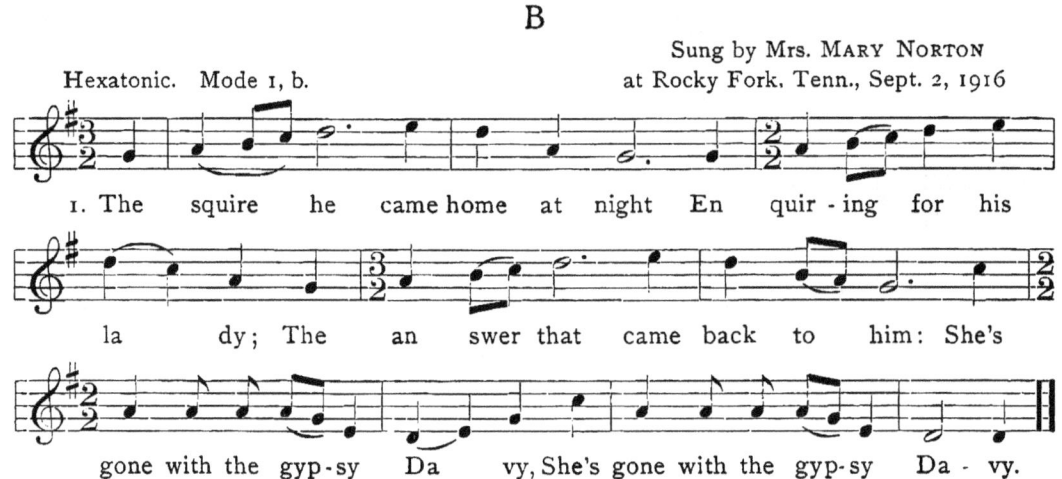

Hexatonic. Mode 1, b.

Sung by Mrs. MARY NORTON
at Rocky Fork, Tenn., Sept. 2, 1916

1. The squire he came home at night En quir-ing for his la-dy; The an-swer that came back to him: She's gone with the gyp-sy Da-vy, She's gone with the gyp-sy Da-vy.

2 Go saddle up my milk-white horse,
  And go saddle up my pony,
  And I will ride both night and day
  Till I overtake my lady.

3 How can you leave your house and land
  And how can you leave your baby?
  And how can you leave your kind husband
  To go with the gypsy Davy?

4 It's I can leave my house and land
  And I can leave my baby;
  And I can leave my kind husband
  To go with the gypsy Davy.

5 Go pull off them high-heeled pumps
  That's made of Spanish leather,
  And give me your lily-white hand.
  We'll bid farewell for ever.

C

Heptatonic. Mode 1, a + b
(mixolydian).

Sung by Mrs. HESTER HOUSE
at Hot Springs, N. C., Sept. 15, 1916

1. Go catch up my old grey horse, My blan-ket is so speed-y, O; I'll

The Gypsy Laddie

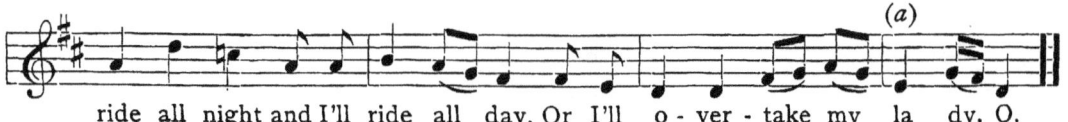

2 It's he caught up his old grey horse,
His blanket being so speedy, O.
He rode all night and he rode all day
And he overtaken of his lady, O.

3 It's come go back, my dearest dear,
Come go back, my honey, O;
Come go back, my dearest dear,
And you shall never lack for money, O.

4 I won't go back, my dearest dear,
Nor I won't go back, my honey, O.
For I wouldn't give a kiss from the gypsy's lips
For the sake of you and your money, O.

5 It's go pull off those snow-white gloves
That's made of Spanish leather, O.
And give me your lily-white hand,
And bid me farewell for ever, O.

6 It's she pulled off them snow-white gloves
That's made of Spanish leather, O,
And give to him her lily-white hand,
And bid him farewell for ever, O.

7 I once could have had as many fine things,
Fine feather-beds and money, O.
But now my bed is made of hay
And the gypsies a-dancing around me, O.

8 She soon went through with many fine things,
Fine rockum (morocco) shoes and stockings, O.
She soon went through with her finger rings
And the breast pin off her bosom, O.

Hexatonic. Mode 4, b.

Sung by Mrs. JANE GENTRY
at Hot Springs, N. C., Sept. 14, 1916

The Gypsy Laddie

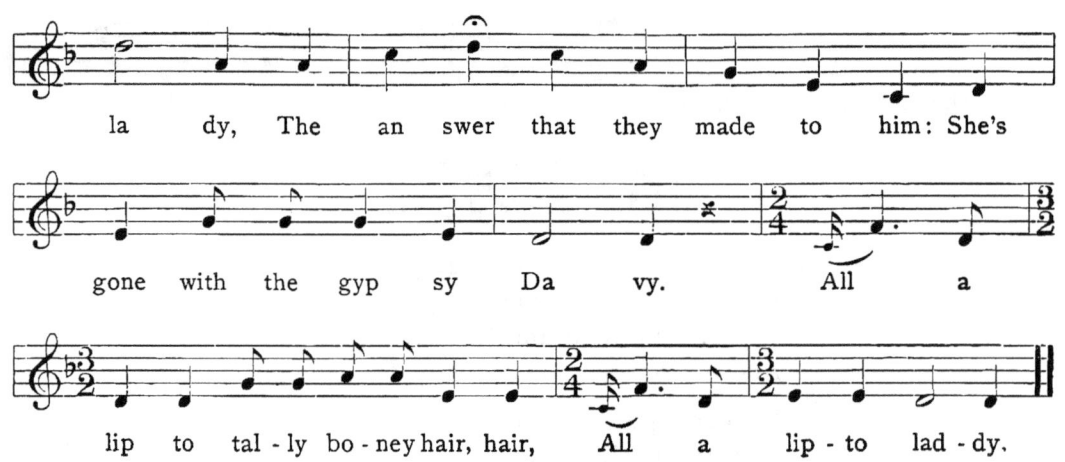

2. It's will you forsake your house and land?
   And will you forsake your baby?
   And will you forsake your own wedded lord
   And go with the gypsy Davy?

3. I'll forsake my house and land,
   And I'll forsake my baby;
   And I'll forsake my own wedded lord
   And go with the gypsy Davy.

4. The night before last I lay on a feather bed,
   Lord Thomas he lay with me.
   Last night I lay on a cold straw bed
   And with the calves a-bawling all around me.

E

Hexatonic. Mode 1, b.

Sung by Mrs. KITTY GWYNNE
at Rocky Fork, Tenn., Sept. 5, 1916

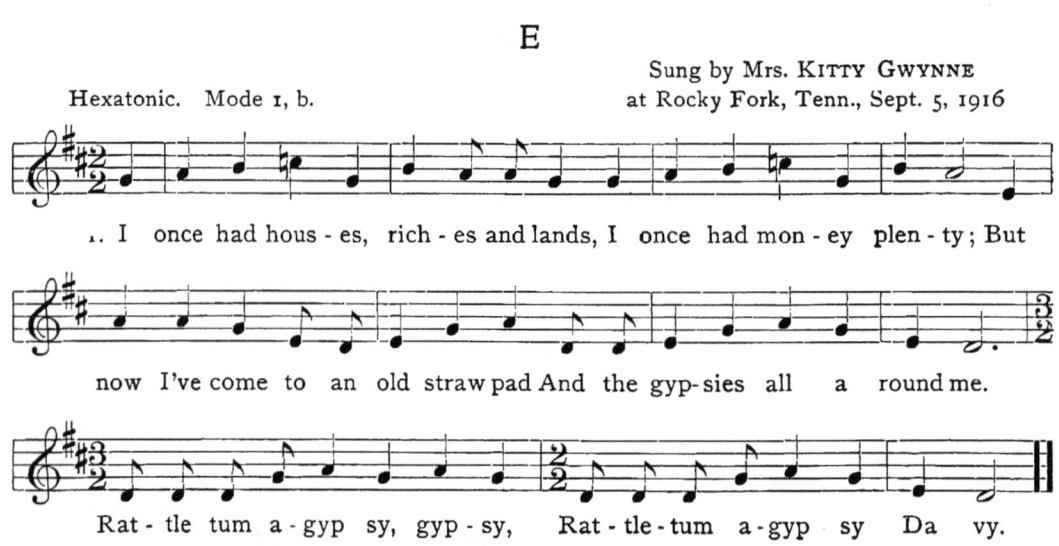

The Gypsy Laddie

I

Heptatonic. Mixolydian.

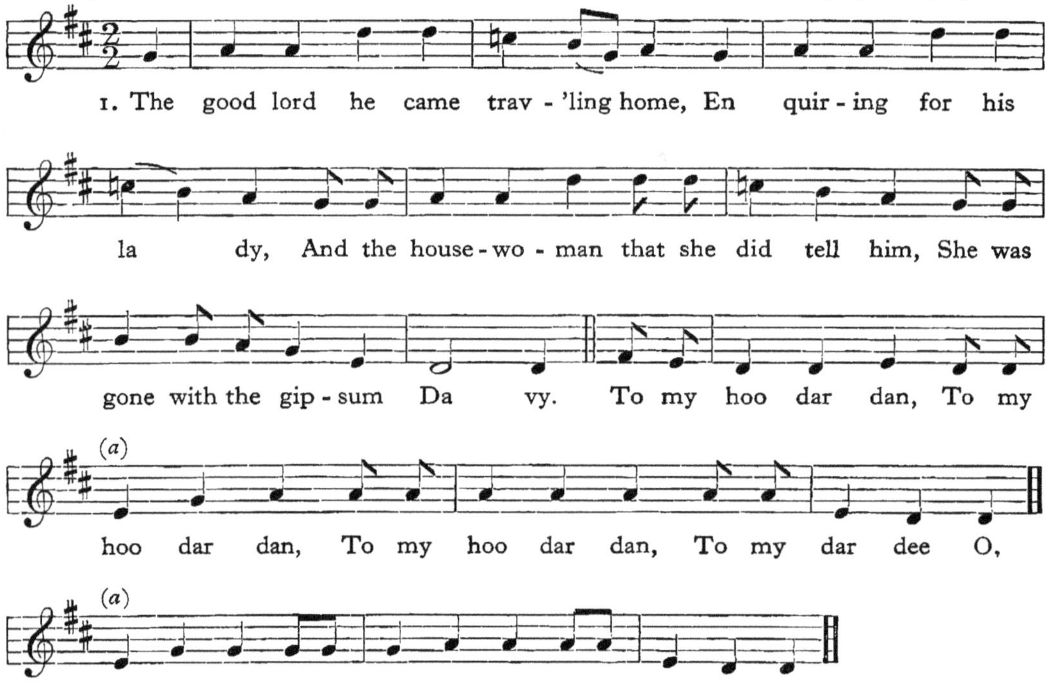

Sung by Mrs Lizzie Gibson
at Cròzet, Va., April 26, 1918

1. The good lord he came trav-'ling home, Enquiring for his lady, And the house-wo-man that she did tell him, She was gone with the gip-sum Davy. To my hoo dar dan, To my hoo dar dan, To my hoo dar dan, To my dar dee O,

2 It's go and get it's my grey nag
And draw them saddles all around her.
I'll ride all night till the broad daylight,
Or overtake my lady.

3 As he was riding up the road,
The rain poured down so muddy,
The first thing he spied up the road,
O there he spied his lady.

4 Come go back with me, my pretty Miss,
Come go back with me, my honey.
I'll swear by the sword that hangs by my side
You never shall want for money.

The Gypsy Laddie

5 I won't go back with you, my love,
I won't go back with you, my honey;
For I'd rather have a kiss from gipsum's lips
Than all your land and money.

6 Pull off, pull off your high-heel-ed shoes,
What's made of Spanish leather,
And hand you down your lily-white hand,
We'll bid farewell for ever.

7 She pull-ed off her high-heeled shoes,
Was made of Spanish leather,
She handed him down her lily-white hand,
And bid him farewell for ever.

8 Last night she lied on a soft feather bed
With the good lord by the side of her;
To-night she's a-lying on the damp, cold ground
With the gypsies all around her.

J

Sung by Mrs. Delie Hughes
at Cane River, Burnsville, N. C., Oct. 5, 1918

Hexatonic. Mixolydian.

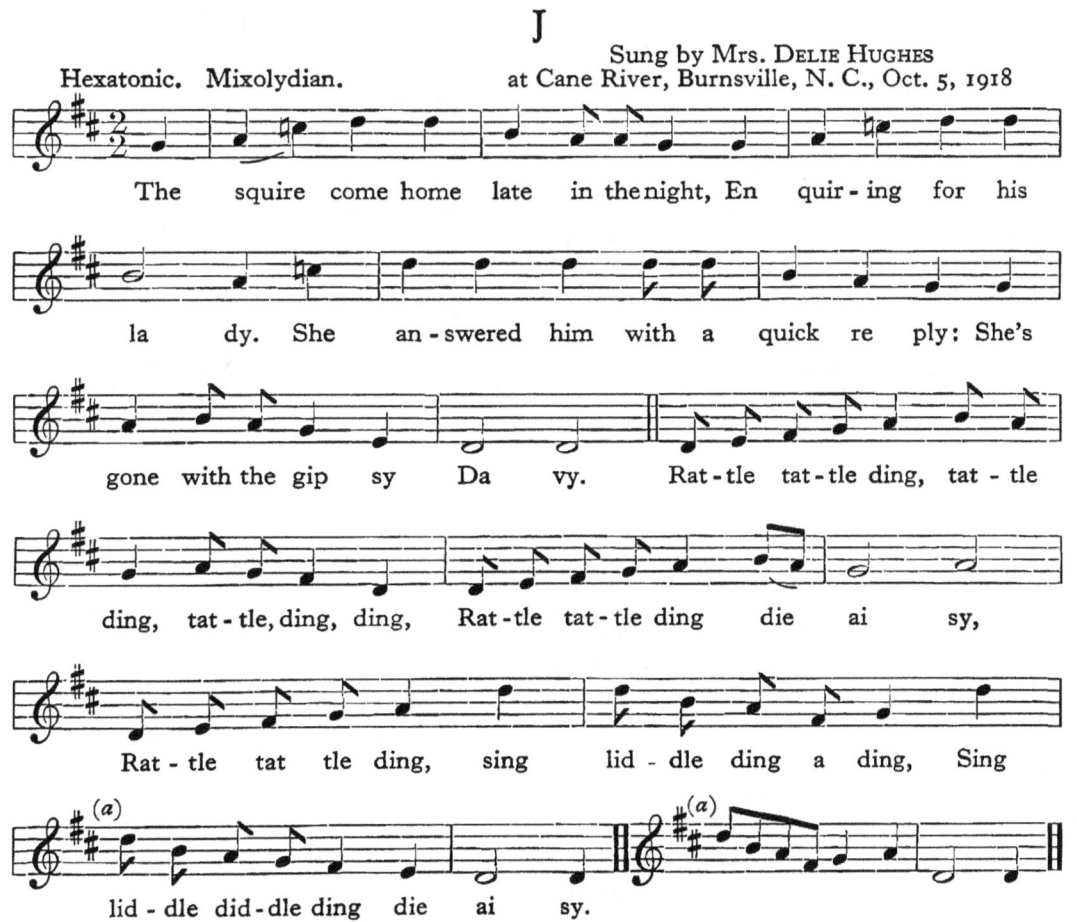

The squire come home late in the night, Enquiring for his lady. She answered him with a quick reply: She's gone with the gipsy Davy. Rattle tattle ding, tattle ding, tattle, ding, ding, Rattle tattle ding die ai sy, Rattle tat tle ding, sing lid-dle ding a ding, Sing lid-dle did-dle ding die ai sy.

No. 34

Geordie

A

Hexatonic. Mode 3, b
(Tonic A).

Sung by Mr. WILLIAM F. WELLS
at Swannanoah, N. C., Sept. 9, 1916

1. As I crossed o ver Lon-don's bridge One morn-ing bright and ear-ly, I spied a maid for-bide the way La-ment-ing for poor Char-lie.

(2D VERSE)

2. Char lie was the son of a poor man Who was lov-ed by a fair la dy. It's by his own con-fes sion he must die. May the Lord have mer cy on him.

(a) 3d Verse

3 Charlie never murdered any one.
  He stole sixteen of the king's white staff
  And sold them in Virginee.

4 The king looked over his right shoulder
  And thus he says to Charlie:
  It's by your own confession you must die.
  May the Lord have mercy on you.

5 The king looked over his left shoulder
  And thus he says to Charlie:
  It's by your own confession you must die.
  Jinny have mercy on you.

Geordie

B

Hexatonic. Mode 2, a.

Sung by Mrs. Jane Gentry
at Hot Springs, N. C., Sept. 14, 1916

1. As I went over London's bridge One morning bright and early, I saw a maid forbide the way Lamenting for poor Charlie.

2 It's Charlie's never robbed the king's high court,
   Nor he's never murdered any,
   But he stole sixteen of his milk-white steeds
   And sold them in old Virginia.

3 Go saddle me my milk-white steed,
   The brown one ain't so speedy,
   And I'll ride away to the king's high court
   Enquiring for poor Charlie.

4 She rode, she rode to the king's high court
   Enquiring for poor Charlie.
   Fair lady you have come too late,
   For he's condemned already.

5 It's Charlie's never robbed the king's high court,
   Nor he's never murdered any,
   But he stole sixteen of his milk-white steeds
   And sold them in old Virginia.

6 It's will you promise me? she said,
   O promise me, I beg thee,
   To hang him by a white silk cord
   That never has hung any.

C

Pentatonic. Mode 3.

Sung by Mrs. Sarah Buckner
at Black Mountain, N. C., Sept. 19, 1916

1. She saddled up her milk-white steed, She rode bright and gaily, She rode till she came to the king's high court, Lamenting for poor Charlie.

Geordie

D

1. As I came over new London Bridge, One misty morning early, I overheard a tender-hearted girl A-pleading for the life of Georgie.

2 Come saddle unto me my milk-white steed,
   Come saddle unto me quite gaily,
   That I might ride the livelong night
   A-pleading for the life of Georgie.

3 Georgie was hung with a silken rope,
   Such ropes they was not many,
   But Georgie came of a noble race
   And was loved by a virtuous lady.

E

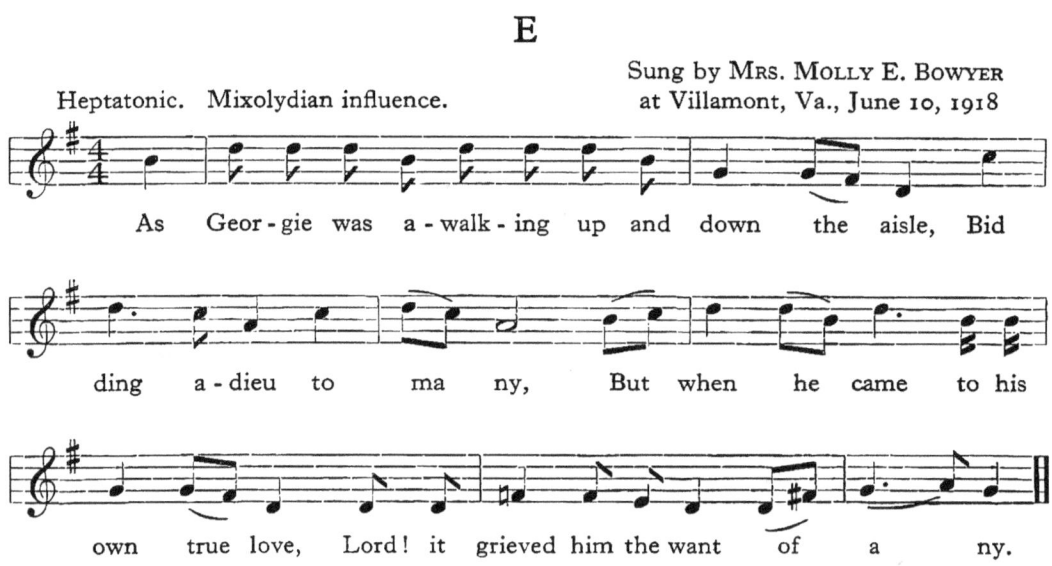

As Georgie was a-walking up and down the aisle, Bidding adieu to many, But when he came to his own true love, Lord! it grieved him the want of any.

Geordie

F

Pentatonic. Mode 4.

Sung by Mrs. Julie Boone
at Micaville, N. C., Oct. 3, 1918

(1st verse)

She rode up in the Court-house yard Lawyer's mo-ney plen-ty. Fee your selves if it takes it all To save the life of my Geor-gie.

(Subsequent verses)

2 It's rise up George, and plead for yourself,
  For I cannot plead any longer.
  Your own confession's hang-ed you,
  The Lord have mercy on me.

3 It's I've not robbed no store-houses,
  Nor done any murder,
  But I stole sixteen of the king's fair steeds,
  And I stole them in I-O-Bandy.

4 The own free cash was paid in my hand,
  It all be paid in style-ee,
  The own free cash was paid in my hand
  To save the life of my Georgie.

No. 35

The Daemon Lover

A

Heptatonic. Mode 4, a + b (dorian).*

Sung by Mrs. Mary Sands at Allanstand, N. C., Aug. 1, 1916

1. If you could have married the King's daughter dear, You'd better have married her, For I've lately got married to a nouse-carpenter And I'm sure he's a fine young man.

literally thus.

2 If you will forsaken your house-carpenter
  And go along with me,
  I will take you away where the grass grows green
  On the banks of sweet Da Lee.

3 She picked up her tender little babe
  And give it kisses three.
  Stay here, stay here, my tender little babe,
  And keep your papa company.

4 She dressed herself as in a yellow rose,
  Most glorious to behold,
  And she walked the streets all round and about,
  And shined like glittering gold.

5 They had not been on the sea more than two weeks,
  I'm sure it was not three,
  Till she begin to weep and mourn
  And wept most bitterly.

6 Are you weeping for your gold?
  Or are you for your store?
  Or are you weeping for your house-carpenter
  That you never shall see no more?

* If F be tonic :— Mode 3, a + b (ionian).

The Daemon Lover

7 I'm neither weeping for my gold,
　Nor neither for my store;
　I'm weeping about my tender little babe
　I left a-sitting on the floor.

8 And if I had it's all the gold
　That ever crossed the sea,
　So free would I give it to see land again
　And my tender little babe with me.

9 If you had all the gold
　You should give it all to me,
　For you shall never see land any more,
　But stay here for ever with me.

10 Don't you see yon light cloud arising
　As light as any snow?
　That's the place called heaven, she says,
　Where all righteous people go.

11 Don't you see yon dark cloud arising
　As dark as any crow?
　That's the place called hell, she says,
　Where I and you must go.

12 They had not been on the sea more than three weeks,
　I'm sure it was not four,
　Till the ship sprung a leak, to the bottom it went,
　And it went to rise no more.

B

Hexatonic. Mode 4, a.

Sung by Mrs. SARAH BUCKNER
at Black Mountain, N. C., Sept. 18, 1916

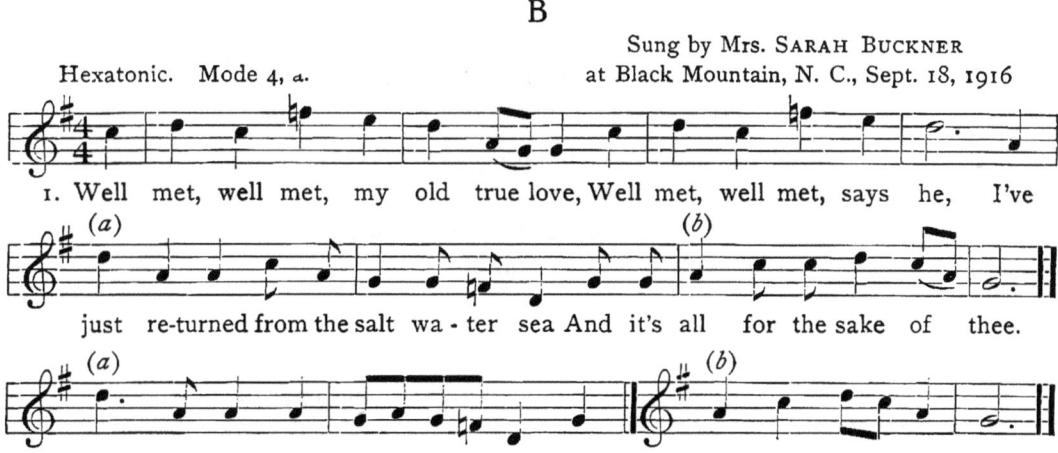

1. Well met, well met, my old true love, Well met, well met, says he, I've just re-turned from the salt wa-ter sea And it's all for the sake of thee.

2 We've met, we've met, my old true love,
　We've met, we've met, says she,
　I have just married a house-carpenter,
　A nice young man is he.

The Daemon Lover

3 If you'll forsake your house-carpenter
   And go along with me,
   I'll take you where the grass grows green
   On the banks of sweet Tennessee.

4 She picked up her tender little babe
   And kisses give it three.
   Stay here, stay here, my tender little babe,
   And keep your pa company.

5 They hadn't been a-sailing but about two weeks,
   I'm sure it was not three,
   Till this fair damsel began for to weep,
   She wept most bitterly.

6 O what are you weeping for, my love?
   Is it for my gold or store?
   Or is it for your house-carpenter,
   Whose face you'll see no more?

7 I'm neither weeping for your gold,
   Nor neither for your store,
   But I'm weeping for my tender little babe
   Whose face I'll see no more.

8 What banks, what banks before us now
   As white as any snow?
   It's the banks of Heaven, my love, she replied,
   Where all good people go.

9 What banks, what banks before us now
   As black as any crow?
   It's the banks of hell, my love, he replied,
   Where I and you must go.

10 They hadn't been sailing but about three weeks,
   I'm sure it was not four,
   Till that fair ship begin for to sink,
   She sank and riz' no more.

C

Hexatonic. Mode 4, a.

Sung by Mrs. BISHOP
at Clay Co., Kentucky, July 16, 1909

1. Well met, well met, my own true love, Well

The Daemon Lover

met, well met, says he; O I am from a foreign land, All alone for the sake of thee.

2 I could have been married to the Queen's daughter,
And she would a-married me,
But I've forsaken her and her gold
All alone for the sake of thee.

3 If you could have married the Queen's daughter
And she would a-married you,
I'm sure you must be for to blame,
For I am married to a little house-carpenter,
And I think him a neat young man.

4 O will you forsake that house-carpenter
And go, O go along with me?
And I will take you where the grass grows green
On the banks of old Willie.

5 What have you got to maintain me?
And what have you got? says she;
O what have you got to maintain me on
While sailing on the sea?

6 Seven vessels all on shore,
Seven more on sea;
And I have got one hundred and ten neat young men
All alone for to wait on thee.

7 She dressed herself in finest silk,
Her baby she kissed, 'twas one, two, three.
O stay, O stay, O stay at home
And bear your father company.

8 She hadn't sailed but a day or two,
I'm sure it was not three,
Till she began to weep
And wept most bitterly.

9 Are you a-weeping for my gold and my silver?
Or are you a-weeping for my store?
Or are you a-weeping for that house-carpenter
That you will never see no more?

The Daemon Lover

10 I'm neither weeping for your gold nor your silver,
    I'm neither weeping for your store;
    I'm a-weeping for my poor little baby
    That I will never see no more.

11 Cheer up, cheer up, my pretty, fair maid,
    Cheer up, cheer up, cried he,
    For I will take you where the grass grows green
    On the banks of the sweet Willie.

12 They did not sail but a day or two,
    I'm sure it was not four
    Till the vessel sprung a leak and began to sink,
    And sank for to rise no more.

D

Hexatonic. Mode 4, a.

Sung by Mr. WM. RILEY SHELTON
at Alleghany, N. C., Aug. 29, 1916

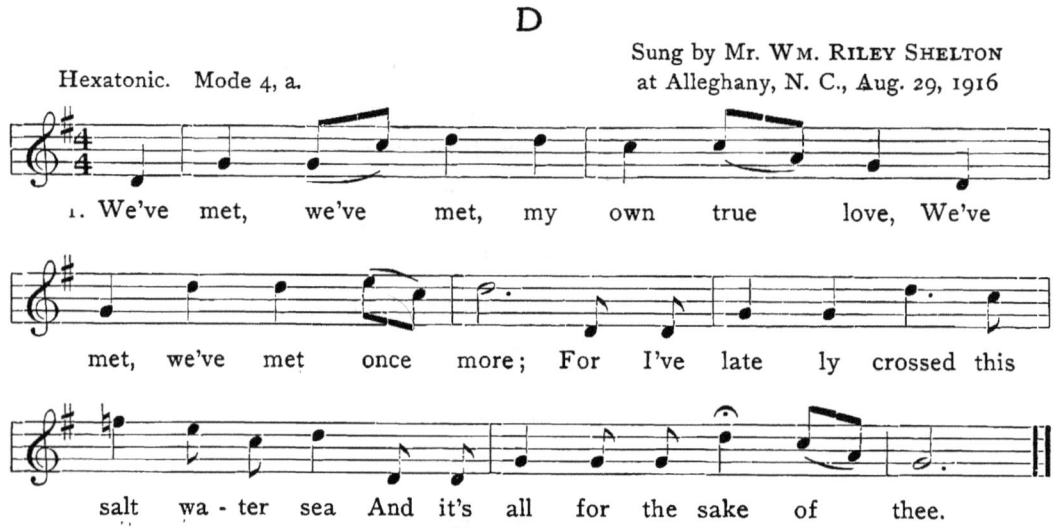

1. We've met, we've met, my own true love, We've met, we've met once more; For I've lately crossed this salt water sea And it's all for the sake of thee.

2 It's I could have married the king's daughter dear,
   I'm sure she'd have married me;
   But I forsaken them crowns of gold,
   And it's all for the sake of thee.

3 If you could have married the king's daughter dear,
   I'm sure you ought to have married then;
   For I am married to the house-carpenter,
   I'm sure he's a fine young man.

4 If you'll forsake your house-carpenter
   And go along with me,
   I'll take you where the grass grows green
   All on the banks of sweet Lillee.

The Daemon Lover

5 If I forsake my house-carpenter
   And goes along with thee,
   Pray tell me the wealth you have on board
   To keep me from slavery?

6 I have three ships all sailing on the sea,
   All making for dry land,
   And besides three hundred jolly sailor boys,
   You can have them at your command.

7 She catched her tender little babes in her arms,
   Kisses give them, one, two, three,
   Saying: Stay at home with your papee,
   I'm sure he'll be good to thee.

8 They hadn't been sailing but a day or two,
   Not more than two or three,
   Till she began to weep and mourn
   And she weep most bitterly.

9 Are you weeping about my gold, said he?
   Are you weeping about my stores?
   Or are you weeping about your house-carpenter
   That you shall never see no more?

10 I'm neither weeping for your gold,
   Nor neither for your store;
   But I am weeping about my tender little babe
   That I never shall see any more.

E

Heptatonic. Mode 4, a + b (mixolydian).

Sung by Mrs. Sylvaney Ramsey at Flag Pond, Tenn., Sept. 1, 1916

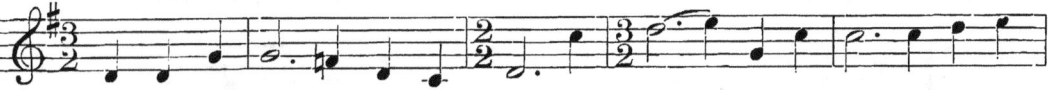

1. Well met, well met, my own true love, It's well met, said he. I've just re-

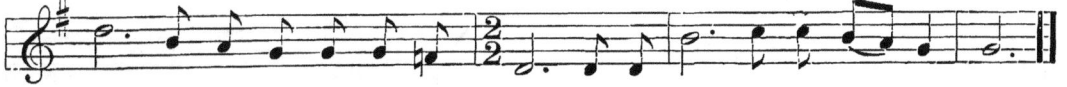

turned from the State of Ten-ne-see, And it's all for the sake of thee.

2 O who will clothe my little babe,
   And who will shoe its feet,
   And who will sleep in its lily-white arms
   While we're sailing for dry land?

The Daemon Lover

3 Its papa will kiss its little cheek,
And also shoe its feet,
And also sleep in its lily-white arms
While we're sailing for dry land.

5 She picked up her little babe,
And kissed it on the cheek,
She laid it down on a soft bed of down
And bid it go to sleep.

F

Heptatonic. Mode 1, a + b
(Tonic C. Mixolydian influence).

Sung by Mr. Frankland B. Shelton
at Allanstand, N. C., July 31, 1916

We've met, we've met, my own true love, We've met, we've met once more. I've lately crossed the salt wa-ter sea And it's all for the love of thee.

G

Hexatonic. Mode 4, a.

Sung by Mrs. Tempa Shelton
at Spillcorn, N. C., Sept. 6, 1916

We've met, we've met, my own true love, We've met, we've met once more. I have lately crossed the salt wa-ter sea And it's all for the sake of thee.

The Daemon Lover

H

Hexatonic. Mode 4, a.

Sung by Mrs. Jane Gentry
at Hot Springs, N. C., Sept. 12, 1916

O come you home, my own true love, O come you home from sea? It's are you married? he said. Yes, I am married to a house-car-pen-ter And I think he is a nice young man.

*The passage between asterisks not repeated in subsequent verses.

literally, or

I

Heptatonic. Mode 1, a + b
(mixolydian influence).

Sung by Mrs. Hester House
at Hot Springs, N. C., Sept. 15, 1916

Well met, well met, my own true love, Well met, well met, says he. I've just re-turned from the salt wa-ter sea And it's all for the sake of thee.

251

The Daemon Lover

The Daemon Lover

2 If you will leave your house-carpenter
   And come and go with me,
   I'll take you where the grass grows green
   On old sweet Cavalry.

3 If I should leave my house-carpenter,
   Go strolling along with thee,
   What have you to keep and clothe me with
   And to keep me from slavery?

4 I have a ship on the ocean a-sailing.
   A-sailing for dry land,
   Over one hundred and ten jolly men
   Are here at your command.

5 She went, picked up her sweet little babe,
   And kisses she gave it three.
   Stay at home, stay at home with your papa, little love,
   And give him company.

6 She dressed herself in scarlet red,
   Her belt was in green,
   And every station that she came through
   Her glittering gold was seen.

7 They hadn't been on sail but about two weeks,
   I'm sure it was not three,
   Till she began to weep and she began to mourn,
   She wept most bitterly.

8 O are you weeping for gold, my love,
   O are you weeping for fee,
   Or are you weeping for your house-carpenter
   That you love much better than me?

9 I neither weep for gold, my love,
   I neither weep for fee,
   But I weep to return back again
   My sweet little babe to see.

10 You need not weep for gold, my love,
   You need not weep for store,
   You need not weep for your sweet little babe;
   You'll see it never no more.

11 They hadn't been on sail but about three weeks,
   I'm sure it was not four,
   Till the ship sprang a leak and to bottom began to sink.
   I'm sinking to rise no more.

The Daemon Lover

12 Farewell, farewell to my sweet little babe,
   Farewell to my friends on the shore,
   Farewell, farewell to the man that parted me,
   I'm sinking to rise no more.

13 What banks, what banks is that, my love,
   As black as any crow?
   The banks, the banks of hell, my love,
   Where you and I shall go.

14 What banks, what banks is that, my love,
   As white as any snow?
   The banks, the banks of heaven, my love,
   Where all tender little babes shall go.

M

Sung by Mrs. VIRGINIA BENNETT
at Burnsville, N. C., Sept. 13, 1918

Hexatonic (no 3rd).

1. Well met, well met, my own true love, Well met, well met, said he. I've just re-turned from the salt, salt sea, And it's all for the sake of thee, It's all for the sake of thee. I've just re-turned from the salt, salt sea, And it's all for the sake of thee.

2 I could have married a king's daughter fair,
  I'm sure she would have married me,
  But I refused those golden crowns,
  And it's all for the sake of thee.

3 If you could have married a king's daughter fair,
  I'm sure you are to blame,
  For I am married to a house-carpenter,
  And I think he's a nice young man.

The Daemon Lover

4 I pray you leave your house-carpenter
  And go away with me;
  I'll take you down where the grass grows green
  On the banks of the Aloe Dee.

5 Have you anything to support me on
  To keep me from slavery?
  Have you anything to supply my wants
  To keep me from slavery?

6 I have three ships on the ocean wide,
  Sailing towards dry land;
  Three hundred and sixty sailor men
  Shall be at your command.

7 She took her babe up in her arms,
  And kisses gave it three,
  Saying: Stay at home with your papa dear,
  And keep him company.

8 She dressed herself in silk so fine,
  Most beautiful to behold.
  As she marched down by the brine water side,
  Bright shined those glittering golds.

9 She had not been on the sea two weeks,
  I'm sure it was not three,
  Till she lay on deck of her true lover's boat
  And wept most bitterly.

10 Are you weeping for your silver and gold,
   Or is it for your store,
   Or is it for your house-carpenter
   You never shall see any more?

11 I'm not weeping for my silver and gold,
   Neither for my store;
   'Tis all for the love of my darling little babe
   I never shall see any more.

12 She had not been on sea but three weeks,
   I'm sure it was not four,
   Till a leak sprung in her true lover's boat,
   And sank it to rise no more.

13 Accursed, accursed be all sea-men,
   Accursed for ever more.
   They've robbed me of my darling little babe,
   I never shall see any more.

The Daemon Lover

* This D was sometimes definitely natural, never sharp, but occasionally neutral.

The Daemon Lover

T

Heptatonic. Mixolydian.

Sung by Mr. H. D. Kinnard
at Berea, Madison Co., Ky., May 27, 1917

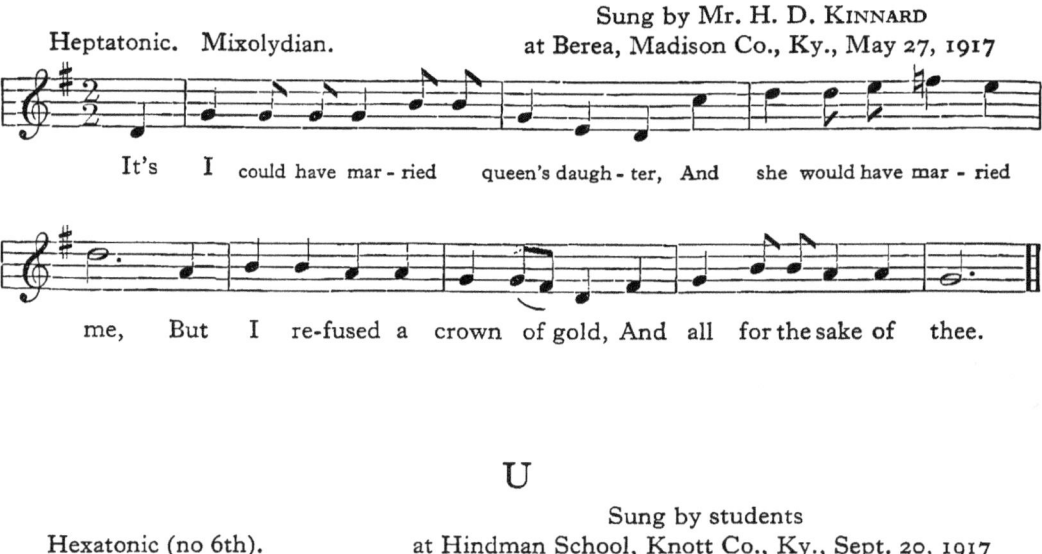

It's I could have mar-ried queen's daugh-ter, And she would have mar-ried me, But I re-fused a crown of gold, And all for the sake of thee.

U

Hexatonic (no 6th).

Sung by students
at Hindman School, Knott Co., Ky., Sept. 20, 1917

Well met, well met, my own true love, Well met, well met, says he. I've just re turned from the old salt sea, And its all for the sake of thee, And it's all for the sake of thee.

V

Pentatonic. Mode 4.

Sung by Mrs. Julie Boone
at Micaville, N. C., Oct. 3, 1918

She picked up her sweet lit-tle babe, And gave it kiss-es three; Set it down and told it to stay And keep its Pa-pa com-pan-y.

No. 36

The Grey Cock

Heptatonic. Mode 3, a + b
(mixolydian).

Sung by Mrs. JANE GENTRY
at Hot Springs, N. C., Aug. 24, 1916

1. All on one sum-mer's eve-ning when the fe-ver were a-dawn-ing I

heard a fair maid make a mourn. She was a-weep-ing for her fa-ther and a-

griev-ing for her moth-er, And a-think-ing all on her true love John. At

last John-ny came and he found the doors all shut, And he

ding led so low at the ring. Then this fair maid she rose and she

hur-ried on her clothes To make haste to let John-ny come in.

2 All around the waist he caught her and unto the bed he brought her,
   And they lay there a-talking awhile.
   She says: O you feathered fowls, you pretty feathered fowls,
   Don't you crow till 'tis almost day,
   And your comb it shall be of the pure ivory
   And your wings of the bright silveree (*or* silver grey).
   But him a-being young, he crowed very soon,
   He crowed two long hours before day;
   And she sent her love away, for she thought 'twas almost day,
   And 'twas all by the light of the moon.

The Grey Cock

3 It's when will you be back, dear Johnny,
   When will you be back to see me?
   When the seventh moon is done and passed and shines on yonder lea,
   And you know that will never be.
   What a foolish girl was I when I thought he was as true
   As the rocks that grow to the ground;
   But since I do find he has altered in his mind,
   It's better to live single than bound.

No. 37

The Suffolk Miracle

A

Heptatonic. Mode 1, a+b (Mixolydian).

Sung by Mrs. Mary Sands at Allanstand, N. C., July 31, 1916

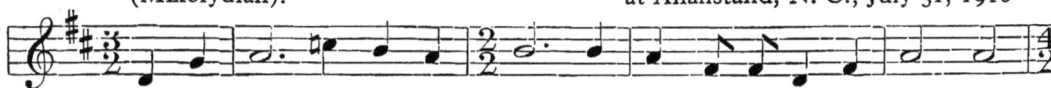

1. Come you peo ple old and young, Pray don't do as I have done; Pray

let your chil-dren have their way For fear that love breeds a de cay.

2 When her old father came this to know
  That she did love young Villian so,
  He sent her off three hundred miles or more,
  And swore that back home she should come no more.

3 This young man wept, this young man cried,
  In about six months for love he died;
  Although he had not been twelve months dead
  Until he rode a milk-white steed.

4 He rode up to his uncle's home
  And for his true love he did call.

5 Here's your mother's coat and your father's steed:
  I've come for you in great speed.
  And her old uncle, as he understood,
  He hoped it might be for her good.

6 He jumped up, and her behind,
  And they rode faster than the wind;
  And when he got near her father's gate
  He did complain that his head did ache.

7 A handkerchief she pulled out
  And around his head she tied it about,
  And kissed his lips and thus did say:
  My dear, you're colder than the clay.

8 Get down, get down, get down, says he,
  Till I go put this steed away.
  While she was knocking at the door
  The sight of him she saw no more.

The Suffolk Miracle

9 Get up, get up, get up, says he,
   You're welcome home, dear child, says he,
   You're welcome home, dear child, says he,
   What trusty friend did come with thee?

10 Dear old father, do you know,
   The one that I once loved before.
   The old man knowing he had been twelve months dead
   It made the hair rise on his head.

11 He summoned clerks and clergies too,
   The grave was to open and him to view.
   Although he had been twelve months dead
   The handkerchief was around his head.

12 Come all of ye, both young and old,
   Who love your children better than gold,
   And always let them have their way
   For fear that love might prey (?) decay.

B

Heptatonic. Mode 1, a + b (mixolydian).

Sung by Mr. T. Jeff Stockton at Flag Pond, Tenn., Sept. 4, 1916

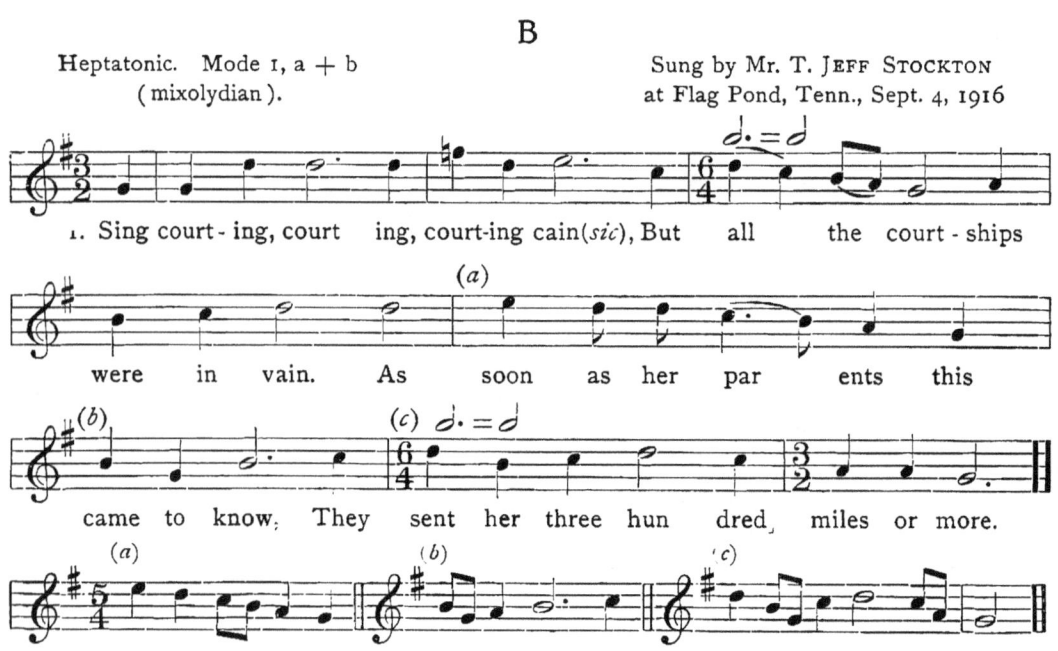

1. Sing court-ing, court ing, court-ing cain(sic), But all the court-ships were in vain. As soon as her parents this came to know, They sent her three hun dred miles or more.

2 It's first they vowed and then they swore
   Back home she should not come no more.
   This young man was taken sad,
   No kind of news could make him glad.
   His day had come, his hour had passed,
   Unto his grave he must go at last.

The Suffolk Miracle

3 Although he has twelve months been dead
He arose and rode this milk-white steed.
Your mother's cloak, your father's steed,
My love, I've come for you with great speed.

4 They rode more swifter than the wind.
At last, at last, three hours or more,
At last, at last, three hours or more,
He sot her at her father's door.

5 Just as they got within the gate,
He did complain his head did ache.
She drew her handkerchief from around her neck
And bound it round her lover's head.

6 She reached around to kiss his lips.
She says: My love, you're colder than the clay.
When we get home some fire we'll have;
But little did she know he'd come from the grave.

7 Go in, go in, my love, go in,
Till I go put this steed away.
Her knocking at her father's door —
The sight of her love she saw no more.

8 This old man arose, come putting on his clothes,
Saying: You're welcome home, dear child, to me;
You're welcome home, dear child, to me.
What trusty friend did come with thee?

9 Did you not send one I did adore,
I loved so dear, could love no more?
Him a-knowing he had twelve months been dead,
It made the hair rise on the old man's head.

10 The very next morning this was to do,
This young man raise and him to view.
Although he had twelve months been dead,
The handkerchief was around his head.

11 Come parents all, both old and young,
Your children love more precious than gold.
For in love let them have their way,
For love brings many to their grave.

2 A many a squire came this way,
   This handsome lady for to see;
   But at length there were a widow's son,
   'Twas found he were her chosen one.

The Suffolk Miracle

3 It's when her folks came this to know
   They sent her two thousand miles from home,
   Which broke this young man's tender heart
   To think that he and his love must part.

4 It were on a cold and stormy night,
   He started for his heart's delight;
   He rode till he came to the place he knew,
   Says he: My love, I've come for you.

5 It's your father's request, your mother's heed,
   I've come for you all in great speed,
   And in two weeks or a little more,
   I'll set you safe at your father's door.

6 They rode till they came to the old man's gate,
   He did complain his head did ache.
   With a handkerchief that she had out,
   With it she tied his head about.

7 They rode till they came to the old man's stile,
   Says he: My love, let's tarry awhile.
   Alight, alight, alight, says he,
   And I will put your steeds away.

8 She knocked upon her father's door,
   The sight of her lover she saw no more.
   It's welcome home, my child, says he.
   What trusty friend hath come with thee?

9 It's the one I love, I love so well,
   I love him better than tongue can tell.
   Which made the hair stand on the old man's head,
   To think that he'd been twelve months dead.

10 Then princes grand and judges too
   Were sent for to witness this great one do (wonder?)
   It's although he had been twelve months dead,
   The handkerchief were around his head.

11 Now this is warning to young and old
   Who love your children better than gold;
   For if you love them give them their way
   For fear that love will lead astray.

The Suffolk Miracle

E

Pentatonic. Mode 2. Sung by Mrs. Frances Richards at St. Peter's School, Callaway, Va., Aug. 16, 1918

1. Twelve months he rose, put on his clothes, Then after

her he then did go.

(*Usually thus.*)

2. Here's your mother's cloak and your father's steed,
That's sent for you within great speed.

3. He mounted on and she got behind him,
And they rode swiftly as the wind.

4. Before she got to her father's gate,
He did complain his head did ache.

5. She taken her own handkerchief
And around his head she bound it around.

6. He set her at her father's door
The sight of him she saw no more.

7. Come in, come in, dear daughter, dear,
You are welcome, dear child, to me.

8. Saying: Do you send thee any more,
Whom I once loved till I could love no more.

9. It made the hair rise on this old man's head
In knowing he had been twelve months dead.

10. This old man rose, put on his clothes,
Saying: This young man's grave is to be undone.

11. And when they undone this young man's grave
The handkerchief bound round his head.

12. Saying: If love can bring the dead decay,
I say pray give to them their way.

13. And ain't this warning to both young and old
To love their children better than gold.

No. 38

Our Goodman

A

Pentatonic. Mode 3 (no 6th).

Sung by Mrs. JANE GENTRY
at Hot Springs, N. C., Sept. 16, 1916

3 Old woman, etc.
Boots on the floor where my boots ought to be.
You old fool, etc.
It's nothing but a churn, sir, your mammy sent to me.
Miles I have travelled, etc.
Heels on a churn, sir, I never saw before.

Our Goodman

4 Old woman, etc.
   A hat on a table where my hat ought to be.
   You old fool, etc.
   It's nothing but a nightcap your mammy sent to me.
   Miles I have travelled, etc.
   Fur round a nightcap I never saw before.

5 Old woman, etc.
   A man in the bed where I ought to be.
   You old fool, etc.
   It's nothing but a baby your mammy sent to me.
   Miles I have travelled, etc.
   Hair on a baby's face I never saw before.

B

Hexatonic. Mode 3, a.

Sung by Mrs. Tom Rice
at Big Laurel, N. C., Aug. 18, 1916

1. Whose horse is that horse, where my horse ought to be? You old fool, you blind fool, can't you never see? It's nothing but a milk cow my mother sent to me. It's miles I have travelled, some forty miles or more, A milk-cow with a saddle on I never saw before.

2 Whose coat is that coat where my coat ought to be?
   You old fool, etc.
   It's nothing but a bed-quilt my mother sent to me.
   It's miles, etc.
   A bed-quilt with buttons on I never saw before.

Our Goodman

3 Whose boots is those boots where my boots ought to be?
  It's nothing but a cabbage head my mother sent to me.
  A cabbage head with boot heels on I never saw before.

4 Whose hat is that hat where my hat ought to be?
  It's nothing but a dish rag my mother sent to me.
  A dish rag with a hat band on I never saw before.

5 Whose pants are those pants where my pants ought to be?
  It's nothing but a petticoat my mother sent to me.
  A petticoat with a gallices (suspenders) on I never saw before.

6 Who's that in the bed where I ought to be?
  It's nothing but a baby child my mother sent to me.
  A baby child with mushtash (moustachios) on I never saw before.

C

Sung by Mrs. Tom Rice
at Big Laurel, N. C., Aug. 17, 1916

Mode 3, b (no 6th).

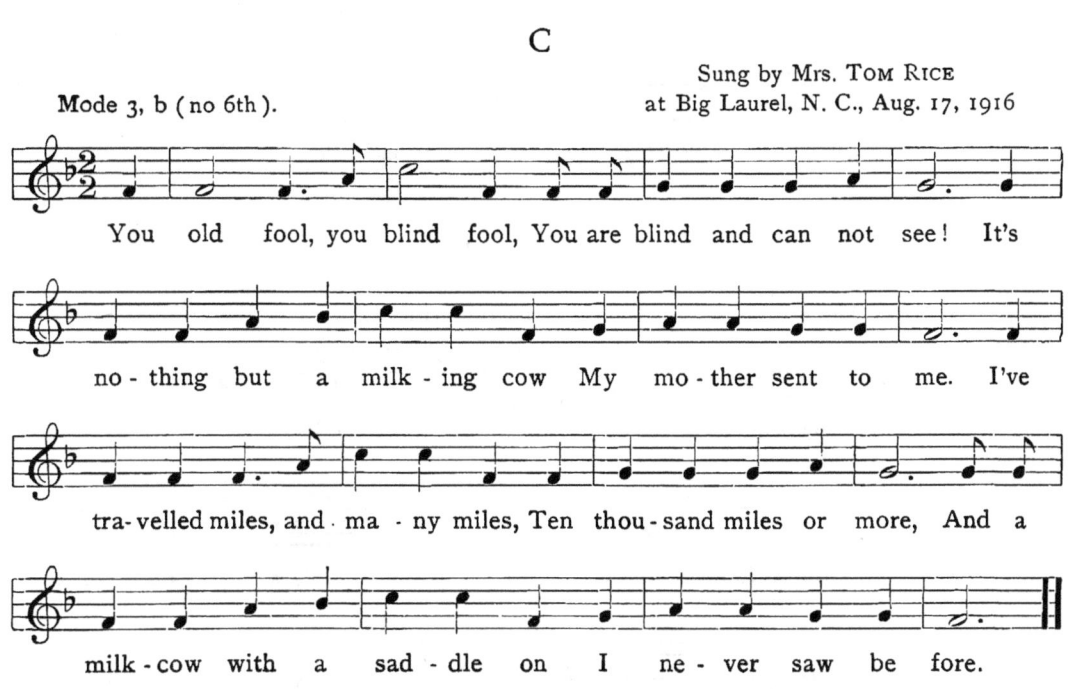

You old fool, you blind fool, You are blind and can not see! It's nothing but a milking cow My mother sent to me. I've travelled miles, and many miles, Ten thousand miles or more, And a milk-cow with a saddle on I never saw before.

D

Sung by Mrs. Wilson
at Pineville, Bell Co., Ky., June 5, 1917

Pentatonic. Mode 3 (Tonic F).

Old man come home at night, The place he ought to be; An-

No. 39

The Wife Wrapt in Wether's Skin
A

Hexatonic. Mode 3, b.

Sung by Mr. N. B. Chisholm
at Woodridge, Va., Sept. 21, 1916

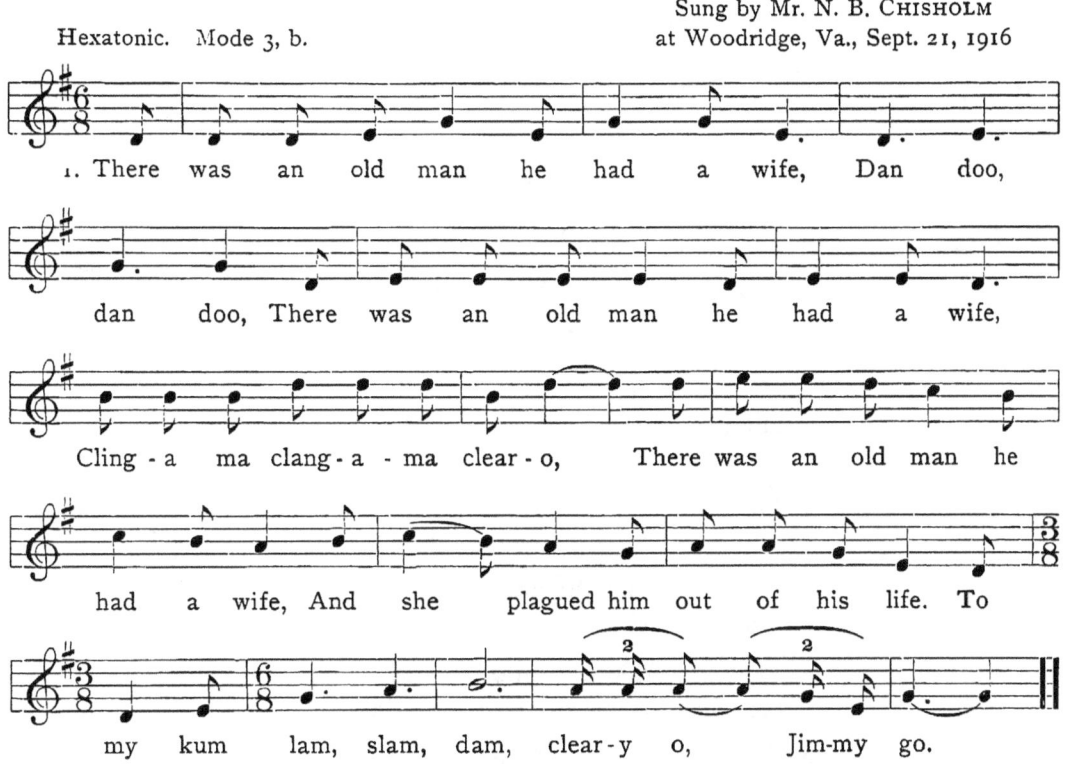

1. There was an old man he had a wife, Dan doo, dan doo, There was an old man he had a wife, Cling-a ma clang-a-ma clear-o, There was an old man he had a wife, And she plagued him out of his life. To my kum lam, slam, dam, clear-y o, Jim-my go.

2 When this old man came in from plough,
   Says: Have you got my breakfast now?

3 She says: There's a piece of bread upon the shelf;
   If that don't do, go bake it yourself.

4 This old man went out to his sheep-pen,
   And soon had off an old wether's skin.

5 He placed it on his old wife's back,
   And with two sticks went wickety whack.

6 I'll tell your daddy and mammy and all your kin,
   How you tanned your wether's skin.

B

Pentatonic. Mode 3 (no 2nd).

Sung by Miss Mary Large
at Lee Co., Ky., June, 1916

1. There was a man lived in the West, Dan dù, dan dù, There

The Wife Wrapt in Wether's Skin

2 She put a cold slice on the shelf:
If you want any more you can get it yourself.

3 The man went out to his sheep-fold,
And caught the wether tough and old.

4 He threw the skin round his wife's back,
And that old sheep's hide he did whack.

5 The wife cried out unto her kin:
He's beating me on my bare skin.

6 The man he grinned and he replied:
I'm only tanning my old sheep's hide.

C

Sung by Mrs. Margaret Dunagan
at St. Helen's, Lee Co., Ky., Sept. 9, 1917

Hexatonic (no 3rd).

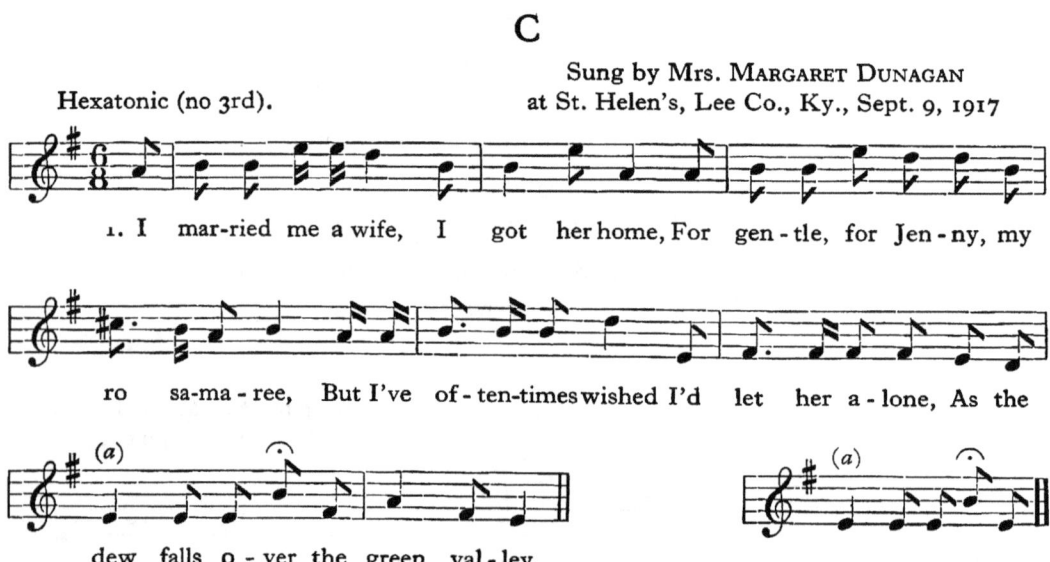

The Wife Wrapt in Wether's Skin

2 Then I come in it's from my plough,
    For gentle, etc.
  O now, my kind wife, is my dinner ready now?
    As the dew, etc.

3 There's a piece of bread upon the shelf,
  If you want any more you can bake it yourself.

4 I gets me a knife and I went to the barn,
  And I cut me hickory just as long as my arm.

5 Then I come back it's to the house,
  I make my hickory go wickechy whack.

6 Then I come it's from my plough.
  O now, my kind wife, is my dinner ready now?

7 She flew around, the board it was spread,
  And every word it was 'Yes, sir' and 'No, sir'

D

Heptatonic. Dorian.

Sung by Miss POLLY ANN KELLY
at Hindman School, Knott Co., Ky., Sept. 20, 1917

1. I married me a wife and took her home, For gentle, for Jenny, for rosamaree, I often wish I'd left her alone, As the dew flies over the green valley.

2 For fear of spoiling her new cloth shoes,
  All in the kitchen she would not use.

3 First day at noon came in from plough.
  My dearest wife, is my dinner ready now?

4 Lays a piece of bread upon the shelf.
  If you want any dinner go get it yourself.

5 Next day at noon came in from plough.
  My dearest wife, isn't dinner ready now?

The Wife Wrapt in Wether's Skin

6 Get out of here, you dirty scamp (?).
  If you want any dinner go get it yourself.

7 Took my knife and went to the barn.
  I cut me hickory as long as my arm.

8 As I went back to the house,
  Around her back I made it crack.

9 I'll tell my father and all my kin
  That you have hit me with a hickory limb.

10 You can tell your father and all your kin;
   I've whipped you once and I'll whip you again.

E

Sung by Mrs. ELIZA PACE
at Hyden, Leslie Co., Ky., Oct. 1, 1917

Pentatonic. Mode 3.

1. The old man he came in from plough, Dan doo, The old man he came in from plough, And a hump ty did dle dy dan doo. He says: Old wo-man, have you got din-ner now? To my ha lem, ga lem, wil ter ha lem ban go.

2 A piece of cold bread upon the shelf;
  If you want anything else you can get it yourself.

3 He went out to his sheep-fold;
  He got him a wether both tough and old.

4 He took it out to his wife's back;
  He took a little stick and he made it crack.

5 She says: I'll tell my father and all my kin
  That you whipped me with your old wether's skin.

6 If you do I'll tell you lied.
  I was a-dressing my old wether-hide.

No. 40

The Farmer's Curst Wife

A

Pentatonic. Mode 3.

Sung by Mrs. Sarah Buckner
at Black Mountain, N. C., Sept. 19, 1916

3 His wife she had ten hens in the lot,
  Sing halifor band if I do,
  Sing bands and rebels, and rebels and troubles,
  Sing new, new.

The Farmer's Curst Wife

4 And every day had one in the pot,
   Sing halifor, etc.

5 He prayed for the devil to come get them all,
   Sing halifor, etc.

6 One day the old devil he come,
   Sing halifor, etc.

7 Says: Now, old man, I've come after your wife,
   Sing halifor, etc.

8 He picked her up all on his back,
   And away he went to old tample (*or* temple) shack,
   Sing halifor, etc.

9 He took her down unto his den,
   Sing halifor, etc.

10 Where he had bells, blubs, blinds and chains,
   Sing halifor, etc.

11 She picked up the axe and mauled out his brains,
   Sing halifor, etc.

12 He picked her up all on his back,
   And away he went to old tample shack,
   Sing halifor, etc.

13 Says: Here, old man, you may have your wife,
   She's almost plagued me out of my life,
   Sing halifor, etc.

14 And now you see what women can do,
   They can conquer men and the devil too,
   Sing halifor, etc.

B

Hexatonic. Mode 1, b.

Sung by Mr. N. B. CHISHOLM
at Woodridge, Va., Sept. 21, 1916

1. There was an old man lived un-der the hill, Sing ti ro rat tle ing day, If he ain't moved a way he's

The Farmer's Curst Wife

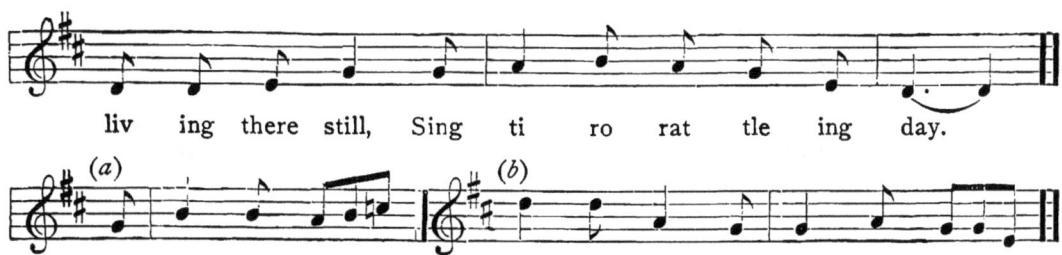

2. This old man went out to his plough,
   To see the old devil fly over his mow.

3. The old man cries out: I am undone,
   For the devil has come for my oldest son.

4. It's not your oldest son I want,
   But your damned old scolding wife I'll have,

5. He took the old woman upon his back,
   And off he went with her packed in a sack.

6. He packed her back in one corner of hell,
   Saying: I hope the old devil will use you well.

7. Twelve little devils came walking by,
   Then she up with her foot and kicked eleven in the fire.

8. The odd little devil peeped over the wall,
   Saying: Take her back, daddy, or she will kill us all.

9. She was six months going and eight coming back,
   And she called for the mush she left in the pot,

10. The old man lay sick in the bed.
    With an old pewter pipe she battered his head.

11. The old man cries out: I am to be cursed,
    She has been to hell and come back worse.

C

Sung by Miss SABRINA RITCHIE
at Hindman School, Knott Co., Ky., Sept. 20, 1917

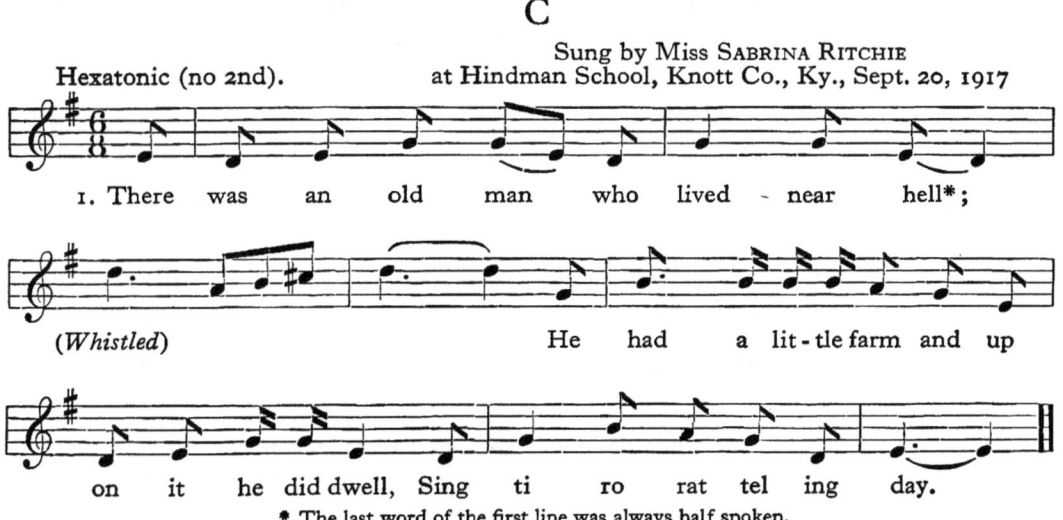

* The last word of the first line was always half spoken.

The Farmer's Curst Wife

2 The devil came to him to his plough one day,
  Saying: One out of your family I'll have to have now.

3 It's neither your son nor your daughter I crave,
  But your old scolding wife and I have to have her now.

4 He harvest her up all on his back,
  Like an old pedlar went packing his pack.

5 He carried her down to the high gates of hell,
  Saying: Rake back the coals and we'll roast her well.

6 Two little devils came rattling their chains,
  She hauled back her cudgels and hauled out their brains.

7 Two more little devils peeped over the wall,
  Saying: Take her back, daddy, she'll kill us all.

8 So he harvest her up all on his back,
  And went like a bold pedlar went packing her back.

9 Seven years gone and seven a-coming back,
  She called for the 'bacca' she left in the crack.

10 The women they are so much better than men,
  When they go to hell they're sent back again.

D

Sung by Mr. SANDY STUART STOREY
at Mt. Smoky Academy,
Sevier Co., Tenn., April 19, 1917

Pentatonic. Mode 3.

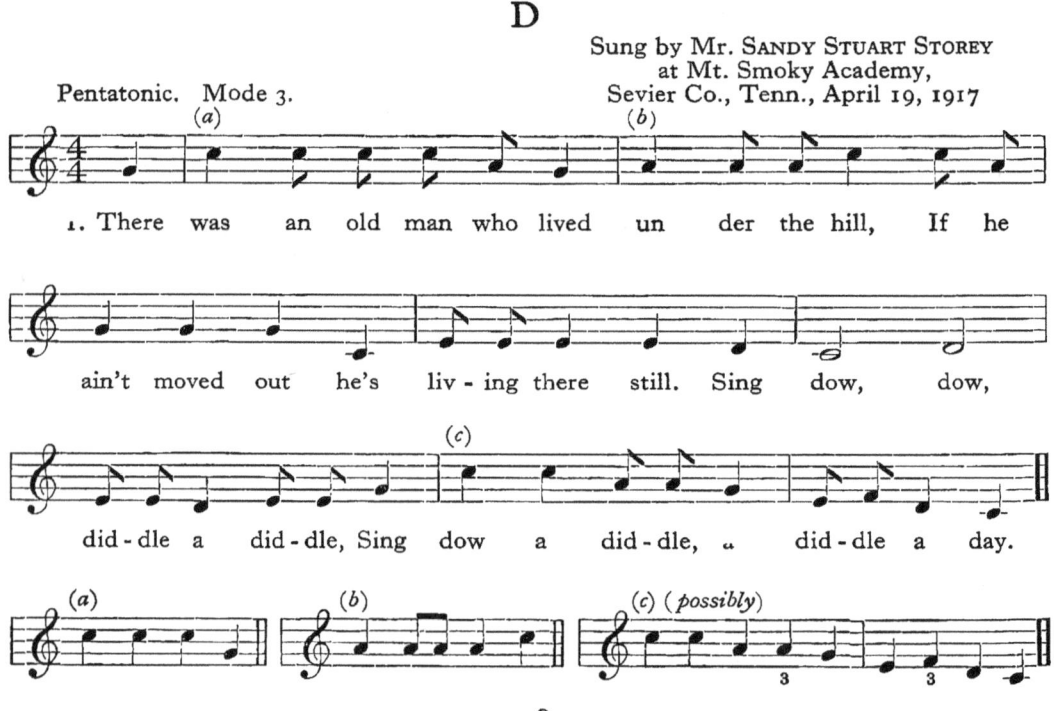

1. There was an old man who lived under the hill, If he ain't moved out he's living there still. Sing dow, dow, diddle a diddle, Sing dow a diddle, a diddle a day.

The Farmer's Curst Wife

2 He geared up his hogs and went out to plough,
And how he got along I hardly know how.

3 One day the old devil came down the field,
Said: One of your family I'm going to steal.

4 He got her up upon his back,
He looked like a pedlar with a pack on his back.

5 He carried her till he came to the road.
Get down, old lady, you're a terrible load.

6 He carried her till he came to the gate.
Get down, old lady, right here's the place.

7 As he was binding her down with chains,
She grabbed up a pick and split out his brains.

8 Seven little devils came out from the wall,
Saying: Take her back, daddy, she'll murder us all.

9 And now you see what a woman will do;
She can out the devil and her husband too.

E

Heptatonic. Mixolydian.

Sung by Miss SUSAN MOBERLY
at Oneida, Clay Co., Ky., Aug. 20, 1917

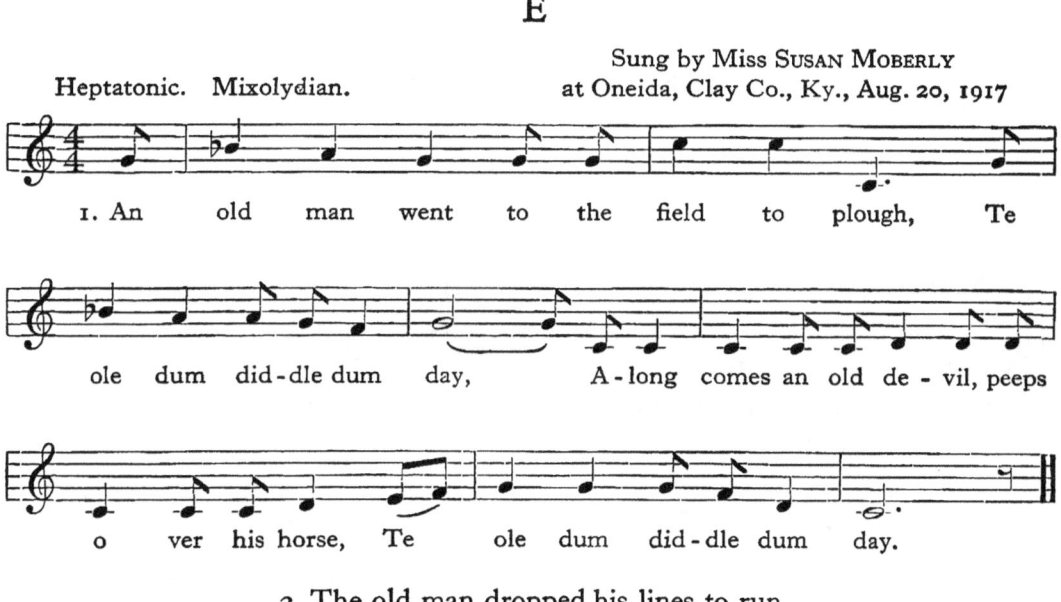

1. An old man went to the field to plough, Te ole dum did-dle dum day, A-long comes an old de-vil, peeps over his horse, Te ole dum did-dle dum day.

2 The old man dropped his lines to run.
He's right now after my oldest son.

3 It's not your oldest son I want,
But your old hump-back-ed wife I crave.

The Farmer's Curst Wife

4 Take her, O take her with all your heart,
And leave me with hopes that you'll never depart.

5 He picked her up all on his back,
Like an old pedlar went wagging his pack.

6 He carried her on to the forks of the road,
Says: Good lady, you're a pretty good load.

7 He carried her on to the devil's back-door,
He put her down there to carry no more.

8 The old devil laid far back on the bed.
With an old pewter pot she mellered his head.

9 Ten little devils hanging up by a chain;
With her old pewter pipe she picked out their brains.

10 Seven little devils peeped over the wall,
Says: Take her back, daddy, she'll murder us all.

11 He picked her up all on his back,
Just like an old fool went wagging her back.

12 He carries her on to the foot of the hill.
She says: If the devil won't have me, don't know who will.

13 Seven years there and three years back,
She called for the bread-crust she left in the crack.

F

(No 6th or 7th.) Sung by Mrs. Eliza Pace
at Hyden, Leslie Co., Ky., Oct. 1, 1917

1. There was an old fellow lived under the hill, There was an old fellow lived under the hill, If he hain't moved away he's living there still, Sing ti ro rat tel ing day.

The Farmer's Curst Wife

2 One day the old man went out to plough,
  The devil flew over his old grey mare.

3 He dragged his plough, it broke and he ran.
  The devil's come after my oldest son.

4 It's not your oldest son I pray,
  It's your old scolding wife I'll have.

5 He took her down to the gates of hell,
  He gave her a kick, saying: Go there.

6 Nine little devils come rattling their chains.
  She up with the poker and knocked out their brains.

7 One little devil peeped over the wall,
  Saying: Take her back, daddy, or she'll kill us all.

8 He humped her up all on his poor back,
  And away the old fool went walking her back.

9 Her husband lying sick on the bed,
  She took her old pewter pot, battered his head.

10 She's six months going and nine coming back;
   Called for the mush she left in the pot.

11 What I can do I never can tell;
   I ain't fit for heaven and they won't have me in hell.

G

Sung by Mr. WILLIAM MORGAN
at Short Creek, Hyden, Leslie Co., Ky., Oct. 5, 1917

Hexatonic (no 3rd).

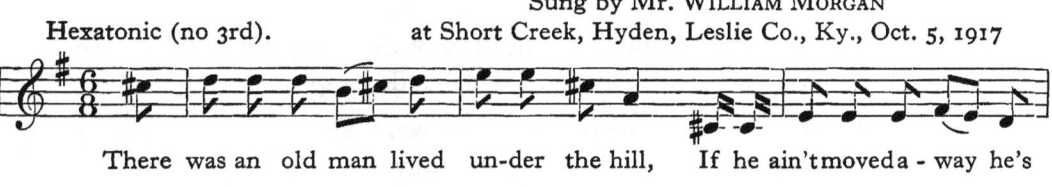

There was an old man lived un-der the hill, If he ain't moved a-way he's

liv ing there still, Sing ti ro rat tel ing day.

No. 41

The Golden Vanity

A

Heptatonic. Mode 4,
a + b (dorian).*

Sung by Mrs. Jane Gentry
at Hot Springs, N. C., Sept. 12, 1916

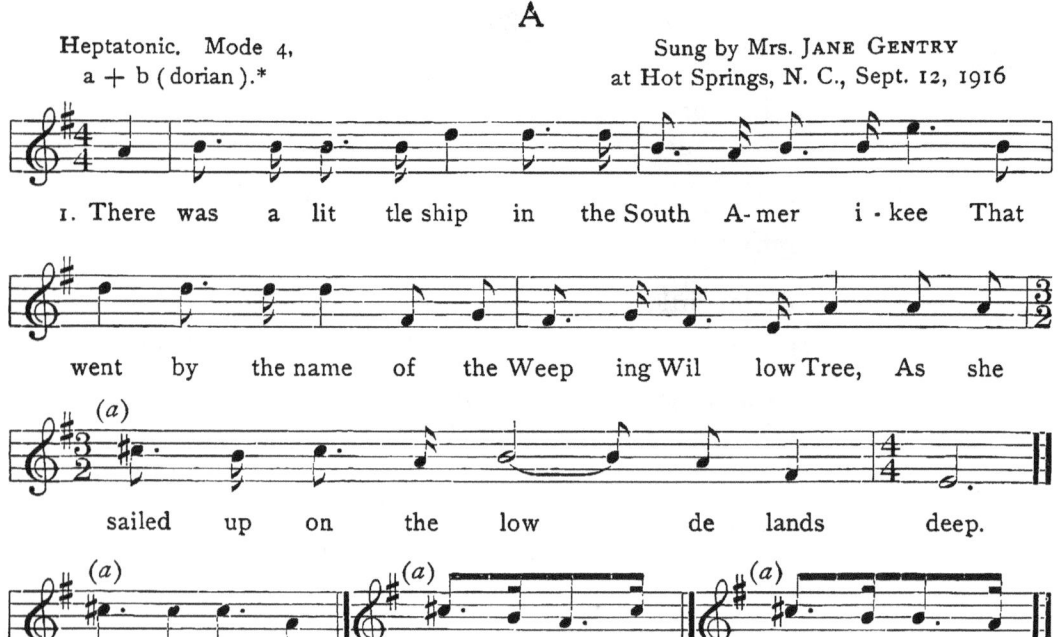

1. There was a little ship in the South A-mer-i-kee That went by the name of the Weeping Willow Tree, As she sailed upon the low-de-lands deep.

2 There was another ship in the North Amerikee,
She went by the name of the Golden Silveree,
As she sailed upon the low-de-lands deep.

3 O captain, O captain, what'll you give to me,
If I'll go and sink the ship of the Weeping Willow Tree,
As she sailed upon the low-de-lands deep?

4 I will give you gold and I'll give to you a fee,
Give to you my daughter and married you shall be,
As we sailed upon the low-de-lands deep.

5 He bent to his breast and away swum he,
He swum and he sunk the ship of the Weeping Willow Tree,
As they sailed upon the low-de-lands deep.

6 He bent to his breast and back swum he,
Back to the ship of the Golden Silveree,
As they sailed upon the low-de-lands deep.

7 O captain, O captain, pray take me on my board,
For I have been just as good as my word,
I sunk her in the low-de-lands deep.

* If A be tonic — Mode 1, a + b (mixolydian).

The Golden Vanity

8 I know that you've been just as good as your word,
But never more will I take you on board,
As we sailed upon the low-de-lands deep.

9 If it wasn't for the love that I have for your girl,
I'd do unto you as I did unto them,
I'd sink you in the low-de-lands deep.

10 But he turned upon his back and down went he,
Down, down, down to the bottom of the sea,
As they sailed upon the low-de-lands deep.

B

Pentatonic. Mode 4.

Sung by Mrs. SARAH BUCKNER
at Black Mountain, N. C., Sept. 18, 1916

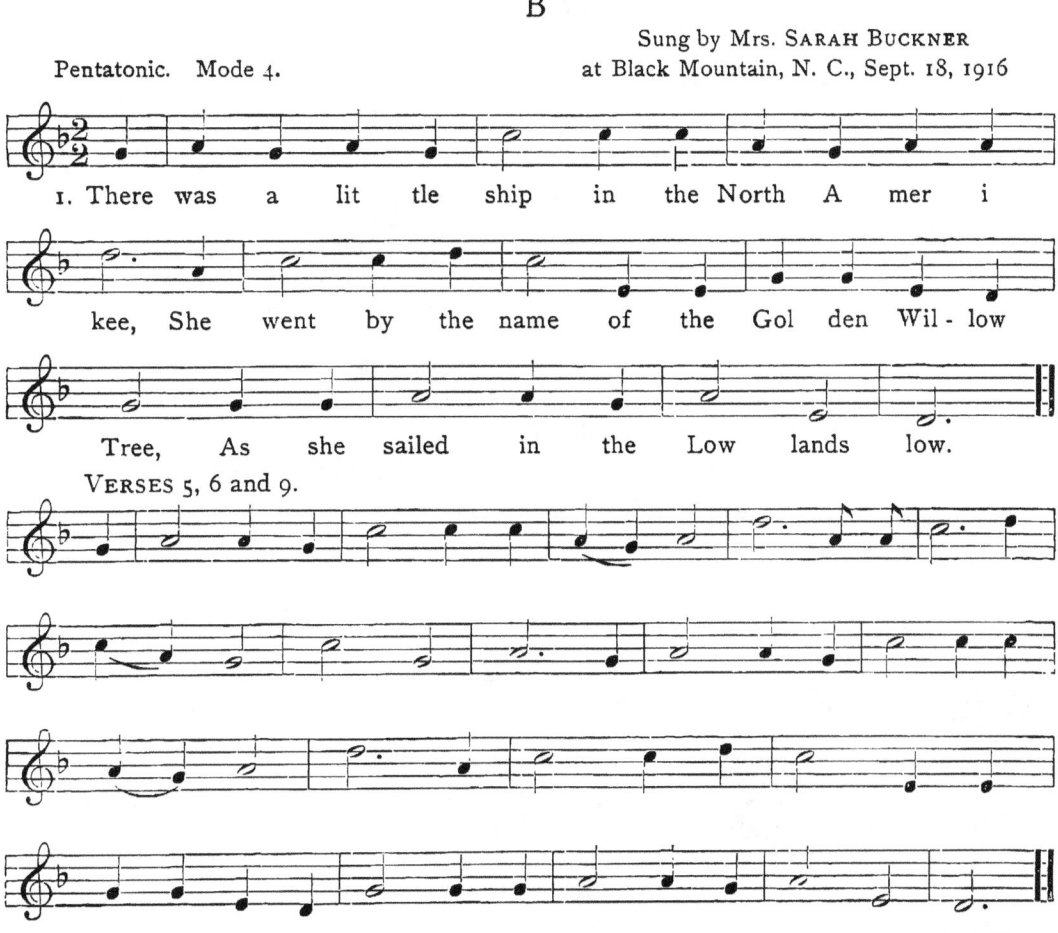

1. There was a little ship in the North Amerikee, She went by the name of the Golden Willow Tree, As she sailed in the Lowlands low.

VERSES 5, 6 and 9.

2 There was another ship in the South Amerikee,
She went by the name of the Turkey Silveree,
As she sailed in the Lowlands low.

3 O captain, O captain, what will you give to me
To sink the ship of the Golden Willow Tree,
As she sails in the Lowlands low?

The Golden Vanity

4 I will give you gold, I will give you fee,
   I'll give you my daughter and a-married you shall be,
   If you sink her in the Lowlands low.

5 He turned on his back and away swam he,
   Crying: O this Lowland lies so low.
   He turned on his breast and away swam he,
   He swam till he came to the Golden Willow Tree,
   As she sailed on the Lowlands low.

6 He turned on his back and away swam he,
   Crying: O this Lowland lies so low.
   He turned on his breast and away swam he,
   He swam till he came to the Turkey Silveree,
   As she sailed on the Lowlands low.

7 O captain, O captain, pray take me on board,
   For I have been just as good as my word,
   I have sunk her in the Lowlands low.

8 I know you have been just as good as your word,
   But never no more will I take you on board,
   While I sail on the Lowlands low.

9 He turned on his back and down swum he,
   Crying: O this Lowland lies so low.
   He turned on his breast and down swum he,
   He sank before he came to the Turkey Silveree,
   Till she sailed on the Lowlands low.

C

Pentatonic. Mode 1.

Sung by Mrs. Hester House
at Hot Springs, N. C., Sept. 15, 1916

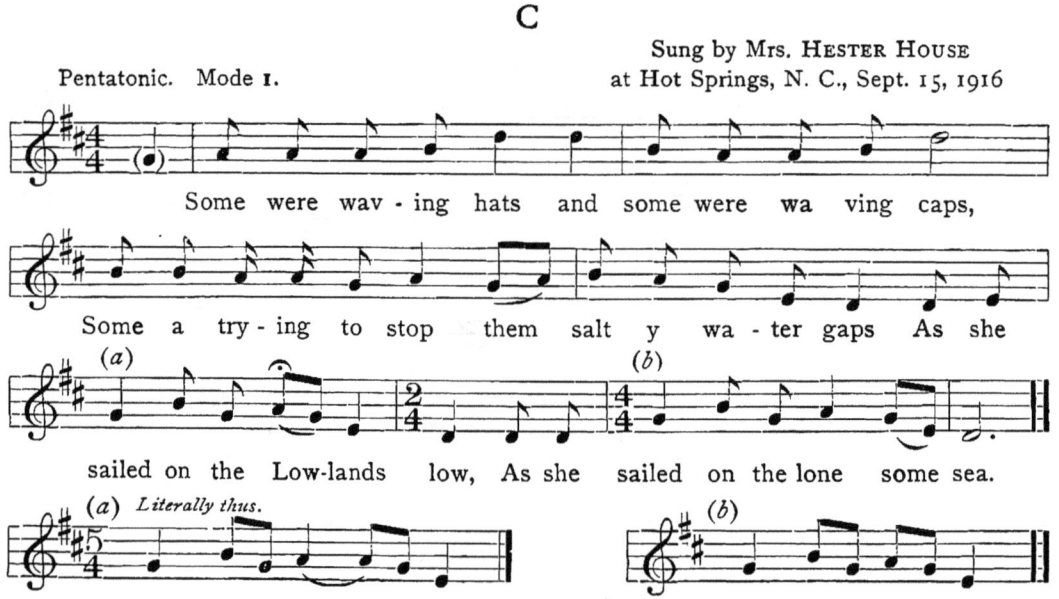

Some were wav-ing hats and some were wa ving caps,
Some a try-ing to stop them salt y wa-ter gaps As she
sailed on the Low-lands low, As she sailed on the lone some sea.

(a) *Literally thus.*

The Golden Vanity

D

Sung by Mr. LUTHER SHADOIN
at Lexington, Ky., Sept. 3, 1917

Hexatonic (no 6th).

1. There was a ship sailed from the North A-mer-i-kee, Cry-ing

O the lone-some low-lands low, There was a ship sailed from the

North A-mer-i-kee, And she went by the name of the Green Willow Tree, As she

sailed from the low-lands low.

2 She'd only been a-sailing for two weeks or three,
   O ho, the lonesome lowlands low,
   She'd only been a-sailing for two weeks or three
   Till she was overtaken by the Turkish Revelee,
   As she sailed from the lowlands low.

3 Then cried the captain: What shall we do?
   Crying O the lonesome lowlands low.
   Then cried the captain: What shall we do?
   The Turkish Revelee will surely cut us in two,
   As we sailed from the lowlands low.

4 Up spake a sailor boy: What will you give to me?
   Crying O the lonesome lowlands low.
   Up spake a sailor boy: What will you give to me
   If I will go and sink for you the Turkish Revelee?
   As we sail from the lowlands low.

5 I'll give you gold, I'll give you fee,
   Crying O the lonesome lowlands low.
   I'll give you gold, I'll give you fee
   And my only daughter for your wedded wife to be,
   As we sailed from the lowlands low.

The Golden Vanity

6 The lad leaped down and away swam he,
    Crying O the lonesome lowlands low,
  The lad leaped down and away swam he,
  And he swam till he came to the Turkish Revelee,
    As we sailed from the lowlands low.

7 There were some playing cards and some playing checks,
    As we sailed from the lowlands low,
  There were some playing cards and some playing checks,
  And before they cleared the boards they were in water to their necks,
    As we sailed from the lowlands low.

8 Then the lad turned back and away swam he,
    Crying O the lonesome lowlands low,
  Then he fell upon his breast and away swam he,
  And he swam till he came to the Green Willow Tree,
    As we sailed from the lowlands low.

9 Cried he: Kind captain, I have done your decree,
    Crying O the lonesome lowlands low,
  Cried he: Kind captain, I have done your decree,
  Now take me on board ere I perish in the sea,
    And we sailed from the lowlands low.

10 Nay, nay, sailor-boy, I'll never take you on board,
    Crying O the lonesome lowlands low,
  Nay, nay, sailor-boy, I'll never take you on board,
  Never will I be to you as good as my word,
    As we sailed from the lowlands low.

11 'Tis only the respect that I have for your crew,
    O ho, the lonesome lowlands low,
  'Tis only the respect that I have for your crew,
  Or I'd sink your ship and you with it too,
    As we sailed from the lowlands low.

12 Then he fell upon his breast and away swam he,
    Crying O the lonesome lowlands low,
  Then he fell upon his breast and away swam he.
  Adieu, adieu to the Green Willow Tree,
    Adieu to the lowlands low.

The first stanza only was noted from Mr. Shadoin's singing. The remaining stanzas were copied from Professor Raine's collection, he having noted the text of the song from Mr. Shadoin on a former occasion.

The Golden Vanity

E

Pentatonic. Mode 3.

Sung by Miss N. F. Stoton
at Berea, Madison Co., Ky., May 29, 1917

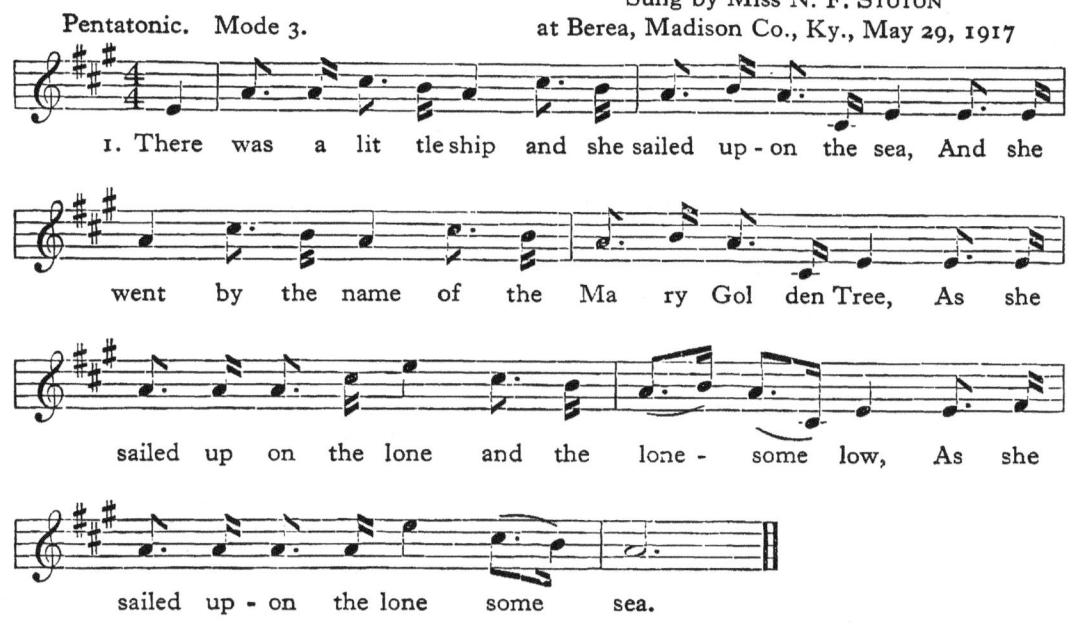

1. There was a lit-tle ship and she sailed up-on the sea, And she went by the name of the Ma-ry Gol-den Tree, As she sailed up on the lone and the lone-some low, As she sailed up-on the lone-some sea.

2 There was another ship and she sailed upon the sea
And she went by the name of the Turkish Robberee,
   As she sailed upon the lone, etc.

3 Up stepped a little sailor, unto his captain said:
O captain, O captain what will you give to me
   If I'll sink them in the lone and the lonesome low,
   If I'll sink them in the lonesome sea.

4 Ten thousand dollars I'll given unto thee,
And my oldest daughter I'll wedden' unto thee,
   If you'll sink them in the lone, etc.

5 He bowed upon his breast and away swam he
Till he came to the ship of the Turkish Robberee,
   As she sailed upon the lone, etc.

6 Then out of his pocket an instrument he drew,
And he bored nine holes for to let the water through,
   As they sailed upon the lone, etc.

7 O some had hats and some had caps,
And they tried for to stop those awful water gaps,
   For they're sinking in the lone, etc.

8 He bowed upon his breast and away swam he
Till he came to the ship of the Mary Golden Tree
   As she sailed upon the lone, etc.

9 O captain, O captain, won't you take me on board?
O captain, O captain, be as good as your word,
   For I've sank them in the low, etc.

The Golden Vanity

10 O no, I will neither be as good as my word,
    O no, I will neither take you on board,
        For I'm sailing on the lone, etc.

11 If it wasn't for the love of your daughter and your men,
    I would do unto you as I done unto them,
        I would sink you in the lone, etc.

12 He turned on his back and down sank he.
    Farewell, farewell to the Mary Golden Tree,
        For I'm sinking in the lone and the lonesome low,
        For I'm sinking in the lonesome sea.

The Golden Vanity

The Golden Vanity

K

Sung by Mrs. Laura Beckett
at St. Peter's School, Callaway, Va., Aug. 16, 1918

Heptatonic (no 6th).

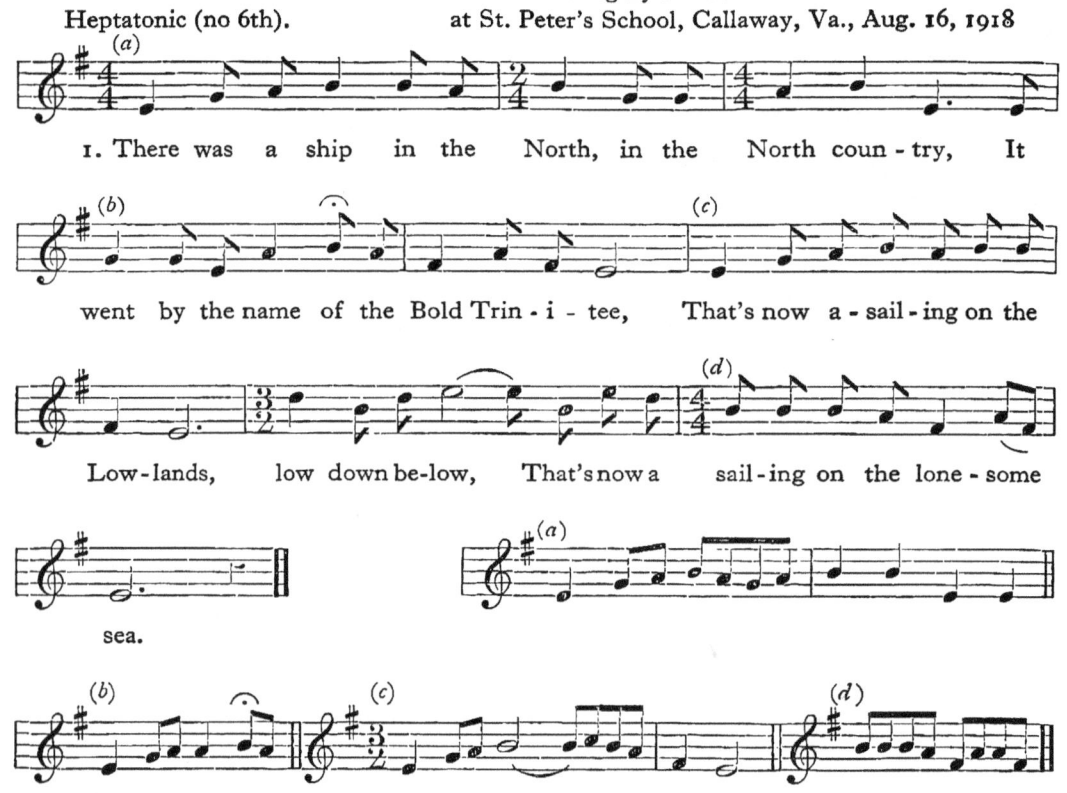

1. There was a ship in the North, in the North country, It went by the name of the Bold Trin-i-tee, That's now a-sail-ing on the Low-lands, low down be-low, That's now a sail-ing on the lone-some sea.

2 He had a little auger just fit for the work,
He bored nine holes in the bottom of the Turk
That's now a-sailing, etc.

3 Out on his back and away swam he,
He swam till he came to the Bold Trinity.

4 Captain, O captain, take me on board
And be unto me just as good as your word
As we're now a-sailing, etc.

5 O no, cried the captain, can't take you on board
Nor neither can I be unto you as good as my word,
But I'll leave you in the Lowlands, etc.

6 If it wasn't for your daughter and the sake of your men
I'd do unto you as I did unto them,
For I'd sink you in the Lowlands low down below,
For I'd sink you on the lonesome sea.

No. 42

The Mermaid

A

Sung by Mrs. Leona Melton
at Mackintosh Creek, Hyden, Leslie Co., Ky.,
Oct. 2, 1917

Heptatonic. Ionian.

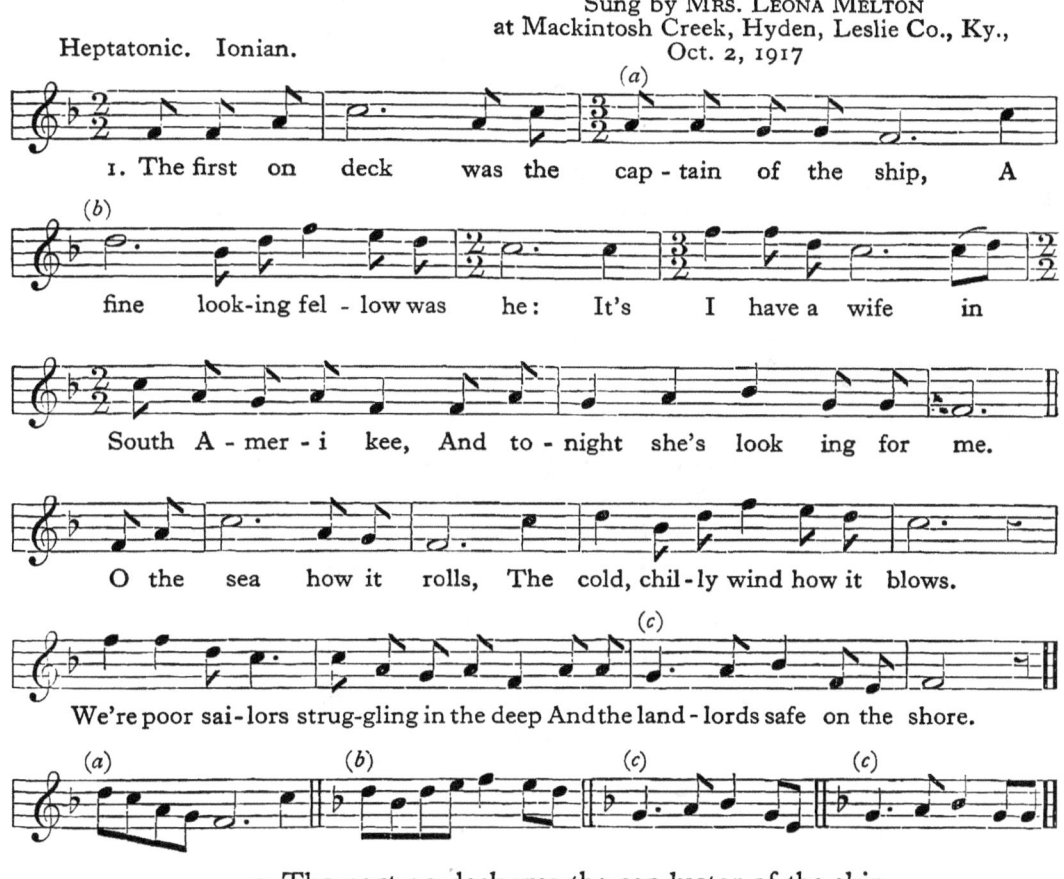

1. The first on deck was the captain of the ship,
A fine looking fellow was he: It's I have a wife in South Ameri kee, And tonight she's looking for me.
O the sea how it rolls, The cold, chilly wind how it blows.
We're poor sailors struggling in the deep And the landlords safe on the shore.

2 The next on deck was the conductor of the ship,
A fine looking fellow was he:
I have a wife and three little babes,
And to-night they're looking for me.
   O the sea how it rolls, etc.

3 The next on deck was the doctor of the ship,
A fine looking fellow was he:
I have two patients on the next deck below,
And to-night they're looking for me.

4 The next on deck was a little boy,
A wretched looking fellow was he;
He said: I care no more for my wife and little babes
Than I do for the fish in the sea.

5 Nine times around sailed the little ship,
Nine times around sailed she,
Nine times around sailed the little ship,
And sank to the depths of the sea.

The Mermaid

B

Pentatonic. Mode 2.

Sung by Mrs. Eliza Pace
at Hyden, Leslie Co., Ky., Oct. 3, 1917

1. As I walked out one eve-ning fair Out of sight of land, There I saw a mer-maid a-sit-ting on a rock With a comb and a glass in her hand.

2 A-combing down her yellow hair,
   And her skin was like a lily so fair;
   Her cheeks were like two roses and her eyes were like a star,
   And her voice were like a nightingale clear.

3 This little mermaid sprung into the deep.
   The wind it began for to blow.
   The hail and the rain were so dark in the air.
   We'll never see land no more.

4 At last came down the captain of the ship
   With a plumb and a line in his hand.
   He plumbed the sea to see how far it was
   To the rock or else to the sand.

5 He plumbed him behind and he plumbed him before,
   The ship kept turning around.
   Our captain cried out: Our ship it does wreck,
   For the measles (*sic*) runs around.

6 Come throw out your lading as fast as you can,
   The truth to you I'll tell.
   This night we all must part
   To heaven or else to hell.

7 Come all you unmarried men that's living on the land,
   That's living at home at your ease.
   Try the best you can your living for to gain
   And never incline to the seas.

The Mermaid

C

Hexatonic (no 7th).
Sung by Mrs. Sina Boone
at Shoal Creek, Burnsville, N. C., Sept. 28, 1918

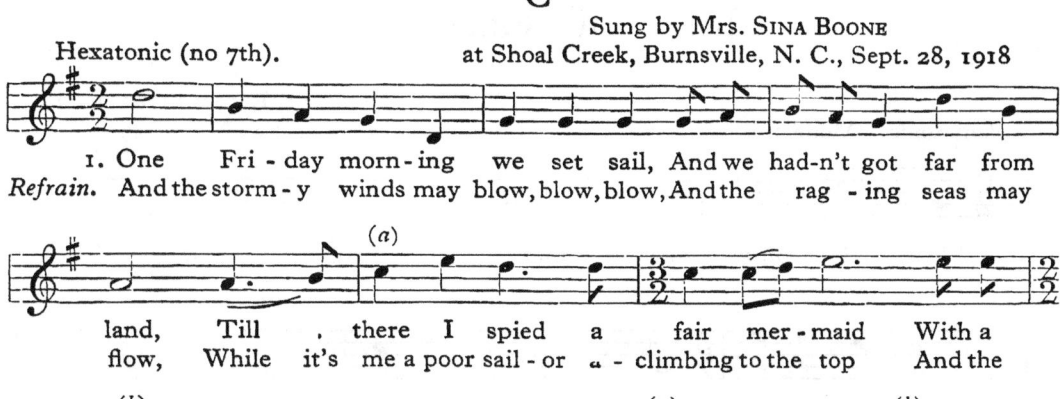

2. Then it's up said the captain of our gallant ship,
   And a well-looking boy was he;
   I've a father and a mother in my native land,
   And this night they're weeping for me.
     And the stormy winds, etc.

3. It's up said the captain of our gallant ship,
   And a well-looking man was he;
   I've a wife and a child in my own native land,
   And this night a widow may be.

4. Then three times around went our gallant ship,
   And three times around went she;
   And the third time that she sailed round,
   She sank to the bottom of the sea.

D

Hexatonic (no 4th).
Sung by Miss Lulu Fulmiller
at Blue Ridge Springs, Va., June 2, 1918

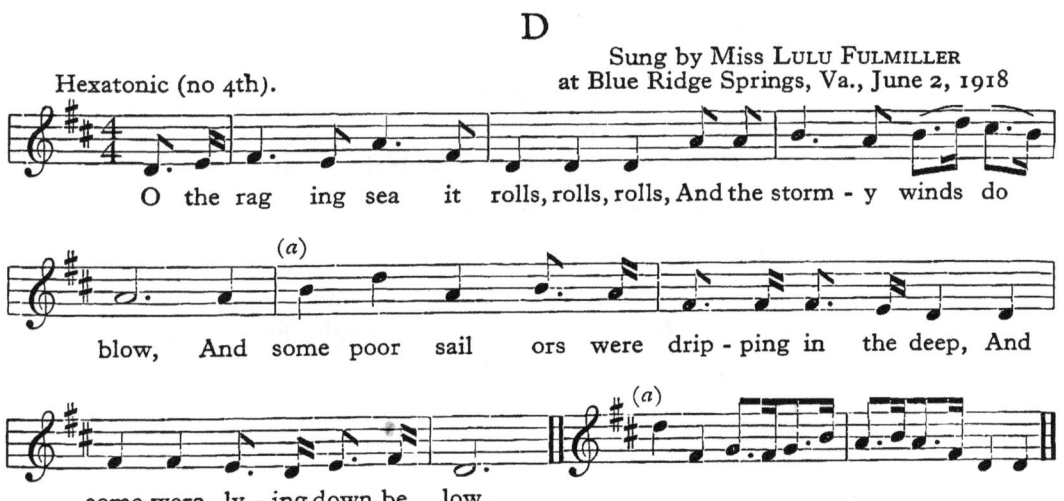

No. 43

John of Hazelgreen

Sung by Mr. LLOYD FITZGERALD
at Nash, Va., May 9, 1918

Pentatonic. Mode 3.

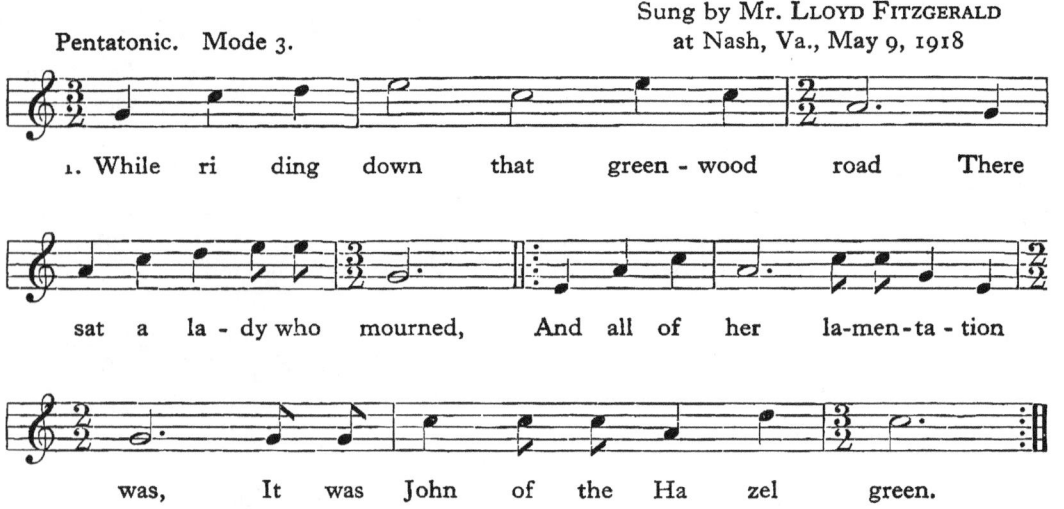

2 You are welcome home with me, kind Miss,
   You are welcome home, said he,
   And you may have my oldest son ⎫ (bis)
   A husband for to be.   ⎭

3 O I don't want your oldest son,
   He's neither lord nor king.
   I intend to be the bride of none
   But John of the Hazelgreen.

4 For he's tall and his shoulders broad,
   He's the lord of all our kin,
   His hair hangs down like the links of gold,
   He's John of the Hazelgreen.

5 While riding down that lengthy lane,
   That lane that leads to town,
   O up stepped John of the Hazelgreen
   And holped his lady down.

6 Forty times he kissed her ruby lips,
   And forty times he kissed her chin,
   And forty times he kissed her ruby lips
   And let (or led) his lady in.

No. 44

The Brown Girl

A

Pentatonic. Mode 3.

Sung by Mrs. Mary Sands
at Allanstand, N. C., July 31, 1916

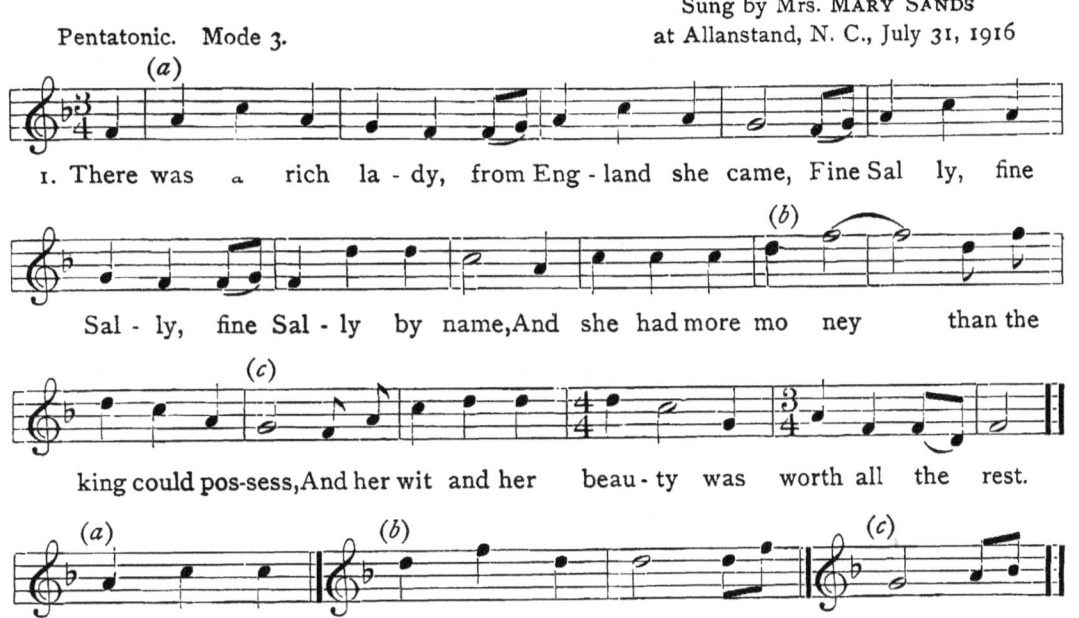

1. There was a rich lady, from England she came, Fine Sally, fine Sally, fine Sally by name, And she had more money than the king could possess, And her wit and her beauty was worth all the rest.

2 There was a poor doctor who lived hard by,
And on this fair damsel he cast his eye.
Fine Sally, fine Sally, fine Sally, says he,
Can you tell me the reason our love can't agree?
I don't hate you, Billy, nor no other man,
But to tell you I love you I never can.

3 Fine Sally took sick and she knew not for why,
And she sent for this young man that she was to deny.
He says: Am I the doctor that you have sent for,
Or am I the young man that you once did deny?
Yes, you are the doctor can kill or can cure
And without your assistance I'm ruined, I'm sure.

4 Fine Sally, fine Sally, fine Sally, says he,
Don't you remember when you slighted me?
You slighted me highly, you used me with scorn,
And now I reward you for what's passed and gone.

5 What's passed and gone, love, forget and forgive,
And spare me a while longer in this wide world to live.
I don't want you, Sally, in the durance of my breath,
But I'll dance on your grave when you're laid in the earth.

The Brown Girl

6 Off from her fingers pulled diamond rings three.
   Here, take these rings and wear them when you're dancing on me,
   Then fly from your colour and be no more seen
   When you have done dancing on Sally your queen.

B

Heptatonic. Mode 3, a+b.

Sung by Mrs. Tom Rice
at Big Laurel, N. C., Aug. 17, 1916

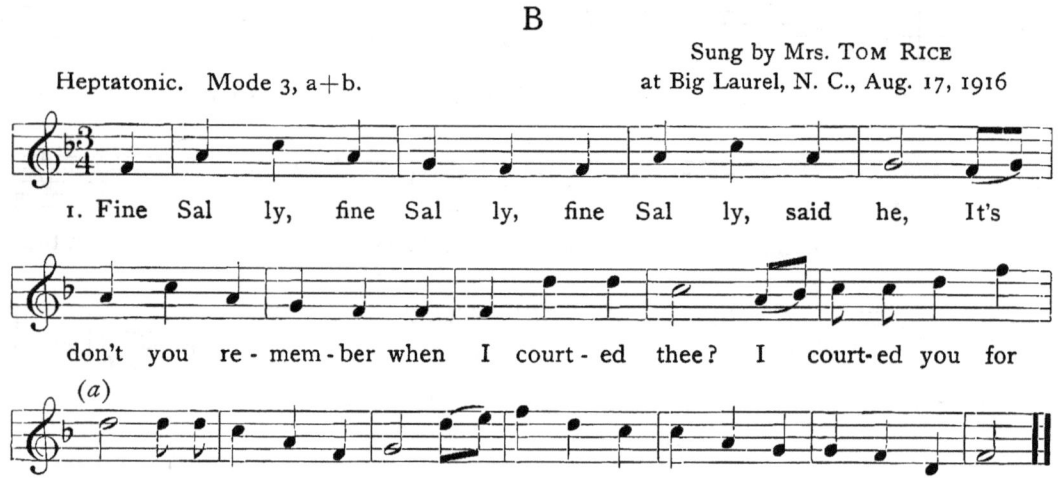

1. Fine Sally, fine Sally, fine Sally, said he, It's don't you re-mem-ber when I court-ed thee? I court-ed you for love, you de-nied me with scorn, And now I'll re-ward you for things past and gone.

2 For things past and gone, love, forget and forgive,
  And grant me a little longer on this earth to live.
  I never will forgive you in the durance of my breath,
  And I'll dance on your grave when you're lying in the earth.

3 Then off her fingers pulled diamond rings three,
  Says: O wear these for my sake when you're dancing on me,
  And fly from your colours and be no more seen
  When you're done dancing on Sally your queen.

4 Farewell to old father and old father's friends,
  Farewell to this young man. God make him amends
  Farewell to this whole world and all

C

Hexatonic. Mode 3, a.

Sung by Mr. Mitchell Wallin
at Allanstand, N. C., Aug. 4, 1916

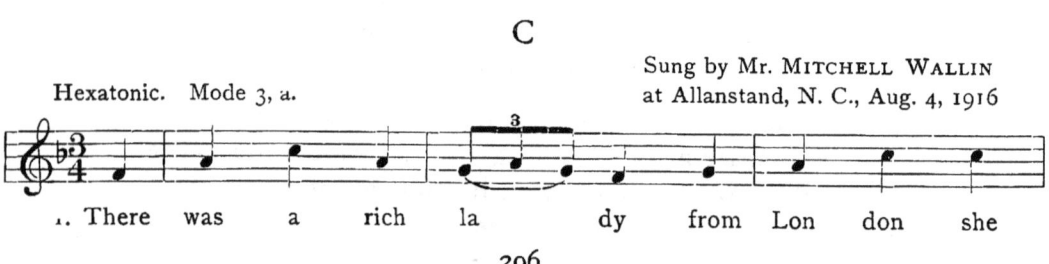

1. There was a rich la-dy from Lon-don she

The Brown Girl

The Brown Girl

F

Sung by Mrs. MOORE, Rabun Co., Ga., May 2, 1909. (Tune not noted.)

1 There was a young doctor, from London he came,
 He courted a damsel called Sarah by name.
 Her wealth it was more than the king could possess;
 Her beauty it was more than her wealth at the best.

2 O Sarah, O Sarah, O Sarah, said he,
 I am truly sorry that we can't agree,
 But if your heart don't turn unto love,
 I fear that your beauty my ruin will prove.

3 O no, I don't hate you, and no other man,
 But to say that I like you is more than I can.
 So now you may stop with all your discourse,
 For I never 'low to have you unless I am forced.

4 After twenty-eight weeks had done gone and passed,
 The beautiful damsel she fell sick at last.
 She sent for the young man she once did deny,
 For to come and see her before she did die.

5 Am I the young man that you sent for here?
 Or am I the young man that you loved so dear?
 You're the only young doctor can kill or can cure,
 And without your assistance I'm ruined, I'm sure.

6 O Sarah, O Sarah, O Sarah, said he,
 Don't you remember you once slighted me?
 You slighted, deviled me, you slighted me with scorn,
 And now I'll reward you for things past and gone.

7 Forget and forgive, O lover, said she,
 And grant me some longer a time for to live.
 O no, I won't, Sarah, enduring your breath,
 But I'll dance on your grave when you lay in cold death.

8 Gold rings off her finger ends she pulled three,
 Saying: Take these and wear them when you dance on me.
 Ten thousand times over my folly I see.

9 Now pretty Sarah is dead, as we all may suppose.
 To some other rich lady willed all her fine clothes.
 At last she made her bed in the wet and cold clay;
 Her red, rosy cheeks is moulderin' away.

The Brown Girl

G

Pentatonic. Mode 3 (Tonic A).

Sung by Mr. H. D. Kinnard
at Berea, Madison Co., Ky., May 27, 1917

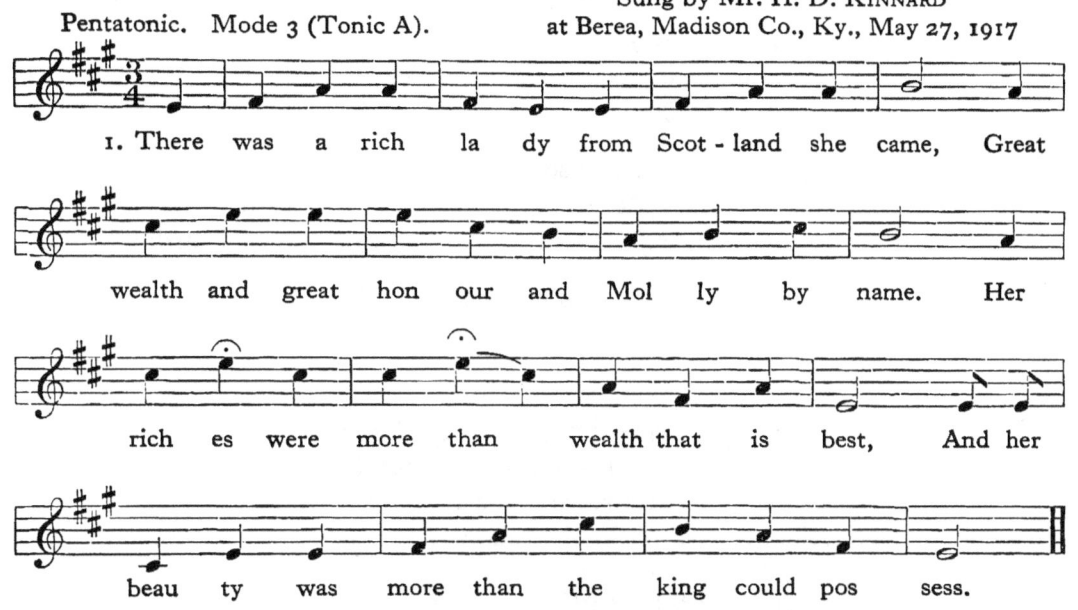

1. There was a rich lady from Scotland she came, Great wealth and great honour and Molly by name. Her riches were more than wealth that is best, And her beauty was more than the king could possess.

2 There was a poor boy who came to court her,
His wages was only one thousand a year.
This lady being wealthy, so noble and high,
And on this poor boy she scarce cast an eye.

3 O Molly, O Molly, O Molly, says he,
I'm sorry that your love and mine don't agree.
Unless all your hatred should turn into love,
Your beauty is my ruin, I'm sure it will prove.

4
But as for to love you is more than I can,
So you may retire in your discourse,
For I never will have you until I am forced.

5 No forcement, dear madam, and this you may know,
There's plenty of others all living alone.
I'll go court some other and hope you may rue.
So fare you well, Molly, I bid you adieu.

6 Six weeks had scarce come, six weeks had scarce passed,
This beautiful damsel lay sick at the last.
In anger, in love, she knew not why,
She sent for the young man she once did deny.

7 O am I the doctor you sent for me here?
Or am I the boy once courted you, dear?
You are the doctor can kill or can cure,
Without your assistance I'm ruined, I'm sure.

The Brown Girl

8 O Molly, O Molly, O Molly, says he,
   It's don't you remember when I once courted thee?
   I courted you lovely, was slighted and scorned;
   And it's I'll reward you for what's passed and gone.

9 For what's passed and gone, love, forget and forgive,
   And grant me assistance some longer to live.
   No, that I won't, Molly, while you do draw breath,
   And I'll dance on your tomb when you're laid in the earth.

10 Then off of her fingers gold rings she pulled three,
   Saying: Take these and wear them while you're dancing on me.

11 This beautiful damsel was laid in the tomb,
   Sweet William was taken on hearing her doom.
   His heart broke with sorrow, his soul it did weep,
   He called for his Molly, but she was asleep.

12 O Molly, O Molly, O Molly, says he,
   You're dead, but in death I am crying for thee.
   I, too, shall die and be laid at your side,
   I'll wed you in death and will make you my bride.

H

Pentatonic. Mode 3 (Tonic C).

Sung by Mr. JOE BLACKETT
at Meadows of Dan, Va., Aug. 28, 1918

1. There was a young lady from London she came, And Sally and Sally, and Sally was her name. Her portion was more than the king he possessed, Her beauty was more than the worth it could fetch.

The Brown Girl

2 Every night in the city (?) for more than one year
  I courted this damsel and straightway did steer.
  But Sally being scornful, her portion being high,
  All on this young knight she'd scarce cast an eye.

3 O Sally, O Sally, O Sally, said he,
  I'm sorry that your love and mine can't agree,
  For I'm sure that you will my ruin prove,
  Unless your great hatred all turns into love.

4 I've no hatred for you, nor no other man,
  But as for to fancy you, I never can.
  So drop your attire and end your discourse,
  For I never will marry you unless I am forced.

5 Before two years had come, or two years had passed,
  He heard of this young lady's misfortune at last,
  She sent for this young man she had slighted and scorned,
  She was pierced through the heart and she knew not wherefrom.

6 Then to her he came to the side of her bed:
  A pain in your side, or a pain in your head?
  O no, kind sir, the rights you've not guessed,
  The pain that I feel presses (*or* pierces) me through the breast.

7 Am I then the doctor you sent for me here?
  Yes, you are the doctor, she cried, my dear.
  You are the man that first caused my woe,
  Then without your assistance I'm ruined, I know.

8 O Sally, O Sally, O Sally, said he,
  Don't you remember how you slighted me?
  The words you have spoken you slighted with scorn,
  And now I'll reward you for things past and gone.

9 For things past and gone, I hope you'll forgive.
  God grant me that blessing each day that I live.
  No, I never will forgive you while I have breath.
  I'll dance on your grave when you're laid in the earth.

10 Then off of her fingers pulled diamond rings three,
   Keep these for my sake when you're dancing on me.
   I'll freely forgive you although you won't me,
   Ten thousand times over my folly I see.

11 Then fare you well, friends, and fare you well, foes,
   Likewise to my sweetheart wherever he goes.
   For ever I must lie in this cold bed of clay.
   My red rosy lips must mould away.

The Brown Girl

I

Hexatonic (no 3rd).

Sung by Mrs. Virginia Bennett
at Burnsville, N. C., Sept. 13, 1918

1. A young Irish lady from London she came, A beautiful creature, fair Sally by name; Her riches was more than the king did possess, Her beauty was more than her wealth at the last.

2 There was a young squire who lived right near,
  A-courting this lady to make her his dear.
  But she was so wealthy, so lofty and high,
  That on this young man she would scarce cast an eye.

3 O Sally, O Sally, O Sally, said he,
  I fear that your beauty my ruin will be
  Unless that your hatred is turned into love,
  I fear that your beauty my ruin will prove.

4 No hatred for you, sir, nor any other man,
  But to say that I love you is more than I can.
  So quit your intentions and mend your discourse,
  For I never will wed you unless I am forced.

5 He said no more to her, but quickly turned home,
  Saying: You shall be sorry for what you have done.
  For what's past and gone I'll never forgive,
  But when you've been buried I will dance on your grave.

6 Before six weeks had scarce come and passed,
  This beautiful creature lay sick at the last.
  She sent for this young man she once did deny.
  She was pierced to the heart and she knew not for why.

The Brown Girl

7 He came to her softly, walked to her bedside.
  Have you a pain in your head or a pain in your side?
  O no, sir, dear young man, the rights you've not guessed,
  The pain is a-piercing all in my left breast.

8 O Sally, O Sally, O Sally, said he,
  O don't you remember that you once slighted me?
  I courted for love, you slighted with scorn,
  Now I'll reward you for what you have done.

9 For what's passed and done, sir, I hope you'll forgive,
  And grant me some longer in this wide world to live.
  That I'll ne'er do, Sally, while I do draw breath,
  But I'll dance on your grave when you're laid in the earth.

10 Farewell father and mother, all foes and all friends,
   Farewell dear young man, God make you amends.
   I'd freely forgive you although you won't me.
   Ten thousand times over my folly I see.

J

Pentatonic. Mode 2. Sung by Mrs. Frances Richards at St. Peter's School, Callaway, Va., Aug. 16, 1918

1. Poor Sally was taken Afflicted to her bed; There's no one knows what ails her, Or could relieve her from pain.

2 King Henry was sent for
  On horseback and speed,
  In the need of poor Sally,
  In the time of her need.

The Brown Girl

3 Am I the doctor
　Was sent for to-day?
　O yes, you're the doctor
　Can kill or can cure,
　And without your assistance
　I am ruined, yes, I'm sure.

4 I courted you with honour,
　You slighted me with scorn.
　I'll remind you of things, girl,
　Of the time past and gone.

5 Of the time past and gone,
　Forget and forgive,
　And 'low me two minutes
　And let me still live.

6 I'll allow you no minutes
　Nor years to live,
　But dance on your grave
　Whilst you lie in cold clay.

7 It's off of her fingers
　Pulled diamond rings twice three.
　Here take those and wear them
　While you're dancing on me.

8 O black was the mourning,
　And yellow was the band,
　And white was poor Sally,
　Poor Sally of time.

K

(No 6th or 7th.) Sung by Mrs. POLLY PATRICK
at Manchester, Clay Co., Ky., Aug. 14, 1917

O am I the doc tor you sent for so shy? Or
am I the young man that you once did de-ny? O you are the doc-tor can
kill or can cure, And with-out your re-lief I am ru ined I'm sure.

No. 45

The Trooper and the Maid

A

Hexatonic. Mode 2, a.

Sung by Mrs. Tom Rice
at Big Laurel, N. C., Aug. 18, 1916

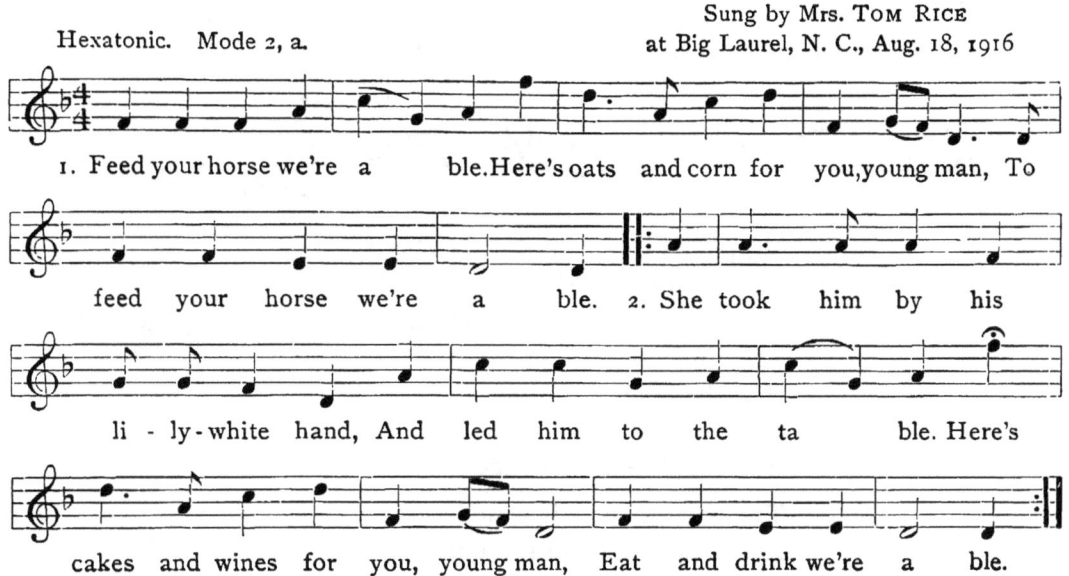

1. Feed your horse we're able. Here's oats and corn for you, young man, To feed your horse we're able. 2. She took him by his lily-white hand, And led him to the table. Here's cakes and wines for you, young man, Eat and drink we're able.

3 She pulled off her lily-white gown
And laid it on the table.
The soldier off with his uniform
And into the bed with the lady.

4 They hadn't been laying in bed but one hour
When he heard the trumpet sound.
She cried out with a thrilling cry:
O Lord, O Lord, I'm ruined.

B

Hexatonic. Mode 2, b.

Sung by Mr. T. Jeff Stockton
at Flag Pond, Tenn., Sept. 4, 1916

1. Here's cakes and wines for you, young man, To eat and drink we're able. Here's cakes and wines for you, young man, To eat and drink we're able. Yes, we're able, we're able, Here's

The Trooper and the Maid

cakes and wines for you, young man, To eat and drink we're a ble.

(a) Last verse

2 He pulled off his shoe-boot clothes
As he rose from the table,
He pulled off his shoe-boot clothes
And into the arms of the lady.
Yes, the lady, the lady,
He pulled off his shoe-boot clothes
And into the arms of the lady.

3 The trumpet now is sounding,
And I must go and leave you.
O soldier, my dear, don't you leave me here,
For if you do I'm ruined for ever.
Yes, for ever, for ever,
O soldier, my dear, don't you leave me here,
For if you do I'm ruined for ever.

4 O when will you come back, my love,
Or when will we get married?
When conk-shells turn to silver bells,
O then, my love, we'll marry.
Yes, we'll marry, we'll marry,
When conk-shells turn to silver bells,
O then, my love, we'll marry.

The Trooper and the Maid

C

Pentatonic. Mode 2.

Sung by Mrs. Effie Mitchell
at Burnsville, N. C., Sept. 29, 1918

2. She took him by the bri-dle rein, She led him to the sta ble.

Here's oats and corn for your horse, young man. To feed your horse we're a ble.

1 I knew a soldier by his horse
  Although I love him dearly.

2 She took him by the bridle rein,
  She led him to the stable.
  Here's oats and corn for your horse, young man,
  To feed your horse we're able.

3 She took him by the lily-white hand,
  She led him to the table.
  Here's cakes and wines for you, young man,
  To eat and drink we're able.

4 She pulled off her lily-white gown
  And fold it on the table;
  He pulled off his bugle-clothes
  And jumped into bed with the lady.

5 They hadn't been there but three hours long
  Till he heard a bugle blowing,
  Saying: O my love, I must go,
  But surely you are ruined.

6 O when shall we meet again,
  Or when shall we get married.
  When conk-shells turn to silver bells,
  O then, my love, we'll marry.

No. 46

The Blind Beggar's Daughter

Heptatonic. Mixolydian.

Sung by Mrs. Ef. Chrisom
at Cane Branch, Burnsville, N. C., Oct. 3, 1918

1 There was a blind beggar, he lost his sight,
He had a daughter both beauty and bright.
Shall I seek for my fortune, kind father, said she.

2 O who be your father, come tell unto me.

3 My father is every day to be seen.

4 If you're the blind beggar's daughter of Bethnal Green,
For I never intend to let any one see,
No, I never intend to let any one see
The blind beggar's daughter my lady shall be.

No. 47

The Babes in the Wood

Sung by Mr. Philander Fitzgerald
at Nash, Va., May 9, 1918

Hexatonic (no 4th).

1. And then those pret-ty lit-tle babes Did wan-der up and down, And ne-ver more did see that man Ap proach ing from the town.

1 And then those pretty little babes
  Did wander up and down,
  And never more did see that man
  Approaching from the town.

2 Their little lips with blackberries
  Were all besmeared and dyed,
  And when the darksome night came on
  They set them down and cried.

3 In each other's arms they died,
  Grim death did end their grief.
  Little Robin Redbreast pitiful-lie
  Covered them up with leaves.

No. 48

In Seaport Town

A

Sung by Miss STELLA SHELTON
at Alleghany, N. C., July 29, 1916

Mode 3, b (no 6th).

1. In Sea-port town there lived a mer-chant, He had three sons and a daugh-ter dear, And a-mong them all was the pret-ti-est boy, He was the daugh-ter's dear-est dear.

2 One evening late they were in the room courting.
  Her oldest brother perchance did hear;
  He went and told his other brothers:
  Let's deprive her of her dearest dear.

3 They rose up early the next morning,
  A game of hunting for to go;
  And upon this young man they both insisted
  For him to go along with them.

4 They wandered over the hills and mountains
  And through a many of a place unknown,
  Till at last they came to a lonesome valley
  And there they killed him dead alone.

5 When they return back the next evening,
  Their sister ask for the servant man.
  Saying: We lost him on a game of hunting;
  No more of him it's could we find.

6 While she lie on her bedside slumbering,
  The servant man did appear to her,
  Saying: Your brother killed me rough and cruel
  All wallowed in a score of blood.

7 She rose up early the next morning;
  She dressed herself in a rich array,
  Saying: I'll go and find my best beloved
  All wallowed in a score of blood.

In Seaport Town

8 She wandered over the hills and mountains
And through a many of a place unknown,
Till at last she came to the lonesome valley,
And there she found him dead alone.

9 Saying: Your eyes look like some bloody butcher,
Your eyes look like some salt or brine.
She kissed his cold, cold lips and, crying,
Said: You are the darling bosom friend of mine.

10 Since my brothers been so cruel
As to force your sweet love away,
One grave shall preserve us both together,
As long as I have breath I will stay with you.

11 When she return back the next evening,
Her brothers ask her where she'd been.
O hold your tongue, you deceitful villains,
For one alone you both shall hang.

12 Her brothers then they came convicted
To jump in a boat and a-finally leave.
The wind did blow and the waves came o'er them;
They made their graves in the deep blue sea.

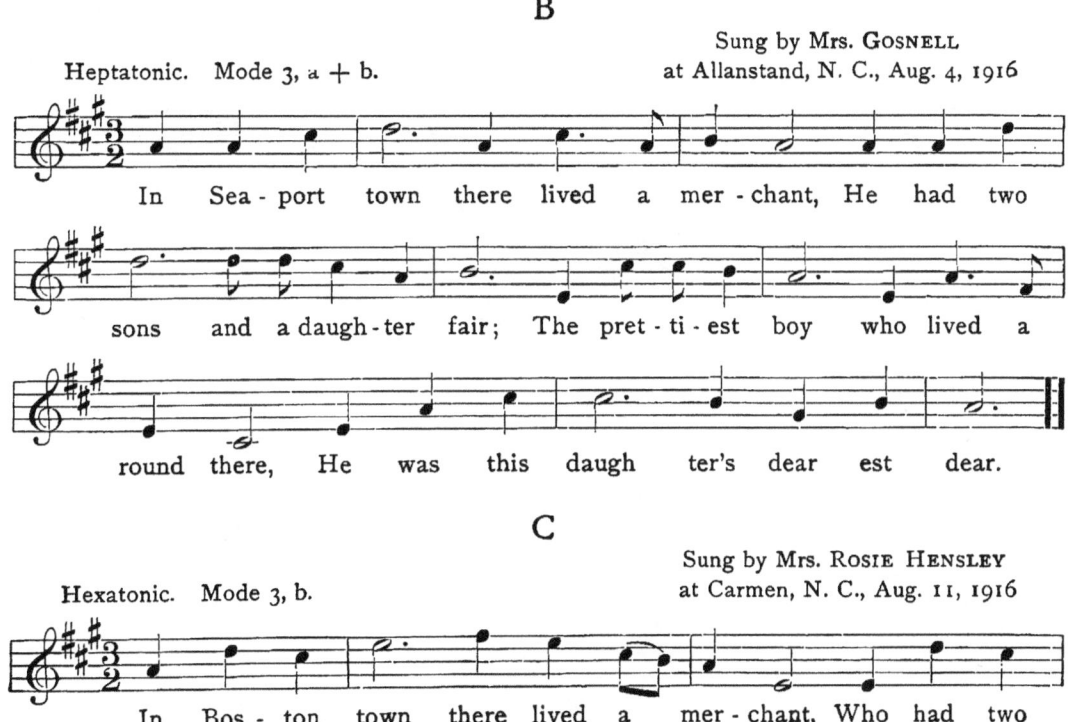

B

Heptatonic. Mode 3, a + b.

Sung by Mrs. GOSNELL
at Allanstand, N. C., Aug. 4, 1916

In Sea-port town there lived a mer-chant, He had two sons and a daugh-ter fair; The pret-ti-est boy who lived a round there, He was this daugh-ter's dear-est dear.

C

Hexatonic. Mode 3, b.

Sung by Mrs. ROSIE HENSLEY
at Carmen, N. C., Aug. 11, 1916

In Bos-ton town there lived a mer-chant, Who had two

In Seaport Town

D

Heptatonic. Mode 4, a + b
(mixolydian).

Sung by Mrs. Jane Gentry
at Hot Springs, N. C., Sept. 14, 1916

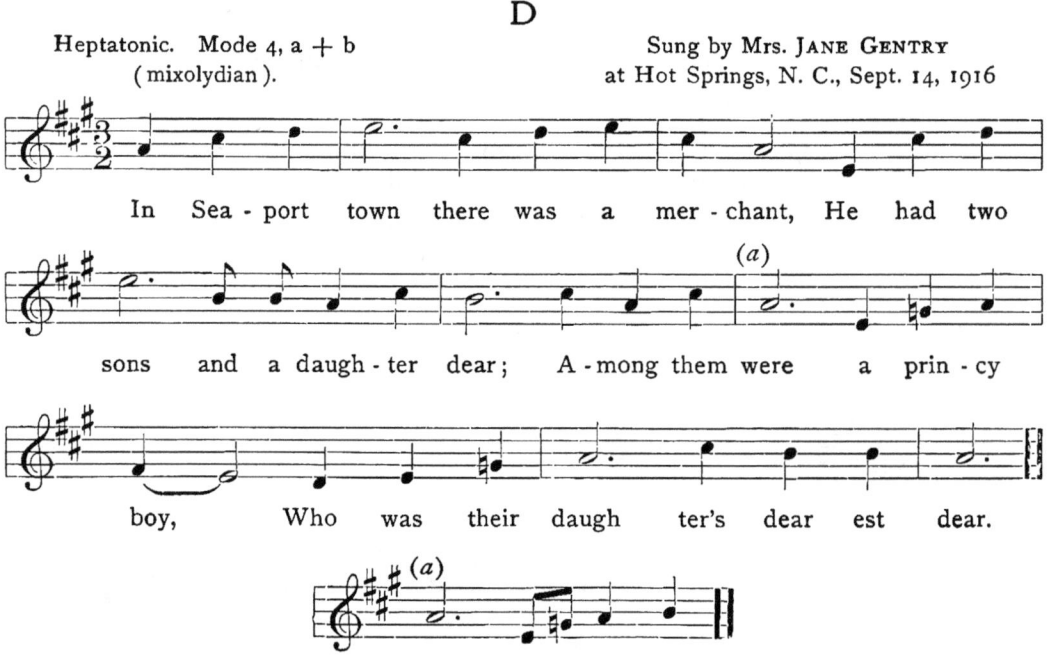

In Seaport Town

E

Heptatonic. Mixolydian influence.

Sung by Mrs. Eliza Pace
at Hyden, Leslie Co., Ky., Oct. 3, 1917

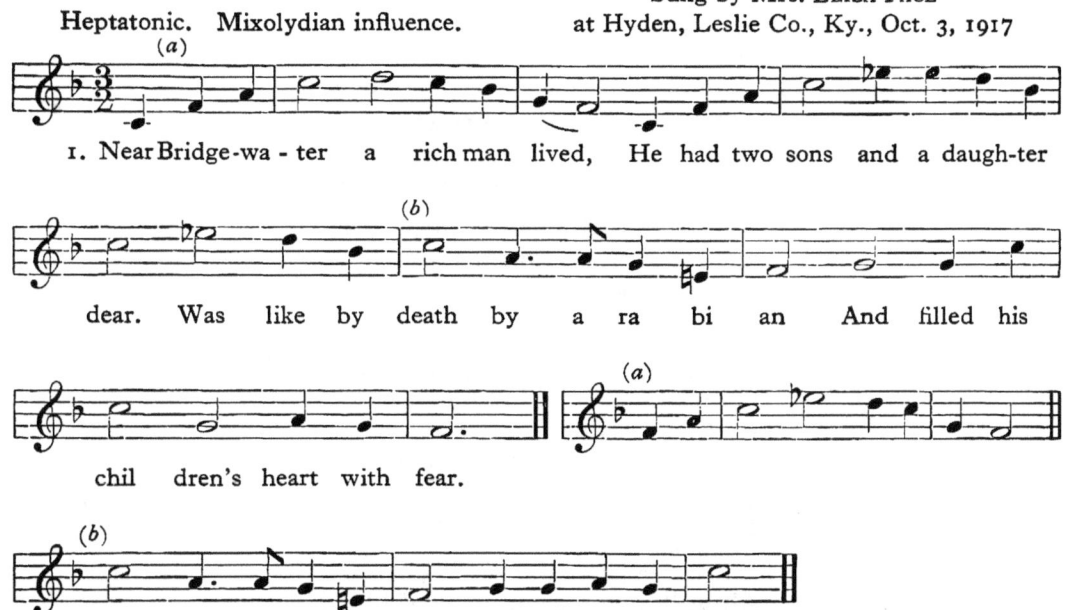

1. Near Bridgewater a rich man lived,
   He had two sons and a daughter dear.
   Was like by death by arabian (*sic*)
   And filled his children's heart with fear.

2. These young men to the sea did venture
   To bring whatever was for gain.
   He was a prencess bound and strong indebted,
   They sent him factory over the sea.

3. This youth was neat and comely,
   Straight and complete in every limb.
   Their sister placed her heart's affections
   On this young man unbeknownst to them.

4. One day it chanced her youngest brother
   For to see them court and play.
   He told the secret to the other,
   This to him then he did say:

5. O now he thinks he'll gain our sister,
   Perhaps he thinks her for to have,
   But their courtship will soon be ended.
   We'll press him headlong to the grave.

In Seaport Town

6 Now for to end this cruel matter
   And fill their sister's heart with woe,
   This poor young man they did flatter
   With them a-hunting for to go.

7 In the backwoods where no one used
   The briers they were overgrown,
   O there they made a bloody slaughter,
   There they had him killed and thrown.

8 They returned home to their sister.
   She asked where was the servant-man.
   I ask because you seem to whisper.
   Tell me, brothers, if you can.

9 We lost him at our game a-hunting,
   We never more could him see.
   I tell you plainly I'm afrighted.
   What makes you examine me?

10 The next night as she lie sleeping
   He came to her bed-side and stood,
   All covered o'er in tears a-weeping,
   All wallowed o'er in gores of blood.

11 The next morning she got up
   With many a sigh and bitter groan.
   To the place she then returned,
   Where she found him killed and thrown.

12 She said: My love, I will stay with you
   Until my heart doth burst with woe.
   She felt sharp hunger creeping;
   Homewards she was obliged to go.

13 She returned to her brothers.
   They asked her what made her look so orn.
   O by the loss you've acted treason
   In killing your poor servant man.

F

Sung by Mrs. MOLLIE BROGHTON
at Barbourville, Knox Co., Ky., May 8, 1917

Pentatonic. Mode 3.

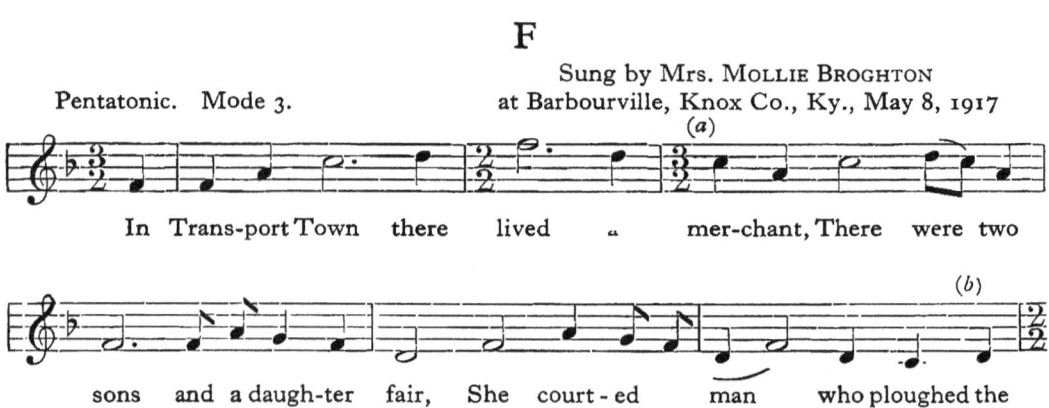

In Trans-port Town there lived a mer-chant, There were two sons and a daugh-ter fair, She court-ed man who ploughed the

In Seaport Town

o cean. It was their mind to be strong the same.

G

Pentatonic. Mode 3.

Sung by Mr. Hillard Smith
at Hindman, Knott Co., Ky., Sept. 20, 1917

A - long at eve ning as she re turned Her bro - thers

asked her where she'd been. You two hard heart ed de - ceit ful

vil - lains, For him a lone you both shall swing.

315

In Seaport Town

H

Hexatonic (no 3rd).
Sung by Mrs. Laurel Wheeler at Buena Vista, Va., May 2, 1918

She tra-velled o-ver hills and moun-tains, Trav-'ling by her-self a lone. She tra-velled till she came to a ditch of bri-ers where his bo-dy was slain and thrown.

I

Pentatonic. Mode 4.
Sung by Mrs. Sina Boone at Shoal Creek, Burnsville, N. C., Sept. 28, 1918

In Sea-port Town there lived a mer-chant, Who had two sons and a daugh-ter dear, And a-mong them all was the ser-vant boy Who was the daugh-ter's dear-est dear.

No. 49

The Cruel Ship's Carpenter
A

Hexatonic. Mode 4, b

Sung by Mrs. Tom Rice
at Big Laurel, N. C., Aug. 16, 1916

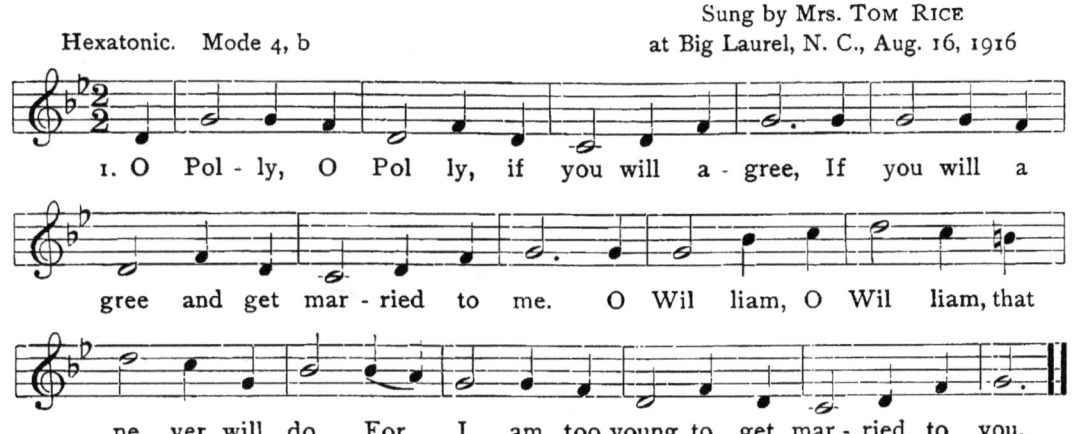

1. O Polly, O Polly, if you will agree, If you will agree and get married to me. O William, O William, that never will do, For I am too young to get married to you.

2. O Polly, O Polly, if you will agree,
   It's I have a friend that we will go and see.
   He led her over mountains and valleys so deep,
   Till at length pretty Polly began for to weep.

3. O William, O William, you're leading me astray
   On purpose my innocent heart to betray.
   O Polly, O Polly, I guess you spoke right,
   I were digging your grave the best part of last night.

4. She fold her arms around him without any fear.
   How can you bear to kill the girl that loves you so dear?
   Polly, O Polly, we've no time to stand,
   And instantly drew a short knife in his hand.

5. He opened her bosom all whiter than snow,
   He pierced her heart and the blood it did flow,
   And into the grave her fair body did throw.
   He covered her up and away did go,
   He left nothing but small birds to make their sad mourn.

6. He entered his ship all upon the salt sea so wide,
   And swore by his Maker he'd sail to the other side.
   Whilst he was sailing on in his full heart's content,
   The ship sprung a leak and to the bottom she went.

7. Whilst he was lying there all in his sad surprise,
   He saw pretty Polly all in a gore of blood.
   O William, O William, you've no time to stay,
   There's a debt to the devil that you're bound to pay.

The Cruel Ship's Carpenter

B

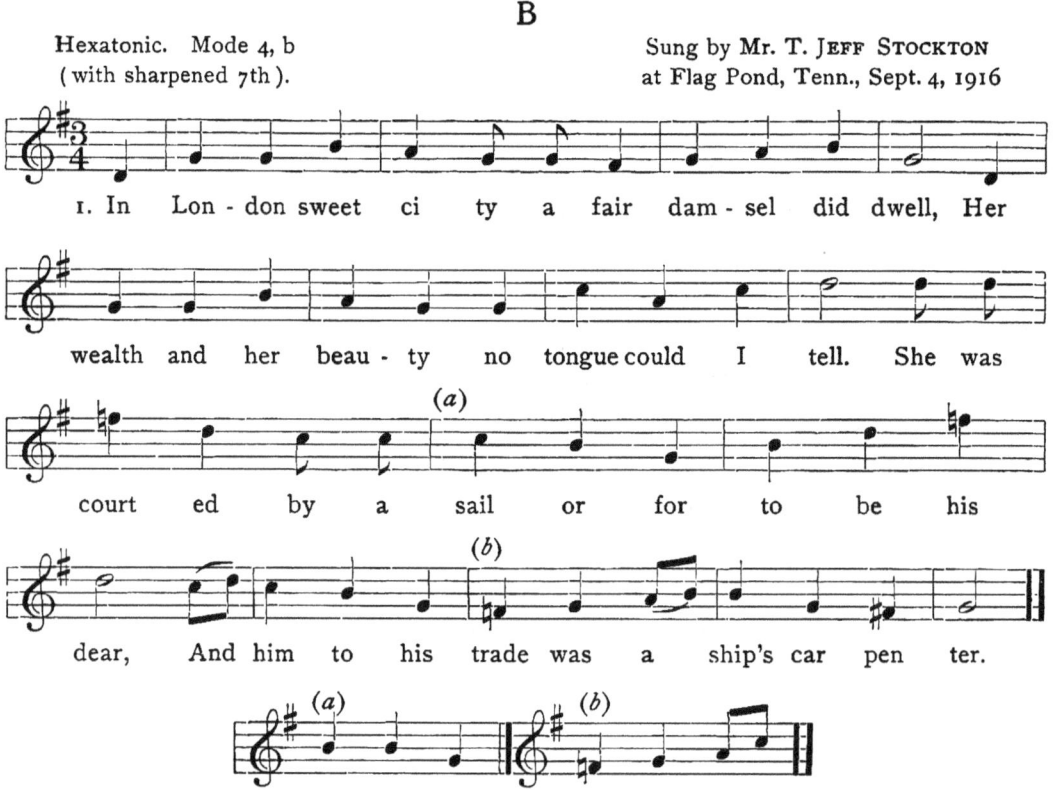

Hexatonic. Mode 4, b (with sharpened 7th).

Sung by Mr. T. Jeff Stockton at Flag Pond, Tenn., Sept. 4, 1916

1. In London sweet city a fair damsel did dwell, Her wealth and her beauty no tongue could I tell. She was courted by a sailor for to be his dear, And him to his trade was a ship's carpenter.

2 He says: My Miss Mary, if you will agree,
If you will consent and go along with me,
I will ease you from trouble or sorrow and fear,
If you will but marry a ship's carpenter.

3 Through 'braces and kisses they parted that night.
She started next morning for to meet him by light.
He led her through ditches and valleys so deep,
Till at length this fair damsel begin for to weep.

4 She says: My sweet William, you've led me astray
On purpose my innocent life to betray.
He says: My Miss Mary, you have guessed right,
For I was digging your grave all last night.
She turned her head and her grave she there spied,
Saying: Is this the bright bed for which me you've provide?

5 O pardon, sweet William, and spare me my life.
Let me go distressed if I can't be your wife.
For pardon sweet William is the worst of all men,
For the Heavens will reward you when I am dead and gone.

The Cruel Ship's Carpenter

6 No time for to weep nor no time for to stand.
  He instantly taken his knife in his hand.
  Into her bright body his knife he there stole,
  And the blood from her body like a fountain did flow.

7 He covered her all up, straight home he returned,
  Left no one to mourn but the small birds alone,
  And pled forth the paymount for to plough the whole sea.

8 The captain then summoned his whole-y ship crew.
  He said: My brave boys, I'm afraid some of you
  Have murdered some damsel before we came away,
  That will cause us to be hate upon the whole sea.

9 And he that did do it the truth he'll deny.
  We'll hang with God in yon gallows so high;
  But he that confess it his life we'll not take,
  But we'll leave him on the very next island we'll meet.

10 Poor William, poor William then fell to his knees,
   The blood in his veins with horror did freeze.
   And no one did see it but this wicked wretch,
   And he went distracted and died that same night.

C

Hexatonic. Mode 4, b
(with sharpened 7th).

Sung by Mr. HILLIARD SMITH
at Hindman, Ky., Aug. 10, 1910

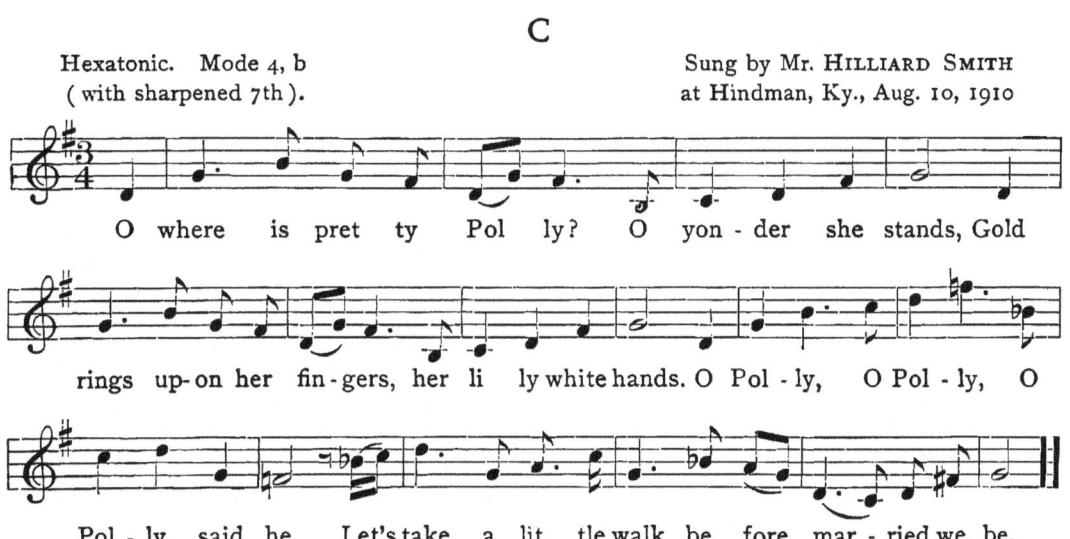

O where is pretty Polly? O yonder she stands, Gold rings up-on her fingers, her lily white hands. O Polly, O Polly, O Polly, said he, Let's take a little walk before married we be.

2 O William, O William, I don't want to go.
  Your people are all against it and that you well know.
  He led her over high hills and hollows so steep,
  At length pretty Polly began for to weep.

The Cruel Ship's Carpenter

3 O William, sweet William, O William, said she,
I fear your intention is for to murder me.
O Polly, O Polly, you have guessed about right,
I was digging your grave the best part of last night.

4 They went on a little farther and she began to shy.
She saw her grave dug and the spade a-sitting by.
She threw her arms around him, saying: I am in no fear,
How can you kill a poor girl that loves you so dear?

5 O Polly, O Polly, we have no time for to stand.
He drew his revolver all out in his hand.
He shot her through the heart which caused the blood to flow,
And into her grave her fair body he did throw.
He threw her in the grave, straightway he did run,
Left no one to weep but some small birds to mourn.

6 The ship setting ready all on the sea-side,
He swore by his Maker he'd sail the other side.
All on whilst he was sailing the ship she sprang a leak,
And away to the bottom sweet William he sank.

7 There he met with pretty Polly all in the gores of blood,
In her lily-white arms an infant of mine.
Such screaming and hollering, it all passed away.
A debt to the devil he surely had to pay.

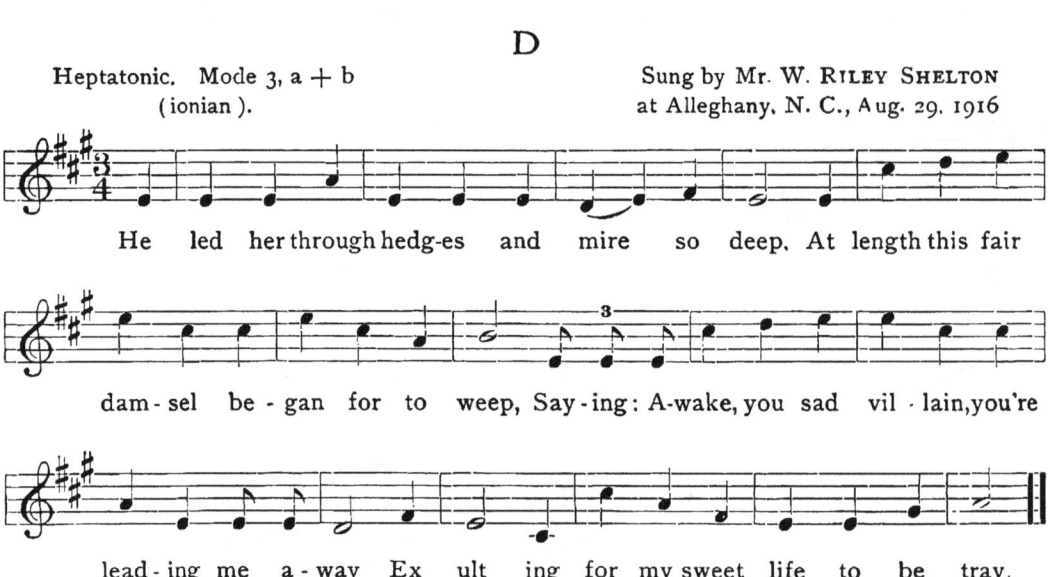

D

Heptatonic. Mode 3, a + b (ionian).

Sung by Mr. W. RILEY SHELTON at Alleghany, N. C., Aug. 29, 1916

He led her through hedges and mire so deep, At length this fair damsel began for to weep, Saying: A-wake, you sad villain, you're leading me away Exulting for my sweet life to betray.

The Cruel Ship's Carpenter

E

Pentatonic. Mode 2.

Sung by Mrs. SARAH BUCKNER
at Black Mountain, N. C., Sept. 18, 1916

There was a ma-son who lived by his trade, And he had for his daugh-ter a beau-ti-ful maid. For wit and for beau-ty there was none to com-pare; For her old sweet-heart was a ship's car-pen-ter.

F

Pentatonic. Mode 2.

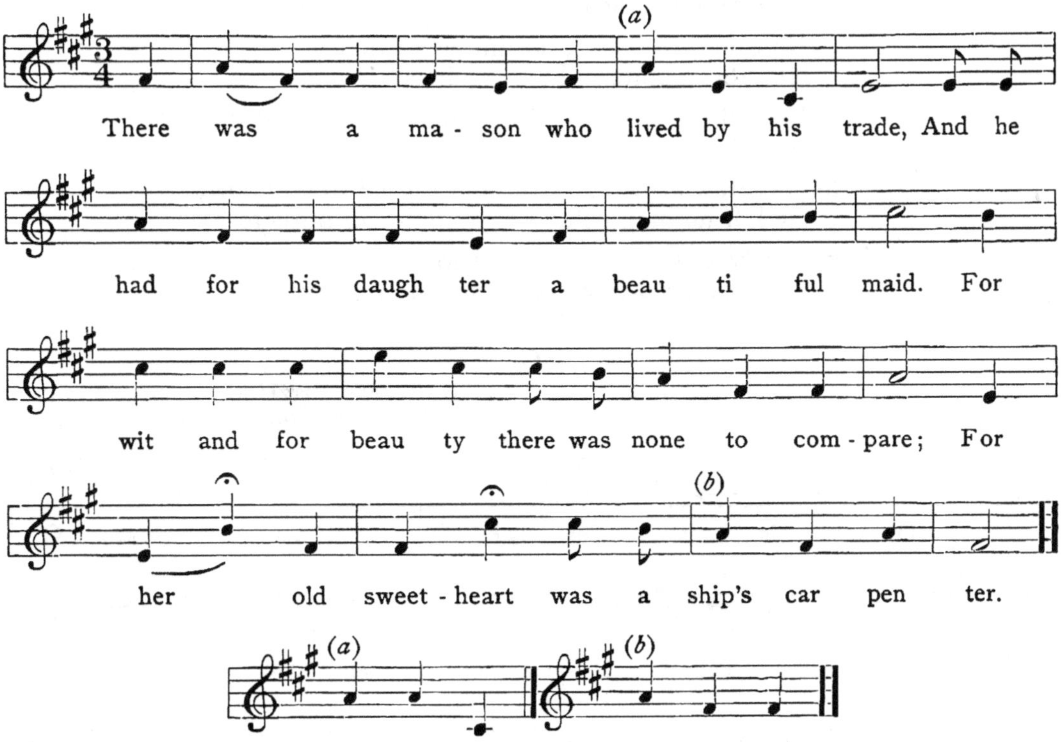

Sung by Mrs. ALICE SLOAN
at Barbourville, Knox Co., Ky., May 6, 1917

1. O Pol-ly, pret-ty Pol-ly, come and go with me, O Pol-ly, pret-ty Pol-ly, come and go with me, Be-fore we get mar-ried some plea-sure to see.

The Cruel Ship's Carpenter

2 He led her over valleys and valleys so deep,
  He caused pretty Polly to mourn and to weep.

3 A few steps further pretty Polly she spied
  A grave was dug and the spade a-laying by.

4 No time is to weep, no time is to stand,
  He drew a knife in his right hand.

5 He stabbed her to the heart and the blood it did flow,
  Into the grave pretty Polly did go.

6 He threw some dirt over and turned to go home,
  He left nothing behind him but small birds to roam.

7 A debt to the devil I've got to pay
  For stealing pretty Polly and running away.

The Cruel Ship's Carpenter

I

Sung by the Misses Sarah
and Docia Hylton and Abby Moseley
at Berea College, Madison Co., Ky., May 21, 1917

Pentatonic. Mode 2.

O where is pret-ty Pol ly, O yon der she stands. O where is pret-ty Pol ly, O yon-der she stands; Gold rings on her fin gers and li ly-white hands.

J

Sung by Mrs. Maud Kilburn
at Berea, Madison Co., Ky., May 31, 1917

Pentatonic. Mode 2.

Pret-ty Pol ly, pret-ty Pol ly, come go a-long with me, Be fore we get mar ried some plea-sures to see, Pret-ty Pol ly, pret-ty Pol ly, come go a-long with me, Be fore we get mar-ried some plea-sures to see.

K

Sung by Mrs. Vestie Thompson
at Pineville, Bell Co., Ky., June 2, 1917

Hexatonic (no 7th).

She threw her arms a round him in a hug and a fear, Say-ing: How can you kill the poor girl when she loves you so

The Cruel Ship's Carpenter

The Cruel Ship's Carpenter

T

Hexatonic (no 6th).

Sung by Mrs. Frances Richards
at St. Peter's School, Callaway, Va., Aug. 16, 1918

She threw her arms round him, she suf-fered no fear, She threw her arms round him, she suf-fered no fear. How can you kill the girl that has loved you so dear?

U

Pentatonic. Mode 2.

Sung by Mr. K. Freeman
at Marion, N. C., Sept. 3, 1918

There liv ed a ma-son who liv ed by trade, He had for his daugh-ter a beau ti ful maid, For wit and for beau-ty there was none to com-pare, For her old sweet-heart was a ship's car pen ter.

No. 50

Shooting of His Dear
A

Pentatonic. Mode I (no 6th).
Sung by Mrs. JANE GENTRY
at Hot Springs, N. C., Aug. 25, 1916

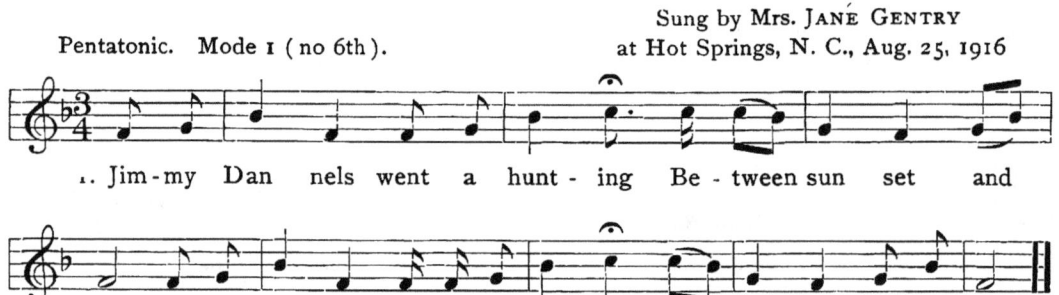

1. Jim-my Dan-nels went a-hunting Between sunset and dark. Her white apron over her shoulder, He took her for a swan.

2. He throwed down his gun
   And to her he run.
   He hugged her, he kissed her
   Till he found she was dead.

3. Then dropping her down
   To his uncle he run.
   Good woe and good lasses,
   I've killed poor Polly Bam.

4. O uncle, O uncle, what shall I do?
   For woe and good lasses,
   I've killed poor Polly Bam.
   Her white apron over her shoulder,
   But woe and good lasses,
   It was poor Polly Bam.

5. Stay in your own country
   And don't run away.

6. The day before trial
   The ladies all appeared in a row.
   Polly Bam 'peared among them
   Like a fountain of snow.

7. Don't hang Jimmy Dannels,
   For he's not to blame.
   My white apron over my shoulder
   He took me for a swan;
   But woe and good lasses,
   It was me, poor Polly Bam.

Shooting of His Dear

2 Molly Bander were a-walking and a shower came on.
She stopped under a beech-tree tho' shower to shun.
Jimmy Randal were a-hunting, he were a-hunting in the dark;
He shot his own true love, and he missed not her heart.

Shooting of His Dear

3 And then he run to her and he found her quite dead,
  And in her own bosom finding tears he had shed.
  He took his gun in his hand, to his uncle did go,
  Saying: Uncle, dear uncle, I've killed Molly Ban;
  I shot her and killed her. She was the joys of my life.
  I always intended for to make her my wife.

4 Up stepped his old father with his head all so grey,
  Saying: Randal, Jimmy Randal, don't run away.
  Stay in your own country till your trial comes on;
  You shall not be hanged; I'll spend my whole farm.

5 On the day of his trial her ghost did appear,
  Saying: Randal, Jimmy Randal, Jimmy Randal, go clear.
  He spied my apron pinned around me, he killed me for a swan.
  He shot me and killed me. My name's Molly Ban.

D

Sung by Mrs. FLORENCE FITZGERALD
at Royal Orchard, Afton, Va., April 27, 1918

Hexatonic (no 6th).

1. Jim-my Ran-dal went hunt-ing All a-bout in the dark. He shot Mol-ly Varn, And he not missed his mark.

2 He ran out up to her,
  When he found she were dead,
  And over her bosom
  A many tear he shed.

3 He picked up his gun,
  To his uncle's house did run.
  Says: Uncle, dear uncle,
  I've shot Molly Varn.

Shooting of His Dear

4 I've shot that fair damsel,
The joy of my life.
I always intended
For to make her my wife.

5 Up stepped Jimmy's father
Whose locks were turning grey,
Says: Jimmy, dear Jimmy,
Do not run away.

6 Stay with your old country
Till your trial comes on.
You will never be punished
For shooting Molly Varn.

7 The day of Jimmy's trial
Molly's ghost did appear,
Says: Gentlemen of the jury,
Jimmy Randal go clear.

8 All of the city girls
Were placed in a row.
Molly Varn showed among them
Like a mountain of snow.

E

Sung by Mrs. Eliza Pace
at Hyden, Leslie Co., Ky., Oct. 6, 1917

Hexatonic (no 6th).

Three ladies in a cambric and eight in a row, Pretty Polly in the middle like a mountain of snow. Jimmy Randals, remember to the day that you die I saved you from hanging with the rope that did tie.

Shooting of His Dear

F

Heptatonic. Ionian.

Sung by Mrs. Margaret Dunagan
at St. Helen's, Lee Co., Ky., Sept. 9, 1917

Jim-my Ran-dles was a hunt-ing, A hunt-ing in the dark. He shot his own true love, And missed not the spot. With her a-pron white a round her He had ta-ken her for a swan; He shot her, and killed her, And her name was Mol-ly Bon.

No. 51

The Lady and the Dragoon
A

Hexatonic. Mode 4, a.

Sung by Mrs. Mary Sands
at Allanstand, N. C., Aug. 1, 1916

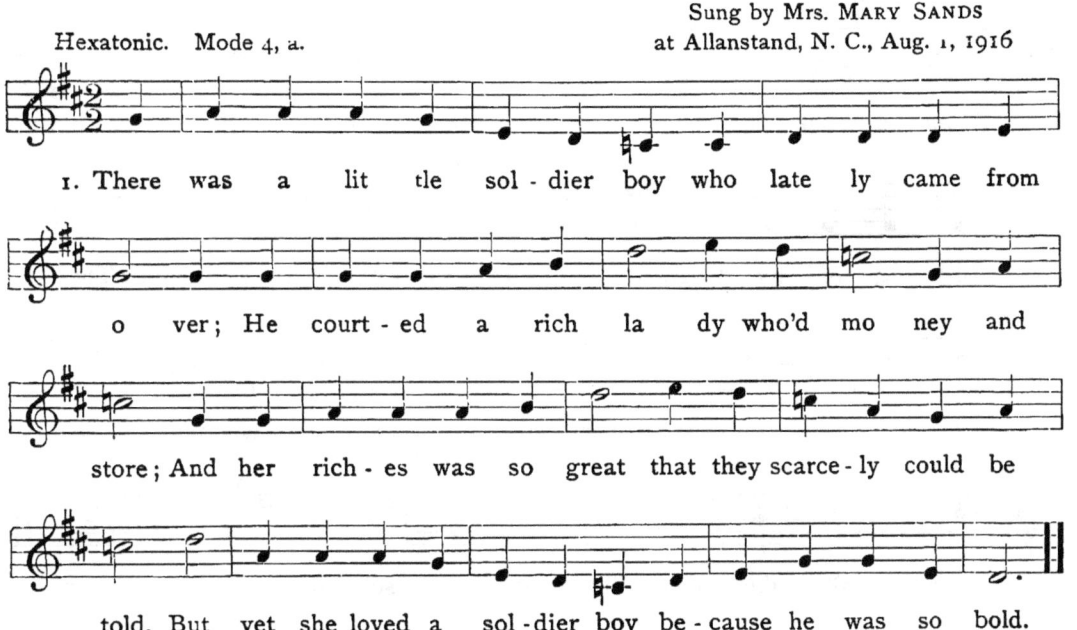

1. There was a little soldier boy who lately came from over; He courted a rich lady who'd money and store; And her riches was so great that they scarcely could be told, But yet she loved a soldier boy because he was so bold.

2 She says: My little soldier, I would freely be your wife,
  If I knowed my cruel old father would surely spare your life.
  He drew his pistol and sword and hung them by his side,
  And swore he would get married, let what would be tried.

3 As they had been to church and returning home again,
  Out slipped her cruel old father and seven armed men.
  Saying: Since you are determined to be the soldier's wife,
  Way down in the valley I will surely take his life.

4 O, says the little soldier, I have no time to tattle;
  I am here in this world in no fix for battle.
  But he drew his pistol and sword and caused them to rattle,
  And the lady held the horse while the soldier fought the battle.

5 The first one he come to he run him through the main,
  And the next one he come to he served him the same.
  Let's run, says the rest, I'll see we'll all be slain,
  To fight the valiant soldier I see it all in vain.

6 Up step this old man, speaking mighty bold;
  You shall have my daughter and a thousand pound of gold.
  Fight on, says the lady, the pile is too small.
  O stop, says the old man, and you shall have it all.

The Lady and the Dragoon

B

Heptatonic. Mode 4, a + b (mixolydian)

Sung by Mr. T. Jeff Stockton at Flag Pond, Tenn., Sept. 1916

Con-cern-ing of a sol-dier who has late-ly come from war, He is court-ing of my daugh-ter with great rich-es and a store. The daugh-ter loved the sol-dier be-cause he is poor; Be-yond all the gen-tle-men her sol-dier goes be-fore.

C

Hexatonic (no 6th).

Sung by Mrs. Martha Stamper at Hindman, Knott Co., Ky., Sept. 18, 1917

There was a lit-tle sol-dier, just late-ly come from war; He court-ed a rich la-dy, and mo-ney she had in store. Her rich-es they were so great-ly, they scarce-ly could be told. But yet she loved the sol-dier be-cause he were so bold.

The Lady and the Dragoon

D

Sung by Mr. Clinton FitzGerald
at Royal Orchard, Afton, Va., April 28, 1918

Hexatonic (no 6th).

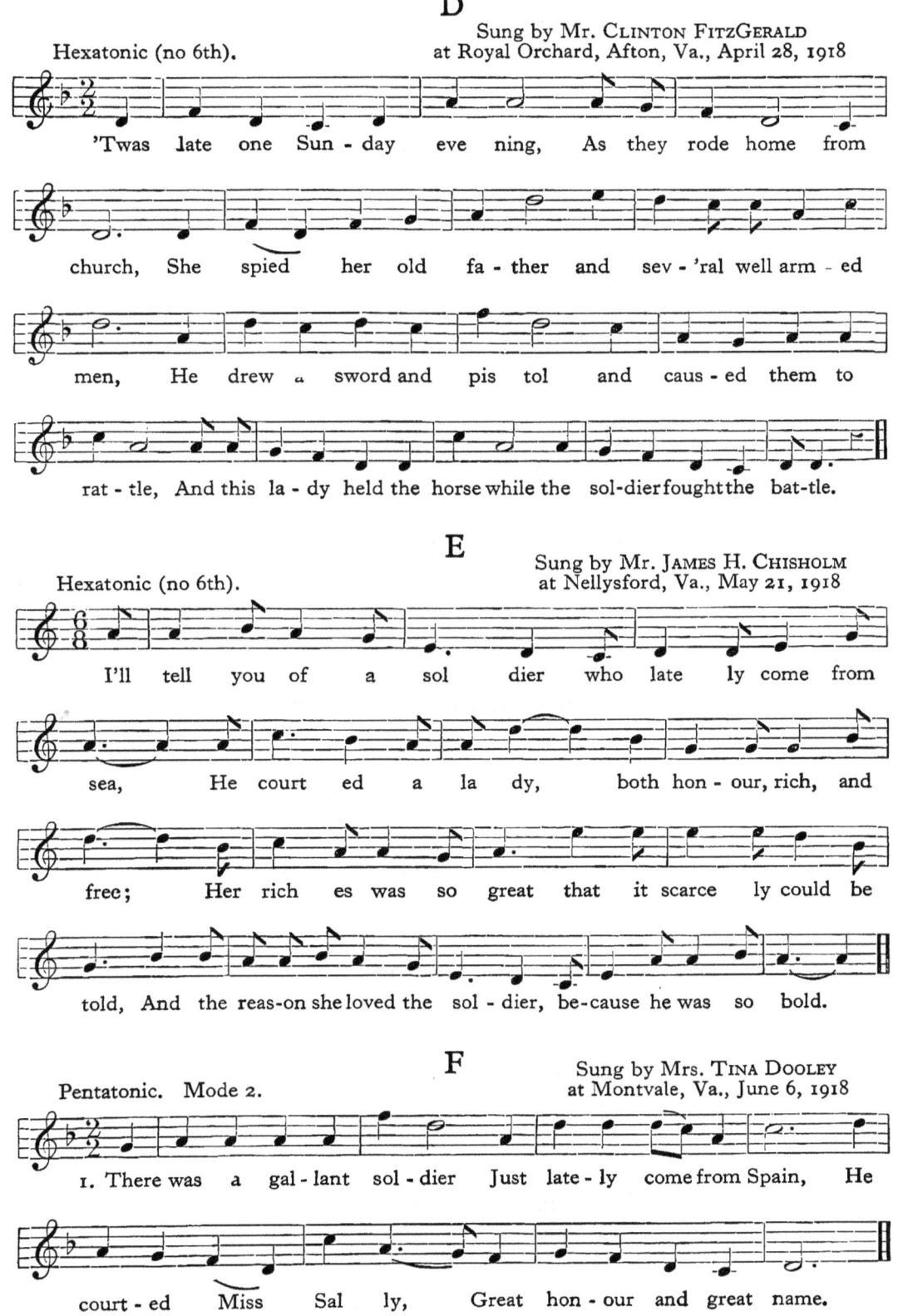

'Twas late one Sunday evening, As they rode home from church, She spied her old father and sev-'ral well arm-ed men, He drew a sword and pistol and caus-ed them to rat-tle, And this la-dy held the horse while the sol-dier fought the bat-tle.

E

Sung by Mr. James H. Chisholm
at Nellysford, Va., May 21, 1918

Hexatonic (no 6th).

I'll tell you of a soldier who lately come from sea, He courted a lady, both hon-our, rich, and free; Her rich-es was so great that it scarce-ly could be told, And the reas-on she loved the sol-dier, be-cause he was so bold.

F

Sung by Mrs. Tina Dooley
at Montvale, Va., June 6, 1918

Pentatonic. Mode 2.

1. There was a gal-lant sol-dier Just late-ly come from Spain, He court-ed Miss Sal-ly, Great hon-our and great name.

335

The Lady and the Dragoon

2 Her riches was so greatly
  They scarcely could be told,
  Although she loved the soldier
  Because he was so bold.

3 See here, my little Duel,
  I'd vainly be your wife,
  But my hard-hearted father
  Will shortly end your life.

4 He drew his sword and pistol,
  He placed her by his side,
  He swore that he'd get married
  At their own heart's content.

5 They got on their horses
  And to the church they went,
  And there they got married
  At their own heart's content.

6 They got on their horses,
  Returning home again,
  They met their cruel father
  And seven arm-ed men.

7 See here, my little Duel,
  Do you make this lady your wife,
  Down in some lonesome valley
  I'll shortly take your life.

8 Ride on, ride on, said the lady,
  I have no flatter (?),
  I am but one soldier
  Not fitten for a battle.

9 See here, my little Duel,
  You bring my daughter so low,
  For to marry a soldier
  And he's so poor.

10 He drew his sword and pistol,
   He caused them to rattle.
   The lady held the horses
   While the soldier fought the battle.

11 The first one he came to
   He pierced him through the main,
   The next one he came to
   He served him the same.

The Lady and the Dragoon

12 Stop, stop, says the old man,
   It's labour all in vain
   To fight this gallant soldier,
   For we will all be slain.

13 See here, my little Duel,
   You must not be so bold.
   O you may have my daughter
   And ten thousand pounds of gold.

No. 52

The Boatsman and the Chest

A

Hexatonic (no 6th).

Sung by Mrs. Mary Sands at Allanstand, N. C., Aug. 4, 1916

1. There was a little boatsman, wherever he did dwell, And he had a little wife and the tailor loved her well, And he could not step more than one inch out of the way Till a trick upon his wife the little tailor he would play. Singing fol de dol the day long.

2. The boatsman came home when he come at night,
   And he knocked on the door and he knocked just right.
   This stirred the little tailor from his sleep:
   O kind Miss, where can I creep?

3. She put him in the chest and bid him lie still:
   You're just as safe there as a mouse in a mill.
   She trippled downstairs and she opened the door,
   And in come her husband and three or four more.

4. She looted to him and give to him a kiss,
   Saying: O kind Sir, what's the meaning of this?
   I haven't come here for to disturb you of your rest,
   But to come to bid you good-bye and to take away my chest.

The Boatsman and the Chest

5 The boatsman being young and very stout and strong,
   He picked up the chest and he carried it along.
   But he had not got more'n half through the town,
   Till the weight of the little tailor boy made him lie it down.

6 He opened the lid and says to them all:
   Here lies a little tailor like a pig in a stall.
   I'll take him to the king and make you serve your time with him;
   See if that will put an end to this night's cuckolding.

B

Sung by Mrs. Margaret Dunagan
at St. Helen's, Kentucky., Sept. 6, 1916

Hexatonic (no 6th).

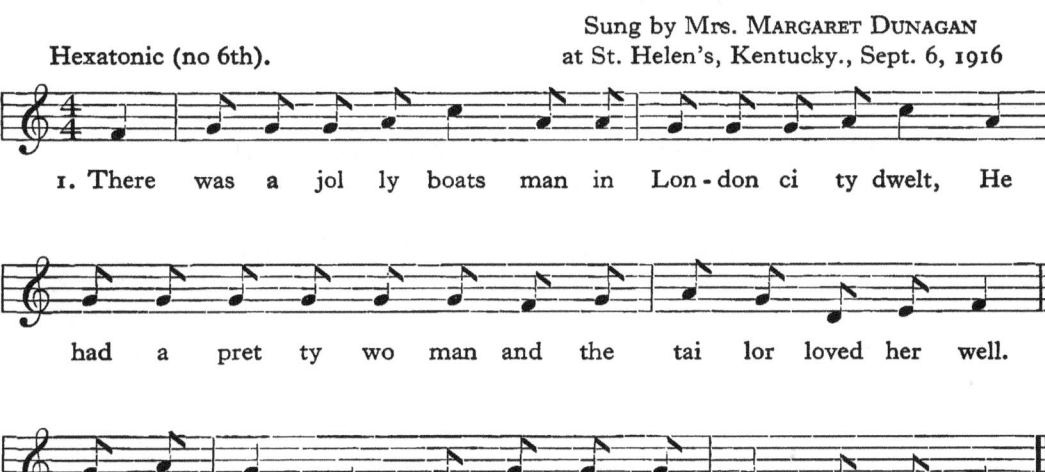

1. There was a jolly boatsman in London city dwelt, He had a pretty woman and the tailor loved her well. Sum a ti rum rod-dy, Sum a tire lar di day.

2 She was a-walking the London street,
  And she and the little tailor did a-chancey to meet.

3 My husband has left me, he's gone to sea,
  And this very night you can stay with me.

4 They hadn't been together but a half a night or more
  Till the jolly boatsman drops loudly at the door.

5 She waked the little tailor out of his sounder sleep.
  It's dear beloved woman, O where shall I creep?

6 There sits a chest at my bedside,
  It's there you shall creep and there you shall hide.

7 He jumped in the chest as limber as a deer.
  My dear beloved woman, there's nothing more to fear.

The Boatsman and the Chest

8 She run downstairs and opened up the door,
   And there stood her husband and several ever more.

9 He gave her a weapon and she gave him a call,
   My dear beloved woman, here's the meaning of it all.

10 I'm not come to disturb you nor rob of your rest,
    I'm a-going on sea and I've come for my chest.

11 Stepped in the jolly boatsman, a-being very strong,
    He picked up the chest and marched right along.

12 They never got it half over town
    Till this little tailor brought the sweat a-pouring down.

13 Let's all sit down and take a moment's rest.
    Said one to the other: The devil's in the chest.

14 They heard little tailor give such a loud a' knock,
    They sent for the captain the chest to unlock.

15 Yander comes the captain and several others too;
    It's none but the captain the chest to undo.

16 He opened up the door in the presence of them all,
    There laid the tailor like a pig in a stall.

17 Now I have got you, I'll thrash you on sea,
    I won't leave you here cutting capers under me.

No. 53
The Holly Twig
A

Hexatonic. Mode 3, a.

Sung by Mr. N. B. Chisholm
at Woodridge, Va., Sept. 23, 1916

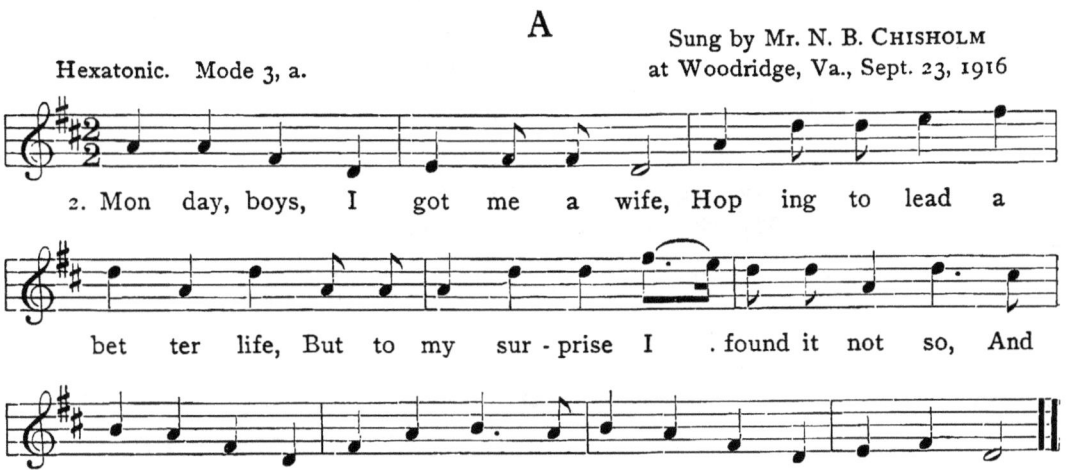

1. When I was a bachelor bold and brave,
   I wanted for nothing my heart could crave;
   But kisses and guineas I made them fly,
   I slipped on my beaver hat and who was like I?
   or
   When I was a bachelor bold and young,
   I courted a girl with a flattering tongue;
   The kisses I give her was a hundred and ten,
   Promised to marry, but didn't tell her when.

2. Monday, boys, I got me a wife,
   Hoping to lead a better life;
   But to my surprise I found it not so,
   And all my pleasure turned to woe.

3. Tuesday, boys, to my surprise,
   Just before the sun did rise,
   She riz in a fit and scolded me more
   Than ever I was scolded before.

4. Wednesday, boys, I went to the woods
   To get me some hickories to make her good.
   As I passed by the willow so green,
   I cut me the toughest that ever was seen.

5. Thursday, boys, I laid them by,
   Resolving Friday for to try.
   If she's no better the better may be,
   The devil may take her and keep her for me.

The Holly Twig

6 Saturday, boys, I lammed her well,
   I kicked her and cuffed her to the lowest pits of hell.
   The ruby and the booby and two little devils came,
   They carried her off in a fire of flame.

7

   My biggest bottle is my best friend,
   My week's work is all at an end.

B

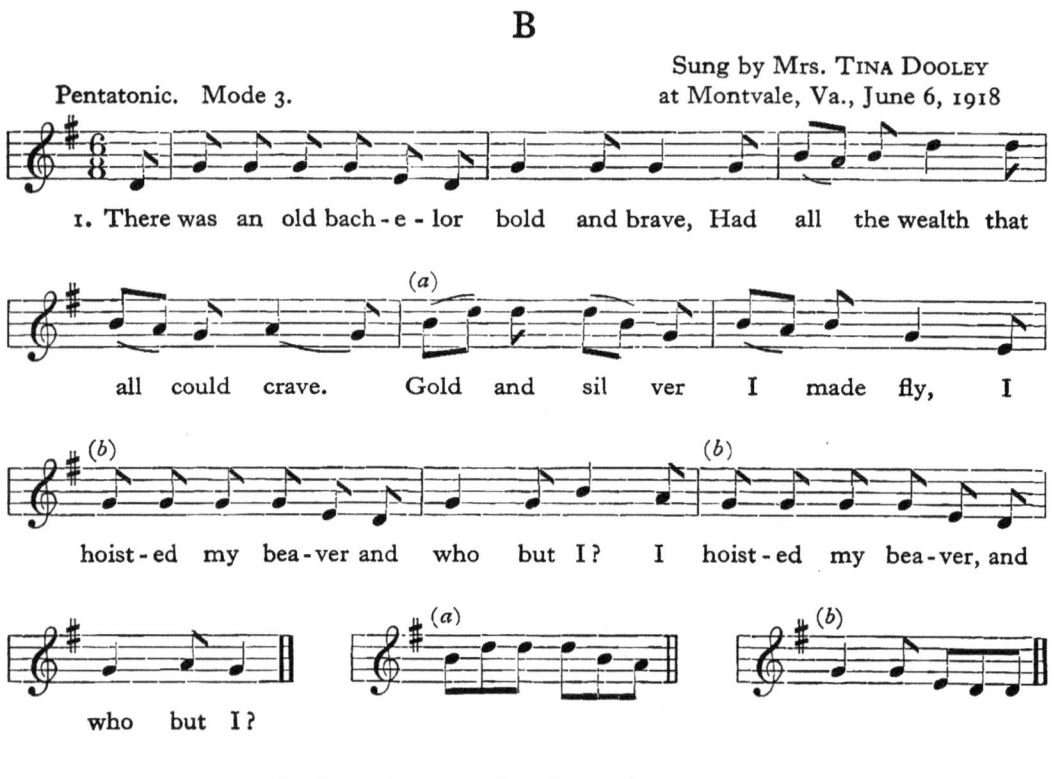

Sung by Mrs. Tina Dooley
at Montvale, Va., June 6, 1918

Pentatonic. Mode 3.

1. There was an old bach-e-lor bold and brave, Had all the wealth that all could crave. Gold and sil-ver I made fly, I hoist-ed my bea-ver and who but I? I hoist-ed my bea-ver, and who but I?

2 On Monday morning I married me a wife,
   Thought I'd begin the joys of life;
   My fife and drum so merrily played
   To think how happy I'd been made.

3 On Tuesday morning I carried her home,
   Instead of a wife a scold and groan.
   On Wednesday I walked to the woods
   To see if I could do her a little good.

The Holly Twig

4 I cut me some hickory so tough and so keen,
I think it was the toughest I ever had seen.

5 On Thursday morning I banged her well,
The truth to you, young ladies, I'll tell.
If she jaws me any more I'll bang her again,
I'll bang her again.

6 On Friday morning away before day
On her scolding pillow she lay.
Two little angels came down with wings
And carried her away in a gust of wind.

7 On Saturday morning had breakfast alone,
I had no wife to scold and groan.
My week's work was then at an end.
My whisky bottle is my best friend.

C

Sung by Mr. Joe Blackett
at Meadows of Dan, Va., Aug. 28, 1918

Pentatonic. Mode 3.

O cut me a stick both crook-ed and brown, The crook-ed-est stick that e ver was seen. On Tues day morn-ing laid it by, Think-ing of her old back to try.

No. 54

Polly Oliver

A

Pentatonic. Mode 3.

Sung by Mrs. MARY SANDS
at Allanstand, N. C., Aug. 4, 1916

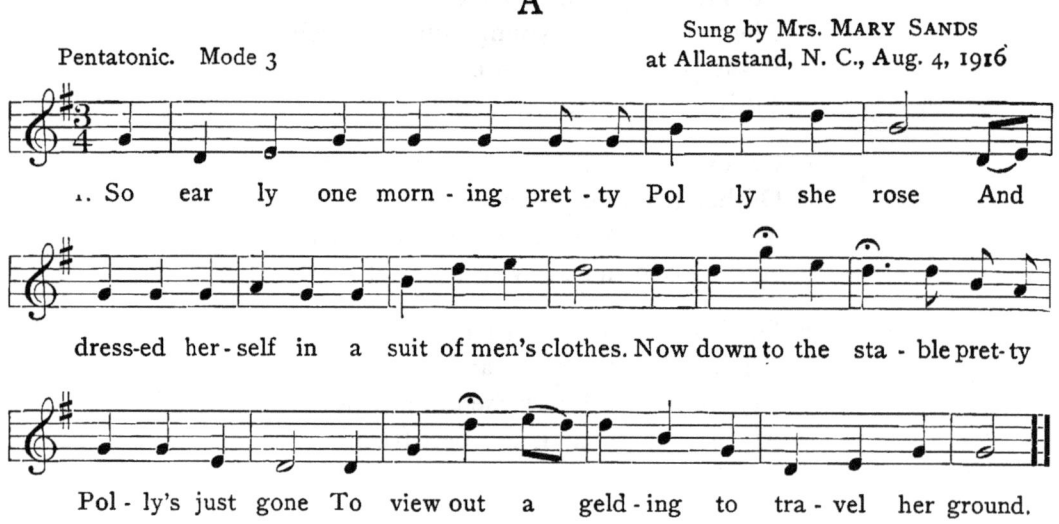

1. So early one morning pretty Polly she rose And dressed herself in a suit of men's clothes. Now down to the stable pretty Polly's just gone To view out a gelding to travel her ground.

2 In riding all day and riding in speed
 The first thing she come to was her captain indeed.
 She stepped up to him. What news do you bear?
 Here's a kind, loving letter from Polly your dear.

3 In breaking this letter ten guineas he found.
 He drunk his own health with the soldiers all round;
 And reading the letter, he sit and did cry,
 Not a-thinking Polly was nigh.

B

Heptatonic. Mixolydian.

Sung by Mrs. MOLLIE BROGHTON
at Barbourville, Knox Co., Ky., May 8, 1917

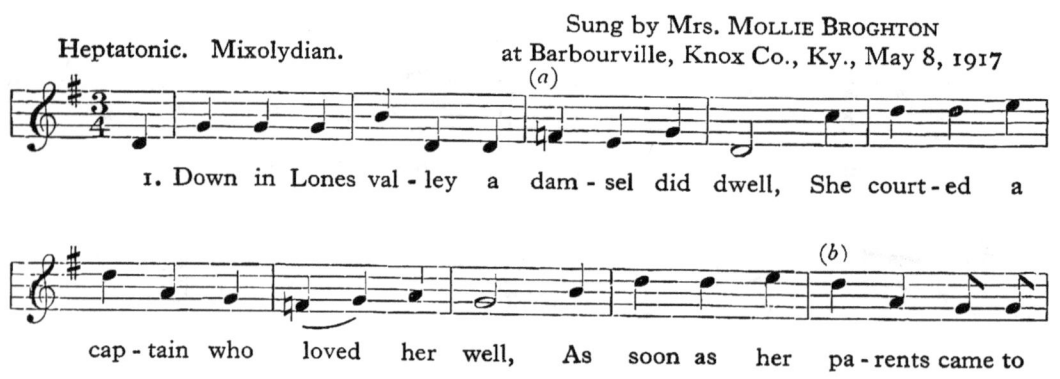

1. Down in Lones valley a damsel did dwell, She courted a captain who loved her well, As soon as her parents came to

Polly Oliver

hear how she proved They part-ed pret-ty Mol-ly and her roy-al true love.

2 Pretty Molly lies musing all on her downy bed,
   Such notions and projects still run through her head.
   Neither father nor mother can make me forsworn,
   I'll dress like a soldier and follow my love.

3 She went to the stables and viewed all around;
   She caught the best gelding that measured the ground.
   She dressed herself in men's clothes and followed her true love,
   Her long yellow hair reached down her back,
   Her sword and her pistol a-hanging to her side.

4 She rode till she came to the town of renown,
   And there let off to the side of the street.
   The first that come in was a brave English lord,
   And the next one come in was pretty Molly's true love.

5 Here is a letter from Molly, your dear,
   In the middle of that letter is a guinea and a crown
   For you and your soldiers to drink Molly's health around.

6 In reading this letter, he sat, sighed and cried,
   No word did he speak but his Molly did hear.
   O Molly, pretty Molly, O Molly, my dear,
   O what would I give if pretty Molly were here.

7 Pretty Molly felt drowsy, she hung down her head,
   She asked for a candle to light her to bed.
   Here's a bed, says the captain, here's a bed at your ease
   Mayn't I lie with you, countryman, if you please?

8 Shall I lie with a captain? It's dangerous then.
   Ninety young squires go fight for your king.
   I'll fight for my kingdom, I'm shepherd on door.
   O Molly is a girl I always adore.

Polly Oliver

9 So early next morning pretty Molly she rose,
And dressed herself inside of her own clothes.
She come showing downstairs like an angel above.
O here's pretty Molly, your royal true love.

10 Pretty Molly's now married, she lives at her ease.
She goes when she wants and comes when she please.

C

Heptatonic. Aeolian.

Sung by Mrs. Florence FitzGerald
at Royal Orchard, Afton, Va., April 25, 1917

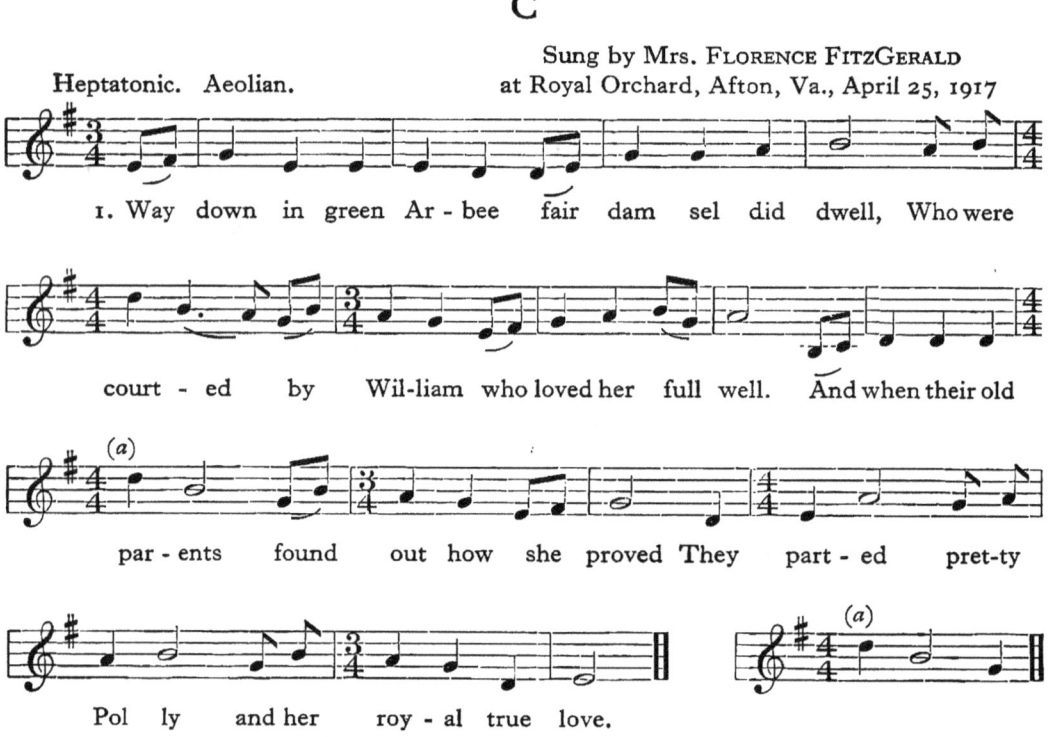

1. Way down in green Ar-bee fair dam-sel did dwell, Who were court-ed by Wil-liam who loved her full well. And when their old par-ents found out how she proved They part-ed pret-ty Pol-ly and her roy-al true love.

2 So early next morning pretty Polly she rose,
She dressed herself up in a suit of men's clothes,
With her long wavy hair and a sword in her hand,
In every degree she looked like a man.

3 She went o'er the stable and she viewed the stall around
Until she found a horse that could travel the ground;
With a pair of brass pistols and a sword by her side,
Pretty Polly, pretty Polly like a trooper did ride.

4 She rode, she rode till she came to the hall,
And there she put off with the lief of them all.
And the first man that entered were the bravest landlord,
And the next man that entered were Polly's true love.

Polly Oliver

5 Here's a letter from Polly, from Polly, your dear,
  I pray you for to take it and read it with care,
  For under the sealing a guinea to be found,
  That you and your soldiers may drink a health round.

6 He taken the letter and he read it full slow,
  Then the tears from his eyes like a fountain did flow.
  With one arm extended and one by his side,
  Says: Wherever I meet her I will make her my bride.

7 Pretty Polly being sleepy she hung down her head,
  She called for a candle for to light her to bed.
  We have a bed empty, you can lie at your ease,
  And you may lie with me, kind sir, if you please.

8 To lie with a captain is a dangerous thing,
  But I am a captain, I'll fight for my king,
  I'm a captain on land, I'm a captain on shore,
  How royal, how royal I prove.

9 'Twas early next morning pretty Polly she rose,
  She dressed herself up in a suit of her clothes;
  With her long wavy hair came tripping downstairs,
  Good morning, good morning, kind sir.

10 Pretty Polly is married and lives at her ease,
   And goes when she wants and comes when she please.
   She left her old parents to lament and to mourn.
   Welcome home, pretty Polly, you're welcome back home.

11 Now William is married and lives at his ease,
   And goes when he wants and comes when he please.
   He left his old parents to lament and to mourn.
   Welcome home, gallant soldier, you're welcome back home.

No. 55

The Rich Old Lady

A

Heptatonic. Mode 4,
„ + b (dorian).

Sung by Mrs. Gosnell
at Allanstand, N. C., Aug. 4, 1916

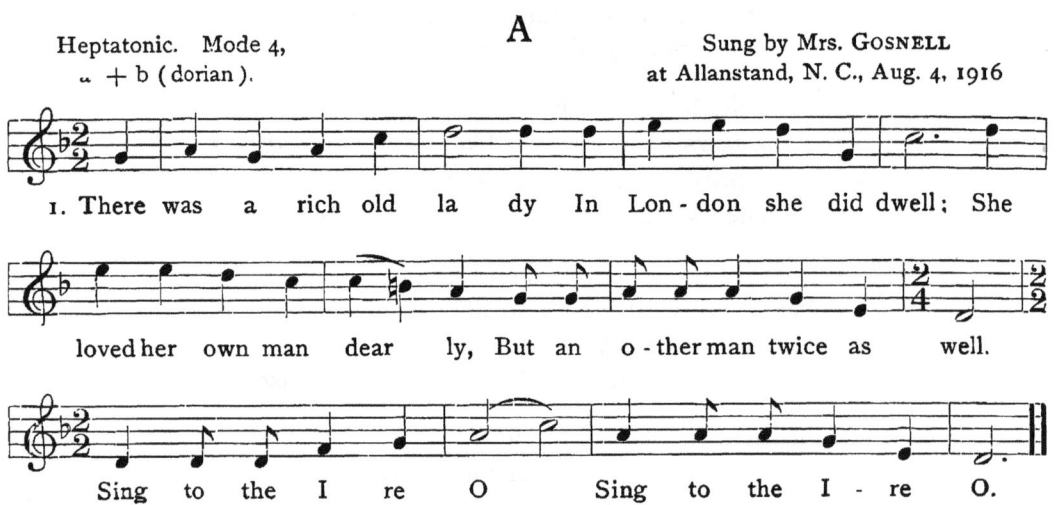

1. There was a rich old lady In London she did dwell; She loved her own man dearly, But another man twice as well. Sing to the I re O Sing to the I-re O.

2 She went to the doctor's shop,
  As hard as she could go,
  To see if there was anything she could find
  To turn her old man blind.

3 She got two walloping mar' bones
  And made him eat them all.
  He says: O my dear beloved wife,
  I can't see you at all.

4 If I could see my way to go,
  I'd go to the river and drown.
  She says: I'll go along with you
  For fear you go astray.

5 She got up behind him
  Just ready for to plunge him in;
  He stepped a little to one side,
  Headlong she went in.

6 She begin to kick and scream
  As loud as she could bawl.
  He says: O my dear beloved wife,
  I can't see you at all.

7 Him being tender-hearted
  And thinking she could swim,
  He got him a great, long pole
  And pushed her away out in.

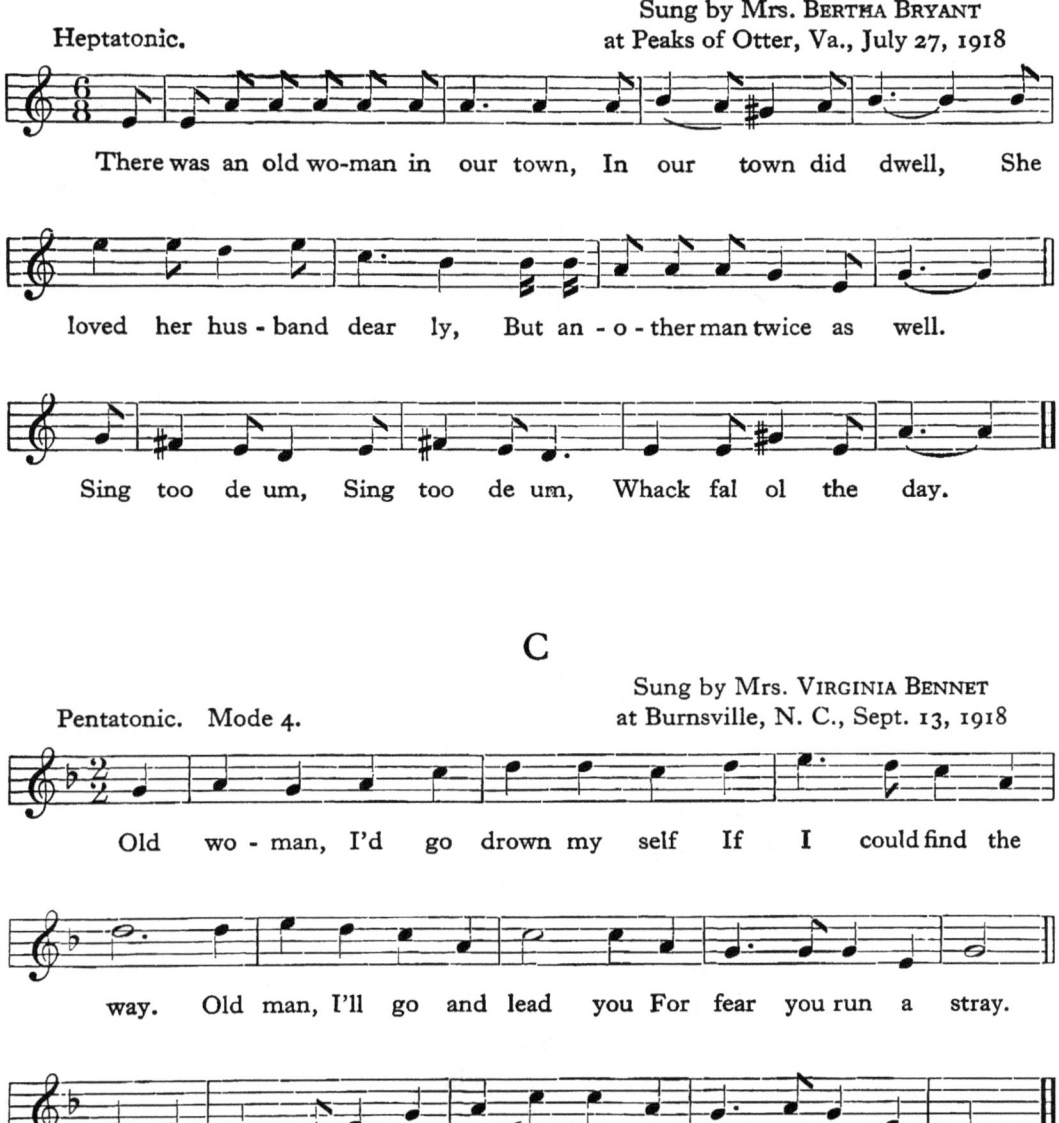

No. 56

Edwin in the Lowlands Low
A

Pentatonic. Mode 1.

Sung by Mrs. JANE GENTRY
at Hot Springs, N. C., Aug. 25, 1916

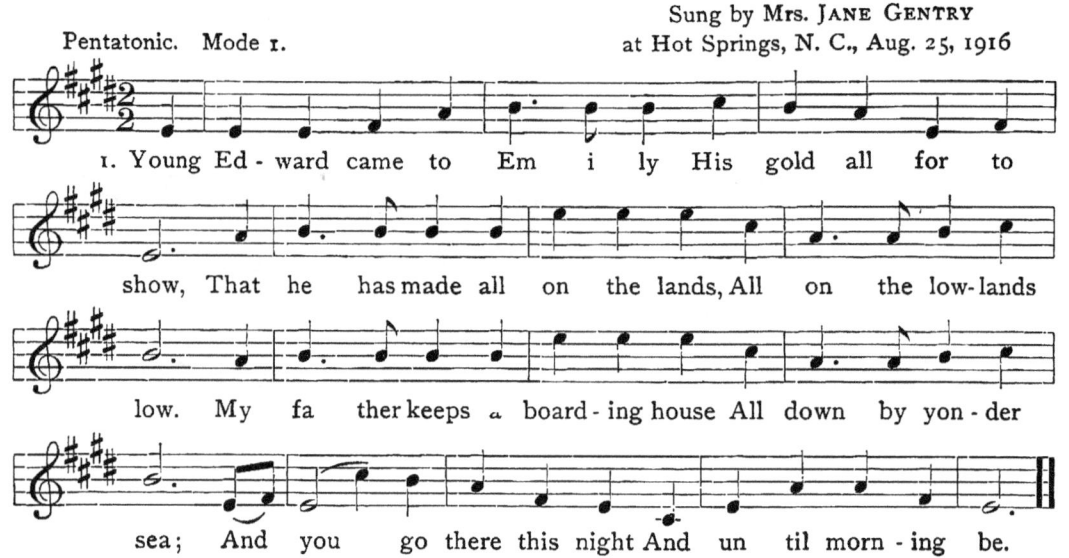

2 Young Emily in her chamber,
   She dreamed an awful dream;
   She dreamed she saw young Edward's blood
   Go flowing like the stream.
   She rose so early in the morning
   And dressed herself although
   To go and see young Edward,
   Who ploughed the lowlands low.

3 O father, where's that stranger
   Came here last night to dwell?
   His body's in the ocean
   And you no tales must tell.
   O father, O father, you'll die a public show
   For the murdering of young Edward
   Who ploughed the lowlands low.

4 Away then to some councillor
   To let the deeds be known.
   The jury found him guilty
   His trial to come on.
   On trial they found him guilty
   And hanged was to be
   For the murdering of young Edward,
   Who ploughed the lowlands low.

Edwin in the Lowlands Low

5 The fish that's in the ocean
   Swims over young Edward's breast,
   While his body's in the ocean
   I hope his soul's at rest,
   For his name it was young Edward,
   Who ploughed the lowlands low.

B

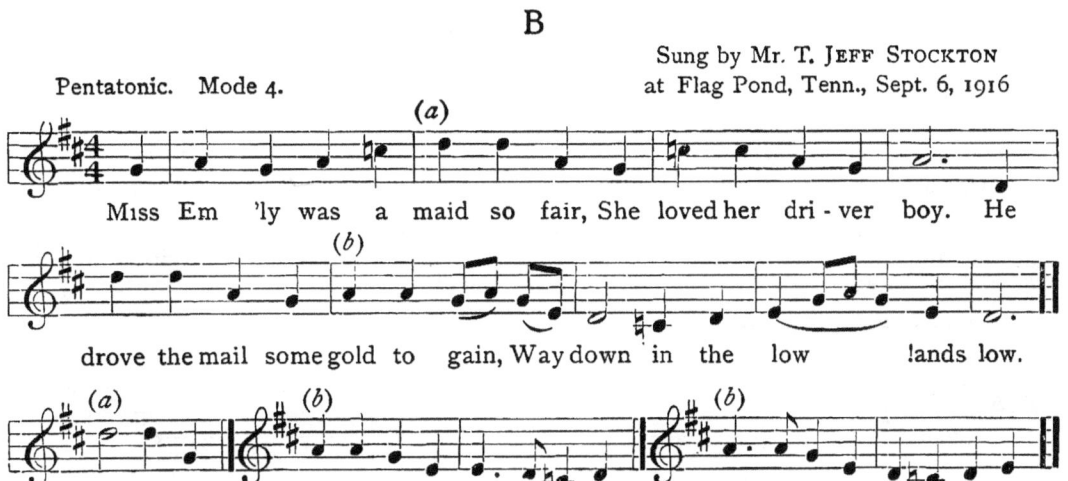

Pentatonic. Mode 4.

Sung by Mr. T. Jeff Stockton
at Flag Pond, Tenn., Sept. 6, 1916

Miss Em'ly was a maid so fair, She loved her dri-ver boy. He drove the mail some gold to gain, Way down in the lowlands low.

2 My father keeps a public house
   On yonders river side.
   Go ye, go there and enter in
   And there this night abide.

3 Be sure that you tell nothing,
   Nor let my parents know
   That your name it is young Edmund,
   Who drove in the lowlands low.

4 Young Edmund fell a-drinking
   When time for to go to bed.
   He did not know that his sword that night
   Would part his neck and head.

5 Miss Emily up next morning,
   The sun was shining bright,
   Saying: I am going to marry the driver boy,
   Who come here to stay last night.

6 O daughter, dear daughter Emily,
   His gold we will make sure.
   I've here sent his body a-drowning
   Way down in the ocean low.

Edwin in the Lowlands Low

7 O dear, dear, cruel father,
You shall die a public show
For murdering of my old true love,
Who drove in the lowlands low.

8 There's a coach on yonders mountain,
It tosses to and fro.
It 'minds me of my driver boy
Who drove in the lowlands low.

C

Hexatonic. Mode 4, b
(with sharpened 7th).

Sung by Miss McKinney
at Habersham Co., Ga., May 28, 1910

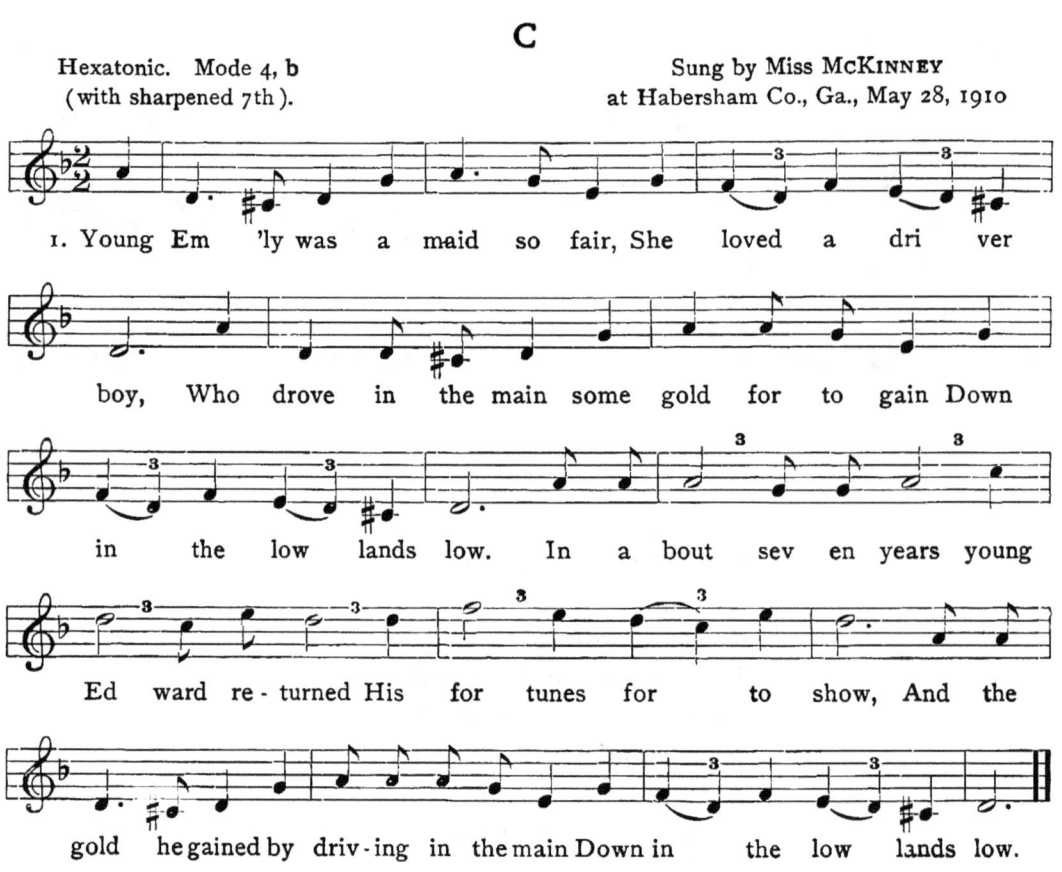

1. Young Em'ly was a maid so fair, She loved a driver boy, Who drove in the main some gold for to gain Down in the lowlands low. In about seven years young Edward returned His fortunes for to show, And the gold he gained by driving in the main Down in the lowlands low.

2 Young Edward fell a-drinking,
It was time for to go to bed,
Although he wasn't a-thinking
The custom came around his head.
Young Emily fell asleep that night;
She dreamed a frightful dream;
She dreamed that her love was bleeding,
The blood ran down in streams.

Edwin in the Lowlands Low

3 Next morn she rose, put on her clothes,
  And to her parents did go,
  Enquiring for her driver boy,
  Who drove in the lowlands low.
  O mother, where is my driver boy
  Who came last night for to stay?
  He's gone for to dwell no tongue can tell
  How cruel your father did say.

4 O father, cruel father,
  You'll die a public show,
  For killing of my driver boy,
  Who drove in the lowlands low.

5 My love is in the ocean
  While fish play o'er his breast.
  His body's in a constant motion;
  I hope his soul's at rest.
  His coaches are in the mountain,
  The rivers are all aflow.
  It reminds me of my driver boy,
  Who drove in the lowlands low.

D

Sung by Mrs. SARAH BUCKNER
at Black Mountain, N. C., Sept. 14, 1916

Hexatonic. Mode 4, a.

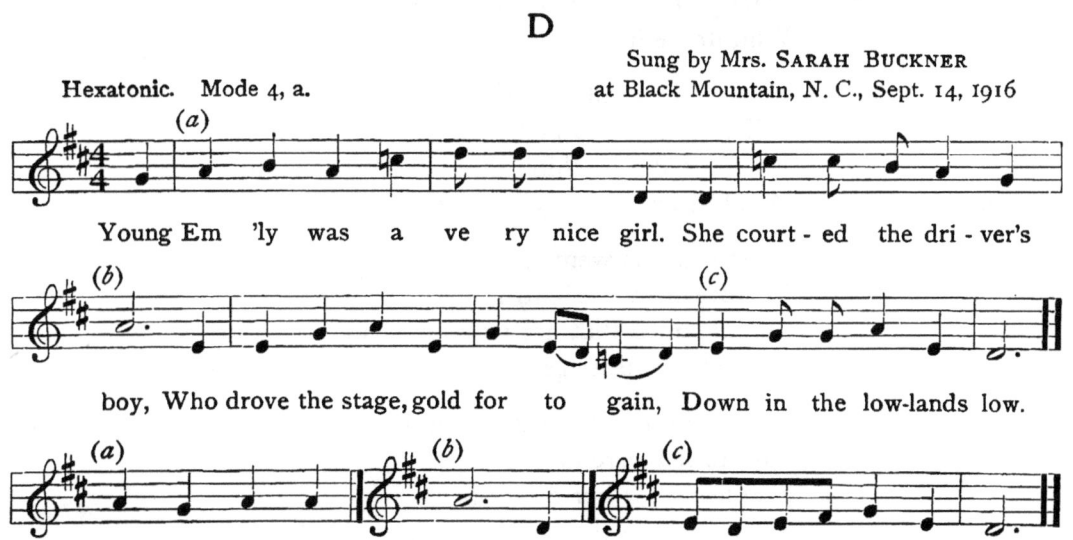

Young Em 'ly was a ve-ry nice girl. She court-ed the dri-ver's boy, Who drove the stage, gold for to gain, Down in the low-lands low.

Edwin in the Lowlands Low

E

Pentatonic. Mode 4.

Sung by Mrs. SINA BOONE
at Shoal Creek, Burnsville, N. C., Sept. 28, 1918

1. Young Em-ma she's a pret-ty fair maid, And she loves the dri-ver boy, Who

drove the mail some gold for to gain, Way down in the low-lands low.

2 My father keeps a boarding-house
All on yon riverside.
Go you, go there and venture in,
And there all night abide.

3 Be sure don't tell them nothing,
Or let my parents know
That your name is young Edna
Who drove in the lowlands low.

4 Young Edna fell to drinking
Till time to go to bed;
But little did he think that sword that night
Would part his body and head.

5 Young Emma went to bed that night,
She dreamed a frightful dream;
She dreamed that her true love had gone away
To never return again.

6 She rose up early next morning,
And to her parents did go,
Enquiring for her driver boy
Who drove in the lowlands low.

7 O daughter, dear daughter,
What makes you treat me so,
To leave your dear old mother
And with a drunkard go?

Edwin in the Lowlands Low

8 O mother, dear mother,
   I know I love you well,
   But the love I have for the driver boy
   No human tongue can tell.

9 O father, dear father,
   You shall die a public show,
   For murdering my poor driver boy
   Who drove in the lowlands low.

10 O father, dear father,
   You may think it wrong or right,
   That I love the driver boy
   Who drove in the lowlands low.

11 There is a coach on yonders mountain
   That looks so black and true;
   It makes me think of the driver boy
   Who drove in the lowlands low.

12 The fish that's in the ocean
   Swims over my true love's breast;
   His body's in a gentle motion,
   And I hope his soul's at rest.

F

Heptatonic. Mixolydian influence.

Sung by Mrs. Maud Kilburn
at Berea, Madison Co., Ky., May 31, 1917

Young Em'-ly was a maid so fair, She loved a dri-ver boy, Who drove the mail some gold to gain Down in the Low-lands low.

Edwin in the Lowlands Low

Edwin in the Lowlands Low

J

Hexatonic (no 3rd).
Sung by Mrs. MARY BLANKENSHIPP
at Price's Creek, Burnsville, N. C., October 5, 1918

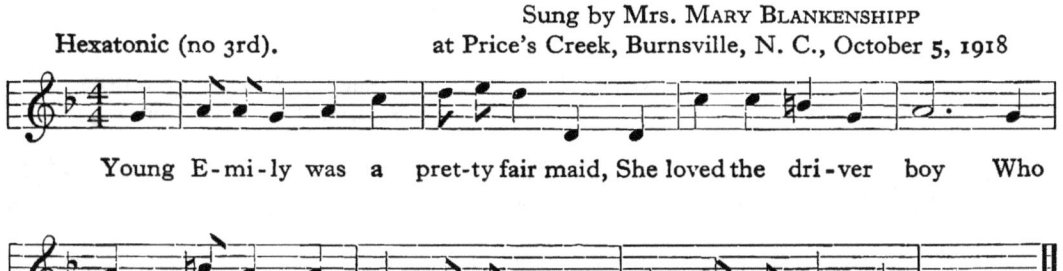

Young E-mi-ly was a pret-ty fair maid, She loved the dri-ver boy Who drove the stage the gold for to gain Down in the low-lands low.

K

Hexatonic (no 3rd).
Sung by Mr. LUTHER SHADOIN
at Lexington, Ky., Sept. 3, 1917

No. 57

Awake! Awake!

A

Pentatonic. Mode 3.

Sung by Mrs. MARY SANDS
at Allanstand, N. C., Aug. 1, 1916

1. A-wake! a-wake! you drow-sy sleep-er, A-wake! a-wake! it's al most

day; How can you lie and sleep and slum-ber And your true love go-ing far a - way?

2 Say, my love, go ask your mother
   If you my bride, my bride shall be;
   And if she says No, love, come and tell me;
   It will be the last time I'll bother thee.

3 I'll not go and ask my mother,
   For she lies on her bed at rest,
   And in her hands she holds a paper
   That speaks the most of my distress.

4 Say, my love, go ask your father
   If you my bride, my bride shall be;
   And if he says No, love, come and tell me;
   It will be the last time I'll bother thee.

5 I will not go and ask my father,
   For he lies on his bed at rest,
   And in his hands he holds a weapon
   To kill the man that I love best.

6 I'll go down in some lone valley
   And spend my weeks, my months, my years,
   And I'll eat nothing but green willow,
   And I'll drink nothing but my tears.

7 Then come back, come back, my own true lover,
   Come back, come back, in grief cried she,
   And I'll forsake both father and mother
   And I'll cry, love, and pity thee.

Awake! Awake!

B

Pentatonic. Mode 3.

Sung by Mrs. Anelize Chandler
at Alleghany, N. C., Aug. 28, 1916

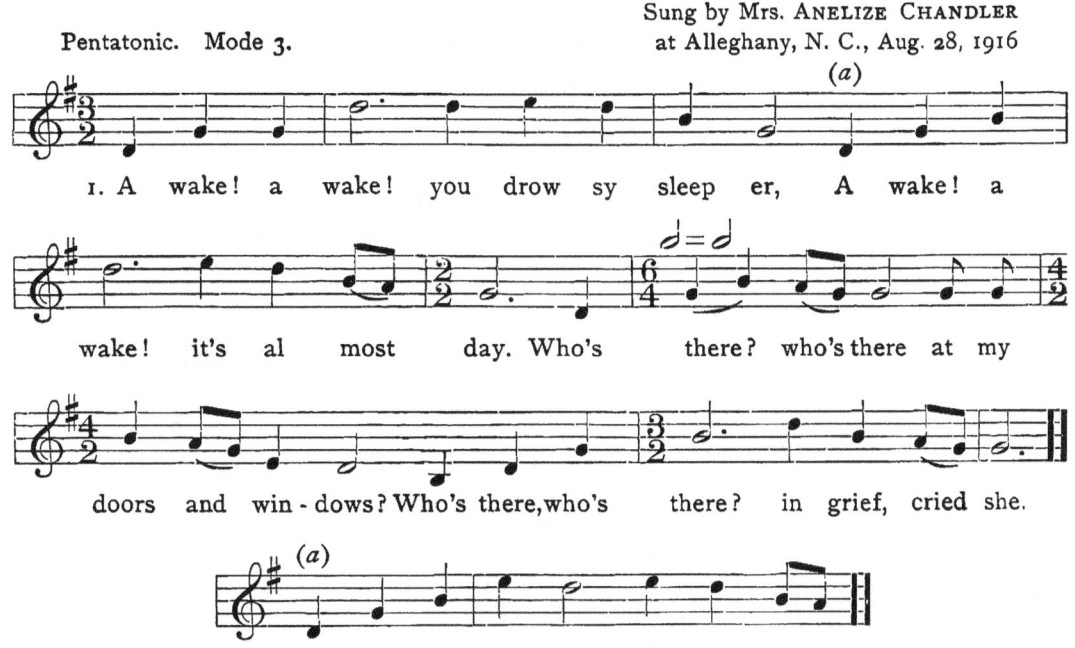

1. Awake! awake! you drowsy sleeper,
   Awake! awake! it's almost day.
   Who's there? who's there at my doors and windows?
   Who's there, who's there? in grief, cried she.

2. It's me alone, your own true love,
   He's just now here going away.
   Go away, go away from my doors and windows,
   Go away, go away, in grief, cried she.

3. It's you go, love, and ask your father
   If you my bride, my bride shall be;
   And if he says No, love, come and tell me;
   And this'll be the last time I'll bother thee.

4. It's I will not go and ask my father,
   For he's on his bed at rest a-sleeping,
   And in his hands he holds a weapon
   That will be a grief to thee.

5. It's you go, love, and ask your mother
   If you my bride, my bride shall be;
   And if she says No, love, come and tell me;
   And this'll be the last time I'll bother thee.

6. I'll not go in and ask my mother,
   For she's on her bed at rest a-sleeping,
   For in her hand she holds a card, love,
   That'll be bad news to thee.

Awake! Awake!

7 It's rise you up, love, come and pity me,
   For I'm going away to some sandy river bottom,
   And while I spend my days, my weeks, my months and years,
   I'll eat nothing but green willow and drink nothing but my tears.

8 Come back, come back, my love, and let me tell you.
   If you will go with me,
   I will forsake both father and mother
   And go along with you and spend my life for ever.

C

Pentatonic. Mode 3.

Sung by Mrs. Carrie Ford
at Black Mountain, N. C., Sept. 19, 1916

1. O Ka-tie dear, go ask your fa-ther If you may be a bride of mine; If he says No, please come and tell me; And I'll no long-er trou-ble you.

2 O Willie dear, it's no use to ask him.
   He's in his room and taking his rest.
   By his side a golden dagger
   To kill the one that I love best.

3 O Katie dear, go ask your mother
   If you may be a bride of mine;
   If she says No, please come and tell me;
   And I'll no longer trouble you.

4 O Willie dear, it's no use to ask.
   She's in her room and taking her rest.
   By her side a silver dagger
   To kill the one that I love best.

5 O he picked up a silver dagger,
   He pierced it through his wounded breast.
   Farewell, Kitty, farewell, darling,
   I'll die for the one that I love best.

6 She picked up the bloody weapon,
   She pierced it through her snow-white breast.
   Farewell, mamma, farewell papa,
   I'll go with the one that I love best.

Awake! Awake!

D

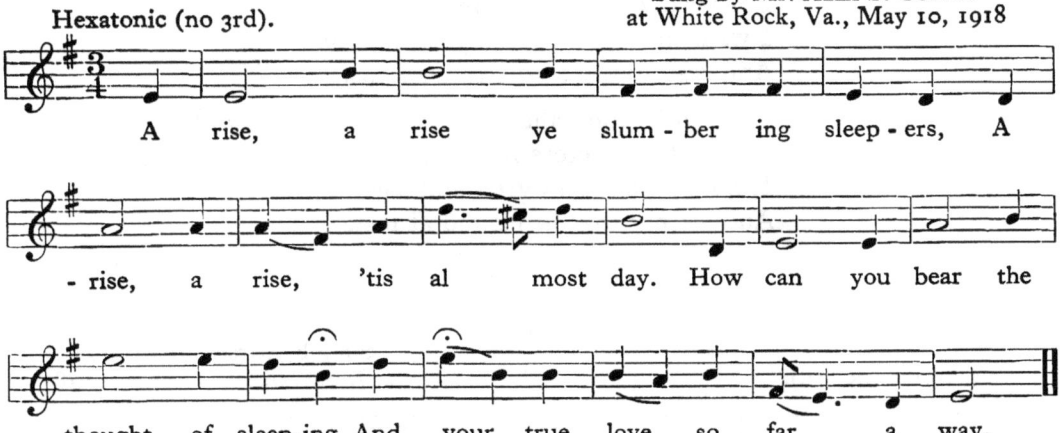

Sung by Mr. ALEX S. COFFEY
at White Rock, Va., May 10, 1918

Hexatonic (no 3rd).

A rise, a rise ye slum-ber-ing sleep-ers, A-rise, a rise, 'tis al most day. How can you bear the thought of sleep-ing, And your true love so far a way.

E

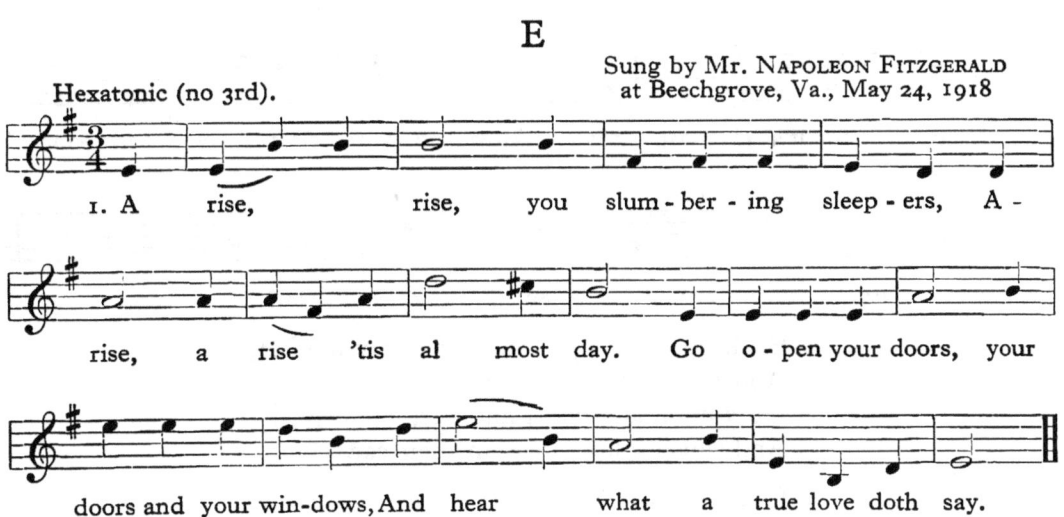

Sung by Mr. NAPOLEON FITZGERALD
at Beechgrove, Va., May 24, 1918

Hexatonic (no 3rd).

1. A rise, rise, you slum-ber-ing sleep-ers, A-rise, a rise 'tis al most day. Go o-pen your doors, your doors and your win-dows, And hear what a true love doth say.

2 O who is this that knocks at my window,
That speaks my name so familiarly?
'Tis James, 'tis James, your own true lover,
That wants to speak one word with thee.

3 Go away from my window, you'll waken my father,
He's lying now a-taking his rest,
And in his right hand he holds a weapon
To pierce the one that my heart loves best.

4 Go away from my window, you'll waken my mother,
Such tales of love she scorns to hear;
You'd better go court, go court some other,
She kindly whispered in my ear.

Awake! Awake!

5 I won't go court, go court some other,
   For what I say I mean no harm;
   I want to win you from your mother,
   And rest you in a true love's arms.

6 O down in yon valley there grows a green willow,
   I wish it was across my breast;
   It might cut off all grief and sorrow
   And set my troubled mind at rest.

F

Sung by Mrs. RHODA GREY
at Montvale, Va., Aug. 3, 1918

Hexatonic (no 6th).

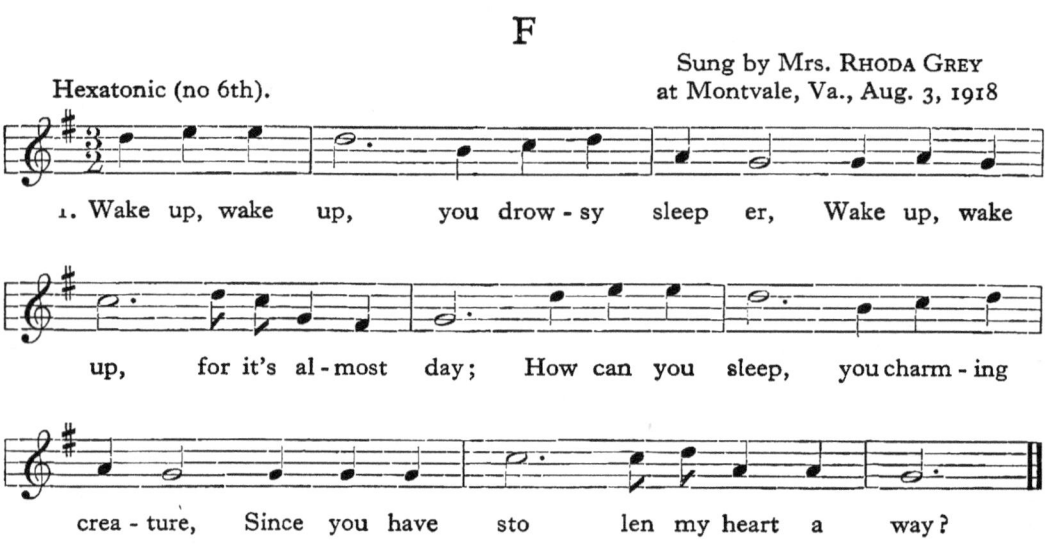

1. Wake up, wake up, you drow-sy sleep-er, Wake up, wake up, for it's al-most day; How can you sleep, you charm-ing crea-ture, Since you have sto-len my heart a-way?

2 Hush up, hush up, you'll wake my mother,
   And that will be sad news to her;
   Go you off and court another,
   And whisper low, love, in their ear.

3 I won't, I won't, I won't go off,
   For what I say I mean no harm;
   I've come to win you from your mother
   And rest you in your true love's arms.

4 Hush up, hush up, you'll wake my father,
   And that will break him of his night's rest;
   He holds a weapon in his right hand
   To kill the one that I love best.

5 The sea's so wide I cannot wade it,
   Nor neither have I wings to fly;
   I wish I had feet like a sparrow
   And wings like a little dove,
   I'd fly away off from the hills of sorrow
   And light on some low lands of love.

Awake! Awake!

6 Hand me down pen, ink, and paper,
   And set me down here for to write;
   I'll write a grief which is siley under (*sic*)
   That troubles me both day and night.

7 There sticks an arrow in yons wa';
   I wish the same was in my breast;
   I'd bid adieu to sin and sorrow,
   While my poor soul would be at rest.

G

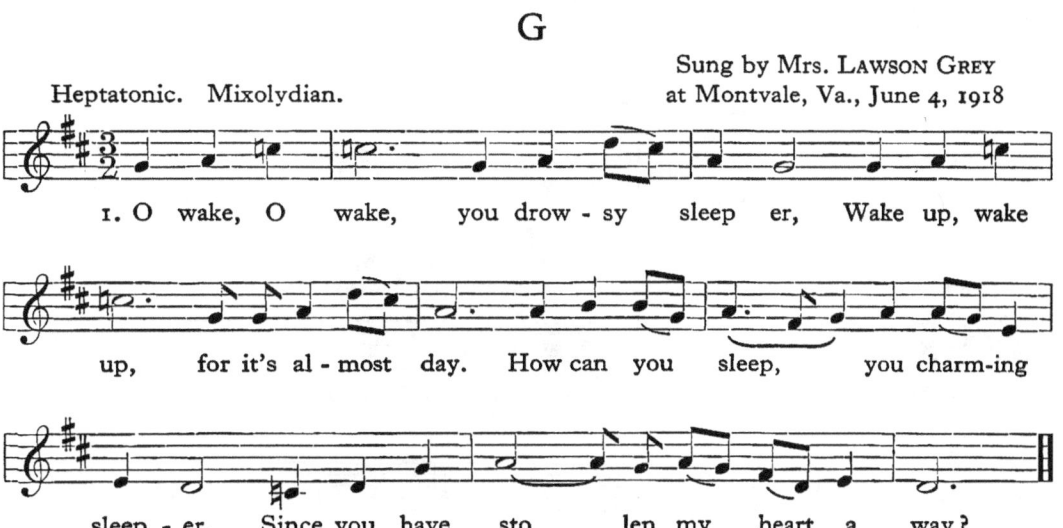

Heptatonic. Mixolydian.

Sung by Mrs. Lawson Grey
at Montvale, Va., June 4, 1918

1. O wake, O wake, you drow-sy sleep-er, Wake up, wake up, for it's al-most day. How can you sleep, you charm-ing sleep-er, Since you have sto-len my heart a-way?

2 O hush, O hush, my mother will hear you,
   And that will be sad news to her;
   Go off, go off, and court some other,
   And whisper low, love, in her ear.

3 I won't, I won't, I won't go away,
   For what I say I mean no harm;
   I've come to wean (*or*, win) you from your mother,
   And lie and rest you in your true love's arms.

4 O hush, O hush, you'll wake my father,
   And that will break him from his night's rest;
   He holds a weapon in his right hand
   To kill the one that I love best.

5 I wish I was on yonders mountain,
   There to spend both months and years;
   My food should be all grief and sorrow,
   My drink shall be of troubles tears.

6 If I had feet like a sparrow,
   If I had wings like a lonesome dove,
   I'd fly away over the hills of sorrow,
   I'd lie and rest in some low lands of love.

No. 58

The Green Bed

A

Hexatonic. Mode 4. b.

Sung by Mrs. Jane Gentry
at Hot Springs, N. C., Sept. 12, 1916

1. O come you home, dear John- ny, O come you home from sea? Last night my daugh-ter Pol- ly was dream-ing of thee.

2 O what for luck, dear Johnny?
  No for luck, says he;
  I lost my ship and cargo
  All on the raging sea.

3 Go bring your daughter Polly
  And set her down by me.
  We'll drink a melancholy
  And married we will be.

4 My daughter's busy
  And can't come in to thee;
  Except you wait an hour,
  It's one, two and three.

5 O Johnny, being drowsy,
  He dropped down his head.
  He called for a candle
  To light him to bed.

6 My beds they are full
  And has been all the week,
  And now for your lodging
  Out of doors you may seek.

7 It's bring here your reckoning book,
  Johnny he did say,
  And let me pay my reckoning bill
  Before I go away.

The Green Bed

8 'Twas then forty guineas
   Polly did behold,
   And out of his pockets
   Drawed handfuls of gold.

9 The old woman she vowed,
   And she vowed in a tusk,
   Saying what she had said
   Had been through a joke.

10 My green beds they are empty
   And have been all this week,
   Awaiting for you and daughter Polly
   To take a pleasant sleep.

11 It's you and your daughter Polly
   Both deserves to be burned,
   And before I lodge here
   I would lodge in a barn.

12 Be careful of your money, boys,
   And lay it up in store,
   And when you have no money, boys,
   You're turned out of doors.

B

Sung by Mrs. DELIE KNUCKLES
at Barbourville, Knox Co., Ky., May 16, 1917

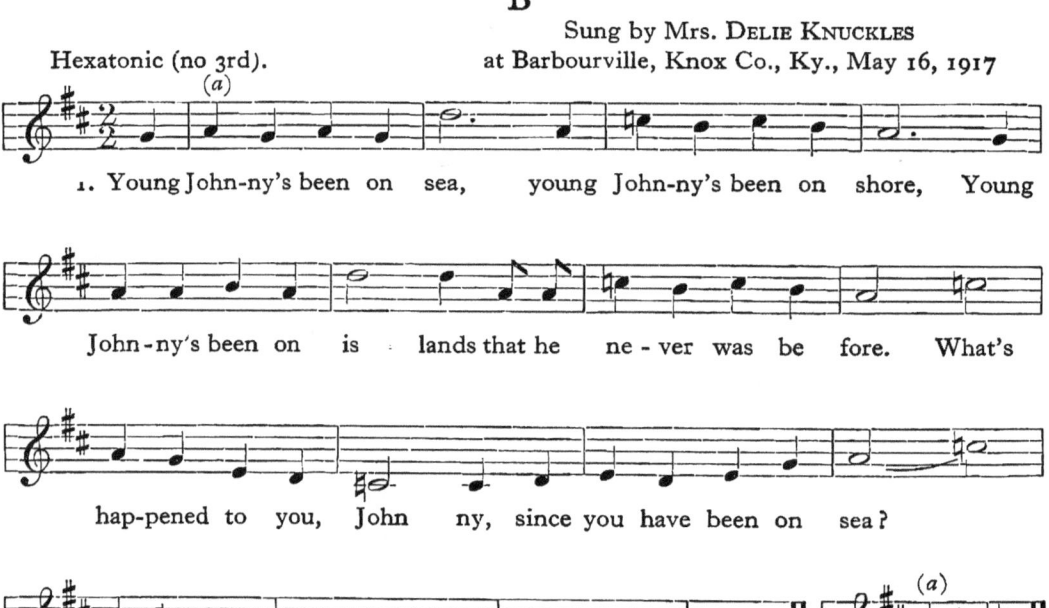

1. Young Johnny's been on sea, young Johnny's been on shore, Young Johnny's been on islands that he never was before. What's happened to you, Johnny, since you have been on sea? Nothing in this wide world only what you see on me.

The Green Bed

2 Young Johnny being wearied he hung down his head,
   He called for a candle to light himself to bed.
   Our beds is full of strangers, it's been for a week or more;
   You'll have to seek of your lodging in some other store.

3 Go bring your daughter Polly and place her down by me.
   Our daughter Polly's absent; she hain't been seen to-day.
   If she was here, Johnny, she'd cast you far away.

4 Young Johnny he got up, he struggled across the hall,
   Says: For the debts I owe I have the money all.
   Three thousand of the young and four of the old,
   He drew out his two hands full of gold.

5 Young Polly ran downstairs, a very pretty Miss,
   She threw her arms around him for him to hug and kiss
   O when I was a poor boy my lodging for to seek,
   Before I'd lie in your big beds, I'd lie all in the street.
   But now I have the money I'll roam the tavern through
   With a bottle of peach brandy and a pretty girl on each knee.

C

Heptatonic. Mixolydian.

Sung by Mrs. Mollie Broghton
at Barbourville, Knox Co., Ky., Aug. 25, 1917

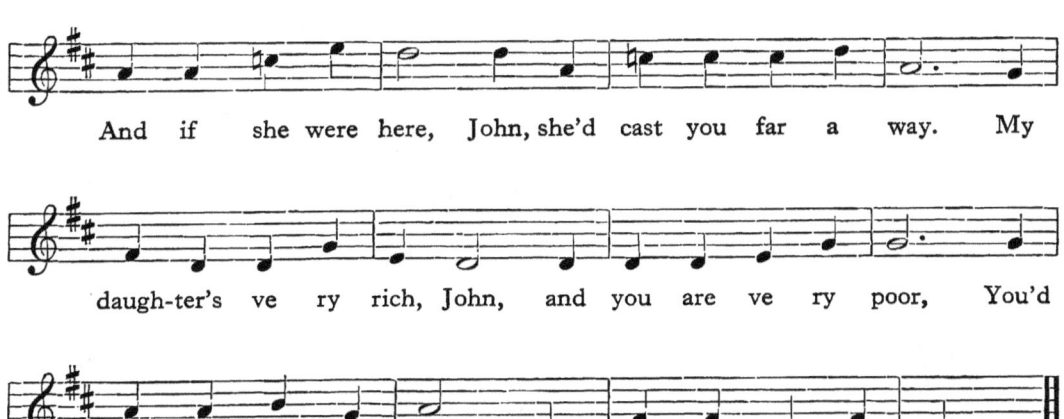

My daugh-ter has been ab-sent, John, and has-n't been seen to day,
And if she were here, John, she'd cast you far a way. My
daugh-ter's ve ry rich, John, and you are ve ry poor, You'd
bet ter seek your lodg ing in some o ther store.

The Green Bed

D

Heptatonic. Aeolian.

Sung by Mrs. Laurel Wheeler
at Buena Vista, Va., May 1, 1918

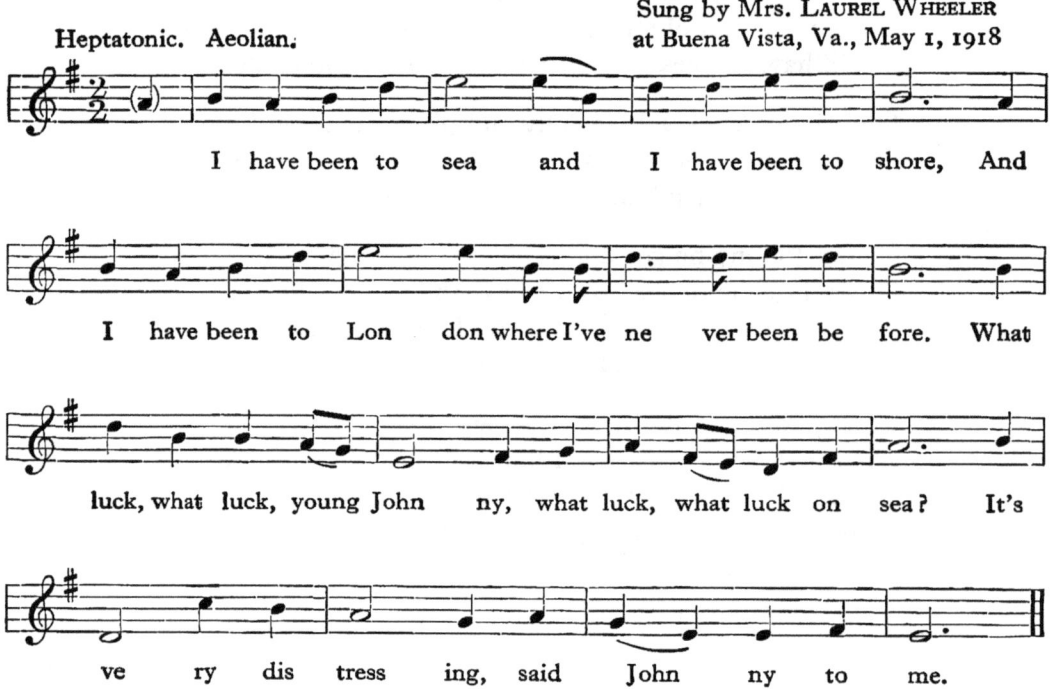

I have been to sea and I have been to shore, And I have been to London where I've never been before. What luck, what luck, young Johnny, what luck, what luck on sea? It's very distressing, said Johnny to me.

No. 59

The Simple Ploughboy

Sung by Mr. N. B. Chisholm
at Woodridge, Va., Sept. 27, 1916

Major mode.

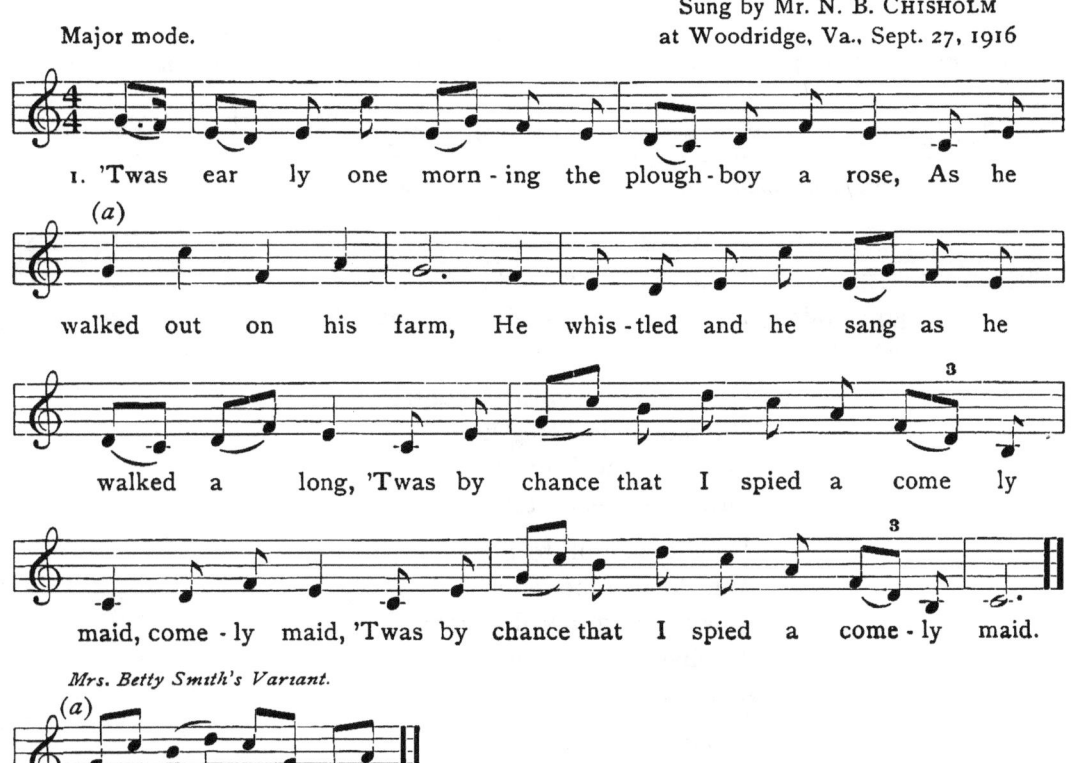

1. 'Twas early one morning the plough-boy a rose, As he walked out on his farm, He whis-tled and he sang as he walked a long, 'Twas by chance that I spied a come-ly maid, come-ly maid, 'Twas by chance that I spied a come-ly maid.

Mrs. Betty Smith's Variant.

2 Saying: Supposing you fall in love and your parents won't approve,
  Straightway they'll send you to sea.
  They'll press force against you and hurry you away,
  And send you to the wars to be slain.

3 She dressed herself in men's clothes, so costly and so fine,
  Her pockets well filled with gold.
  She walked up to London and she walked back again
  Enquiring for her sailor boy.

4 He has 'listed on the deep and is rolling on the sleet
  And has gone to the wars to be slain.

5 O she threw it on the deck and caught him round his neck,
  And she kissed him till she brought him safe on shore,
  Saying: The bells may loudly ring and the fair maids may sing;
  I'll get married to the lady I adore.

No. 60

The Three Butchers

A

Pentatonic. Mode 3 (no 6th).

Sung by Mr. DANA NORTON
at Flag Pond, Tenn., Aug. 31, 1916

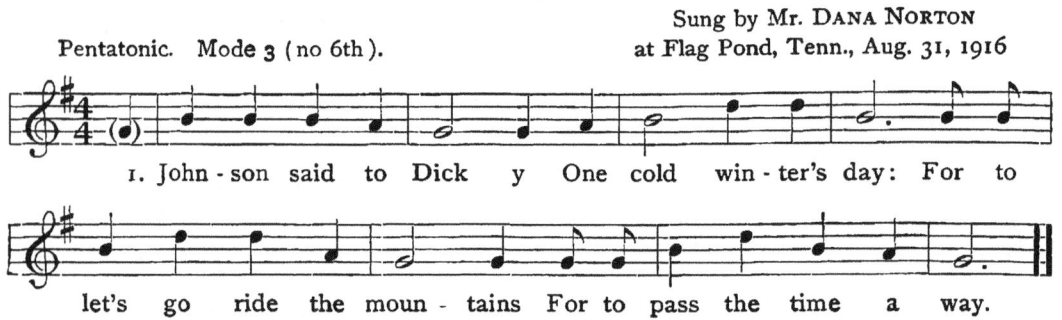

1. Johnson said to Dicky One cold winter's day: For to let's go ride the mountains For to pass the time away.

2 They rode up on the mountain,
   The mountain being high.
   Dicky said to Johnson:
   I heard a woman cry.

3 They looked off to the right
   And then to the left;
   Dicky seen a naked woman
   All chained down by herself.

4 Dicky, being kind
   To all the female kind,
   He wropt a great coat round her
   And took her on behind.

5 They rode on a little piece farther
   To a certain point of the road.
   She slapped three fingers over her eyes
   And gave three screams and a cry.

6 Out stepped seven robbers
   With weapons in their hands,
   Took Dicky by the bridle,
   Said: Young man, your life is mine.

7 Johnson said to Dicky:
   Let's take wings and fly.
   Dicky said to Johnson:
   I'll die before I fly.

8 And from that morning
   Till the sun set that night,
   Dicky killed six of the robbers
   And made the seventh take flight.

The Three Butchers

9 Dicky being tired,
   He laid down to rest.
   That woman stole his dagger
   And stuck it in his breast.

10 Good woman, good woman,
   Can you tell me the crime you have done?
   You have killed the bravest soldier
   That ever fought the gun.

B

Pentatonic. Mode 3.

Sung by Miss LINNIE LANDERS
at Carmen, N. C., Sept. 5, 1916

1. Dick-y said to John-son One cold win-ter's day: Let's go and ride the moun-tain And pass the time a-way.

C

Heptatonic. Mixolydian.

Sung by Master JAMES AGY
at Barbourville, Ky., May 7, 1917

1. John-son said to Jack-son on one ho-li-day:
   You get your ri-fle and I'll get my gun.

2 And ride around this mountain and have a little fun,
  Ride around this mountain one hundred miles or more.

3 They rode around this mountain for a hundred miles or more,
  Spied a wounded woman all bound down on the floor.

The Three Butchers

4 Dear woman, dear woman, what are you doing here?
  Robbers have robbed me and left me here to die.

5 Jackson was free-hearted like a young man kind,
  Threw his arms all around her and brought her on behind

6 They rode around this mountain for a hundred miles or more,
  Spied six old robbers all standing in a row.

7 Johnson says to Jackson: You'd better take wings and fly.
  Jackson says to Johnson: Before I'd fly I'd die.

8 The battle commenced at six o'clock,
  At seven till the sun went down.

9 Jackson he got wounded and he lay down to rest.
  Up stepped this dear little woman and stabbed him in the breast.

10 Dear woman, dear woman, just look what you have done;
   Killed the bravest soldier that ever borrowed a gun.

11 I shoulder my rifle, my pistol in my hand,
   I'll go up on this mountain and there I'll take my stand.

12 I see the captain a-coming, O what are you coming for?
   I killed me one soldier and I killed me another man.

13 Sends me to old England and sends me to be hung,
   Tell him I killed one soldier, I've killed my last one.

D

Hexatonic (no 6th).

Sung by Mrs. Mary F. Gross
at Peaks of Otter, Va., July 26, 1918

They had not gone but nine miles, but nine miles on the way, When Dick-son said to John-son: I hear some hu-man cry.

No. 61

William Taylor

A

Pentatonic. Mode 3.

Sung by Mrs. Rosie Hensley
at Carmen, N. C., Aug. 28, 1916

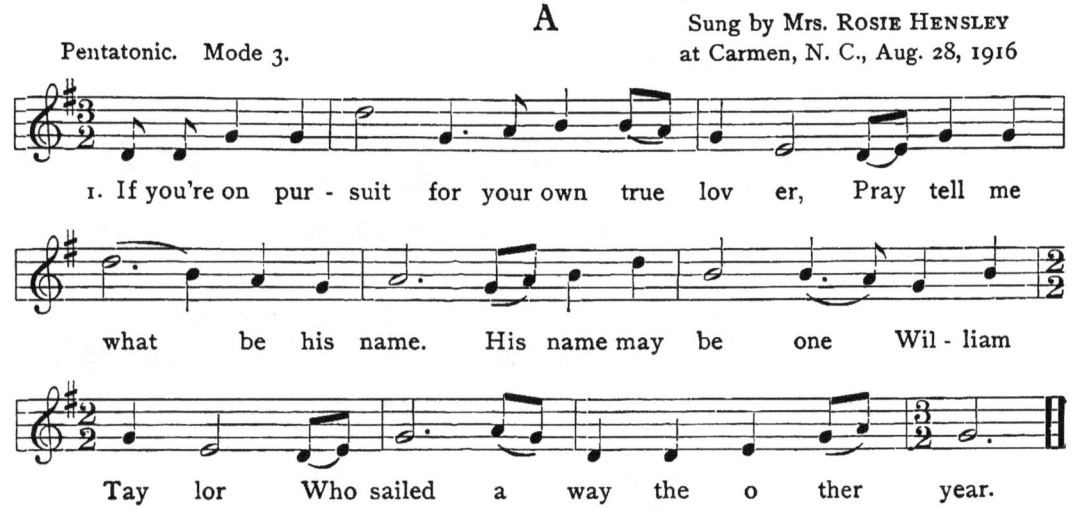

1. If you're on pur-suit for your own true lov-er, Pray tell me what be his name. His name may be one Wil-liam Tay-lor Who sailed a-way the o-ther year.

2 If his name may be one William Taylor,
  Very like, very like I know the man.
  If you'll rise early in the morning,
  You'll see him walking down the strand.

3 As she rose early the very next morning,
  Just about the break of day,
  And she saw her own dear William Taylor
  A-walking with his lady gay.

4 If this here is my William Taylor,
  Good lord, good lass, what shall I do?
  She wrung her lily-white hands and crying,
  And overboard her body threw.

B

Pentatonic. Mode 3.

Sung by Mrs. Talithah Powell
at Berea, Madison Co., Ky., May 28, 1917

1. O Wil-liam be-ing a youth-ful lov-er, In all pride and youth-ful ways, But when his love was first dis

William Taylor

2 She dressed herself in a soldier's jacket,
And to the sea for to sail.
O may I eat only bread and water
Till I see his face again.
Good lass, good lass, what is the matter?
What the fortune's brought you here?
I'm in pursuit of my true lover,
Who sailed away the other year.

3 If you're in pursuit of your true lover,
And, kind Miss, tell me his name.
His name is loving William Taylor
Who sailed away the other year.
If his name is loving William Taylor
Very like I know the man.
If you'll rise early in the morning,
You'll see him walking on the strand.

4 She rose early in the morning,
She rose just at the break of day,
And there she saw loving William Taylor
Walking with that lady gay.
If that be loving William Taylor,
Goodness, goodness, what shall I do?
She wrung her hands and cried for mercy,
And overboard her body threw.

William Taylor

C

Sung by Mrs. Francis Carter
at Beattyville, Lee Co., Ky., Sept. 7, 1917

Hexatonic (no 3rd).

1. One day on board rose a dread-ful scream-ing, And she be-ing

one a-mong the rest, A sil-ver but-ton flew off her

jack-et, The sail-ors spied her snow-y white breast.

2 O pray, kind Miss, what is the matter,
   Or what misfortune's brought you here?
   I am in pursuit of my own true love
   Who sailed away the other year.

3 If you're in pursuit of your own true love,
   It's pray, kind Miss, tell me his name,
   For I have very lately crossed the ocean,
   Perhaps I have this young man seen.

4 Why, sir, his name is Willie Taylor,
   He sailed away from the I-O-Green.
   Well, if his name be Willie Taylor,
   So very well I know the man.
   If you'll rise early in the morning
   You'll see him walking up the strand.

5 So she rose early the next morning,
   'Twas just about the break of day,
   And there she spied her love, Willie Taylor,
   A-walking with a lady gay.

6 O is this you, young Willie Taylor?
   All by your side is this your wife?
   The one that's got you never shall enjoy you.
   For your wicked crime I'll end your life.

William Taylor

7 She called for a sword and a band of pistols,
  And they were brought to her command.
  And there she shot her love, Willie Taylor,
  As he were holding her by the hand.

8 Then she was highly recommended
  For the wicked deed that she had done.
  They made her head and chief commander
  Over the ship called the Youlie Anne.

9 One day she was sitting in a very deep study,
  And overboard she threw herself.
  The whole ship's crew they strove to save her;
  They strove, they strove, but it was in vain.

10 Now Willie's shot and Polly's drownded.
  These two true lovers they had to part.
  Now let young men be very cautious
  How they treat their old sweethearts.

No. 62

The Golden Glove

A

Heptatonic. Mode 3, a + b (ionian).

Sung by Mrs. MARY SANDS at Allanstand, N. C., Aug. 2, 1916

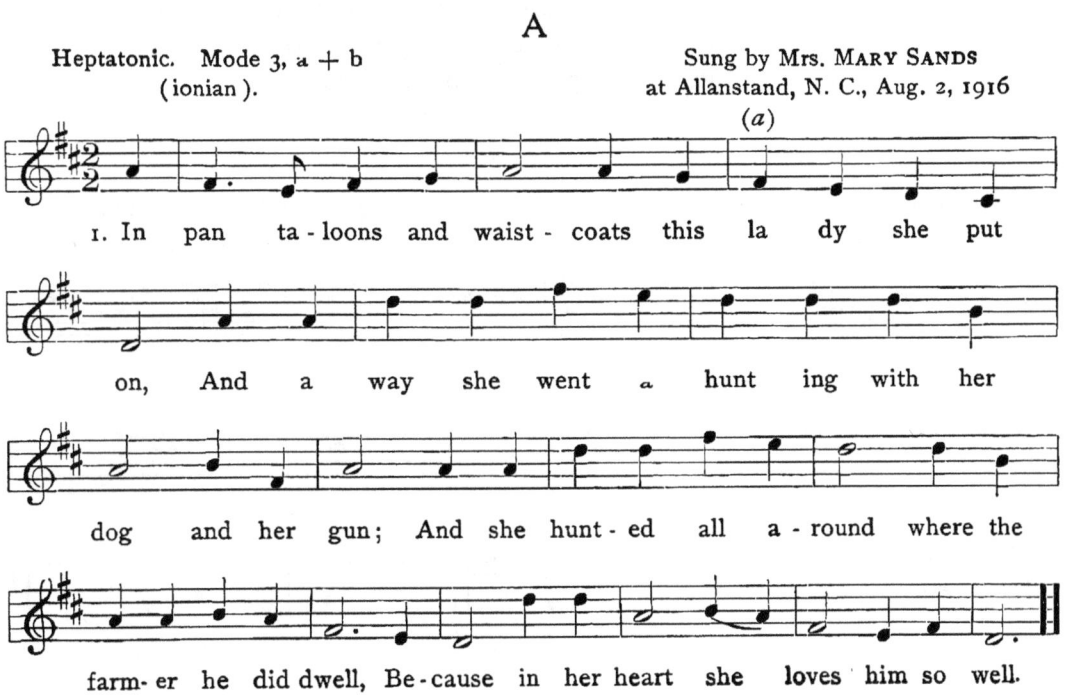

1. In pantaloons and waistcoats this lady she put on, And away she went a-hunting with her dog and her gun; And she hunted all around where the farmer he did dwell, Because in her heart she loves him so well.

2 In firing one time but nothing did kill,
Out came the farmer and whistled to his field.
She step-ped up to him, these words she did say:
Why wasn't you at the wedding, the wedding to-day?
Why wasn't you at the wedding to wait upon the Squire
And to give to him his bride?

3 Back to this lady the farmer replied:
I will not give her up for I love her too well.
This pleased this young lady in hearing him so bold.
She gave to him her glove that was covered in gold.

4 I picked it up as I came along,
As I came a-hunting with my dog and my gun;
Returning back home with her heart all filled with love,
Put out the new oration that she had lost her glove.
And if any man will find it and bring it to me,
Him I will marry and his lady I will be.

The Golden Glove

5 Now I am married I will tell to you my fun,
How I hunted up my farmer with my dog and my gun,
And now I have got him so closely in a share,
I will not give him up I vow and declare.

B

Heptatonic. Mode 3, a + b
(ionian).

Sung by Mr. N. B. CHISHOLM
at Woodridge, Va., Sept. 27, 1916

No. 63

Pretty Nancy of Yarmouth

Hexatonic. Mode 1, b.

Sung by Mrs. MARY SANDS
at Allanstand, N. C., July 31, 1916

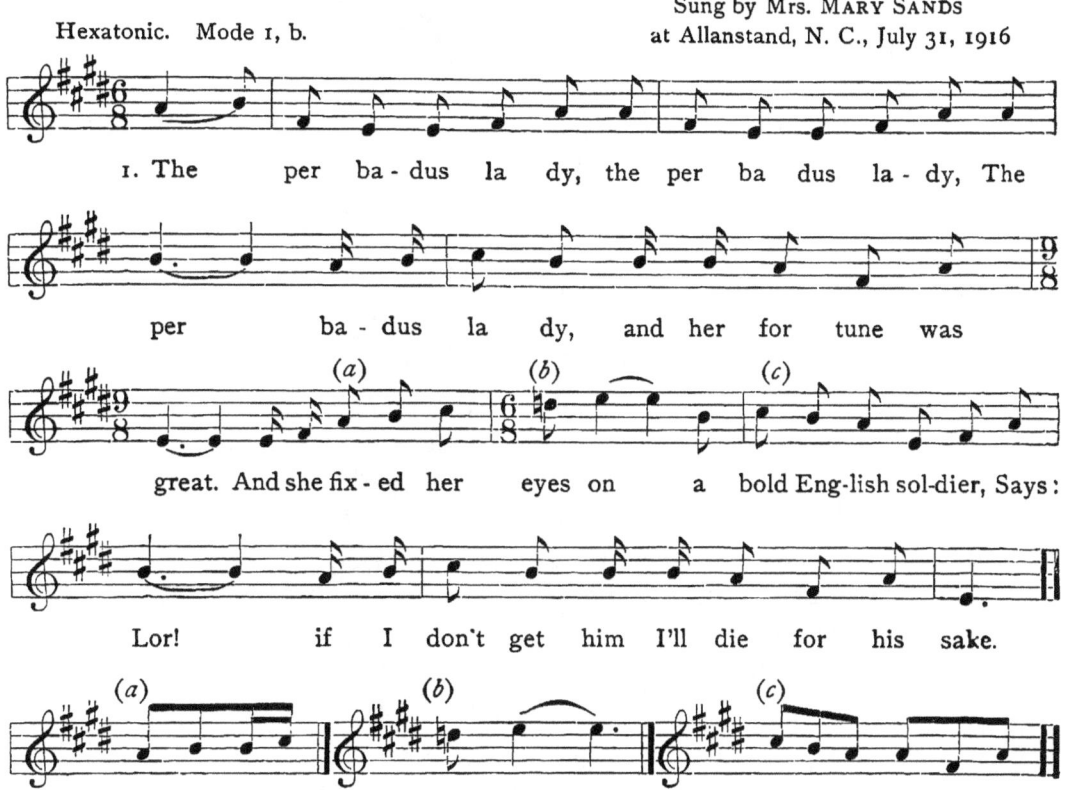

1. The per ba-dus la-dy, the per ba-dus la-dy, The per ba-dus la-dy, and her for-tune was great. And she fix-ed her eyes on a bold Eng-lish sol-dier, Says: Lor! if I don't get him I'll die for his sake.

2. A | perbadus lady, a | perbadus lady,
   A | perbadus | lady was deep to de- | ny.
   But in old English | land I | vowed to a lady,
   And | at my re- | turn I must make her my | bride.

3. She | dressed herself in | many' rich 'tires
   And | in costly | diamonds she plaited her | hair;
   A hundred of | slaves she | took to wait on her
   And | with her two | maidens she went to him | there.

4. Saying: | Now if you fancy a | perbadus lady,
   A | perbadus | lady and her fortune is | great.
   Saying: Now if you can | fancy a | perbadus lady,
   You shall have | music to | charm you to your silent | sleep.

5. A | perbadus lady, a | perbadus lady,
   A | perbadus | lady was deep to | deny.
   But in old English | land I | vowed to a lady,
   And | at my re- | turn I must make her my | bride.

Pretty Nancy of Yarmouth

6 Whilst | he was a-sailing back | to his true lover,
   She | wrote a | letter to the boatswain her | friend,
   Saying : A handsome re- | ward I | surely will give you
   If | you the | life of young Jemmy will | end.

7 For the | sake of the money and for the | wit of the beauty,
   As | they were a- | lonely the same did com- | plete,
   And as they were a- | lonely a-| sailing together,
   He | suddenly | did plant him into the | deep.

8 In the | dead time of night when they | all lie a-sleeping,
   A | trouble it | did to her window appear,
   Saying : Rise you up | here, it's | here, pretty Nancy,
   And | 'fer to the | vows that you made to your | dear.

9 She | raised her head off her | soft downy pillow
   And | straight to her | gazement (casement) she did ap- | pear,
   And the | moon being | bright and so | clearly shining :
   That | surely | must be the voice of my | dear.

10 O | yes, dearest Nancy, I | am your true lover,
   | Dead or a- | live you know you're my | own,
   And now for your | promises | I am pursuing
   To | follow me | down to the watery | tomb.

11 O | yes, dearest Jemmy, I'll | soon be a-going,
   I'll | soon plunge | into your arms a- | sleep.
   And no sooner this | unfortuned | lady she spoken,
   She | suddenly | did plunge herself into the | deep.

12 Then | at the sea-side he was | tried for the murder
   And | at the ship's | arms he was hung for the | same ;
   And the old man's heart was | broke and he | died for his daughter
   Be | fore the | ship into the harbour it | came.

No. 64

The Silk Merchant's Daughter
A

Hexatonic. Mode 2, a.

Sung by Mrs. Mary Sands
at Allanstand, N. C., July 31, 1916

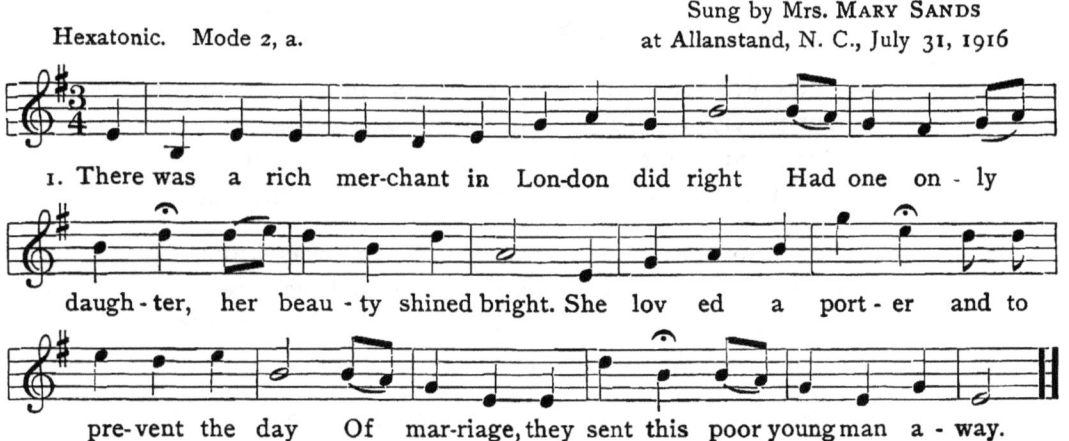

1. There was a rich merchant in London did right Had one only daughter, her beauty shined bright. She loved a porter and to prevent the day Of marriage, they sent this poor young man away.

2 O now he is gone for to serve his king,
It grieves this lady to think of the thing.
She dressed herself up in rich merchant's shape,
She wandered away her true love for to seek.

3 As she was a-travelling one day, almost night,
A couple of Indians appeared in her sight,
And as they drew nigh her, O this they did say:
Now we are resolved to take your life away.

4 She had nothing by her but a sword to defend,
These barbarous Indians murder intend.
But in the contest one of them she did kill
Which caused the other for to leave the hill.

5 As she was a-sailing over the tide,
She spied a city down by the sea-side.
She saw her dear porter a-walking the street,
She made it her business her true love to meet.

6 How do you do, sir, where do you belong?
I'm a-hunting a diamond and I must be gone.
He says: I'm no sailor, but if you want a man,
For my passage over I'll do all I can.

7 Then straightway they both went on board.
Says the captain to the young man: What did you do with your sword?
On account of long travel on him she did gaze.
Once by my sword my sweet life did save.

The Silk Merchant's Daughter

8 Then straightway to London their ship it did steer,
   Such utter destruction to us did appear.
   It was all out on main sea, to our discontent,
   Our ship sprung a leak and to the bottom she went.

9 There was four and twenty of us contained in one boat,
   Our provision gave out and our allowance grew short.
   Our provisions gave out and death drawing nigh,
   Says the captain: Let's cast lots for to see who shall die.

10 Then down on a paper each man's name was wrote,
   Each man ran his venture, each man had his note.
   Amongst the whole ship's crew this maid's was the least,
   It was her lot to die for to feed all the rest.

11 Now, says the captain, let's cast lots and see
   Amongst the ship's crew who the butcher will be.
   It's the hardest of fortune you ever did hear,
   This maid to be killed by the young man, her dear.

12 He called for a basin for to catch the blood
   While this fair lady a-trembling stood,
   Saying: Lord, have mercy on me, how my poor heart do bleed
   To think I must die, hungry men for to feed.

13 Then he called for a knife his business to do.
   She says: Hold your hand for one minute or two.
   A silk merchant's daughter in London I be;
   Pray see what I've come to by loving of thee.

14 Then she showed a ring betwixt them was broke.
   Knowing the ring, with a sigh he spoke:
   For the thoughts of your dying my poor heart will burst,
   For the hopes of your long life, love, I will die first.

15 Says the captain: If you love her you'll make amend,
   But the fewest of number will die for a friend,
   So quicken the business and let it be done.
   But while they were speaking they all heard a gun.

16 Says the captain: You may now all hold your hand,
   We all hear a gun, we are near ship or land.
   In about half an hour to us did appear
   A ship bound for London which did our hearts cheer.
   It carried us safe over and us safe conveyed,
   And then they got married this young man and maid.

The Silk Merchant's Daughter

B

Hexatonic. Mode 2, a.

Sung by Mrs. Tom Rice
at Big Laurel, N. C., Aug. 17, 1916

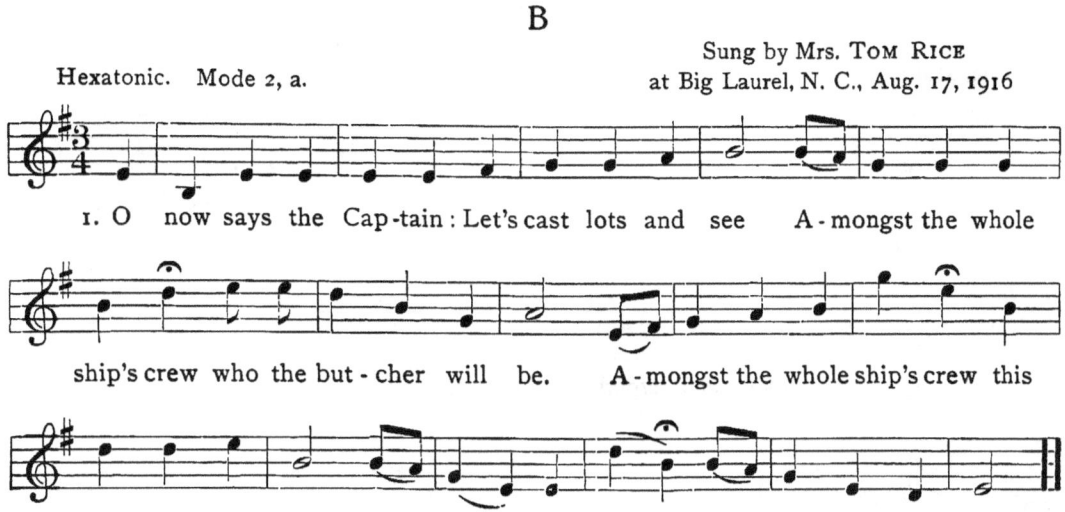

1. O now says the Captain: Let's cast lots and see Amongst the whole ship's crew who the butcher will be. Amongst the whole ship's crew this maid was the last And she must die. to feed all the rest.

C

Hexatonic (no 7th).

Sung by Mrs. Kate Thomas
at St. Helen's, Lee Co., Ky., Sept. 12, 1917

There was a silk-merchant in London did dwell, He had one only daughter none could excel. She loved a young porter and to permit the day Her cruel old parents forced her away.

The Silk Merchant's Daughter
D

No. 65

Jack Went A-Sailing

A

Pentatonic. Mode 3.

Sung by Mrs. Gentry
at Hot Springs, N. C., Aug. 26, 1916

1. Jack went a-sailing With trouble on his mind, To leave his native country And his darling dear behind. Sing ree and sing low, So fare you well, my dear.

2 She dressed herself in men's array,
And apparel she put on;
Unto the field of battle
She marched her men along.

3 Your cheeks too red and rosy,
Your fingers too neat and small,
And your waist too slim and slender
To face a cannon ball.

4 My cheeks are red and rosy,
My fingers neat and small,
But it never makes me tremble
To face a cannon ball.

5 The battle being ended,
She rode the circle round,
And through the dead and dying,
Her darling dear she found.

6 She picked him up all in her arms,
She carried him down to town,
And sent for a London doctor
To heal his bleeding wounds.

7 This couple they got married,
So well they did agree;
This couple they got married,
And why not you and me?

Jack Went A-Sailing

B

Heptatonic. Mode 2,
a + b (æolian).

Sung by Mrs. Combs
at Knott County, Ky., August, 1908

1. There was a wealthy merchant, In London he did dwell, He had one lovely daughter, The truth to you I'll tell, O the truth to you I'll tell.

2 She had sweethearts a-plenty,
She courted both day and night,
Till all on the sailor boy
She placed her heart's delight.

3 Her father heard the callin',
So quickly he came in.
Good morning, Mrs. Frasier,
Is that your sweetheart's name?

4 I will lock you in my dungeon,
Your body I'll confine,
If there is none but Jacky Frasier
That will ever suit your mind.

5 You can lock me in your dungeon,
It is hard to be confined,
But there is none but Jacky Frasier
That will ever suit my mind.

6 O daughter, O daughter,
If you will quit that boy to-day,
I'll pay him forty shillings
To bear him far away.

7 She answered him quickly, quickly,
I'll quit that boy to-day;
But yet all in her heart
She loved her darling still.

Jack Went A-Sailing

8. When her father saw him coming,
   He flew in an angry way.
   She gave him forty shillings
   To bear him far away.

9. He sailed East, and he sailed West
   All across the deep blue sea,
   So safely he got landed
   In the wars of Germany.

10. This girl being a girl of honour
    With money in her hand,
    She set her resolution
    To visit some foreign land.

11. She went down to a tailor's shop
    And dressed all in men's gray,
    And laboured for the captain
    To bear her far away.

12. Your waist is too long and slender,
    Your fingers too long and small,
    Your cheeks too red and rosy
    To face the cannon ball.

13. It's true my waist is long and slender,
    My fingers they are small;
    It would not change my countenance
    To see ten thousand fall.

14. Kind sir, your name I would like to know
    Before aboard you go.
    She smiled all in her countenance:
    They call me Jackaro.

15. She sailed all over the ocean,
    All over the deep blue sea;
    So safely she got landed
    In the wars of Germany.

16. She went out to the battlefield,
    She viewed it up and down;
    Among the dead and wounded
    Her darling boy she found.

17. She picked him up all in her arms
    And carried him to the town,
    Enquiring for a doctor
    To heal his bloody wound.

Jack Went A-Sailing

18 So here's a handsome couple
So quickly did agree.
How stylish they got married,
And why not you and me?

C

Hexatonic. Mode 3, a.

Sung by Miss MacKinney
at Habersham Co., Ga., May 28, 1910

1. There was a silk merchant In London town did dwell, He had one only daughter, And the truth to you I'll tell. Sing li li, li li, O, O li li, li li, O.

2 This young lady she was courted
By men of high degree;
There was none but Jack the sailor
Would ever do for she.

3 As soon as her waiting-maid
Heard what she did say,
She went unto her father
With her heart content.

4 Dear daughter, if this be true
What I have heard of you,
It's Jackie shall be vanished
And you confined shall be.

5 This body you may have,
My heart you can't confine;
There's none but Jack the sailor
That can have this heart of mine.

6 Poor Jackie, he's gone sailing
With trouble on his mind,
A-leaving of his country
And darling girl behind.

Jack Went A-Sailing

7 Poor Jackie, he's gone sailing,
His face we shall see no more.
He's landed at San Flanders
On the dismal sandy shore.

8 She went into the tailor shop
And dressed in men's array,
And went into a vessel
To convey herself away.

9 Before you step on board, sir,
Your name I'd like to know.
She smiled all over her countenance:
They call me Jack Monroe.

10 Your waist is light and slender,
Your fingers neat and small,
Your cheeks too red and rosy
To face the cannon ball.

11 I know my waist is light and slender,
My fingers are neat and small,
But I never change my countenance
To face the cannon ball.

12 The wars being over,
She hunted all around
Among the dead and wounded,
And her darling boy she found.

13 She picked him all up in her arms
And carried him to the town,
And sent for a physician
Who quickly healed his wounds.

14 This couple they got married,
So well did they agree.
This couple they got married,
And why not you and me?

D

Sung by Mr. N. B. CHISHOLM
at Woodridge, Va., Sept. 23, 1916

Hexatonic. Mode 4, a.*

Jack he went a sail ing, With trou ble on his mind, To

*If A be tonic: — Mode 2, a.

Jack Went A-Sailing

Jack Went A-Sailing

Jack Went A-Sailing

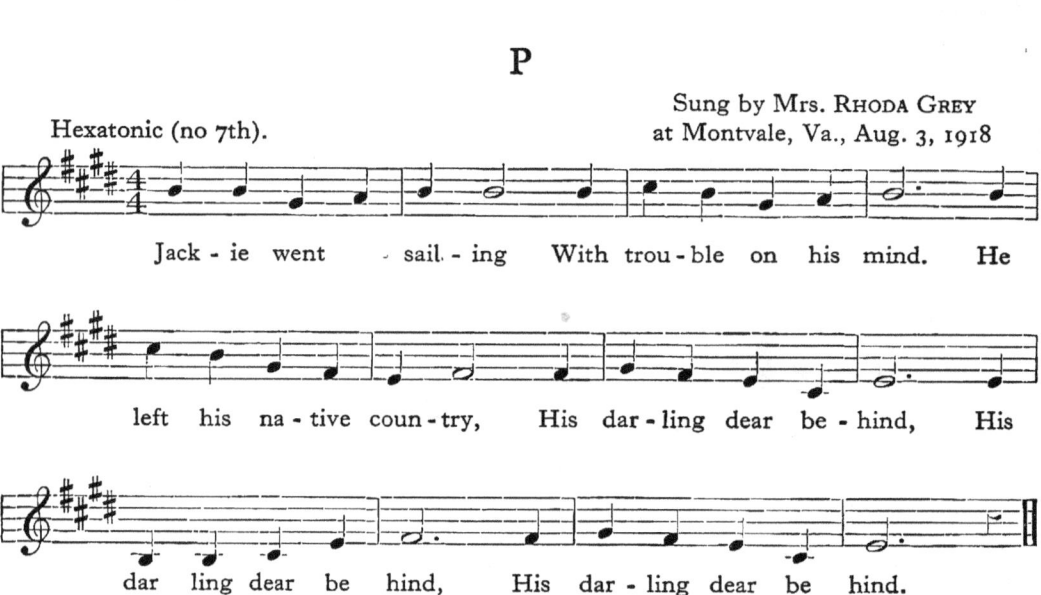

P

Hexatonic (no 7th). Sung by Mrs. Rhoda Grey at Montvale, Va., Aug. 3, 1918

Jack-ie went sail-ing With trou-ble on his mind. He left his na-tive coun-try, His dar-ling dear be-hind, His dar-ling dear be-hind, His dar-ling dear be-hind.

Q

Hexatonic (no 3rd). Sung by Mrs. Ef. Chrisom at Cane Branch, Burnsville, N. C., Oct. 3, 1918

Jack he's gone a sail-ing With trou-ble on his mind, A leav-ing of his coun-try, His dar-ling dear be-hind. Go lay the lil I you, Go lay the lil I you.

No. 66

The Bold Lieutenant

A

Pentatonic. Mode 3.

Sung by Mrs. JENNY L. COMBS
at Berea, Madison Co., Ky., May 30, 1917

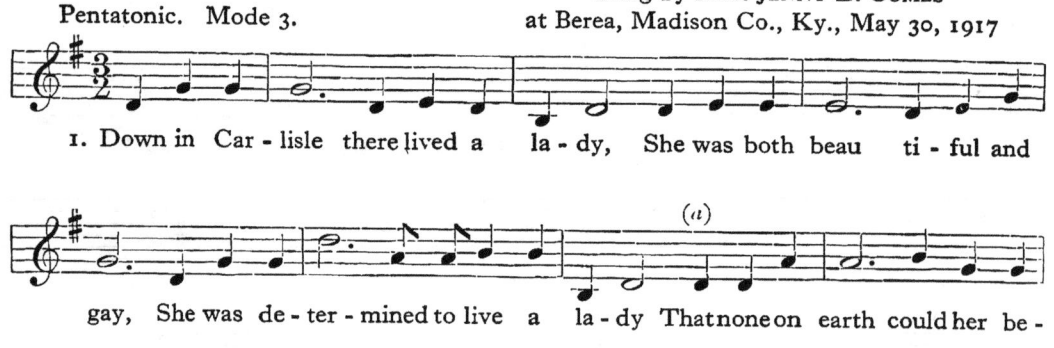

1. Down in Car-lisle there lived a la-dy, She was both beau-ti-ful and gay, She was de-ter-mined to live a la-dy That none on earth could her be-

-tray.

2 Unless he was a man of honour,
   A man of honour on land or sea.
   Until at length two loving brothers
   Came this fair lady for to see.

3 One he was a brave lieutenant,
   A man of honour and man of war;
   The other was a bold sea-captain,
   Belonging to a ship called Colonel Carr.

4 Then up spoke this noble lady,
   Saying: I cannot but be one man's bride;
   So come you both in the morning early,
   There we will this case decide.

5 She ordered her a coach and horses,
   A coach and horses at her command,
   And then off rode these three true lovers
   Until they came to a lion's den.

6 There they paused and there they halted,
   While these two brothers stood gazing round,
   And for the space of half an hour
   The girl stood speechless on the ground.

The Bold Lieutenant

7. Then up rose this noble lady,
   And threw her fan in the lion's den,
   Saying: Which of you to gain this lady
   Will return to me my fan again?

8. Then up spoke the brave lieutenant,
   Saying: O madam, of this I don't approve.
   I know I am a man of honour,
   But I will not lose my life for love.

9. Then up spoke the brave sea-captain,
   He raised his voice most rattling high:
   I know I am a man of honour,
   And I'll return your fan or die.

10. Down in the lion's den he entered,
    Where the lions rage so fierce and grim.
    He raged and raged around among them,
    And then returned out again.

11. When she saw her true love coming
    And saw to him no harm was done,
    She threw herself all on his bosom,
    Saying: Here's the prize that you have won.

12. Then up spoke the brave lieutenant,
    Just like one all troubled in mind,
    Saying: In some lonesome woods I'll wander
    Where none on earth my body can find.

B

Sung by Mrs. MINNIE POPE
at Clear Creek, Wasioto, Bell Co., Ky., May 1, 1917

Pentatonic. Mode 2.

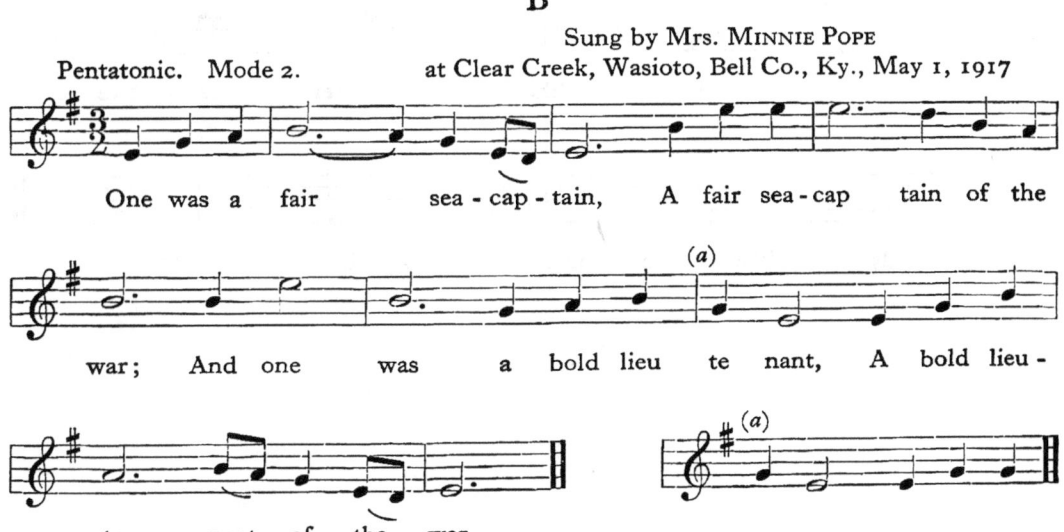

One was a fair sea-cap-tain, A fair sea-cap tain of the war; And one was a bold lieu te nant, A bold lieu-te nant of the war.

The Bold Lieutenant

C

Pentatonic. Mode 4.   Sung by Mrs. Margaret Dunagan at St. Helen's, Lee Co., Ky., Sept. 9, 1917

D

Hexatonic (no 6th).   Sung by Mrs. Berry Creech at Greasy Creek, Pine Mountain, Harlan Co., Ky., Aug. 31, 1917

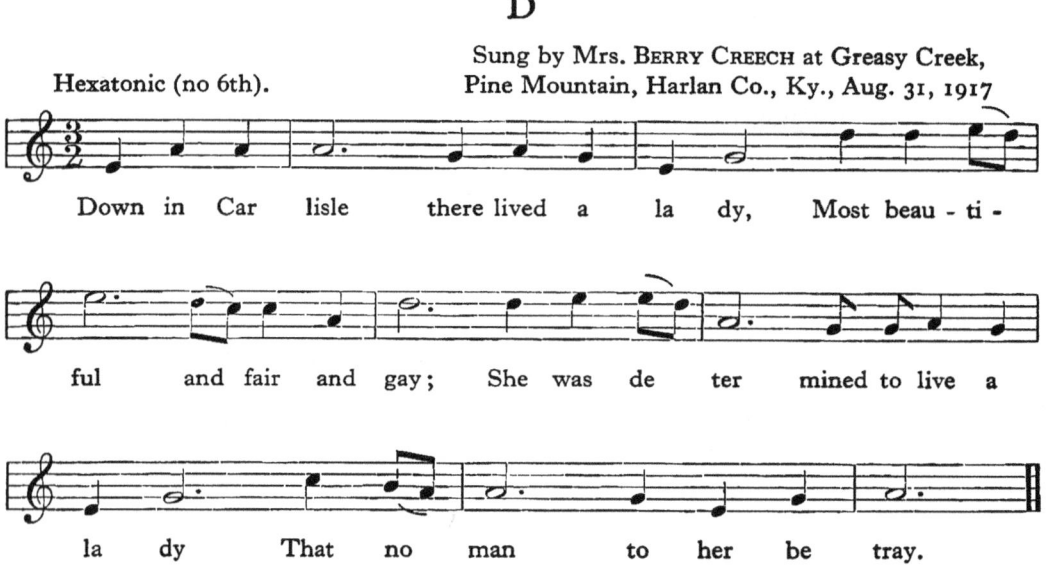

No. 67

The Banks of Sweet Dundee

A

Pentatonic. Mode 2.

Sung by Mrs. DAN BISHOP
at Teges, Clay Co., Ky., Aug. 21, 1917

1. I'll tell you a sad story which happened in this land,
   It was of a handsome female as you may understand,
   Who never knew her mother, but likewise a gay young man.

2. Her father died and left her ten thousand pounds of gold.
   She lived with her uncle, the cause of all her woes.
   Her uncle had a ploughboy which Mollie liked right well,
   And in her uncle's garden their tender love did tell.

3. So early one morning this old man he rose
   And at Mollie's room door he hastened on his clothes,
   Saying: Arise, you handsome female, and married you shall be,
   For the squire is now a-waiting on the banks of sweet Dundee.

4. A fig to all you squires, to lord and Jews likewise,
   For William 'pears like diamonds a-glittering in my eyes.
   You never shall have sweet Willie, nor happy shall you be,
   For I mean to banish Willie from the banks of sweet Dundee.

5. The first crowd came on Willie when he was all alone.
   He fought full hard for his liberty, but there were eight to one.
   Pray kill me now, says Willie, pray kill me now, says he,
   For I'd rather die for Mollie on the banks of sweet Dundee.

The Banks of Sweet Dundee

6 As Mollie was walking, lamenting for her love,
   She meets the wealthy squire all in her uncle's grove.
   Stand off, stand off, says Mollie, stand off, you man, says she,
   For I'd rather die for Willie on the banks of sweet Dundee.

7 He threw his arms around her and crushed her to the ground.
   There she spied two pistols and his sword beneath his morning-gown.
   The pistols she slipped slily and the sword she used free,
   She shot and killed the squire on the banks of sweet Dundee.

8 Her uncle overheard them, come hastening to the grove,
   Saying: You've killed the wealthy squire, prepare for your death-blow.
   Stand off, stand off, says Mollie, stand off, you man, says she,
   So the trigger drew and her uncle slew on the banks of sweet Dundee.

9 The doctor being sent for, he knew that they were killed,
   Also there came a lawyer to write the old man's will.
   He willed his gold to Mollie, because she fought so free,
   Then closed his eyes to write no more on the banks of sweet Dundee.

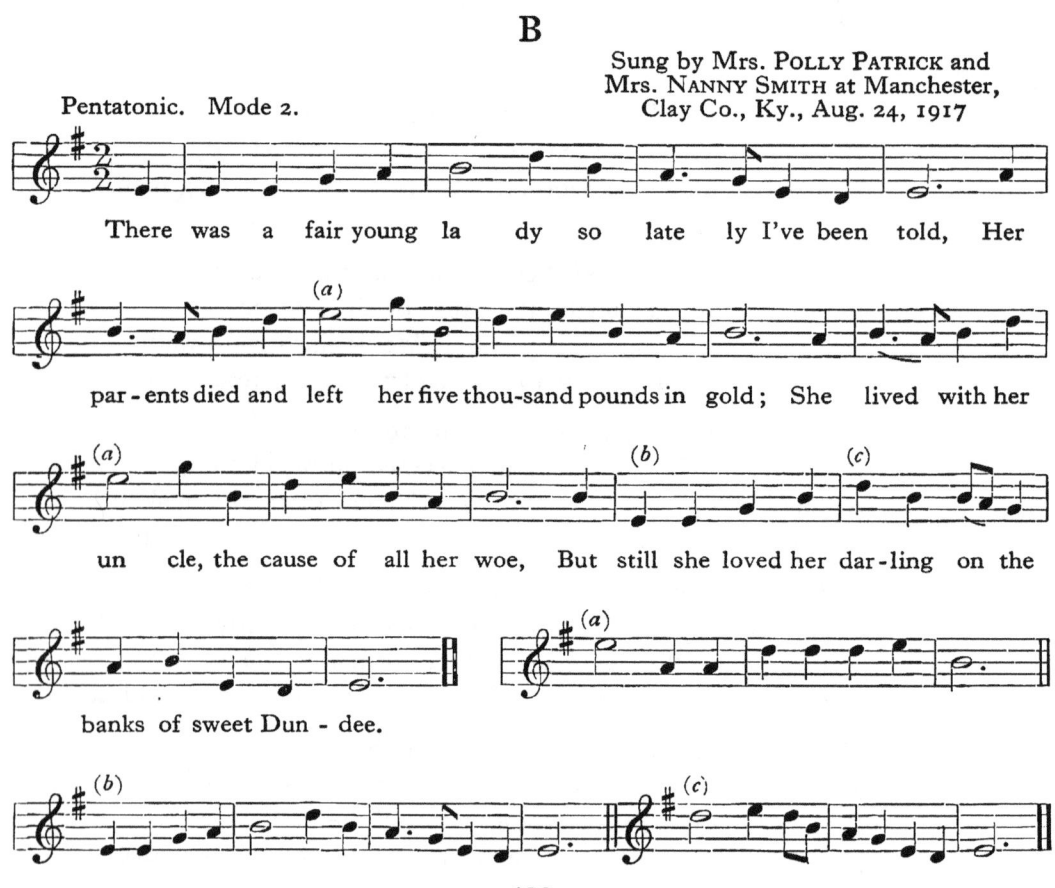

B

Sung by Mrs. POLLY PATRICK and Mrs. NANNY SMITH at Manchester, Clay Co., Ky., Aug. 24, 1917

Pentatonic. Mode 2.

There was a fair young lady so lately I've been told, Her parents died and left her five thousand pounds in gold; She lived with her uncle, the cause of all her woe, But still she loved her darling on the banks of sweet Dundee.

The Banks of Sweet Dundee

C

Sung by Miss May Ray
at Lincoln Memorial University, Harrogate,
Claiborne Co., Tenn., April 25, 1917

Heptatonic. Mixolydian influence.

There lived a rich old mer-chant, in Lon-don he did dwell; He

had the on-ly daugh-ter, the truth to you I'll tell, She

went to live with her un-cle in spite of all her woe, I'll

tell you now of a dis-tant maid may prove her o-ver-throw.

No. 68

The Councillor's Daughter

Pentatonic. Mode 3.

Sung by Mr. W. M. MAPLES
at Sevierville, Sevier Co., Tenn., April 16, 1917

1. There was a coun - cil - lor a-fright, He had a come-ly daugh-ter; She

was a charm - ing beau-ty bright. But mark what fol - lowed af - ter.

2 Her uncle died and left to her
  A sumptious great possession;
  Her father was to take a care
  Until his own transgression.

3 Both lords and earls had courted her
  Of higher lands descended;
  She was courted by a many a fair,
  But none could gain this lady.

4 At length the squire's youngest son
  In private came a-courting;
  And when he had her favour won
  She feared he was at his ruin.

5 It's O, my dearest dear, said she,
  I must confess I love you,
  But there is none in all this world
  That I do prize above you.

6 But since you've been so good and kind,
  I fear you'll be so careless,
  I fear you'll be condemned to die
  For stealing of an heiress.

7 O up bespoke this young man then
  With a   pollution (?):
  Your father is a councillor;
  I'll tell him my condition.

8 Away went the young man then
  The day following after;
  But he never let the lawyer know
  The lady was his daughter.

The Councillor's Daughter

9   But when the lawyer saw the gold
    And knew he was the gainer,
    A pleasant trick to him he told
    To safely to obtain her.

10 Let her provide a horse, he cried,
    And you get on behind her;
    Unto the squire quickly ride
    Before her friends find her.

11 If she steals you, you may complain,
    This will abate all fury,
    For this is law that I maintain
    Before either judge or jury.

12 Thank you, kind sir, said he,
    By you I've been befriended.
    To your house I'll bring this girl
    Whenever the work is ended.

13 Away went the young man then,
    This news with him he carried.
    This lady her father's counsel took
    And firmly she got married.

14 And when they'd spent the night in mirth
    And joy beyond expression,
    They both returned upon their knees
    Asking their father's blessing.

15 But when the lawyer saw them both
    He flew like one distracted;
    He vowed in wrath he'd have revenge
    For the way they both had acted.

16 Up bespoke the young man then:
    There can be no indicting,
    For this is law which we have done;
    Here is your own handwriting.

17 Both lords and earls had courted her
    Of higher lands descended;
    Since you had my darling in your eye,
    I should not be offended.

18 Ten thousand pounds her fortune was,
    Left to her by my brother,
    And when I die she shall have more,
    For child I have no other.

No. 69

Caroline of Edinboro' Town

Sung by Mrs. Dan Bishop
at Teges, Clay Co., Ky., Aug. 21, 1917

Pentatonic. Mode 3.

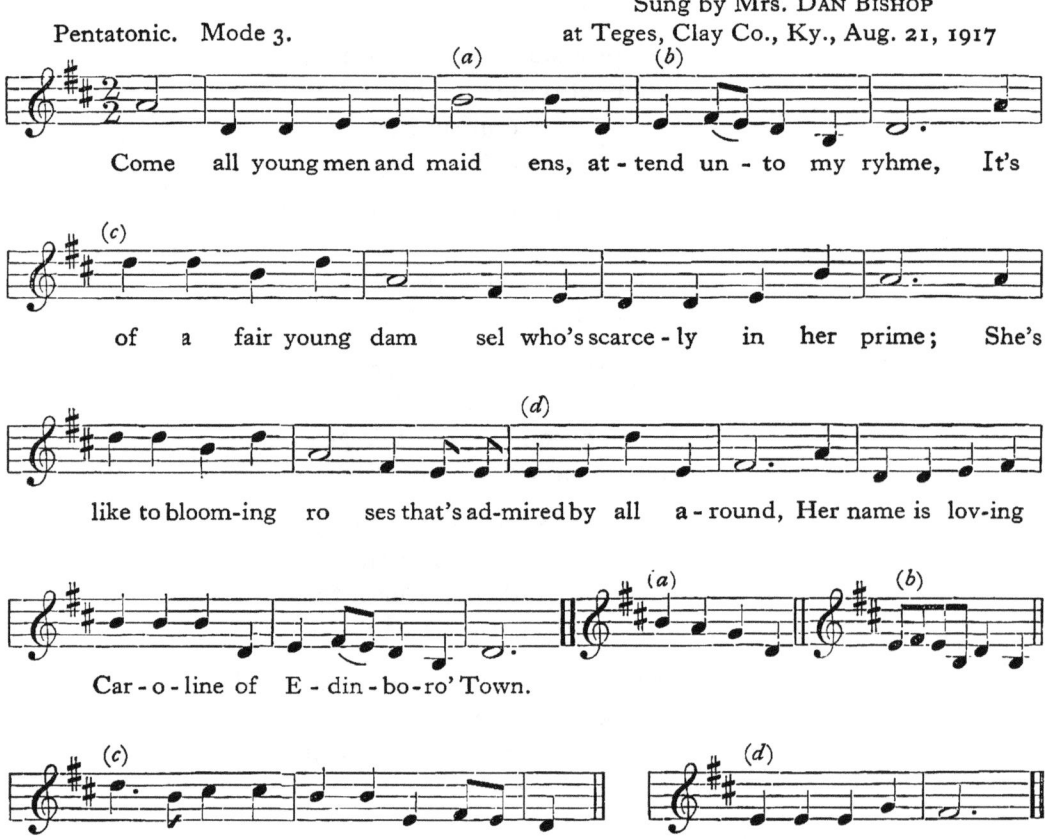

No. 70

The Clothier

Heptatonic. Mixolydian.

Sung by Mr. William Cullen Wooton
at Hindman, Knott Co., Ky., Sept. 21, 1917

1. There was a fair damsel in Carlchester, To me rod-dle ol a dock, to me rod-dle ol a day, And there a clothier courted her, To me rod-dle ol a dock, to me rod-dle ol a day, For three months' space, both night and day, To me rod-dle ol a dock, to me rod-dle ol a day, And yet the damsel still said Nay, To me rod-dle ol a dock, to me rod-dle ol a day.

2 It was at ten o'clock or more,
   She to a tanner went therefore,
   And there she borrowed an old cow-hide
   With crooked horns both large and wide.

3 She to a lonesome field did stray.
   At length the clothier came that way,
   And at her he did surely scare,
   For he thought it was old Lucifer.

The Clothier

4 With a hairy hide, horns on her head,
   And them three feet asunder spread,
   With that he saw a long, black tail.
   He strove to run, but his feet did fail.

5 Then she with a grum and doleful note,
   She quickly seized him by the throat.
   She says: Young man, whether you will or no,
   Into my gloomy region go.

6 Since you have left poor Kate, I hear,
   And wooed with a lawyer's daughter dear;
   And if young Kate she doth complain,
   O soon you'll hear from me again.

7 O master devil, spare me now,
   And I'll perform my former vow;
   I'll make young Kate my lawful bride.
   See that you do, the devil cried.

8 When they had twelve months married been,
   She told it at her lying-in.
   Her husband laughed as well as they.
   Wasn't that a joyful marriage day?

No. 71

The Miller's Apprentice, or The Oxford Tragedy
A

Sung by Mrs. MARY WILSON and Mrs. TOWNSLEY at Pineville, Bell Co., Ky., May 1, 1917

Hexatonic (no 3rd).

2 I fell in love with a Knoxville girl,
 Her name was Flora Dean.
 Her rosy cheeks, her curly hair,
 I really did admire.

3 Her father he persuaded me
 To take Flora for a wife;
 The devil he persuaded me
 To take Flora's life.

4 Up stepped her mother so bold and gay,
 So boldly she did stand:
 Johnny dear, go marry her
 And take her off my hands.

5 I went unto her father's house
 About nine o'clock at night,
 A-asking her to take a walk
 To do some prively talk.

6 We had not got so very far
 Till looking around and around,
 He stooping down picked up a stick
 And knocks little Flora down.

7 She fell upon her bended knees,
 For mercy she did cry:
 O Johnny dear, don't murder me,
 For I'm not fit to die.

The Miller's Apprentice, or The Oxford Tragedy

8 I took her by her lily-white hands
   A-slung her around and around;
   I drug her off to the river-side,
   And plunged her in to drown.

9 I returned back to my miller's house
   About nine o'clock at night,
   But little did my miller know
   What I had been about.

10 The miller turned around and about,
   Said: Johnny, what blooded your clothes?
   Me being so apt to take a hint:
   By bleeding at the nose.

11 About nine or ten days after that,
   Little Flora she was found,
   A-floating down by her father's house
   Who lived in Knoxville town.

B

Sung by Mrs. POFF
at Barbourville, Knox Co., Ky., May 8, 1917

Heptatonic.*

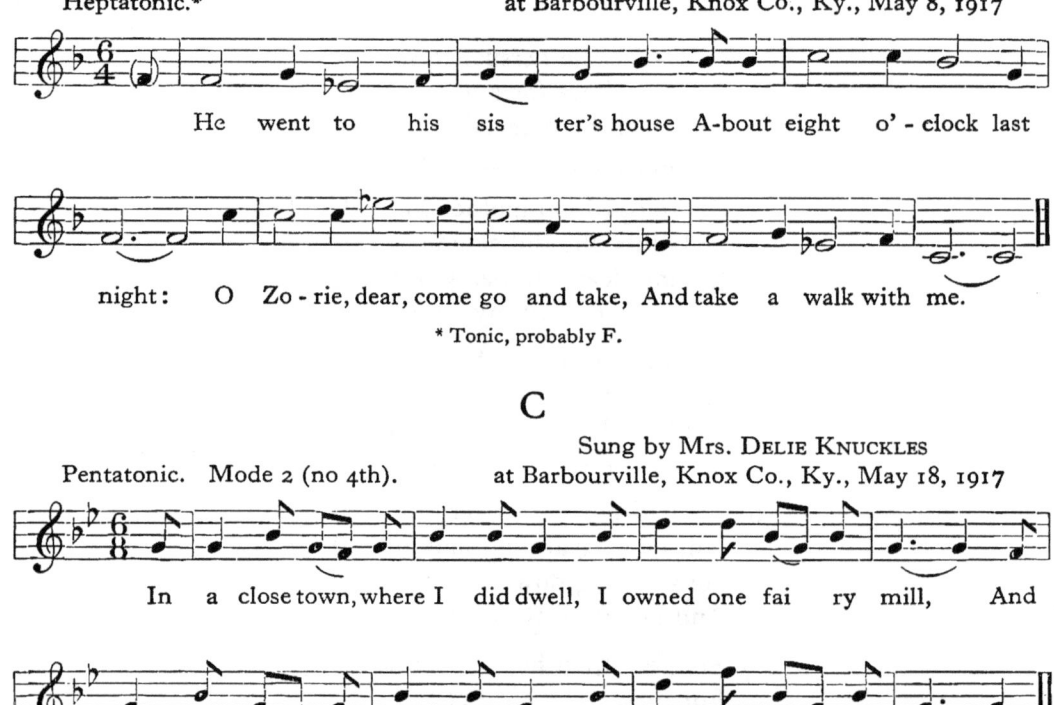

He went to his sister's house A-bout eight o'-clock last night: O Zo-rie, dear, come go and take, And take a walk with me.

* Tonic, probably F.

C

Sung by Mrs. DELIE KNUCKLES
at Barbourville, Knox Co., Ky., May 18, 1917

Pentatonic. Mode 2 (no 4th).

In a close town, where I did dwell, I owned one fai-ry mill, And there I spied a milk fond girl With dark and roll-ing eyes.

The Miller's Apprentice, or The Oxford Tragedy

D

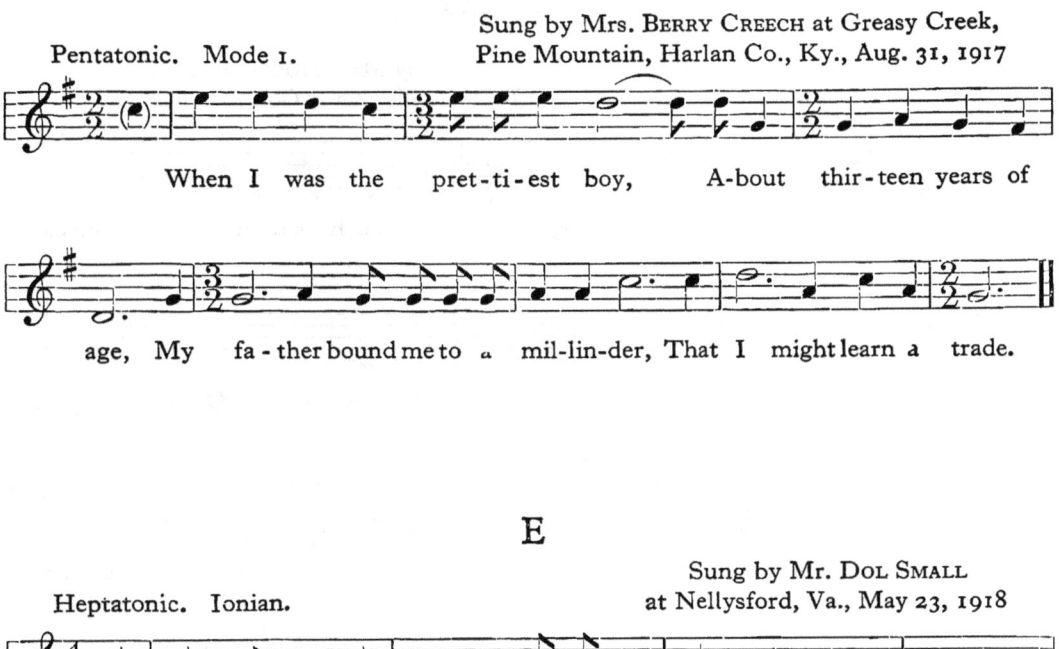

E

No. 72

Still Growing

Sung by Mrs. Mollie Broghton
at Barbourville, Knox Co., Ky., May 8, 1918

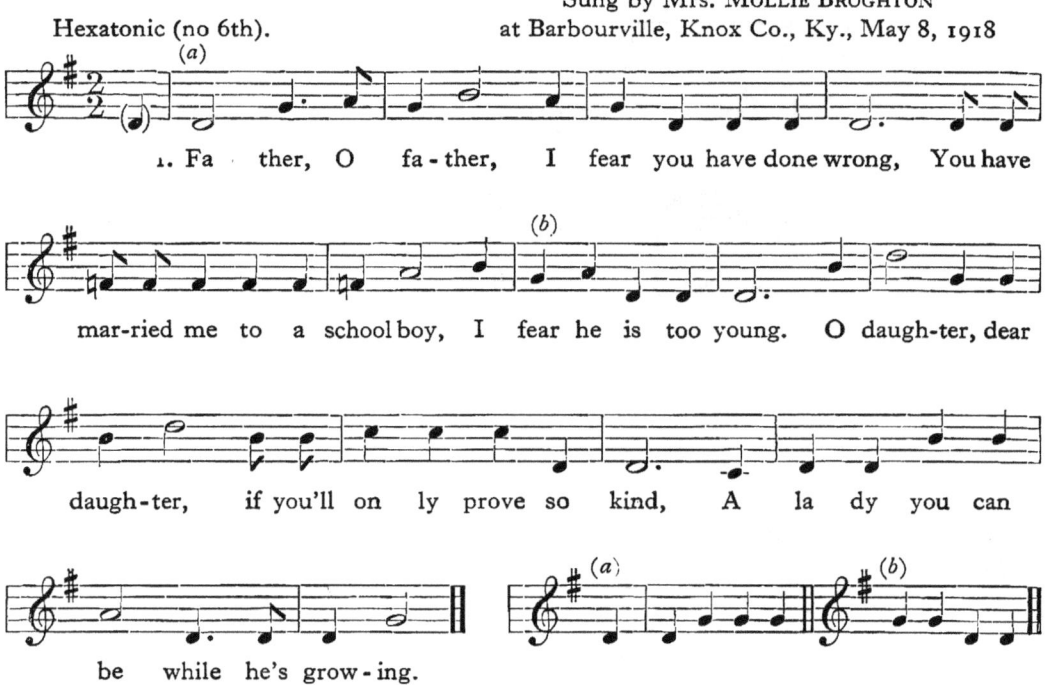

1. Father, O father, I fear you have done wrong, You have married me to a schoolboy, I fear he is too young. O daughter, dear daughter, if you'll only prove so kind, A lady you can be while he's growing.

2. I'll send him to the college for a year or two,
I'll send him to the college and see what he will do.
The only one, the one succeeds them all
Was my bonny boy, young and a-growing.

3. When I were riding through the Mascot Hall,
Four and twenty schoolboys a-playing bat and ball.
The only one, the one succeeds them all
Was my bonny boy, young and a-growing.

4. At the age of sixteen he was a married man,
At the age of seventeen she proved to him a son,
At the age of eighteen his grave was growing green;
My bonny boy is young and he's quit growing.

NOTES

BALLADS

No. 1. The Elfin Knight.

Texts without tunes:—Child's *English and Scottish Popular Ballads*, No. 2. S. Baring-Gould's *Book of Nursery Songs and Rhymes*, p. 3. R. P. Gray's *Songs and Ballads of the Maine Lumberjacks*, p. 78. *Journal of American Folk-Lore*, xiii. 120; xix. 130; xxiii. 430; xxvi. 174.

Texts with tunes:—*Northumbrian Minstrelsy*, p. 79. Kidson's *Traditional Tunes*, pp. 43 and 172. Gavin Greig's *Last Leaves*, No. 1. *Folk-Songs of England*, Book III, p. 21. C. Sharp's *Folk Songs from Somerset*, No. 64. C. Sharp's *English Folk Songs* (Selected Edition), vol. ii, p. 52. *Songs of the West*, 2nd ed., No. 96. Lucy Broadwood and Fuller Maitland's *English County Songs*, p. 12. *Journal of the Folk-Song Society*, i. 83; ii. 212; iii. 274. *Journal of American Folk-Lore*, vii. 228; xviii. 49 and 212; xxx. 283. *British Ballads from Maine*, p. 3.

No. 2. The False Knight Upon the Road.

Texts without tunes:—Child's *English and Scottish Popular Ballads*, No. 3. Compare, also, 'Harpkin', Chambers's *Popular Rhymes of Scotland*, p. 66. *Journal of American Folk-Lore*, xxiv. 344; xxx. 285. *British Ballads from Maine*, p. 11.

Texts with tunes:—Motherwell's *Minstrelsy*, Appendix, p. xxiv, and tune No. 32. Child's *English and Scottish Popular Ballads*, vol. v, p. 411. Davis's *Traditional Ballads of Virginia*, pp. 61 and 549.

The Introduction to version A, A Knight met a child on the road, sung by the singer by way of preface is very unusual, if not unique.

Version A is published with pianoforte accompaniment in *Folk Songs of English Origin*, 1st Series.

No. 3. Lady Isabel and the Elf Knight.

Texts without tunes:—Child's *English and Scottish Popular Ballads*, No. 4. Gavin Greig's *Folk-Song of the North-East*, ii. art. 106. C. S. Burne's *Shropshire Folk-Lore*, p. 548. A. Williams's *Folk Songs of the Upper Thames*, p. 159. Reed Smith's *South Carolina Ballads*, p. 97. *Journal of American Folk-Lore*, xix. 232; xxii. 65; xxiii. 375; xxiv. 344; xxvii. 90; xxviii. 148; xxxv. 338.

Texts with tunes—*Journal of the Folk-Song Society*, i. 246; ii. 282; iv. 116. *English County Songs*, p. 164. Kidson's *Traditional Tunes*, pp. 27 and 172. *Northumbrian Minstrelsy*, p. 48. *Folk Songs from Somerset*, No. 84 (published also in *English Folk Songs*, Selected Edition, vol. i, p. 29, and *One Hundred English Folk-Songs*, p. 29). A. E. Gillington's *Eight Hampshire Folk Songs*, p. 4. Gavin Greig's *Last Leaves*, p. 2. Wyman and Brockway's *Lonesome Tunes*, p. 82. J. H. Cox's *Folk Songs of the South*, pp. 3 and 521 (see further references). Mackenzie's *Ballads and Sea Songs from Nova Scotia*, No. 1. D. Scarborough's *On the Trail of Negro Folk Songs*, p. 43. *Journal of American Folk-Lore*, xviii. 132; xxii. 76 (tune only) and 374; xxiv. 333. *British Ballads from Maine*, p. 14. Davis's *Traditional Ballads of Virginia*, pp. 62 and 549. Sandburg's *American Songbag*, p. 60.

'My Colleen' in version A may, or may not be, a corruption of the May Colvin, Colven, or Collins, of other versions.

No. 4. Earl Brand.

Texts without tunes:—Child's *English and Scottish Popular Ballads*, No. 7. Gavin Greig's *Folk-Song of the North-East*, i, art. 57.

Notes

Texts with tunes:—*Northumbrian Minstrelsy*, p. 31. Gavin Greig's *Last Leaves*, No. 4. Cox's *Folk Songs of the South*, p. 18. W. R. Mackenzie's *Ballads and Sea Songs from Nova Scotia*, No. 2. *Journal of American Folk-Lore*, xxviii. 152. *British Ballads from Maine*, p. 35. Davis's *Traditional Ballads of Virginia*, pp. 86 and 552.

Miss A. G. Gilchrist points out that to 'cheep' (B, stanza 5) is Scottish 'to speak feebly or quietly, to make a slight sound' (see Chambers's *Scots Dialect Dictionary*, 1911, edited by A. Warrack).

In E, stanza 6, and F, stanzas 2 and 6, it was difficult to determine whether 'better' or 'bitter' was sung, but it sounded more like the former, and according to Miss Gilchrist, 'better' is commonly used in this sense in Lancashire. For instance, an old woman, describing how her daughter had made a strenuous search for a lost pet, said: 'She lait it and better lait it', i.e. 'She searched and searched for it'

Mr Philander Fitzgerald, the singer of version F, is an old Confederate soldier, and is the father of Mr. Clinton Fitzgerald who sang version G.

No. 5. The Two Sisters.

Texts without tunes:—Child's *English and Scottish Popular Ballads*, No. 10. *Journal of American Folk-Lore*, xix. 233.

Texts with tunes:—Christie's *Traditional Ballad Airs*, i, pp. 40 and 42. *Journal of the Folk-Song Society*, i. 253; ii. 282. *English County Songs*, p. 118. *Northumbrian Minstrelsy*, p. 61. Child's *English and Scottish Popular Ballads*, v, pp. 411 and 412 (three tunes). 'Binnorie' arranged by Sir Arthur Somervell. Gavin Greig's *Last Leaves*, No. 6. *Journal of American Folk-Lore*, xviii. 130; xxx. 387. Cox's *Folk Songs of the South*, pp. 20 and 521. *British Ballads from Maine*, p. 40. Davis's *Traditional Ballads of Virginia*, pp. 93 and 552.

Compare the refrain in version A, 'Jury flower gent the rose-berry' with 'Jennifer gentle and rosemaree' in 'Riddles Wisely Expounded' (*Child*, No. 1, B).

Version L was learned by the singer in Ohio.

Version C is published with pianoforte accompaniment in *Folk Songs of English Origin*, 2nd Series.

No. 6. The Cruel Brother.

Texts without tunes:—Child's *English and Scottish Popular Ballads*, No. 11.

Texts with tunes:—Christie's *Traditional Ballad Airs*, i. 109. Gilbert's *Ancient Christmas Carols*, 2nd ed., p. 68. Child's *English and Scottish Popular Ballads*, v. 412. Kidson's *Garland of English Folk Songs*, pp. 24 and 26. *Journal of American Folk-Lore*, xxviii. 300.

The versions given in the texts are close variants of Davies Gilbert's, which was collected in the West of England.

Version A is published with pianoforte accompaniment in *Folk Songs of English Origin*, 1st Series.

No. 7. Lord Randal.

Texts without tunes:—Child's *English and Scottish Popular Ballads*, No. 12. Gavin Greig's *Folk-Song of the North-East*, ii, art. 112. *Journal of American Folk-Lore*, xiii. 115; xxiv. 345.

Texts with tunes:—*Scots Musical Museum*, iii, No. 327. (See Dick's *Notes on Scottish Song*.) L. Broadwood's *Traditional Songs and Carols*, p. 96. *A Garland of Country Song*, No. 38. *Journal of the Folk-Song Society*, ii. 29; iii. 43; v. 117, 122, and 245. *Folk Songs from Somerset*, Nos. 13 and 14. (No. 13 also published in *English Folk Songs*, Selected Edition, vol. 2, p. 2, and *One Hundred English Folk-*

Notes

Songs, p. 44.) *English and Scottish Popular Ballads*, v, pp. 412 and 413. Gavin Greig's *Last Leaves*, No. 7. Dick's *Songs of Robert Burns*, p. 324. *Journal of the Welsh Folk-Song Society*, ii. 48. Cox's *Folk Songs of the South*, p. 23. Reed Smith's *South Carolina Ballads*, p. 101. *Journal of American Folk-Lore*, xvi. 258-64; xviii. 195 and 303; xxii. 75 and 376; xxx. 290; xxxv. 339. *Musical Quarterly*, January 1916, p. 19. *British Ballads from Maine*, p. 47. Davis's *Traditional Ballads of Virginia*, pp. 105 and 556. McGill's *Folk Songs of the Kentucky Mountains*, p. 19.

No. 8. Edward.

Texts without tunes:—Child's *English and Scottish Popular Ballads*, No. 13. *Journal of American Folk-Lore*, xxxix. 93.

Texts with tunes:—Davis's *Traditional Ballads of Virginia*, pp. 105 and 558.

The single stanzas of B and F may, or may not, belong to this ballad.

In version A, the 'you, you, you', which is evidently intended to be 'thee, thee, thee', is a good instance of the folk-singers' disregard of rhyme.

Version A is published with pianoforte accompaniment in *Folk Songs of English Origin*, 1st Series.

No. 9. Sir Lionel.

Texts without tunes:—Child's *English and Scottish Popular Ballads*, No. 18. A. Williams's *Folk Songs of the Upper Thames*, p. 295. *Journal of American Folk-Lore*, xix. 235; xxv. 175; xxx. 291.

Texts with tunes:—Christie's *Traditional Ballad Airs*, i. 110. D. Scarborough's *On the Trail of Negro Folk Songs*, p. 51. Davis's *Traditional Ballads of Virginia*, pp. 125 and 558. McGill's *Folk Songs of the Kentucky Mountains*, p. 83.

No. 10. The Cruel Mother.

Texts without tunes:—Child's *English and Scottish Popular Ballads*, No. 20. C. Burne's *Shropshire Folk-Lore*, p. 540. A. Williams's *Folk Songs of the Upper Thames*, p. 295. *Journal of American Folk-Lore*, xxv. 183; xxxii. 503.

Texts with tunes:—Kinloch's *Ancient Scottish Ballads*, p. 44 and Appendix. Child, v. 413. Christie's *Traditional Ballad Airs*, i. 105 and 107. *Journal of the Folk-Song Society*, ii. 109; iii. 70. *Folk Songs from Somerset*, No. 98 (also published in *English Folk Songs*, Selected Edition, Series 1, p. 35, and *One Hundred English Folk Songs*, p. 35). Gavin Greig's *Last Leaves*, No. 11. Dick's *Songs of Robert Burns*, p. 347. Cox's *Folk Songs of the South*, pp. 29 and 522. W. R. Mackenzie's *Ballads and Sea Songs from Nova Scotia*, No. 3. *British Ballads from Maine*, p. 80. Davis's *Traditional Ballads of Virginia*, pp. 133 and 560. McGill's *Folk Songs of the Kentucky Mountains*, p. 83.

The tune of version B is that of *The Wife of Usher Well*, No. 22.

In version I there appears to be a change of mode from Dorian to Mixolydian. The singer is a brother of Mr. W. B. Chisholm of Woodridge, who sang version D.

Version A is published in *Ballads* (School Songs, Book 261), Novello & Co., London, and version E in *Folk Songs of English Origin*, 2nd Series—both with pianoforte accompaniment.

No. 11. The Three Ravens.

Texts without tunes:—Child's *English and Scottish Popular Ballads*, No. 26. *Journal of American Folk-Lore*, xx. 154. See also D. Scarborough's *On the Trail of Negro Folk Songs*, p. 149.

Texts with tunes:—*Melismata*, No. 20. Motherwell's *Minstrelsy*, Appendix xviii, tune No. 12. Kidson's *Traditional Tunes*, p. 17. Cox's *Folk Songs of the South*,

Notes

pp. 31 and 522 (see also further references). Davis's *Traditional Ballads of Virginia*, pp. 137 and 562.

Version B is published with pianoforte accompaniment in *Folk Songs of English Origin*, 2nd Series.

No. 12. The Two Brothers.

Texts without tunes:—Child's *English and Scottish Popular Ballads*, No. 49. *Journal of American Folk-Lore*, xxiii. 293; xxvi. 361; xxix. 158; xxx. 293. R. P. Gray's *Songs and Ballads of the Maine Lumberjacks*, p. 75. Cox's *Folk Songs of the South*, p. 33 (see also further references).

Texts with tunes:—*British Ballads from Maine*, p. 99. Davis's *Traditional Ballads of Virginia*, pp. 146 and 563. McGill's *Folk Songs of the Kentucky Mountains*, p. 55.

It is worthy of note that versions A, B, and J contain allusions in their earlier stanzas to the sweetheart, the cause of the quarrel; whereas not one of the other published texts makes mention of the sweetheart until the conclusion of the ballad. Mrs. Smith sang her version (B) to the accompaniment of the guitar which possibly may account for the harmonic character of the tune.

It may be that the 'hopping' in stanzas 15 and 16 of version F is a corruption of 'harping' (see version K) and that the 'small hoppers' have been introduced to conform with the altered meaning. However this may be, the variation is certainly very pleasing to the imagination.

Version F is published with pianoforte accompaniment in *Folk Songs of English Origin*, 1st Series.

No. 13. Young Beichan.

Texts without tunes:—Child's *English and Scottish Popular Ballads*, No. 53. A. Williams's *Folk Songs of the Upper Thames*, p. 147. Gavin Greig's *Folk-Song of the North-East*, i, art. 78; ii, art. 112. Logan's *Pedlar's Pack of Ballads*, p. 11. Broadsides by Pitts, Catnach, and Jackson. Burne's *Shropshire Folk-Lore*, p. 547. Garret's *Merrie Book of Garlands*, vol. iii. *Journal of American Folk-Lore*, xviii. 209; xx. 251; xxii. 64; xxviii. 149; xxx. 294; xli. 585. Cox's *Folk Songs of the South*, p. 36.

Texts with tunes:—Kinloch's *Ancient Scottish Ballads*, p. 260 (tune in Appendix). *Child*, v. 415. Christie's *Traditional Ballad Airs*, i, pp. 8 and 31. *Northumbrian Minstrelsy*, p. 64. Kidson's *Traditional Tunes*, p. 33. *English County Songs*, p. 62. *Journal of the Folk-Song Society*, i. 240; iii. 192–200. *Folk Songs from Somerset*, No. 65 (published also in *English Folk Songs*, Selected Edition, i. 22, and *One Hundred English Folk-Songs*, p. 17). Gavin Greig's *Last Leaves*, No. 22. *Sussex Songs*, p. 43. Kidson's *Garland of English Folk Songs*, p. 8. Reed Smith's *South Carolina Ballads*, p. 104. W. R. Mackenzie's *Ballads and Sea Songs from Nova Scotia*, No. 5. Wyman and Brockway's *Lonesome Tunes*, p. 58. *British Ballads from Maine*, p. 106. Davis's *Traditional Ballads of Virginia*, pp. 158 and 565.

No. 14. Lizzie Wan.

Texts without tunes:—Child's *English and Scottish Popular Ballads*, No. 51.

It is possible that versions B and F of No. 8 (Edward) may belong to this ballad.

No. 15. The Cherry-Tree Carol.

Texts without tunes:—Child's *English and Scottish Popular Ballads*, No. 54. Hone's *Ancient Mysteries Described*, p. 90. Gavin Greig's *Folk-Song of the North-East*, ii, art. 160. *Journal of American Folk-Lore* xxiii. 293.

Notes

Texts with tunes:—Husk's *Songs of the Nativity*, p. 194. *English Folk-Carols*, Nos. 3 and 4. *Journal of the Folk-Song Society*, iii. 260; v. 11 and 321; viii. 229. Davis's *Traditional Ballads of Virginia*, pp. 172 and 565. McGill's *Folk Songs of the Kentucky Mountains*, p. 60.

The references to the birthday do not appear in the English texts. It is of interest that the date is given in texts B and C as 'the fifth day of January', which according to 'Old Style' reckoning was the date of Christmas Day between the years 1752 and 1799. In 1751, when a change in the calendar had become expedient, eleven days were dropped out between September 2nd and 14th, 1752, thus making January 5th the date of Old Christmas Day. In 1800, another day was taken from the calendar, and in 1900 still another, so that Old Christmas Day now falls on January 7th. In Miss McGill's version the date is given as the 6th of January.

No. 16. Fair Annie.

Texts without tunes:—Child's *English and Scottish Popular Ballads*, No. 62. *British Ballads from Maine*, p. 446. Comb's *Folk Songs du Midi des États-Unis*, p. 129.

Texts with tunes:—Gavin Greig's *Last Leaves*, No. 25. Davis's *Traditional Ballads of Virginia*, pp. 177 and 566.

No. 17. Lady Maisry.

Texts without tunes:—Child's *English and Scottish Popular Ballads*, No. 65. Davis's *Traditional Ballads of Virginia*, p. 180.

Texts with tunes:—*Journal of the Folk-Song Society*, iii. 74 and 304. *Folk-Songs of England*, i. 36. *Folk Songs from Somerset*, No. 75 (published also in *English Folk Songs*, Selected Edition, i. 26, and *One Hundred English Folk-Songs*, p. 26).

The complete story is not given in any of the oral English versions.

No. 18. Young Hunting.

Texts without tunes:—Child's *English and Scottish Popular Ballads*, No. 68. Cox's *Folk Songs of the South*, p. 42 (see also further references). *Journal of American Folk-Lore*, xx. 252.

Texts with tunes:—*Child*, v. 416. Reed Smith's *South Carolina Ballads*, p. 107. *Journal of American Folk-Lore*, xviii. 295 (tune only); xxx. 289. *British Ballads from Maine*, p. 122. Davis's *Traditional Ballads of Virginia*, pp. 182 and 566. Sandburg's *American Songbag*, p. 64.

Compare 'And you shall have the cheers of the cheer cold girl' of D. 4 with 'Ye shall hae cheer, an charcoal clear' in Child's version K. 4.

Tune H, with text of version G, is published with pianoforte accompaniment in *Folk Songs of English Origin*, 1st Series.

No. 19. Lord Thomas and Fair Ellinor.

Texts without tunes:—Child's *English and Scottish Popular Ballads*, No. 73. Broadside by Catnach. C. S. Burne's *Shropshire Folk-Lore*, p. 545. A. Williams's *Folk Songs of the Upper Thames*, p. 135. *Journal of American Folk-Lore*, xix. 235; xx. 254; xxviii. 152; xxxix. 94. Cox's *Folk Songs of the South*, p. 45 (see also further references).

Texts with tunes:—Kidson's *Traditional Tunes*, p. 40. *English County Songs*, p. 42. E. M. Leather's *Folk-Lore of Herefordshire*, p. 200. Sandys's *Christmas Carols*, tune 18. *Journal of the Folk-Song Society*, ii. 105; v. 130. Rimbault's *Musical Illustrations of Percy's Reliques*, p. 94. C. Sharp's *English Folk Songs* (Selected Edition), ii. 27 (also published in *One Hundred English Folk Songs*, No. 28). Gavin Greig's *Last Leaves*, No. 28. *Scots Musical Museum*, vi, No. 535.

Notes

Reed Smith's *South Carolina Ballads*, No. 6. Wyman and Brockway's *Twenty Kentucky Songs*, p. 14. *Journal of American Folk-Lore*, xviii. 128. *British Ballads from Maine*, p. 128. Davis's *Traditional Ballads of Virginia*, pp. 191 and 568. McGill's *Folk Songs of the Kentucky Mountains*, p. 28. Sandburg's *American Songbag*, p. 156.

No. 20. Fair Margaret and Sweet William.

Texts without tunes :—Child's *English and Scottish Popular Ballads*, No. 74. Ashton's *Century of Ballads*, p. 345. W. R. Mackenzie's *Ballads and Sea Songs from Nova Scotia*, No. 7. *Journal of American Folk-Lore*, xix. 281 ; xxiii. 381 ; xxviii. 154 ; xxx. 303.

Texts with tunes :—Christie's *Traditional Ballad Airs*, i. 117. *Journal of the Folk-Song Society*, ii. 289 ; iii. 64. *Folk-Songs of England*, i, No. 14. Rimbault's *Musical Illustrations of Percy's Reliques*, pp. 117 and 118. Kidson's *Garland of English Folk Songs*, p. 30. Chappell's *Popular Music of the Olden Times*, i. 382. C. Sharp's *English Folk Songs* (Selected Edition), ii. 13. Cox's *Folk Songs of the South*, pp. 65 and 522 (see also further references). Wyman and Brockway's *Lonesome Tunes*, p. 94. *Journal of American Folk-Lore*, xxxi. 74 ; xxxv. 340. *Musical Quarterly*, January 1916. *British Ballads from Maine*, p. 134. Davis's *Traditional Ballads of Virginia*, pp. 221 and 570. McGill's *Folk Songs of the Kentucky Mountains*, p. 71.

No. 21. Lord Lovel.

Texts without tunes :—Child's *English and Scottish Popular Ballads*, No. 75. Gavin Greig's *Folk-Song of the North-East*, art. ii. 159. A. Williams's *Folk Songs of the Upper Thames*, p. 145. Cox's *Folk Songs of the South*, p. 78 (see further references). *Journal of American Folk-Lore*, xix. 283.

Texts with tunes :—*Journal of the Folk-Song Society*, ii. 209 ; iii. 64 ; vi. 31. Child, v, p. 416. Gavin Greig's *Last Leaves*, No. 29. C. Sharp's *English Folk Songs* (Selected Edition), i. 22 (also published in *One Hundred English Folk-Songs*, No. 26). *Journal of American Folk-Lore*, xviii. 291 ; xxxv. 342. Reed Smith's *South Carolina Ballads*, p. 121. D. Scarborough's *On the Trail of Negro Folk Songs*, p. 55. Broadside, G. H. de Marsan, New York. *Musical Quarterly*, January 1916, p. 5. *British Ballads from Maine*, p. 139. Davis's *Traditional Ballads of Virginia*, pp. 240 and 573. McGill's *Folk Songs of the Kentucky Mountains*, p. 10. Sandburg's *American Songbag*, p. 570.

No. 22. The Wife of Usher's Well.

Texts without tunes :—Child's *English and Scottish Popular Ballads*, No. 79. *Journal of American Folk-Lore*, xiii. 119 ; xxiii. 429 ; xxx. 305 ; xxxix. 96. Cox's *Folk Songs of the South*, p. 88.

Texts with tunes :—E. M. Leather's *Folk-Lore of Herefordshire*, p. 198. Davis's *Traditional Ballads of Virginia*, pp. 278 and 576.

See also The Cruel Mother (No. 10), Tune B. McGill's *Folk Songs of the Kentucky Mountains*, p. 5.

Texts A and B are remarkable in that the children cite the mother's 'proud heart' as the reason that has caused them to 'lie in the cold clay', a motive which is absent from other English and Scottish versions.

No. 23. Little Musgrave and Lady Barnard.

Texts without tunes :—Child s *English and Scottish Popular Ballads*, No. 81. Reed Smith's *South Carolina Ballads*, p. 125. Cox's *Folk Songs of the South*, p. 94. *Journal of American Folk-Lore*, xxiii. 371 ; xxv. 182.

Texts with tunes :—Rimbault's *Musical Illustrations of Percy's Reliques*, p. 92. Chappell's *Popular Music of the Olden Times*, i. 170. Motherwell's *Minstrelsy*,

Notes

Appendix, tune No. 21. W. R. Mackenzie's *Ballads and Sea Songs of Nova Scotia*, No. 8. Wyman and Brockway's *Twenty Kentucky Mountain Songs*, pp. 22 and 62. *Journal of American Folk-Lore*, xxx. 309. *British Ballads from Maine*, p. 150. Davis's *Traditional Ballads of Virginia*, pp. 289 and 577.

No. 24. Barbara Allen.

Texts without tunes:—Child's *English and Scottish Popular Ballads*, No. 84. Gavin Greig's *Folk-Song of the North-East*, ii, arts. 165 and 166. Ashton's *Century of Ballads*, p. 173. Miss Burne's *Shropshire Folk-Lore*, p. 543. Garret's *Merrie Book of Garlands*, vol. ii. A. Williams's *Folk Songs of the Upper Thames*, pp. 204 and 206. D. Scarborough's *On the Trail of Negro Folk Songs*, p. 59. *Journal of American Folk-Lore*, xix. 285; xx. 250; xxii. 63; xxviii. 144; xxix. 161.

Texts with tunes:—Christie's *Traditional Ballad Airs*, i. 87 and 89. *Journal of the Folk-Song Society*, i. 111 and 265; ii. 15 and 80. Kidson's *Traditional Tunes*, p. 37. *Journal of the Irish Folk-Song Society*, i. 45. Chappel's *Popular Music of the Olden Times*, ii. 538. Kidston's *Garland of English Folk Songs*, p. 74. Joyce's *Ancient Irish Music*, p. 79. Rimbault's *Musical Illustrations of Bishop Percy's Reliques*, No. 53. Gavin Greig's *Last Leaves*, No. 32. *Folk Songs from Somerset*, No. 22 (also published in *English Folk Songs*, Selected Edition, i. 20, and *One Hundred English Folk-Songs*, p. 20). Thomson's *Scottish Songs*, iii. 29. Cox's *Folk Songs of the South*, pp. 96 and 523. Reed Smith's *South Carolina Ballads*, p. 129. W. R. Mackenzie's *Ballads and Sea Songs of Nova Scotia*, No. 9. Wyman and Brockway's *Lonesome Tunes*, p. 1. *Journal of American Folk-Lore*, vi. 132; xxii. 74 (tune only); xxxv. 343; xxxix. 97 and 211. *Musical Quarterly*, January 1916, p. 20 (tune only). *British Ballads from Maine*, p. 195. Davis's *Traditional Ballads of Virginia*, pp. 302 and 577. McGill's *Folk Songs of the Kentucky Mountains*, p. 40. Sandburg's *American Songbag*, p. 57.

Aunt Maria Jones, the singer of version P, was an old coloured woman of 85 who had been a slave. She sang very beautifully, in a wonderfully musical way and with clear and perfect intonation.

No. 25. Giles Collins.

Texts without tunes:—Child's *English and Scottish Popular Ballads*, No. 85. Cox's *Folk Songs of the South*, p. 110 (see also further references). Reed Smith's *South Carolina Ballads*, p. 129. *Journal of American Folk-Lore*, xxviii. 151; xxxix. 102.

Texts with tunes:—Miss Mason's *Nursery Rhymes and Country Songs*, p. 46. *Journal of the Folk-Song Society*, iii. 299. *Journal of American Folk-Lore*, xxxii. 500. Davis's *Traditional Ballads of Virginia*, pp. 346 and 581.

In a note (*Journal of the Folk-Song Society*, iv. 106), Miss Barbara M. Cra'ster argues that this ballad and Clerk Colvill are complementary or, rather, that they are both descended from a more complete form such as that given in *Journal of the Folk-Song Society*, iii. 299. In the usual form in which Giles Collins is sung (e.g. the versions given in the text), no reason is given for Giles's death, and this, of course, robs the song of its point. This omission is supplied in the version above cited, but so far has not been found in any other variant.

No. 26. The Lowlands of Holland.

Texts without tunes:—Child's *English and Scottish Popular Ballads*, No. 92. Logan's *Pedlar's Pack of Ballads*, p. 23. H. R. Hayward's *Ulster Songs*, p. 54. R. P. Grey's *Songs and Ballads of the Maine Lumberjacks*, p. 88. Combs's *Folk-Songs du midi des États-Unis*, p. 173.

Texts with tunes:—*Scots Musical Museum*, ii, No. 115. Christie's *Traditional*

Notes

Ballad Airs, i. 236. *Folk Songs from Somerset*, No. 44 (also published in *English Folk Songs*, Selected Edition, ii. 16, and *One Hundred English Folk-Songs*, p. 54). *Journal of the Folk-Song Society*, i. 97; iii. 307; v. 170; vii. 63. Ford's *Vagabond Songs*, p. 55. *Songs of the West* (2nd Edition), No. 103. H. Hughes's *Irish Country Songs*, ii. 70. *Journal of the Irish Folk-Song Society*, ii. 31. Joyce's *Old Irish Folk Music and Songs*, p. 214.

No. 27. Lamkin.

Texts without tunes:—Child's *English and Scottish Popular Ballads*, No. 93. *Journal of American Folk-Lore*, xiii. 117; xxix. 162.

Texts with tunes:—Christie's *Traditional Ballad Airs*, i. 61. E. M. Leather's *Folk-Lore of Herefordshire*, p. 199. *Journal of the Folk-Song Society*, i. 212; ii. 111; v. 81. Gavin Greig's *Last Leaves*, No. 34. *Folk-Songs of England*, iv, p. 38 (also published in *English Folk Songs*, Selected Edition, ii. 24, and *One Hundred English Folk-Songs*, p. 62). *Journal of American Folk-Lore*, xxxv. 344. *British Ballads from Maine*, p. 200. Davis's *Traditional Ballads of Virginia*, pp. 354 and 583.

No. 28. The Maid Freed from the Gallows.

Texts without tunes:—Child's *English and Scottish Popular Ballads*, No. 95. A. Williams's *Folk Songs of the Upper Thames*, pp. 281 and 283. Cox's *Folk Songs of the South*, p. 115. *Journal of American Folk-Lore*, xxi. 56; xxvi. 175; xxxix. 105. *Musical Quarterly*, 1916, pp. 10 and 11. *British Ballads from Maine*, p. 206.

Texts with tunes:—*English County Songs*, p. 112. *Folk-Songs from Somerset*, No. 121 (also published in *English Folk Songs*, Selected Edition, ii. 4, and *One Hundred English Folk-Songs*, p. 42). *Journal of the Folk-Song Society*, v. 228. Wyman and Brockway's *Lonesome Tunes*, p. 44. Reed Smith's *South Carolina Ballads*, p. 144. D. Scarborough's *On the Trail of Negro Folk Songs*, pp. 35–42. *Journal of American Folk-Lore*, xxx. 319. *British Ballads from Maine*, p. 483 (tune only). Davis's *Traditional Ballads of Virginia*, pp. 360 and 584. Sandburg's *American Songbag*, pp. 72 and 385.

No. 29. Johnie Scot.

Texts without tunes:—Child's *English and Scottish Popular Ballads*, No. 99.

Texts with tunes:—Motherwell's *Minstrelsy*, Appendix, tune No. 15. *Child*, v, p. 418. Gavin Greig's *Last Leaves*, No. 36. *British Ballads from Maine*, p. 213.

'Taverin'' in the text is 'Italian', 'Tailliant', 'Itilian', or simply 'champion' in other versions. Child throws light upon the incident by quoting a story (Rev. Andrew Hall's *Interesting Roman Antiquities recently Discovered in Fife*, 1823, p. 216) in which James Macgill of Lindores is offered a pardon by Charles II upon condition of his fighting an Italian gladiator or bully. In the contest which ensues, 'the Italian actually leaped over his opponent as if he would swallow him alive, but in attempting to do this a second time Sir James run his sword up through him and then called out, "I have spitted him; let them roast him who will."' A similar story is related of the Breton seigneur Les Aubrays of St. Brieux, who is ordered by the French King to undertake a combat with his wild Moor (Luzel's *Poésies populaires de la France*, MS., vol. i).

No. 30. The Bailiff's Daughter of Islington.

Texts without tunes:—Child's *English and Scottish Popular Ballads*, No. 105. A. Williams's *Folk Songs of the Upper Thames*, p. 174. *Journal of American Folk-Lore*, xxx. 321; xxxix. 106. *British Ballads from Maine*, p. 225.

Texts with tunes:—*Journal of the Folk-Song Society*, i. 125 and 209; vii. 34. Chappell's *Popular Music of the Olden Times*, i. 203. Gavin Greig's *Last Leaves*, No. 41. Rimbault's *Musical Illustrations of Bishop Percy's Reliques*, p. 100.

Notes

Sussex Songs, p. 10. *Folk-Songs of England*, v. 41. C. Sharp's *English Folk Songs* (Selected Edition), ii. 35. Davis's *Traditional Ballads of Virginia*, pp. 383 and 585.

No. 31. Sir Hugh.

Texts without tunes:—Child's *English and Scottish Popular Ballads*, No. 155. C. S. Burne's *Shropshire Folk-Lore*, p. 539. Baring-Gould's *Nursery Songs and Rhymes*, pp. 92 and 94. Cox's *Folk Songs of the South*, p. 120 (see also further references). *Journal of American Folk-Lore*, xix. 293; xxix. 164; xxxix. 108.

Texts with tunes:—M. H. Mason's *Nursery Rhymes*, p. 46. *English County Songs*, p. 86. *Journal of the Folk-Song Society*, i. 264. Rimbault's *Musical Illustrations of Percy's Reliques*, p. 46. Motherwell's *Minstrelsy*, Appendix, xvii, tune No. 7. *Scots Musical Museum*, vi, No. 582. *Folk Songs from Somerset*, No. 68 (published also in *English Folk-Songs*, Selected Edition, i. 22, and *One Hundred English Folk-Songs*, p. 22). Newell's *Games and Songs of American Children*, p. 76. Reed Smith's *South Carolina Ballads*, p. 148. D. Scarborough's *On the Trail of Negro Folk Songs*, pp. 53-5. *Musical Quarterly*, January 1916, p. 15. *Journal of American Folk-Lore*, xxxv. 344; xxxix, 213. Davis's *Traditional Ballads of Virginia*, pp. 400 and 587.

No. 32. The Death of Queen Jane.

Texts without tunes:—Child's *English and Scottish Popular Ballads*, No. 170.

Texts with tunes:—*Journal of the Folk-Song Society*, ii. 221; iii. 67; v. 256. C. Sharp's *English Folk Songs* (Selected Edition), ii. 30 (published also in *One Hundred English Folk-Songs*, No. 68). Gavin Greig's *Last Leaves*, No. 51.

Compare The Brown Girl (No. 44), version J.

No. 33. The Gypsy Laddie.

Texts without tunes:—Child's *English and Scottish Popular Ballads*, No. 200. C. S. Burne's *Shropshire Folk-Lore*, p. 550. Gavin Greig's *Folk-Song of the North-East*, ii, art. 110. Irish and English broadsides. Garret's *Merrie Book of Garlands*, vol. i. A. Williams's *Folk Songs of the Upper Thames*, p. 120. *Journal of American Folk-Lore*, xix. 294; xxiv. 346; xxv. 171-5. Broadside by H. de Marsan, New York (a comic parody).

Texts with tunes:—*Songs of the West*, 2nd ed., No. 50. *Folk Songs from Somerset*, No. 9 (also published *English Folk Songs*, Selected Edition, i. 13, and *One Hundred English Folk-Songs*, p. 13). Gavin Greig's *Last Leaves*, No. 60. *Scots Musical Museum*, ii, No. 181. Cox's *Folk Songs of the South*, pp. 130 and 524. *Journal of American Folk-Lore*, xviii. 191; xxii. 80 (tune only); xxx. 323. *British Ballads from Maine*, p. 269. Davis's *Traditional Ballads of Virginia*, pp. 423 and 590. McGill's *Folk Songs of the Kentucky Mountains*, p. 15. Sandburg's *American Songbag*, p. 311.

Version A is published with pianoforte accompaniment in *Folk Songs of English Origin*, 2nd Series.

The first two lines of the second stanza of text A provide a good instance of the stereotyped idiom of the ballad. Owing to the almost invariable description of a 'steed' as 'milk-white' the term has come to lose its literal significance, and in the mind of the singer a 'milk-white steed' means merely a horse. Similarly the folk will sing without any sense of contradiction of a 'false true lover'.

No. 34. Geordie.

Texts without tunes:—Child's *English and Scottish Popular Ballads*, No. 209. Gavin Greig's *Folk-Song of the North-East*, i, art. 75. Broadside by Such. Cox's *Folk Songs of the South*, p. 135. *Journal of American Folk-Lore*, xxxii. 504. Davis's *Traditional Ballads of Virginia*, p. 435.

Notes

Texts with tunes:—Christie's *Traditional Ballad Airs*, i. 53. *Journal of the Folk-Song Society*, ii. 27, 208; iii. 191; iv. 332. Kidson's *Traditional Tunes*, p. 25. L. Broadwood's *Traditional Songs and Carols*, p. 32. Kinloch's *Ancient Scottish Ballads*, p. 187 and tune. *Folk-Songs of England*, ii, p. 47. *Folk Songs from Somerset*, No. 2 (also published in *English Folk Songs*, Selected Edition, i. 24, and *One Hundred English Folk-Songs*, p. 24). Gavin Greig's *Last Leaves*, No 62. *Scots Musical Museum*, iii, No. 346.

No 35. The Daemon Lover.

Texts without tunes:—Child's *English and Scottish Popular Ballads*, No. 243. Reed Smith's *South Carolina Ballads*, p. 151. *Journal of American Folk-Lore*, xviii. 207; xix. 295; xx. 257; xxvi. 360. Broadside by H. de Marsan, New York. *Musical Quarterly*, January 1916, p. 1.

Texts with tunes:—*Journal of the Folk-Song Society*, iii. 84. Motherwell's *Minstrelsy*, Appendix xv, tune 1. *Songs of the West*, 2nd ed., No. 76. Gavin Greig's *Last Leaves*, No. 84. Cox's *Folk Songs of the South*, pp. 139 and 524. Wyman and Brockway's *Twenty Kentucky Mountain Songs*, p. 54. *Journal of American Folk-Lore*, xxv. 274; xxx. 325; xxxv. 347. *British Ballads from Maine*, p. 304. Davis's *Traditional Ballads of Virginia*, pp. 439 and 592. Sandburg's *American Songbag*, p. 66.

No. 36. The Grey Cock.

Texts without tunes:—Child's *English and Scottish Popular Ballads*, No. 248. *British Ballads from Maine*, p. 310.

Texts with tunes:—*Songster's Companion*, ii. 36, 2nd ed. *Scots Musical Museum*, 1787, No. 76 (see Dick's *Notes on Scottish Songs*). Dick's *The Songs of Robert Burns*, pp. 100 and 386. Herbert Hughes's *Irish Country Songs*, vol. ii, p. 64. Chappell's *Popular Music of the Olden Times*, ii. 731. Thomson's *Scottish Songs*, iii. 2.

No. 37. The Suffolk Miracle.

Texts without tunes:—Child's *English and Scottish Popular Ballads*, No. 272. Cox's *Folk Songs of the South*, p. 152. *British Ballads from Maine*, p. 314.

Each of the three tunes, A, B, and C, is a variant of the carol air, 'Christmas now is drawing near at hand' (see *Journal of the Folk-Song Society*, v, pp. 7-11).

No. 38. Our Goodman.

Texts without tunes:—Child's *English and Scottish Popular Ballads*, No. 274. A. Williams's *Folk Songs of the Upper Thames*, p. 188. Ford's *Vagabond Songs of Scotland*, ii. 31. Cox's *Folk Songs of the South*, p. 154. W. R. Mackenzie's *Ballads and Sea Songs of Nova Scotia*, No. 14. *Journal of American Folk-Lore*, xviii. 294.

Texts with tunes:—*Songs of the West*, 2nd ed., No. 33. Chambers's *Songs of Scotland Prior to Burns*, p. 184. Gavin Greig's *Last Leaves*, No. 91. Reed Smith's *South Carolina Ballads*, p. 159. *Musical Quarterly*, January 1916, p. 17 (tune only). *British Ballads from Maine*, p. 315. Davis's *Traditional Ballads of Virginia*, pp. 485 and 595.

No. 39. The Wife Wrapt in Wether's Skin.

Texts without tunes:—Child's *English and Scottish Popular Ballads*, No. 277. Gavin Greig's *Folk-Song of the North-East*, i, art. 13; and ii, art. 122. Ford's *Song Histories*, pp. 271-4. Cox's *Folk Songs of the South*, p. 159. *Journal of American Folk-Lore*, vii. 253; xix. 298; xxx. 328; xxxix. 109.

Texts with tunes:—*Journal of the Folk-Song Society*, ii. 223; v. 260. *Folk Songs*

Notes

from Somerset, No. 97. Ford's *Vagabond Songs of Scotland*, p. 192. Gavin Greig's *Last Leaves*, No. 93. *British Ballads from Maine*, p. 322.

Version C is published with pianoforte accompaniment in *Folk Songs of English Origin*, 1st Series.

No. 40. The Farmer's Curst Wife.

Texts without tunes:—Child's *English and Scottish Popular Ballads*, No. 278. A. Williams's *Folk Songs of the Upper Thames*, p. 211. H. R. Hayward's *Ulster Songs and Ballads*, p. 32. *Journal of American Folk-Lore*, xix. 298; xxx. 329. Lomax's *Cowboy Songs*, p. 110. Cox's *Folk Songs of the South*, p. 164. W. R. Mackenzie's *Ballads and Sea Songs of Nova Scotia*, No. 15.

Texts with tunes:—*Journal of American Folk-Lore*, xxvii. 68. *Journal of the Folk-Song Society*, ii. 184; iii. 131. Dick's *Songs of Robert Burns*, No. 331. Gavin Greig's *Last Leaves*, No. 94 (tune only). *British Ballads from Maine*, p. 325. Davis's *Traditional Ballads of Virginia*, pp. 505 and 598.

'Bell, blubs', stanza 10, version A, may be a corruption of 'Beelzebubs'. Most of the published versions of this song have whistling refrains. Cf. Burns's 'Kellyburn Braes', Centenary Edition, iii. 129.

Version C is published with pianoforte accompaniment in *Folk Songs of English Origin*, 2nd Series.

No. 41. The Golden Vanity.

Texts without tunes:—Child's *English and Scottish Popular Ballads*, No. 286. A. Williams's *Folk Songs of the Upper Thames*, p. 199. Gavin Greig's *Folk-Song of the North-East*, ii, arts. 116 and 119. Cox's *Folk Songs of the South*, p. 169 (see also further references). *Journal of American Folk-Lore*, xxiii. 429; xxx. 330.

Texts with tunes:—Gavin Greig's *Last Leaves*, No. 101. Kidson's *Garland of English Folk Songs*, p. 72. Tozer's *Fifty Sailors' Songs*, p. 30. *English Folk Songs* (Selected Edition), i. 36 (also published in *One Hundred English Folk-Songs*, p. 36). Christie's *Traditional Ballad Airs*, i. 238. *English County Songs*, p. 182. *Songs of the West*, 2nd ed., No. 64. *Journal of the Folk-Song Society*, i. 104; ii. 244. Ford's *Vagabond Songs of Scotland*, p. 103. *Journal of American Folk-Lore*, xviii. 125. Wyman and Brockway's *Lonesome Tunes*, p. 72. *British Ballads from Maine*, p. 339. Davis's *Traditional Ballads of Virginia*, pp. 516 and 602. McGill's *Folk Songs of the Kentucky Mountains*, p. 97.

No. 42. The Mermaid.

Texts without tunes:—Child's *English and Scottish Popular Ballads*, No. 289. A. Williams's *Folk Songs of the Upper Thames*, p. 84. W. R. Mackenzie's *Ballads and Sea Songs of Nova Scotia*, No. 16. Cox's *Folk Songs of the South*, p. 172 (see also further references). *Journal of American Folk-Lore*, xxvi. 175.

Texts with tunes:—*Journal of the Folk-Song Society*, iii. 47. Chappell's *Popular Music of the Olden Times*, ii. 742. Tozer's *Fifty Sailors' Songs*, p. 92. *British Ballads from Maine*, p. 363. Davis's *Traditional Ballads of Virginia*, pp. 521 and 602. *Journal of American Folk-Lore*, xviii. 136. McGill's *Folk Songs of the Kentucky Mountains*, p. 46.

No. 43. John of Hazelgreen.

Texts without tunes:—Child's *English and Scottish Popular Ballads*, No. 293. Ford's *Song Histories*, p. 282. Gavin Greig's *Last Leaves*, No. 106.

Texts with tunes:—Kinloch's *Ancient Scottish Ballads*, pp. 199 and 206. Christie's *Traditional Ballad Airs*, p. 124. *British Ballads from Maine*, p. 369. Davis's *Traditional Ballads of Virginia*, pp. 529 and 604.

Notes

No. 44. The Brown Girl.

Texts without tunes:—Child's *English and Scottish Popular Ballads*, No. 295. Gavin Greig's *Folk-Song of the North-East*, i, art. 79. Broadside by Such, 'Sally and her True Love Billy' Cox's *Folk Songs of the South*, p. 366 (see also further references). *Journal of American Folk-Lore*, xxvii. 73; xxxii. 502; xxxix. 110.

Texts with tunes:—Christie's *Traditional Ballad Airs*, ii. 241. Kidson's *Garland of English Folk Songs*, p. 20. *Journal of American Folk-Lore*, xviii. 295 (tune only). *Journal of the Folk-Song Society*, viii. 5. *British Ballads from Maine*, p. 418. Davis's *Traditional Ballads of Virginia*, pp. 537 and 604.

'Colours' (Texts A and B) may be a corruption of 'country' as given in *Folk Songs of the South*.

Version J is reminiscent of The Death of Queen Jane (No. 32).

No. 45. The Trooper and the Maid.

Texts without tunes:—Child's *English and Scottish Popular Ballads*, No. 299.

Texts with tunes:—Christie's *Traditional Ballad Airs*, ii. 210. *Songs of the West*, 2nd ed., No. 65. Gavin Greig's *Last Leaves*, No. 108. *British Ballads from Maine*, p. 371. Davis's *Traditional Ballads of Virginia*, pp. 544 and 606.

No. 46. The Blind Beggar's Daughter.

Texts without tunes:—A. Williams's *Folk Songs of the Upper Thames*, p. 255. Dixon's *Songs of the Peasantry*, p. 51.

Texts with tunes:—*Journal of the Folk-Song Society*, i. 202. Chappell's *Popular Music of the Olden Times*, i. 159.

No. 47. The Babes in the Wood.

Texts without tunes:—A. Williams's *Folk Songs of the Upper Thames*, p. 217. Baring-Gould's *Book of Nursery Songs*, p. 40. *Journal of American Folk-Lore*, xxxv. 348 (see also further references).

Texts with tunes:—Christie's *Traditional Ballad Airs*, i. 142. Chappell's *Popular Music of the Olden Times*, i. 200. Rimbault's *Musical Illustrations of Percy's Reliques*, p. 108. M. H. Mason's *Nursery Rhymes and Country Songs*, p. 22. McGill's *Folk Songs of the Kentucky Mountains*, p. 104.

No. 48. In Seaport Town.

Texts without tunes:—*Journal of American Folk-Lore*, xx. 259; xxix. 168. Cox's *Folk Songs of the South*, p. 305 (see also further references).

Texts with tunes:—*Journal of the Folk-Song Society*, i. 160; ii. 42; v. 123. Miss Broadwood's *Traditional Songs and Carols*, p. 28. *Folk Songs from Somerset*, No. 12 (also published in *English Folk-Songs*, Selected Edition, i. 4, and *One Hundred English Folk-Songs*, p. 4). *Journal of American Folk-Lore*, xxxv. 359.

No. 49. The Cruel Ship's Carpenter.

Texts without tunes:—Broadsides by Pitts, Jackson & Son, and Bloomer (Birmingham). Ashton's *A Century of Ballads*, p. 101.

Texts with tunes:—Christie's *Traditional Ballad Airs*, ii. 99. *Journal of the Folk-Song Society*, i. 172. *Folk Songs from Somerset*, No. 83 (published also in *English Folk Songs*, Selected Edition, i. 4, and *One Hundred English Folk-Songs*, p. 4). Cox's *Folk Songs of the South*, pp. 308 (see also furthur references) and 528. Wyman and Brockway's *Twenty Kentucky Mountain Songs*, p. 110, and *Lonesome Tunes*, p. 79. *Journal of American Folk-Lore*, xx. 262.

No. 50. Shooting of his Dear.

Texts without tunes:—*Journal of American Folk-Lore*, xxii. 387; xxxix. 136.

Notes

Texts with tunes:—*Journal of the Folk-Song Society*, ii. 59; vii. 17. *Journal of the Irish Folk-Song Society*, iii. 25. *Songs of the West*, 2nd ed., No. 62. *Folk Songs from Somerset*, No. 16. 'Molly Bān (pronounced Vān) so fair,' Petrie's *Collection of Irish Music*, Nos. 724 and 1171 (tunes only). Joyce's *Ancient Irish Music*, p. 20. *Journal of American Folk-Lore*, xxx. 358. Cox's *Folk Songs of the South*, pp. 339 (see also further references) and 529.

No. 51. The Lady and the Dragoon.

Texts without tunes:—Broadside by Such. A. Williams's *Folk Songs of the Upper Thames*, p. 115. *Journal of American Folk-Lore*, xxiii. 447. Cox's *Folk Songs of the South*, p. 375 (see also further references).

Texts with tunes:—*Journal of the Folk-Song Society*, i. 108. *Journal of American Folk-Lore*, xxxv. 414. *British Ballads from Maine*, p. 377.

No. 52. The Boatsman and the Chest.

Variations of this theme form the subject of many ballad texts.

'To loot' (Text A, stanza 4) is a Scottish word signifying to stoop, to bow, or to curtsy.

No. 53. The Holly Twig.

Texts without tunes:—*West Country Garlands* (c. 1760). *Journal of American Folk-Lore*, xxxix. 156.

Texts with tunes:—*Journal of the Folk-Song Society*, iii. 315. *Songs of the West*, 2nd ed., No. 117.

No. 54. Polly Oliver.

Texts without tunes:—Broadside by Such. W. R. Mackenzie's *Ballads and Sea Songs from Nova Scotia*, No. 55. Cox's *Folk Songs of the South*, p. 387 (see also further references). *Journal of American Folk-Lore*, xii. 248.

Texts with tunes:—Chappell's *Popular Music of the Olden Times*, p. 676. Kidson's *Traditional Tunes*, p. 116. *Journal of American Folk-Lore*, xxiv. 337.

It is possible that the third line of stanza 8, Text B, is a corruption of 'I'll fight for my king on shipboard or shore' In the *Journal of American Folk Lore*, xxii. 248, these lines occur:

> I am a sailor on sea and a soldier on shore,
> But the name of Pretty Polly I always adore.

No. 55. The Rich Old Lady.

Texts without tunes:—Gavin Greig's *Folk-Song of the North-East*, i, art. 13. *Journal of American Folk-Lore*, xxviii. 174; xxix. 179. Cox's *Folk Songs of the South*, p. 464.

Text with tune:—L. J. Wolford's *Play-Party in Indiana*, p. 93.

No. 56. Edwin in the Lowlands Low.

Texts without tunes:—Gavin Greig's *Folk-Song of the North-East*, ii, art. 123. Broadside by Jackson & Son (Birmingham). *Journal of American Folk-Lore*, xx. 274; xxxv. 421. Cox's *Folk Songs of the South*, p. 345. W. R. Mackenzie's *Ballads and Sea Songs of Nova Scotia*, p. 27.

Texts with tunes:—*Journal of the Folk-Song Society*, i. 124; iii. 266; viii. 227. *Journal of the Irish Folk-Song Society*, iii. 24. *Folk-Songs of England*, iii. 38. Wyman and Brockway's *Twenty Kentucky Mountain Songs*, p. 42.

Notes

No. 57. Awake! Awake!

Texts without tunes:—Gavin Greig's *Folk-Song of the North East*, i, art. 54. Broadside (no imprint). *Journal of American Folk-Lore*, xx. 260; xxix. 200. Cox's *Folk Songs of the South*, p. 348 (see also further references).

Texts with tunes:—Christie's *Traditional Ballad Airs*, i. 225. *Journal of the Folk-Song Society*, i. 269; iii. 78. *Songs of the West*, 2nd ed., No. 41. *Folk Songs from Somerset*, No. 99 (published also in *English Folk Songs*, Selected Edition, i. 72, and *One Hundred English Folk-Songs*, p. 106). *Folk-Songs of England*, v. 12. *Journal of American Folk-Lore*, xxv. 282 (tune only); xxx. 338; xxxv. 356. W. R. Mackenzie's *Ballads and Sea Songs of Nova Scotia*, No. 99. Sturgis and Hughes's *Songs from the Hills of Vermont*, p. 30.

No. 58. The Green Bed.

Texts without tunes:—Broadside by Jackson & Son (Birmingham). Gavin Greig's *Folk-Song of the North-East*, ii, art. 115. *Journal of American Folk-Lore*, xxv. 7; xxviii. 156; xxxv. 373. W. R. Mackenzie's *Ballads and Sea Songs from Nova Scotia*, No. 93. Cox's *Folk Songs of the South*, p. 390.

Texts with tunes:—Christie's *Traditional Ballad Airs*, i. 251. *Songs of the West*, 2nd ed., No. 91. *Journal of the Folk-Song Society*, i. 48; iii. 281; v. 68.

No. 59. The Simple Ploughboy.

Texts without tunes:—Gavin Greig's *Folk-Song of the North-East*, ii, art 117. Broadside by Jackson & Son (Birmingham). W. R. Mackenzie's *Ballads and Sea Songs from Nova Scotia*, No. 93.

Texts with tunes:—*Journal of the Folk-Song Society*, i. 132; iv. 304; viii. 2. *Songs of the West*, 2nd ed., No. 59. Joyce's *Old Irish Folk Music and Songs*, p. 223. *Folk-Songs of England*, v. 10.

No. 60. The Three Butchers.

Texts without tunes:—*Roxburghe Collection*, iii. 30 and 496; iv. 80. Broadside by Pitts. Gavin Greig's *Folk-Song of the North-East*, i, art. 36. A. Williams's *Folk Songs of the Upper Thames*, p. 275.

Texts with tunes:—*Journal of the Folk-Song Society*, i. 174. L. Broadwood's *Traditional Songs and Carols*, p. 42. *School Songs*, vii, No. 1316.

No. 61. William Taylor.

Texts without tunes:—Gavin Greig's *Folk-Song of the North-East*, ii, art. 101. Broadside by H. de Marsan. *Ballads and Sea Songs from Nova Scotia*, No. 46. Cox's *Folk Songs of the South*, p. 382 (see also further references). *Journal of American Folk-Lore*, xxviii. 162.

Texts with tunes:—*Journal of the Folk-Song Society*, iii. 214; v. 68 and 161. Petrie's *Collection of Irish Music*, No. 745 (tune only). Christie's *Traditional Ballad Airs*, ii. 209. Joyce's *Old Irish Folk-Music and Songs*, No. 424. *Journal of the Irish Folk-Song Society*, v. 12. *Folk Songs from Somerset*, Nos. 118 and 119 (the latter also published in *English Folk-Songs*, Selected Edition, i. 114, and *One Hundred English Folk-Songs*, p. 160). *Journal of American Folk-Lore*, xxii. 74 (tune only); xxii. 380.

No. 62. The Golden Glove.

Texts without tunes:—Broadsides by Such, Catnach, and Pitts. Gavin Greig's *Folk-Song of the North-East*, ii, art. 95. Bell's *Songs of the Peasantry*, p. 70. C. S. Burne's *Shropshire Folk-Lore*, p. 553. *Journal of American Folk-Lore*, xxix. 172; xxxix. 113.

Texts with tunes:—Christie's *Traditional Ballad Airs*, ii. 115. Kidson's *Traditional*

Notes

Tunes, pp. 49 and 173. *English Folk-Songs for Schools*, 7th ed., No. 15. Kidson's *Garland of English Folk Songs*, p. 16. *Journal of the Folk-Song Society*, vi. 29. Wyman and Brockway's *Lonesome Tunes*, p. 49. W. R. Mackenzie's *Ballads and Sea Songs from Nova Scotia*, No. 21. Cox's *Folk Songs of the South*, p. 384 (see also further references).

No. 63. Pretty Nancy of Yarmouth.

Texts without tunes:—Broadside by W. Wright (Birmingham). Garret's *Merrie Book of Garlands*, vol. ii.

Texts with tunes:—*Journal of the Folk-Song Society*, ii. 113. Christie's *Traditional Ballad Airs*, ii. 282 (tune only).

Mrs. Sands's song is a shortened and condensed version of the broadside ballad—which consists of 56 stanzas, i.e. 224 lines! In the original story, Jemmy's love for Nancy of Yarmouth is opposed by her father, who, however, promises his consent to their marriage if Jemmy returns safely from an ocean voyage. Jemmy accordingly sails for the Barbadoes where his 'comely features' attract the attention, and arouse the love of the 'Perbadus (i.e. Barbadoes) lady whose fortune was great' Jemmy is constant to his first love, and the Perbadus lady, thwarted in her desires, commits suicide. Nancy's father, hearing that Jemmy is returning, writes to his friend the boatswain and promises him a handsome reward if he 'the life of young Jemmy would end'. The boatswain accepts the bribe and 'tumbles' the unfortunate Jemmy 'into the deep' The conclusion of the story is correctly given in the text.

No. 64. The Silk Merchant's Daughter.

Texts without tunes:—*Journal of American Folk-Lore*, xxviii. 160; xxxix. 113. Cf. *Folk Songs from Somerset*, No. 79.

No. 65. Jack Went A-Sailing.

Texts without tunes:—Gavin Greig's *Folk-Song of the North-East*, i, art. 45. Broadside by Such. Garret's *Merrie Book of Garlands*. *Journal of American Folk-Lore*, xii. 249; xx. 270; xxv. 9. Lomax's *Cowboy Songs*, p. 204. Cox's *Folk Songs of the South*, p. 330. Combs's *Folk-Songs du midi des États-Unis*, p. 208.

Texts with tunes:—*Journal of the Folk-Song Society*, ii. 227. *Journal of American Folk-Lore*, xxxv. 377. Wyman and Brockway's *Lonesome Tunes*, p. 38.

Version D is published with pianoforte accompaniment in *Folk Songs of English Origin*, 2nd Series.

The refrain of version G was sung very nasally, giving a weird effect.

No. 66. The Bold Lieutenant.

Text without tune:—Gavin Greig's *Folk-Song of the North-East*, i, art. 68.

Texts with tunes:—*Journal of the Folk-Song Society*, v. 258 (see note). *Folk Songs from Somerset*, No. 56. W. R. Mackenzie's *Ballads and Sea Songs from Nova Scotia*, No. 22.

No. 67. The Banks of Sweet Dundee.

Texts without tunes:—Gavin Greig's *Folk-Song of the North-East*, i, art. 66. Cox's *Folk Songs of the South*, p. 379. W. R. Mackenzie's *Ballads and Sea Songs of Nova Scotia*, No. 23. *Journal of American Folk-Lore*, xxxv. 354.

Texts with tunes:—*Journal of the Folk-Song Society*, i. 232. Christie's *Traditional Ballad Airs*, i. 258. Kidson's *Traditional Tunes*, 54 and 173. *English County Songs*, p. 116. Ford's *Vagabond Songs*, p. 78.

No. 68. The Councillor's Daughter.

Text without tune:—Bell's *Ballads and Songs of the Peasantry*, p. 110.
Text with tune:—*Folk Songs from Somerset*, No. 42.

Notes

No. 69. Caroline of Edinboro' Town.

Texts without tunes:—Gavin Greig's *Folk-Song of the North-East*, i, art. 70. *Journal of American Folk-Lore*, xxxv. 362 (see also further references). W. R. Mackenzie's *Ballads and Sea Songs from Nova Scotia*, No. 28.

No. 70. The Clothier.

Text without tune:—Combs's *Folk-Songs du midi des États-Unis*, p. 157.

No. 71. The Miller's Apprentice.

Texts without tunes:—W. R. Mackenzie's *Ballads and Sea Songs from Nova Scotia*, No. 115. Cox's *Folk Songs from the South*, p. 311 (see also further references). *Journal of American Folk-Lore*, xxxix. 125.

Texts with tunes:—*Journal of the Folk-Song Society*, vii. 23 and 44.

Version E is closely allied to the English tune, which now is a popular hymn in the *English Hymnal*.

No. 72. Still Growing.

Texts with tunes:—*Scots Musical Museum*, iii, No. 377. Dick's *Songs of Robert Burns*, p. 317; cf. 'Lady Mary Anne' in *The Centenary Burns*, iii. 126. *Journal of the Folk-Song Society*, i. 214; ii. 44, 95, 206; v. 190. *Songs of the West*, 2nd ed., No. 4. L. Broadwood's *English Traditional Songs and Carols*, p. 56. *Folk Songs from Somerset*, No. 15 (also published in *English Folk-Songs*, Selected Edition, ii. 20, and *One Hundred English Folk-Songs*, p. 58). Christie's *Traditional Ballad Airs*, ii. 212.

BIBLIOGRAPHY
BOOKS REFERRED TO IN THE NOTES

American Negro Folk-Songs, Newman I. White. Harvard University Press, 1928.
The American Songbag, Carl Sandburg. Harcourt, Bruce and Co., New York, 1927.
Ancient and Modern Scottish Songs, David Herd. 2 Vols. Edinburgh. Printed by John Wotherspoon for James Dickson & Charles Elliot, 1776.
Ancient Irish Music, P. W. Joyce. M. H. Gill, Dublin, 1901.
Ancient Mysteries Described, William Hone. William Reeves, London, 1823.
Ancient Scottish Ballads, G. R. Kinloch. Longman, London, 1827.

A Ballad Book, Charles Kirkpatrick Sharpe. Edinburgh, 1823.
Ballads and Sea Songs from Nova Scotia, W. Roy Mackenzie. Harvard University Press, 1928.
The Ballads and Songs of Derbyshire, ed. by Llewellyn Jewitt. Bemrose & Lothian, London, 1867.
Ballads and Songs of the Peasantry, Robert Bell. Griffin, Bohn & Co., London, 1861.
Ballads Surviving in the United States, C. Alphonso Smith. Reprinted from Musical Quarterly, January, 1916. Schreiner, New York.
A Book of Nursery Songs and Rhymes, S. Baring-Gould. Methuen & Co., London. 2nd and cheaper ed.
British Ballads from Maine, Phillips Barry, Fannie Hardy Eckstorm, Mary Winslow Smyth. Yale University Press, New Haven, and Humphrey Milford, London, 1929.

The Centenary Burns, Henley and Henderson. T. C. & E. C. Jack, Edinburgh, 1896–7. 4 Vols.
A Century of Ballads, John Ashton. Elliot Stock, London, 1887.
Children's Rhymes, Games, Songs and Stories, Robert Ford. Alexander Gardner, Paisley, 1904.
Children's Singing Games, Alice B. Gomme and Cecil J. Sharp. Novello & Co. London, 1909–12. 5 Vols.
Christmas Carols—Ancient and Modern, William Sandys. R. Beckley, London, 1823.
The Complete Collection of Irish Music, George Petrie, edited by Charles Villiers Stanford. Boosey & Co., London, 1903.
Cowboy Songs, John A. Lomax. Sturgis & Walton Co., New York, 1916.

Dictionary of British Folk Lore, Part 1. *Traditional Games*, Vols. 1 & 2, Alice B. Gomme. David Nutt, London, 1894.

Eight Hampshire Folk Songs, Alice E. Gillington. J. Curwen, London.
The English and Scottish Popular Ballads, F. E. Child. Houghton, Mifflin & Co., Boston, 1882–98. 5 Vols.
English County Songs, Lucy Broadwood & J. A. Fuller Maitland. Leadenhall Press, London; Charles Scribner & Sons, New York.
English Folk-Carols, Cecil J. Sharp. The Wessex Press, Taunton; Novello & Co., London, 1911.
English Folk Songs, William Alexander Barrett. Novello, London.
English Folk Songs for Schools, S. Baring-Gould and Cecil J. Sharp. J. Curwen & Sons, London, 1906.
English Folk Songs (Selected Edition), Cecil Sharp. Novello & Co., London, 1921. 2 Vols.

427

Bibliography

English Traditional Songs and Carols, Lucy Broadwood. Boosey & Co., London, 1908.
Fifty Sailors' Songs or Chanties, Ferris Tozer. 3rd ed. Boosey & Co., London.
The Folk-Lore of Herefordshire, Mrs. E. M. Leather. Sidgwick & Jackson, London, 1912.
Folk Songs of the Kentucky Mountains, Josephine McGill. Boosey & Co., New York and London, 1917.
Folk-Song of the North-East (Scotland), Articles contributed to 'The Buchan Observer', Gavin Greig. 'Buchan Observer' Works, Peterhead, 1909 and 1914. 2 Series.
Folk-Songs du midi des États-Unis, Josiah H. Combs. Les Presses Universitaires de France, Paris, 1925.
Folk Songs from Somerset, Cecil J. Sharp and Rev. Charles L. Marson. Schott & Co., London, 1904-9. 5 Series.
Folk Songs from Sussex, George Butterworth. Augener, London; Boston Music Co., Boston, 1912.
Folk-Songs of England, edited by Cecil J. Sharp. Book I, H. E. D. Hammond and Cecil J. Sharp; Book II, Ralph Vaughan Williams; Book III, G. B. Gardiner and Gustav Holst; Book IV, Cecil J. Sharp; Book V, Percy Merrick and Ralph Vaughan Williams. Novello & Co., London, 1908-12.
Folk-Songs of English Origin collected in the Appalachian Mountains, Cecil J. Sharp. Novello & Co., London, 1919-21. 2 Series. (First Series published in U.S.A. under the title *American-English Folk-Songs*, G. Schirmer, New York and Boston, 1918.)
Folk Songs of the South, John Harrington Cox. Harvard University Press, 1925.
Folk Songs of the Upper Thames, Alfred Williams. Duckworth, London, 1923.

Games and Songs of American Children, William H. Newell. Harper & Bros., New York and London. New and enlarged ed. 1903.
A Garland of Country Song, S. Baring-Gould and H. Fleetwood Sheppard. Methuen & Co., London, 1895.
A Garland of English Folk Songs, Frank Kidson. Ascherberg, Hopwood, & Crew, London.

Irish Country Songs, Herbert Hughes. Boosey & Co., London, 1915. 2 Vols.

Journal of American Folk-Lore, American Folk-Lore Society, Boston and New York, 1888-1928. 41 Vols. In progress.
Journal of the Folk-Song Society, 19 Berners Street, London, 1899-1928. 8 Vols. In progress.
Journal of the Irish Folk-Song Society, London, 1904-1926. 23 Vols. In progress.
Journal of the Welsh Folk Song Society, Jarvis & Foster. Bangor, N. Wales. In progress.

Last Leaves of Traditional Ballads and Ballad Airs, Gavin Greig and Alexander Keith. The Buchan Club, Aberdeen, 1925.
Lonesome Tunes, Loraine Wyman & Howard Brockway. The H. W. Gray Co., New York, 1916.

Melismata; Musical Phansies, Thomas Ravenscroft. London, 1611.
Merrie Book of Garlands, see *Right Choyse and Merrie Book of Garlands*.
Minstrelsy: Ancient and Modern, William Motherwell. John Wylie, Glasgow, 1827.
Modern Street Ballads, John Ashton. Chatto & Windus, London, 1888.
Musical Illustrations of Bishop Percy's Reliques, Edward Rimbault. Cramer & Co., London, 1850.
Musical Quarterly, see *Ballads Surviving in the United States*.

Bibliography

The Negro and his Songs, Howard W. Odum and Guy B. Johnson. University of North Carolina, Chapel Hill; Humphrey Milford, London, 1925.
Northumbrian Minstrelsy, Collingwood Bruce and John Stokoe. Society of Antiquaries of Newcastle-upon-Tyne, 1882.
Notes on Scottish Songs by Robert Burns, J. C. Dick. Henry Frowde, London and New York, 1908.
Nursery Rhymes and Country Songs, Miss M. H. Mason. Metzler, London, 1877.
Nursery Rhymes and Nursery Tales of England, James Orchard Halliwell. Warne & Co., London; Scribner & Co., New York, 5th ed.
Nursery Songs from the Appalachian Mountains, Cecil J. Sharp. Novello & Co., London, 1921-4. 2 Series.

Old Irish Folk Music and Songs, P. W. Joyce. Longmans & Co., London, 1909. 3 parts.
Old Nursery Rhymes, Ed. F. Rimbault. Chappell & Co., London. Reprinted.
On the Trail of Negro Folk Songs, Dorothy Scarborough. Harvard University Press, 1925.
One Hundred English Folk Songs, Cecil J. Sharp. The Musicians Library, Oliver Ditson and Co., New York, 1916.

A Pedlar's Pack of Ballads and Songs, W. H. Logan. William Patterson, Edinburgh, 1869.
The Play-Party in Indiana, Leah Jackson Wolford. Indianapolis Historical Commission, 1916.
Popular Music of the Olden Time, William Chappell. Chappell & Co., London, 1855-9. 2 Vols.
Popular Rhymes of Scotland, Robert Chambers. Chambers, Edinburgh, 1826; 3rd ed., 1870.

Right Choyse and Merrie Book of Garlands, William Garret. Newcastle, 1818. 4 Vols.
The Roxburghe Ballads, Hertford, 1871-96. 8 Vols.

School Songs, Sets 1-9. 1-5 and 7-9, Cecil J. Sharp; Set 6, R. Vaughan Williams. Novello & Co., London.
The Scots Musical Museum, James Johnson. 1st ed., Edinburgh, 1787-1803. 6 Vols. 3rd ed., Edinburgh and London, 1853. 4 Vols.
Scottish Songs, G. Thomson. Edinburgh, 1801.
Shropshire Folk Lore, Charlotte S. Burne. Trübner & Co., London, 1884-6.
Some Ancient Christmas Carols, Davies Gilbert. John Nichols & Son, London. 1st ed. 1822; 2nd ed. 1823.
Song Histories, Robert Ford. William Hodge & Co., Glasgow and Edinburgh, 1900.
Song Time, Percy Dearmer and Martin Shaw. J. Curwen & Sons, London, 1915.
Songs and Ballads of the Maine Lumberjacks, Ronald Palmer Gray. Harvard University Press, 1924.
Songs and Ballads of the West, Rev. S. Baring-Gould and Rev. H. Fleetwood Sheppard. Methuen & Co., London. 1st ed., 4 parts, 1889-91; 2nd ed., 1905, entitled *Songs of the West*, under the musical editorship of Cecil J. Sharp.
Songs from David Herd's Manuscripts, Hans Hecht. Wm. J. Hay, Edinburgh, 1904.
Songs from the Hills of Vermont, Edith B. Sturgis and Robert Hughes. G. Schirmer, New York, 1919.
The Songs of Robert Burns, James C. Dick. Henry Frowde, London and New York, 1903.
The Songs of Scotland Prior to Burns, Robert Chambers. W. & R. Chambers, Edinburgh, 1890.

Bibliography

Songs of the Nativity, W. H. Husk. J. C. Holten, London, 187?
Songs of the West, see *Songs and Ballads of the West*.
Songs of Uladh (Ulster), Herbert Hughes. Privately printed.
South Carolina Ballads, Reed Smith. Harvard University Press, 1928.
Sussex Songs, arranged by H. F. Birch Reynardson (collected by Rev. John Broadwood). Stanley, Lucas Weber & Co., London.

Traditional Ballad Airs, Dean Christie. Edmonston and Douglas, Edinburgh, 1876-81. 2 Vols.
Traditional Ballads of Virginia, Arthur Kyle Davis, Jr. Harvard University Press, Cambridge, Mass., and Humphrey Milford, London, 1929.
Traditional Tunes, Frank Kidson. Charles Taphouse & Son, Oxford, 1891.
Twenty Kentucky Mountain Songs, Loraine Wyman and Howard Brockway. Oliver Ditson Co., Boston, 1920.

Ulster Songs and Ballads, H. Richard Hayward. Duckworth, London, 1925.

Vagabond Songs and Ballads of Scotland, Robert Ford. Alexander Gardner, Paisley, new ed., 1904.

NOTE

During the period of twenty years that has elapsed between the first publication and the second impression of this work a number of new folk-song collections have been published, which contain additional versions of the songs given in these two volumes. The following are some of the more important collections that have appeared during the last twenty years and others are referred to in the extensive bibliographies which most of the collections contain.

BELDEN, H. M.: *Ballads and Songs collected by the Missouri Folklore Society*. The University of Missouri Studies, xv, No. 1, Columbia, 1940.
BREWSTER, Paul G.: *Ballads and Songs of Indiana*. Indiana University Publications, Bloomington, Indiana, 1940.
CREIGHTON, Helen, and SENIOR, Doreen: *Traditional Songs from Nova Scotia*. Ryerson Press, Toronto, 1950.
EDDY, Mary O.: *Ballads and Songs from Ohio*. J. J. Augustin, New York, 1939.
FLANDERS, Helen Hartness, BALLARD, Elizabeth, BROWN, George, and BARRY, Phillips: *The New Green Mountain Songster*. Yale University Press, New Haven, 1939.
GARDNER, Emily E., and CHICKERING, Geraldine J.: *Ballads and Songs of Southern Michigan*. University of Michigan Press, Ann Arbor, 1939.
GREENLEAF, Elizabeth B., and MANSFIELD, Grace Y.: *Ballads and Sea Songs from Newfoundland*. Harvard University Press, Cambridge, 1933.
HENRY, Mellinger E.. *Folk-songs from the Southern Highlands*. J. J. Augustin, New York, 1938.
HUDSON, Arthur Palmer: *Folk-songs of Mississippi and their Background*. University of North Carolina Press. Chapel Hill, 1936. (No tunes.)
LINSCOTT, Eloise H.: *Folk songs of Old New England*. The Macmillan Co., New York, 1939.
LOMAX, John and Alan: *American Ballads and Folk-songs*. The Macmillan Co., New York, 1934.
LOMAX, John and Alan: *Our Singing Country*. The Macmillan Co., New York, 1941.
MORRIS, Alton C.: *Folk-songs of Florida*. University of Florida Press, Gainesville, 1950.
RANDOLPH, Vance: *Ozark Folk-songs*, 4 vols. The State Historical Society of Missouri, Columbia, 1946.

For hymns, see:
JACKSON, George Pullen:
    White Spirituals in the Southern Uplands. University of North Carolina Press, Chapel Hill, 1934.
    Spiritual Folk-songs of Early America. J. J. Augustin, New York, 1937.
    Down-East Spirituals and Others. J. J. Augustin, New York, 1939.

INDEX OF TITLES

	PAGE
A Monday was my Courting Day	ii. 277
Awake! Awake!	i. 358
Awful Wedding, The	ii. 83
Babes in the Wood, The	i. 309
Bailiff's Daughter of Islington, The	i. 219
Banks of Sweet Dundee, The	i. 399
Barbara Allen	i. 183
Barbara Buck	ii. 274
Barber's Cry	ii. 276
Battle of Shiloh, The	ii. 172
Betsy	ii. 4
Betty Anne	ii. 37
Billy Grimes	ii. 248
Bird Song, The	ii. 304
Black Girl	ii. 278
Black is the Colour	ii. 31
Blind Beggar's Daughter, The	i. 308
Boatsman and the Chest, The	i. 338
Bold Lieutenant, The	i. 396
Bold Privateer, The	ii. 175
Boney's Defeat	ii. 245
Boy on the Land, The	ii. 228
Brennan on the Moor	ii. 170
Bridle and Saddle, The	ii. 329
Brisk Young Lover, The	ii. 76
Broken Token, The	ii. 70
Brown Girl, The	i. 295
Bye, Bye, Baby	ii. 341
Caroline of Edinboro' Town	i. 404
Carrion Crow, The	ii. 324
Charlie's Sweet	ii. 375
Chase the Buffalo	ii. 372
Cherry-Tree Carol, The	i. 90
Chickens they are Crowing, The	ii. 378
Christ was Born in Bethlehem	ii. 293
Clay Morgan	ii. 274
Clothier, The	i. 405
Cocky Robin	ii. 299
Come all ye Southern Soldiers	ii. 253
Come All You Fair and Tender Ladies	ii. 128
Come All You Young and Handsome Girls	ii. 80
Come my Little Roving Sailor	ii. 279
Councillor's Daughter, The	i. 402
Courting Case, The	ii. 249
Cripple Creek	ii. 352
Crow-fish Man, The	ii. 275
Cruel Brother, The	i. 36
Cruel Mother, The	i. 56
Cruel Ship's Carpenter, The	i. 317
Cuckoo, The	ii. 177
Daemon Lover, The	i. 244

Index of Titles

Daniel in the Lion's Den	ii. 273
Deaf Woman's Courtship, The	ii. 252
Dear Companion, The	ii. 109
Death of Queen Jane, The	i. 230
Derby Ram, The	ii. 184
Devilish Mary	ii. 200
Drummer and His Wife, The	ii. 265
Earl Brand	i. 14
Early, Early in the Spring	ii. 151
Early Sunday Morning	ii. 373
Edward	i. 46
Edwin in the Lowlands Low	i. 350
Elfin Knight, The	i. 1
Eliza Jane	ii. 356
Every Night when the Sun goes in	ii. 268
Fair Annie	i. 95
Fair Margaret and Sweet William	i. 132
False Knight Upon the Road, The	i. 3
False Young Man, The	ii. 51
Farewell Dear Rosanna	ii. 243
Farmer's Curst Wife, The	i. 275
Farmyard, The	ii. 310
Fateful Blow, The	ii. 246
Foggy Dew, The	ii. 174
Foolish Boy, The	ii. 307
Frog He Went A-courting, A	ii. 312
Frog in the Well, The	ii. 320
Gambling Man, The	ii. 204
Geordie	i. 240
George Reilly	ii. 22
Giles Collins	i. 196
Give the Fiddler a Dram	ii. 358
Going to Boston	ii. 371
Golden Glove, The	i. 377
Golden Vanity, The	i. 282
Gone to Cripple Creek	ii. 358
Good Morning, My Pretty Little Miss	ii. 90
Good Old Man, The	ii. 338
Green Bed, The	i. 365
Green Brier Shore, The	ii. 188
Green Bushes	ii. 155
Green Grows the Laurel	ii. 211
Grey Cock, The	i. 259
Ground Hog, The	ii. 340
Gypsy Laddie, The	i. 233
Ha, Ha, Ha	ii. 201
Handsome Sally	ii. 138
Harding's Defeat	ii. 278
Harm Link	ii. 258
Harry Gray	ii. 15
Hicks's Farewell	ii. 142
Higher Up the Cherry-Tree, The	ii. 377
Hog-eyed Man, The	ii. 360
Hold On	ii. 292

Index of Titles

Holly Twig, The	i. 341
Horse's Complaint, The	ii. 220
I Love my Love	ii. 269
I Must and I Will Get Married	ii. 159
I Whipped My Horse	ii. 311
I wish I was a Child again	ii. 383
Ibby Damsel	ii. 137
If You Want to Go A-courting	ii. 6
I'm Going to Georgia	ii. 14
I'm Going to get Married Next Sunday	ii. 189
I'm Seventeen Come Sunday	ii. 156
In Old Virginny	ii. 232
In Seaport Town	i. 310
Irish Girl, The	ii. 254
Jack Went A-Sailing	i. 385
Jackfish, The	ii. 361
Jacob's Ladder	ii. 295
Jesse Cole	ii. 273
John Hardy	ii. 35
John of Hazelgreen	i. 294
Johnie Scot	i. 215
Johnny Doyle	ii. 27
Johnny German	ii. 256
Katie Morey	ii. 119
Keys of Heaven, The	ii. 45
Lady and the Dragoon, The	i. 333
Lady Isabel and the Elf Knight	i. 5
Lady Maisry	i. 97
Lady Leroy	ii. 210
Lamkin	i. 201
Lazarus	ii. 29
Lily of the West, The	ii. 199
Little Musgrave and Lady Barnard	i. 161
Liza Anne	ii. 355
Lizzie Wan	i. 89
Locks and Bolts	ii. 17
Lonesome Grove, The	ii. 197
Lonesome Prairie, The	ii. 236
Lord Lovel	i. 146
Lord Randal	i. 38
Lord Thomas and Fair Ellinor	i. 115
Lost Babe, The	ii. 160
Lover's Lament, The	ii. 103
Loving Nancy	ii. 226
Loving Reilly	ii. 81
Lowlands of Holland, The	i. 200
Lulie	ii. 276
Macafee's Confession, or Harry Gray	ii. 15
Maid Freed from the Gallows, The	i. 208
Mammy Loves	ii. 341
Maria's Gone	ii. 369
Marina Girls	ii. 362
Married and Single Life	ii. 3

Index of Titles

Mermaid, The	i. 291
Miller's Apprentice, The, or Oxford Tragedy, The	i. 407
Miller's Will, The	ii. 221
Mocking Bird, The	ii. 342
My Boy Billy	ii. 38
My Dearest Dear	ii. 13
My Mother Bid Me	ii. 93
My Parents Treated Me Tenderly	ii. 62
Niagara Falls	ii. 231
Nightingale, The	ii. 192
Noble Man, The	ii. 162
No-e in the Ark	ii. 216
Nottamun Town	ii. 270
O This Door Locked	ii. 363
Old Arkansas	ii. 238
Old Bald Eagle	ii. 374
Old Black Duck, The	ii. 332
Old Doc. Jones	ii. 368
Old Grey Goose, The	ii. 345
Old Grey Mare, The	ii. 326
Old Joe Clarke	ii. 259
Old Roger	ii. 370
Old Woman and the Little Pigee, The	ii. 343
One Cold Winter's Morning	ii. 195
Opossum, The	ii. 353
Our Goodman	i. 267
Oxford Tragedy, The	i. 407
Philadelphia	ii. 374
Phoebe in her Petticoat	ii. 346
Polly Oliver	i. 344
Poor Couple, The	ii. 260
Poor Old Maid	ii. 327
Poor Omie	ii. 144
Poor Stranger, The	ii. 212
Porto Rico	ii. 359
Pretty Nancy of Yarmouth	i. 379
Pretty Peggy O	ii. 59
Pretty Saro .	ii. 10
Putman's Hill	ii. 50
Rain and Snow	ii. 122
Reap, Boys, Reap	ii. 380
Rebel Soldier, The, or Poor Stranger, The	ii. 212
Rejected Lover, The	ii. 96
Rich Old Lady, The	i. 348
Riddle Song, The	ii. 190
Rocky Mountain Top, The	ii. 110
Run, Nigger, Run	ii. 359
Sad Condition	ii. 372
St. James's Hospital	ii. 164
Sally and Her Lover, or Lady Leroy	ii. 210
Sally Anne	ii. 351
Sally Buck	ii. 217
Samuel Young	ii. 271

Index of Titles

Saucy Sailor, The	ii. 235
Seven Long Years	ii. 79
Shad, The	ii. 364
Sheffield Apprentice, The	ii. 66
Shoemaker, The	ii. 75
Shooting of His Dear	i. 328
Silk Merchant's Daughter, The	i. 381
Silver Dagger, The	ii. 229
Simple Ploughboy, The	i. 369
Single Girl, The	ii. 32
Sinner-Man	ii. 289
Sir Hugh	i. 222
Sir Lionel	i. 54
Slighted Soldier, The	ii. 247
Snake Baked a Hoe-cake	ii. 346
Soldier Boy for Me	ii. 381
Soldier, Won't You Marry Me?	ii. 40
Some Love Coffee	ii. 383
Sons of Liberty, The	ii. 224
Sourwood Mountain	ii. 305
Springfield Mountain	ii. 166
Squirrel, The	ii. 330
Still Growing	i. 410
Suffolk Miracle, The	i. 261
Sugar Babe	ii. 357
Sunny South, The	ii. 262
Susannah Clargy	ii. 261
Swannanoa Town	ii. 42
Sweet William	ii. 84
Swing a Lady	ii. 379
Tarry Trowsers	ii. 168
Ten Commandments, The	ii. 283
Three Butchers, The	i. 370
Three Huntsmen, The	ii. 303
Three Ravens, The	i. 63
'Tis a Wonder	ii. 294
Tom Bolynn	ii. 202
Tottenham Toad, The	ii. 347
Tree in the Wood, The	ii. 281
Trooper and the Maid, The	i. 305
True Love from the Eastern Shore	ii. 264
True Lover's Farewell, The	ii. 113
Two Brothers, The	i. 65
Two Sisters, The	i. 26
Up She Rises	ii. 368
Virginian Lover, The	ii. 149
Wagoner's Lad, The	ii. 123
Warfare is Raging, The	ii. 111
Waterloo	ii. 176
Way Down the Ohio	ii. 275
What are Little Boys made of?	ii. 334
What'll we do with the Baby?	ii. 336
When Adam was Created	ii. 272
When Boys go A-courting	ii. 205

Index of Titles

Whistle, Daughter, Whistle	ii. 169
Wife of Usher's Well, The	i. 150
Wife Wrapt in Wether's Skin, The	i. 271
Wild Bill Jones	ii. 74
Will the Weaver	ii. 207
Will You Wear Red?	ii. 371
William and Nancy	ii. 20
William and Polly	ii. 139
William Hall	ii. 239
William Taylor	i. 373
Yonder Stands Young Couple	ii. 367
Young Beichan	i. 77
Young Hunting	i. 101

www.ingramcontent.com/pod-product-compliance
Lightning Source LLC
Chambersburg PA
CBHW081846170426
43199CB00018B/2824